A New and Correct PLAN of LONDON,
WESTMINSTER and SOUTHWARK.
With several Additional Improvements,
Not in any former Survey.

London Newspapers
in the Age of Walpole

The Character of a *good* LORD MAYOR by Biſhop Atterbury.

Juſt and wiſe MAGISTRATE is a bleſſing as extenſive as the Community to which he belongs: a bleſſing, which includes all other bleſſings whatſoever, that relate to this life; ſecures to us the poſſeſſion, and enhances the value of them all. He will do nothing that is beneath his high ſtation, nor omit any thing which becomes it. He will not proſtitute his power to mean and undue ends; nor ſtoop to little and low arts of courting the favour of the People, without doing them real ſervice. He will ſtand his ground againſt all the attacks that can be made upon his probity: no man's power ſhall ſcare him from doing his duty; no man's importunities ſhall weary him; no man's flattery ſhall bribe him; no by-views of his own ſhall miſlead him. He will know how to prize his advantages, and to reliſh the honours which he enjoys, as the teſtimonies of publick eſteem, and the rewards of merit. In ſhort, he will in all reſpects diſcharge the high truſt repoſed in him, with integrity, wiſdom, and courage.

Some Magiſtrates are contented, that their Places ſhould adorn them: and ſome alſo there are, who ſtudy to adorn their Places, and to reflect back again the luſtre they receive from thence. Reputation is the great engine, by which Thoſe, who are poſſeſs'd of power, muſt make that power ſerviceable to the ends and uſes of government. The rods and axes of Princes, and their Deputies, may awe many into obedience: but the fame of their goodneſs, and juſtice, and other virtues, will work on more; will make men not only obedient, but willing to obey, and ready to come into every thing that is done, or deſign'd, for the publick advantage, by Thoſe, who (they are ſatisfy'd) ſincerely mean it. An eſtabliſhed character ſpreads the influence of ſuch as move in a high ſphere, on all around, and beneath them; it reaches farther, than their own care and providence, or that of their inferior officers can poſſibly do: it acts for them, when they themſelves ceaſe to act, and renders their adminiſtration both proſperous and eaſy. Great Places are never well filled but by great minds: and it is as natural to a great mind to ſeek honour by a due diſcharge of an high truſt, as it is to little men to make advantages of it.

A good MAGISTRATE, who would endear himſelf to thoſe whom he governs, muſt be endu'd with a publick ſpirit, free from all narrow ſelfiſh views, and diligent in promoting the common good of the Society committed to his care. The wellfare of That is the chief point which he is to carry always in his eye, and by which he is to govern all his counſels, deſigns, and actions. To this good end he muſt ſacrifice his time, his eaſe, and his private advantages; and think all of them well ſpent in obtaining it. He muſt be an impartial Diſtributor of juſtice

Quel portrait eſt ceci? --- C'eſt le noble CHASSEUR;
La terreur de l'Eſpagne, et la joye d' Angleterre;
Qui donne à toute Europe, ou la paix, ou la guerre.
Non non, Je me trompe. --- C'eſt le fameux BRASSEUR,
Les delices du peuple, un veritable Anglois,
Qui gouverne la Ville, et conſerve ſes loix.
Qui ſe montrant nagueres, en moeurs et en ſcience,
Poli comme un HORACE, à la Cour de la France,
Fut le bon Compagnon de l' Arbitre des Rois.

F. Markam pin.   *I. Barlre ſculp.*

Philoſophum non barba facit, non laurea vatem.
  Eſt EQUES, eſt MILES, nobile calcar habens.
Plurimus eſt MILES, qui nunquam prælia tentat;
  Multus EQUES, qui vix pendulus hæret equo.
Emit ſi titulos, auro ſuffragia vendens,
  Hunc EQUITEM AURATUM dicere jure potes.
At noſter non talis EQUES: ſed ſæpius urget
  Venator celerem conſpiciendus equum.
Pro patria in celebri MILES gerit arma Senatu
  Civica: nam patriæ militat omnis amans.
Magnos qui meruit, parvos contempſit honores,
  Ad famam aſcendens nobiliore viâ,
Regalem quamvis humero non ſenſerit ictum,
  ARMIGER, eſt, pluſquam nomine, MILES, EQUES.

Hard is the taſk to ſhine in glorious deeds,
Where BROCAS went before, and CHILD ſucceeds.
PARSONS alone can that high part ſuſtain.
Than whom, the mace, the ſword, the golden chain }
A greater ne'er did grace, nor greater ſhall again.

without reſpect of perſons, intereſts, or opinions. When right is to be done, he will make no diſtinction of ſmall or great, friend or enemy, citizen or ſtranger; he will always countenance right, and diſcountenance wrong, whoever be the injurer, or the ſufferer.

Courteſy and condeſcenſion is another happy quality, which never fails to make its way into the good opinion, and into the very hearts of thoſe who are under his inſpection. By this he doth, as it were, leſſen the diſtance between him and other men, and by that means allay the envy which always attends an high ſtation; when he is eaſy of acceſs, affable, patient to hear, when not only his Door, but his very countenance [and his HEART] is OPEN TO ALL that have any occaſion to approach him.

Bounty muſt be added to heighten his character. There is ſcarce any quality more truly popular than this, or more ſuitable to the publick ſtation in which he ſhines. It includes hoſpitality to the better ſort, and charity to the poor; two virtues that are never exerciſed ſo gracefully and well, as when they accompany each other. When hoſpitality degenerates into profuſeneſs, and ends in madneſs and folly, it ill deſerves the name of virtue: but in the offices of charity there is no danger of exceſs.

But of all good qualities that which recommends and adorns the MAGISTRATE moſt, is his care of religion; which as it is the moſt valuable thing in the world, ſo it gives the trueſt value to them who promote the eſteem and practice of it, by their example, authority, influence, and encouragement. This is the MAGISTRATE's peculiar province, his moſt glorious employment: to give countenance to piety and virtue, and to rebuke vice and prophaneneſs; to put the laws of men in execution againſt ſuch as trample on the laws of God; and to protect religion, and all that belongs to it, from the daring inſults of thoſe who ſit in the ſeat of the ſcorner.

There never was a time, when the interpoſition of the MAGISTRATE was more neceſſary to ſecure the honour of religion, and uphold the authority of thoſe great principles of it, by which his own authority is beſt upheld. For we live in evil days, when the moſt important and confeſs'd truths, ſuch as by the wiſeſt and beſt men in all ages have been revered, are by licentious tongues queſtioned, argued aſide, derided; and theſe things not only whiſper'd in corners, but proclaimed upon the houſe tops; own'd and publiſh'd in defiance of the common perſuaſion, common reaſon, and the common intereſt of mankind, and of all authority both ſacred and civil. Libertiniſm hath erected its ſtandard, hath declared war againſt religion, and openly liſted men on its ſide and party; a general looſeneſs of principles and manners hath ſeized on us like a peſtilence, *a peſtilence that walketh not in darkneſs, but waſteth at noon-day:* the contagion of which hath ſpread itſelf through all ranks and degrees of men; hath infected both the Camp and the Congregation. Who knows what the zeal and courage of a good MAGISTRATE might do towards ſtopping it? *Let Phineas ſtand up and execute judgment, that ſo this plague may be ſtayed.*

The front page of the *Grub Street Journal* **48, Thursday 3 December 1730, containing a portrait of Humphrey Parsons, Lord Mayor of London.**

London Newspapers
in the Age of Walpole

A Study of the Origins of the Modern English Press

Michael Harris

Rutherford ● *Madison* ● *Teaneck*
Fairleigh Dickinson University Press
London and Toronto: Associated University Presses

Associated University Presses
440 Forsgate Drive
Cranbury, NJ 08512

Associated University Presses
25 Sicilian Avenue
London WC1A 2QH, England

Associated University Presses
2133 Royal Windsor Drive
Unit 1
Mississauga, Ontario
Canada L5J 1K5

The paper used in this publication meets the requirements
of the American National Standard for Permanence of Paper
for Printed Library Materials Z39.48-1984.

Library of Congress Cataloging-in-Publication Data

Harris, M. (Michael), 1938–
   London newspapers in the age of Walpole.

   Bibliography: p.
   Includes index.
   1. English newspapers—England—London—History—18th
century.   I. Title.
PN5129.L62H37   1987   072′.1   86-45934
ISBN 0-8386-3273-4 (alk. paper)

Printed in the United States of America

Contents

List of Illustrations   6
Preface   7
Acknowledgments   11
Notes on the Text   13
Abbreviations   15

 1   The Shaping of the London Newspaper   19
 2   The Distribution of the London Newspapers   33
 3   The Finances of the London Press   49
 4   The Booksellers and Group Ownership   65
 5   The Newspaper Printers   82
 6   The Journalists   99
 7   The Press and Politics   113
 8   Political Control of the Press   134
 9   The Content of the London Newspapers
     Part 1: News and Information   155
     Part 2: Instruction and Entertainment   178
10   The London Press in Mid-Century   189

Notes   198
Bibliography   233
Index   248

Illustrations

Map of London, 1761   *Endpapers*

Front page of the *Grub Street Journal*   *Frontispiece*

Front page of *Parker's London News*   24

Page four of the *General Evening Post* Saturday 24 April 1736   62

A satire on newspaper printers from the *Grub Street Journal*   83

Robin's Reign or Seven's The Main   93

Broadside view of Bolingbroke versus Walpole   118

Nicholas Paxton in Newgate in 1742   128

The Politician by William Hogarth   193

Preface

This study began in an attempt to explore the working of public opinion in the political system of the mid-eighteenth century. It was from the first to be based on an analysis of the content of the newspaper press and in particular of those publications produced in London under some form of political supervision. One strand of the completed work remains an attempt to establish a realistic setting for this political activity. However, over time the focus shifted to the newspapers themselves and in the process has led to some reassessment of their character and development in what has turned out to be a crucial formative period.

The view of the English press that emerges from the solid and sometimes useful nineteenth-century histories[1] has not been substantially reworked in the modern period. Stanley Morison's finely illustrated survey suggested a move in a new direction but this was not followed up and the slow accumulation of material since the 1930s has not followed a regular pattern and has produced its own distortions. The preoccupation with the political involvement of the English press and with the attempts at legal restraint has led to the consistent highlighting of periods of crisis. It is mainly against a background of intense political activity, as for example in the Queen Anne period or during the excitements of the Wilkes affair, that the newspapers achieve an erratic visibility during the eighteenth century. This has resulted in the construction of an eccentric chronological framework for the history of the press in which its development is defined largely if not entirely in terms of national politics. Only Laurence Hanson, in a book published in the mid-1930s, has provided a coherent view centered more closely on the London newspapers than on the political events and personalities of the period. Among the side effects of the concern with party political activity is a crude exaggeration of the importance of direct intervention, particularly through subsidy—a line that Arthur Aspinall's generally useful study *Politics and the Press* has tended to encourage.

On the other hand modern studies of the eighteenth-century newspapers themselves, however interesting and well constructed, have produced a picture that is inherently off balance. This is largely the result of a heavy emphasis on the growth of the provincial press. The admirable pioneering works of G. A. Cranfield, R. M. Wiles, and Robert Munter, produced in a flurry of activity in the 1960s, while quite rightly highlighting the expansion of newspaper publication in the provinces, nonetheless left a vacuum at the center. In each study the London press makes recurrent appearances but always remains a hazy element in the background, a powerful but undefined force. One of the few efforts to tune into the developments in the capital was made by R. L. Haig in his book on the *Gazetteer*. However, although of real importance, his study is tightly focused on a single publication and the emphasis, because of the nature of his manuscript sources, is firmly in the second half of the eighteenth century. It is characteristic that some of the most interesting detail for the earlier period is to be found in Wiles's account of serial publication before 1750, where the newspapers are viewed mainly as vehicles for literary material.

At the same time, within the framework of these and other modern studies, there appears a view of the English press that takes the publications of the eighteenth century to be of interest mainly as a prelude to future developments. This is seldom given any clear definition but is implied in an approach that is both optimistic and "whiggish." The concept is one in which more and more newspapers lead to better and better results. 1695, the year that marked the end of prepublication censorship, is held to represent a starting point for the slow but steady emergence of a free press, which found its apotheosis in the tax repeals of the mid-nineteenth century. Such a view implicitly detracts from the importance of the output of earlier periods, trivializes its character, and reduces the publications to the status of "forerunners." This "fourth-estate" view is now collapsing. Work specifically concerned with the history of the press, although dealing largely with the nineteenth century, has been particularly helpful in reconstructing the frame of reference within which the eighteenth-century newspapers can reasonably be placed. Scholars such as Virginia Berridge, James Curran and the late Alan Lee have encouraged a clearer-sighted approach to the underlying themes of organization, control, and the presentation of material. This, in combination with the steady accumulation of information, not least in collections of well-researched essays, has led to the emergence of a new methodology in which newspapers and periodicals are themselves made the focus of coordinated research.

Hitherto the newspapers and related forms of output have suffered from submersion in a variety of disciplines in which their main value has been as an adjunct to other lines of specialist inquiry. Scholars in the fields of history and literature have produced excellent work that has often touched on the development of the London press. In literature in particular Bertrand Goldgar, Pat Rogers, and the cluster of scholars whose attention is centered on the work of Henry Fielding have produced some extremely valuable material.[2] Nonetheless neither here nor in the overlapping areas of bibliography and book-trade history has the newspaper itself emerged as a major theme of investigation. Because of its peculiar character and because of its importance across society, newspaper history requires special treatment. One aim of this study is to make a modest contribution to the slow but observable development of this major area of research.

At this stage the accumulation of detail is of the greatest importance. The lack of even a coherent bibliography of the eighteenth-century newspapers reflects the massive shortage of information facing students of the period. In attempting to fill in some of the blanks on the map and to make sense of a great deal of messy and dispersed information, the focus of this study remains in the middle decades of the century. This subdivision arises partly from the value of distancing the analysis from both the Queen Anne and Wilkes periods, which have absorbed so much miscellaneous attention and which at the same time still require a great deal of close research from the point of view of the press itself. In this latter respect the exclusion of other periods has been a matter of self-preservation—newspapers are long, at least when put together in volumes on a library shelf, and life is short. More important, the period centered on the 1720s, 30s, and 40s, which coincides with the durable administration run by Sir Robert Walpole, was one in which a major shift in the character of the London press took place. Through the build-up of a new management system and the partial integration of the interests of the business community and the political establishment, the press began to assume an entirely new and yet to the modern eye a relatively familiar character. Although the foundations of the modern English press have been located at various points along an extended chronological line, a claim has to be made for the middle years of the eighteenth century. During this period the elements of organization and control were assembled that were to contribute to most of the tensions and conflicts as well as to the more positive developments of the next two hundred years. This process, taking place largely below the surface, was complete by mid-century, when the London press entered a period of commercial stability and political inertia that can be seen as rounding off the first phase in its modern development.

This study offers a detailed and largely descriptive analysis of a complex adjustment through the identification of shifts in management, control, and content. It is as yet too soon to attempt anything like a general reworking of the history of the eighteenth-century newspaper press. Even so this study aims to contribute to the shelving of a number of long-established stereotypes and to the construction of a more complete and realistic view. At the same time it also aims to place the London press firmly at the center of national developments, indicating how the capital, as in all areas of social, political, and economic life, exercised a dominant influence.

Acknowledgments

My particular thanks are due to the staff of the British Library who provided helpful access to the Burney Collection of newspapers on which this study is based and also to the staff of the Guildhall Library. I am grateful in both instances for permission to use the items reproduced here as illustrations.

My thanks are also due to a great many people who over an extended period have helped me with suggestions and support, in particular to Ian Christie for his long-term interest and cogent advice, to Terry Belanger for some now distant conversations, and to Bertrand Goldgar, Michael Tread-well, Joseph Levine, and other friends and colleagues working in the British Library who have kept me in touch with academic reality. None of these, of course, are to blame for the following material or its treatment.

Notes on the Text

The use of an italic type-face for emphasis or to distinguish material of various sorts was general through the London press. In particular notices about the conduct of a newspaper, located under the title or elsewhere, were usually treated in this way. In such italicized sections, roman type became the emphatic form and this usage is reproduced in all quotations cited in the text. The use of capitals is also retained. Much of the flavor of the material published in the newspapers of the Walpole period is dependent on differentiated type. Its omission could therefore have involved some loss of sense.

Throughout, the new-style Gregorian Calendar adopted in 1752 in which the year was held to begin on 1 January rather than on 25 March has been used. The old calendar by which most, but not all, the London newspapers before this time were dated has caused endless confusion to those binding up copies in volumes. As a result some of the sets in the British Library have been put in the wrong sequence; this has been corrected but not noted.

Abbreviations

B.L.	British Library
C.U.L.	Cambridge University Library
D.N.B.	*Dictionary of National Biography*
G.P.O.	General Post Office
H.M.C.	Historical Manuscripts Commission
H. of C.J.	*House of Commons Journal*
N. and Q.	*Notes and Queries*
P.R.O.	Public Record Office, London
Q.C.	Queens College, Oxford
T.B.P.	Printed calendars of Treasury Books and Papers

For abbreviations of the titles of newspapers and magazines see Bibliography, II, Printed Material.

All dates have been adjusted to the new style, with the year running from 1 January.

London Newspapers
in the Age of Walpole

1

The Shaping of the London Newspaper

By the middle of the eighteenth century the physical appearance of the London newspapers as well as the structural relationship between the different forms had reached a reasonable state of equilibrium. This was partly the result of shifts in internal organization centered on issues of ownership and control. But although such developments were crucial in terms of stability, the shape and character of the London press were largely defined by external pressures, most importantly by the financial constraints embodied in parliamentary legislation and sharpened by the brutal exigencies of the market. The collapse of prepublication censorship in 1695, which accompanied the almost absent-minded lapse of the Licensing Act,[1] was followed by a striking rise in the volume of output. London offered a market of unique scale and coherence, and the printers, freed from official restraint, began at once to exploit the considerable demand for news and related forms of cheap reading matter. By 1712 about twenty single-leaf papers were regularly published in the capital each week.[2] Partly through the efforts of London-trained printers squeezed out by increasing competition, newspapers also began to appear in the English provinces and in Ireland, based directly on the pattern of their London counterparts.[3]

This rapid and far-flung expansion based on a combination of commercial speculation and political opportunism conflicted with a variety of vested interests. Consequently, from the beginning of the century members of the London printing trade and politicians in office were linked in enthusiastic support for the reimposition of some form of general restraint.[4] Recurrent attempts to enact legislation failed[5] and in 1712 Lord Bolingbroke compromised by introducing the system of taxation, first proposed in 1704, as an indirect curb on production.[6] The Act (10 Anne c. 19) fell most heavily on the newspapers, which if printed on a whole sheet were to carry a 1d. stamp or if on a half sheet or less, a half-penny stamp. The advertisements, which were already an important source of revenue,[7] were each placed under a duty of 1/-. The measure was universally condemned by the trade and greeted with morbid prophecies of extinction. As the author of the *British Mercury* remarked, *"The new Duty impos'd on printed single Sheets and half Sheets, will doubtless somewhat lessen the Number of English News Papers, and a Peace may perhaps be fatal to such as survive that first Blow."*[8] The immediate impact of the Act in London, as in the provinces, seems to have been considerable and, while a number of papers went out of business, the circulation of the survivors was severely curtailed.[9] However, in spite of the general rise in price of all forms to 1½d. and 2d., and the subsequent absence of war reports, the London papers were able for the most part to reestablish their commercial position. At the same time, the Act contained a sizable loophole that was immediately apparent to the newspaper proprietors and that itself became a critical formative influence on the development of the London press. In failing to define precisely what constituted a newspaper, the Act allowed publications consisting of more than one sheet, however frequently issued or whatever the nature of their content, to be registered as pamphlets and to pay a much lower duty of 2/- a sheet on a single copy of each edition.[10] The *London Gazette* at once began to appear in occasional unstamped issues of six or eight pages, while sporadic attempts were also made by the proprietors of the single-leaf thrice-weeklies to cash in on this device. During 1713 at least two of these papers, *Pax, Pax, Pax: or, a Pacifick Post Boy* and the *Flying Post: or, the Post Master,* introduced a six-page format at the original price of 1½d.[11] In neither case was the experiment maintained and, although the *St. James's Evening Post* was later extended by "a running Title of half a sheet,"[12] postage costs alone prevented any general increase in size among papers of this type. Similarly although the major dailies established at the end of the decade were occasionally published in six unstamped pages,[13] problems of content and production militated against their regular appearance in this form.

Extension to a sheet-and-a-half was most clearly viable in papers published once a week and, although the *Weekly Packet* continued to appear long after 1712 as a four-page paper, carrying the official stamp and selling at twopence, new six-page publications retailing at 1½d, soon began to dominate the weekly output. The earliest moves in this direction were made in the thrice-weekly *British Mercury,* the house publication of the Sun Fire Insurance company. A petition from the proprietors requesting that it should be exempt from the new duty[14] seems to have been rejected and the day after the Act took effect it was announced that the paper would in future appear weekly on one-and-a-half sheets selling at 1½d.[15] The rapid appearance of the *Mercury,* in what was to become the standard journal form, was followed by the publication of Robert Mawson's *Weekly Journal* in 1713 and John Applebee's *Original Weekly Journal* the following year. By the middle of the decade the dramatic rise in the number of six-page Saturday weeklies began to put a considerable strain on the established papers. The author of the *British Mercury* announced in August 1715 that *"Whereas the great Glut of News-Papers, that are of late publish'd on Saturdays, is grown almost*

*as a common Nuisance, these are (at the request of several hundreds of the Subscrib-
ers to this Office) to give Notice, That we shall, as formerly, put out this Paper on
Wednesdays in every Week."*[16] Early the following year the *Mercury* was reconstituted as a quarterly[17] while the increasing pressure seems to have driven
others out of business. In January, Mawson abandoned his journal in favor
of a four-page weekly *News Letter,* ending the first issue with some bitter
remarks at the expense of his successful rivals. "Several Printers in Town
and Country," he stated,

> who have since the first Publication of the *Weekly-Journal,* foisted their
> miserable Political Collections under the Name, now find themselves at
> Liberty to drop or continue their Papers.
> London. January 7.   1715–1716
> *Memorandum.*
> Agreed that Briscoe, Read, Midwinter, or any other Pirating Printer,
> or Pedling Bookseller whatsoever if They will make known their misera-
> ble case to the First Proprietor of that Paper, he will give them free
> Consent under his Hand to Print *Weekly-Journals,* rather than They shall
> hang Themselves for want of other Employ.[18]

The successful publication of extended journals continued but, although
some of these papers appeared in conjunction with a regular mid-week
supplement,[19] few attempts were made to increase the size of an individual
paper to two full sheets. In 1721 the *London Journal* began to appear
occasionally in eight folio pages,[20] but the difficulty of finding suitable
material to fill the extra space probably put an end to the experiment.[21]

While the loophole in the act of 1712 resulted in the appearance of the
extended journals, it also stimulated important developments in cut-price
newspaper publication. From 1717 an increasing number of six-page
thrice-weeklies, unstamped and aimed specifically at the London market,
began to appear at costs well below the standard rate. James Read's *Penny
Post,* first published in March 1717, was among the earliest of these cheap
papers, although it was almost immediately undercut by William Heathcote's *London Post,* offered at the very low price of ½d.[22] The publication of
Heathcote's paper, which consisted of six small folio pages without the
standard two-column division and with the last page left blank, in turn
prompted the appearance of George Parker's rival halfpenny *London News*
the following year,[23] and by the early 1720s several of these cut-price
newspapers were appearing on the market. The publication of the six-page
Penny Weekly Journal in 1720[24] suggests the way in which production at this
level was being extended, and by 1725 a whole stratum of cheap unstamped
papers had come into existence largely as a result of shortcomings in the
law.

The progress of this form of tax evasion was viewed with increasing
concern by the administration, under heavy attack in the weekly press, as
well as by vested commercial interests. As early as 1717 Toland's memorial

had urged the ministry to take steps to tighten up the act, thus at a stroke preventing unfair competition, increasing the revenue, and checking the growth of sedition. Although a more general political suppression seems to have been under official consideration from the early 1720s, the passage of the amended Stamp Act of 1725, intended to close the tax loophole, was perhaps directly stimulated by the activity of a commercial pressure group. In 1724 Samuel Negus in his list of London printers named three half-penny posts published in the capital,[25] while the following year George Parker claimed in a petition to parliament that five printers were at work on such papers and that 20,000 reams of paper per annum were used in their production. The growing success of the halfpenny posts seems to have caused particular concern to the bookseller proprietors of the leading dailies also circulating mainly in the London area but obliged to conform to the letter of the law. According to Parker, the Act of 1725 was the culmination of about three years' agitation and was obtained entirely through *"the long Application and strenuous Efforts of the Owners of Stamp't* News-Papers, *viz.* Daily Courant, Daily Post, Daily Journal etc."* who were *"intending thereby (no doubt) to engross all the Profits gain'd by* News Papers *to themselves."*[26]

The extension of the tax to newspapers of more than one sheet on 25 April (11 George I. c. 8) had a considerable effect on the flourishing weeklies. They were all obliged to undergo an immediate curtailment in size to 4 pages since the newly imposed duty would have added 1½d. per copy to the production costs and priced them off the market. Although the weeklies also cut down the size of the sheet, the increase in tax still meant an overall rise in price to 2d. a copy. *The Weekly Journal or Saturday's-Post,* which immediately appeared with new numbering and the amended title of *Mist's Weekly Journal,* underwent a typical transformation. Its four pages were cut to roughly half the size of the previous issue, the very elaborate heading by Hoffman was replaced by a plain title, and the price was increased. The author complained that "while I look upon myself in this new Dress, the Gracefulness of my Figure seems to suffer some diminution from the Change: Methinks I look like some veteran Soldier, who by the Misfortunes of War, had lost a leg and an Arm in the Service of his Country."[27] These remarks could have been applied to most weekly papers, although attempts were made to rescue some of the features of the old form from the general wreck. The subsidized *London Journal,* for example, kept its folio sheet, while James Read's *Weekly Journal or British Gazeteer,* though in a quarto format, appeared on cheaper paper and attempted unsuccessfully to peg its price at 1½d. In spite of the radical overhaul in appearance and the increase in price, none of the London weeklies ceased publication at this time and in contrast to the English provinces a number of new journals continued to appear during the late 1720s.[28]

The Act was expected, and to some extent intended, to cause the greatest havoc among the burgeoning cheap papers. In a petition to parliament, reprinted in his paper, George Parker claimed that "should a Duty of

Three Half-pence be laid upon these mean *News-Papers*, (which by reason of the Coarseness of the Paper, the generality of Gentlemen are above Conversing with) it would utterly extinguish and suppress the same."[29] In May, after the Act had taken effect, the author of the *Weekly Journal* remarked that the papers wore the stamp like the badge of the poor, "which causeth such a Decay amongst them, that in a short Time, tis very probable, they will be reduced into their former Non-Existence."[30] In the event these remarks were entirely unjustified and as an instrument of restraint the Act proved ultimately as ineffectual as its predecessor. Parker announced his intention of modifying his paper, *Parker's London News*, well in advance of the Act's coming into force[31] and, having published it on Friday 24 April, produced a final issue in the old six-page, small-folio form the following evening. "Being willing," he announced, "to oblige our Readers as far as possibly lay in our Power, we have published the Paper the Evening before the Act takes Place, that they may not be put to a Penny Charge til Wensday [*sic*] next, when we hope they will give a favourable Reception."[32] Subsequently *Parker's Penny Post* appeared, like *Heathcote's Original London Post*, on four quarto pages, under a brief undecorated title and with a two column page division throughout. All three of the papers listed by Negus survived into the 1730s, apparently with some success.

The physical restraints imposed throughout the London press by the Stamp Acts put space at a premium and underlined the need for a utilitarian approach to layout. Prior to 1725 the main London Weeklies had all been characterized by their flamboyant use of decorated titles.[33] These were almost universally abandoned at this point and only occasionally reappeared to advertise a new paper or to underline a change in editorial policy. In 1732, for example, the extremist *Universal Spy* appeared under an allegorical pro-jacobite illustration that had first appeared in the early 1720s,[34] while in 1741 the *Westminster Journal* heralded its adoption of a political line by incorporating an elaborate view of the Houses of Parliament.[35] The only weekly that continued after 1725 to make regular use of such material was *Read's Weekly Journal* which, like the moribund morning posts, appeared with a rather crudely executed block on each side of the title. In the 1740s, following the general extension in the page size, full-priced papers, such as the *Champion*, the *London Courant* and the new *Whitehall Evening Post* were published under elaborate headings, although for the most part extraneous decoration on the front page was limited to a single design around the opening initial.

The need to take maximum advantage of a restricted printing area produced a similar response from the proprietors of all forms of London newspaper. Reduction in the size of print was occasionally attempted. However, although advertisements were universally compressed in this way and although sections of a few papers, for example the *London Evening Post*, the *Daily Post*, and the *Daily Journal*, were sometimes issued in the same very small type,[36] the sacrifice in legibility was not apparently considered to be

[1]   Numb. 1005

Parker's,
LONDON NEWS,
OR THE
Impartial Intelligencer,

Containing the most

Remarkable Occurrences, Foreign and Domestick.

Saturday Evening, *April* 24. 1725.

Arabian Nights Entertainments *continued*, Vol. X. —— No. 355

ALI Baba did not stand long to consider what he should do, but went immediately into the Cave, and as soon as he was in, the Door shut close again, which never disturb'd him, because he knew the Secret to open it again. He never regarded the Silver, but made the best use of his Time in carrying out as much of that Gold which was in bags, at several Times, as he thought his three Asses could carry. When he had done, he gather'd up his Asses which were dispersed about, and when he had loaded them, covered the Bags with green Boughs, and then pronouncing the Words *Shut Sesame*, made the best of his Way to Town.

When *Ali Baba* got home he drove them into a little Yard, and shut the Gates carefully, threw off the Wood that cover'd the *Bags*, carried them into his House, and ranged them in order before his Wife, who sat on a Sofa.

His Wife handled them and finding 'em full of Money, suspected that her Husband had been robbing, insomuch that when he had brought them all in, she could not help saying, *Ali Baba*, Have you been so unhappy as to ——— be quiet Wife interrupted *Ali Baba*, do not frighten your self, I am no Robber, unless he can be one who steals from Thieves. You will no longer entertain an ill Opinion of me, when I shall tell you my good Fortune. Then he emptied the bags, which raised such a great Heap of Gold, as dazzled his Wife's Eyes; and when he had done, told her the whole Story from the beginning to the end, and above all recommended it to her keep it secret.

The Wife, recover'd and cured of her Fears, rejoyced with her Husband for their good Luck, and would count all the Gold, piece by piece. Wife reply'd *Ali Baba*, you don't know what you undertake, when you pretend to count the Money, you'll never have done; I'll go and dig an Hole and bury it, there's no Time to be lost. You are in the right on't Husband, reply'd the Wife, but let us know as nigh as possible, how much we have? I'll go and borrow a Measure in the Neighbourhood, and measure it while you dig a Hole. What signifies

The front page of *Parker's London News* 1005, Saturday 24 April 1725, the last issue published before the Stamp Act of 1725 took effect.

commercially justifiable. One way of making a mass of closely printed and largely undifferentiated type acceptable to the reader was by the use of multiple columns. The practice of subdividing pages in this way became increasingly widespread as the new Stamp Act took effect and all sections of the London press found it a useful means of reconciling the conflicting pressures of supply and demand. The principal weekly journals adopted a three-column page division during 1725,[37] and the following year the leading London dailies, the *Daily Post* and the *Daily Journal*, simultaneously made the same move.[38] In 1728 the proprietors of the *Daily Journal* attempted to introduce an occasional four-column layout on an extended single leaf.[39] However, this proved both unwieldy and uneconomic[40] and consequently they began to experiment with a two-column division on four smaller pages, raising the price from 1½d. to 2d. This change was vigorously opposed by the London coffee men, who, acting in concert with the proprietors of the *Daily Post,* rapidly forced a reversion to the original form and price.[41] It was not until 1733 that any thrice-weekly paper introduced a third column, but at this time both the *London Evening Post* and its newer rival, the *General Evening Post*, announced an extension.[42] Individual variations in layout continued to crop up in the attempt to establish the most economic use of space. In 1729, James Read enlarged the page-size of his journal and reverted to a two-column division, subsequently carrying out several other alterations before reestablishing the more usual three-column style in the mid-1730s. The adoption of this format was often, in the case of less commercially successful papers, either delayed or never attempted. It was not, for example, until 1730 that the *Daily Courant,* supported by a government subsidy, made the change,[43] while the unsuccessful morning posts and the *Whitehall Evening Post* retained their two-column page division during the 1730s until their eventual collapse.

The use of additional columns was linked to a second device, which arose directly from the shortcomings of the 1725 Act itself. Although the legislation seemed to have dealt successfully with the pamphlet-newspaper by extending the duty to news-carrying publications consisting of more than four pages, it failed altogether to define the size of the sheet and hence of the half-sheet on which only the basic newspaper stamp was required. This allowed the proprietors to carry out an unchecked expansion of their page sizes while still claiming for tax purposes that their publications consisted of only a half-sheet of paper. In 1731 Edmund Curll pointed out to the authorities the need for legislation to plug this loophole.[44] However, while no official action seems to have been taken to implement his self-interested proposal, London papers of all types continued to extend the size of the half-sheet at the cost only of the materials used. The principal weeklies were all appearing by the early 1730s in a variable large folio.[45] Similarly, the thrice-weeklies also underwent an erratic extension, following the lead of the *London Evening Post* and the *General Evening Post*, which adopted a journal-size page with the three-column layout in 1733 and were almost simultaneously extended to a large folio in 1744.[46] The most radical extension within the letter of the law, was made by the principal London dailies, which were able to more than offset production costs by the increased revenue from advertisements. The *Daily Journal* seems to have been among the leaders and, after its abortive experiments of the late 1720s, began occasionally to appear on a large half-sheet folded into four pages and selling at 1½d. Such extended issues, carrying only the ½d. stamp and composed mainly of advertisements, became increasingly popular among the successful London dailies during the busy November-to-April period. During the early 1740s, the proportion of "double" issues steadily increased and by 1746 the highly successful *Daily Advertiser* and *General Advertiser* were both appearing continuously in four large folio pages selling at 1½d.[47] The changes in layout and size taking place among the full priced papers were paralleled by similar moves among the cut-price thrice-weeklies. Thomas Read's *Penny London Post* was already appearing in small folio in 1733,[48] while three years later the page size of the newly published *Rayner's Morning Advertiser* was rapidly increased to folio and given a three-column division, a form that became general among papers of this type by the mid-1740s. A further and in the short term more serious shortcoming of the new Stamp Act of 1725 was the continued failure to provide an effective working definition of a newspaper for tax purposes, and variably successful attempts were made to use this ambiguity to evade the law. Prior to its initial appearance in 1726, the proprietors of the *Craftsman* seem to have had hopes that their paper would be accepted by the authorities as a pamphlet. The first number, containing no news or advertising, appeared on six unstamped pages under an old-style, decorated heading. However, the second issue was published as a conventional single-leaf essay-sheet carrying the halfpenny stamp, the author explaining the radical change of format in a lengthy title notice:

> I am sorry that I am obliged so soon to make an apology to the publick, especially to those persons who were disappointed in having this paper, as advertised on Monday last; but they are desired to consider that a private person must submit to the decisions of those in authority. The case stands thus: I had determined, for several reasons, to print this paper in a *sheet and a half,* as I apprehended might be legally done, and that it did not come within the late Act for obliging all *Journals, Mercuries* and NEWS-PAPERS, to be stampt: but it seems that all papers which are published once a week, or oftener, are deem'd NEWS-PAPERS, and accordingly cannot be publish'd without being *Stampt,* for which Reason, it was not thought safe to sell any of these papers, which were inadvertently printed in this manner.[49]

In spite of its length and the total absence of news, the Stamp Office commissioners seem to have had no hesitation in taking action against the *Craftsman,* although it is possible that in this case some political pressure was brought to bear. A few years later, when the position had been considerably complicated by the emergence of a growing number of monthly and weekly magazines, a new attempt to evade the law by an extension in size was less conclusively dealt with. In 1733 the printer Robert Penny added a supplementary sheet to his weekly *British Observator* and issued both sections without stamps, following, it was later claimed, the example of Eustace Budgell's three-sheet magazine, the *Bee*.[50] In what Wiles has described as a test case, Penny was ordered by the commissioners to stamp the news section of his paper, a ruling that was also applied to some of the news-carrying monthlies.[51] In spite of this, the commissioners' judgement allowed the supplementary section of Penny's *Observator* to continue to appear unstamped, and the commercial possibilities of the device seem to have immediately prompted the publication of a second sheet with most, if not all, the penny thrice-weeklies as well as with James Read's full-priced *Weekly Journal*.[52] The rapidly rising tide of news-carrying weeklies and monthlies in a very wide range of forms posed a considerable administrative problem, which the commissioners were not apparently competent to handle. Sporadic action continued to be taken against publications that contained an unstamped news sheet. In 1735, for example, an advertisement for the *Weekly Oracle* announced to readers that "The News Sheet which used to be published with the oracle, being now to be stamp'd, will, for a Time to come be printed by itself under the Title of the *Gentlemans Journal*."[53] Nonetheless, from the mid-1730s the prolixity and obscurity of the pseudo-newspapers seem to have defeated the commissioners' efforts. In 1739 the author of the *Daily Gazetteer* denounced the increase of such publications. "Some there are that print on *Two Sheets* or *a larger Quantity;* and others print *News* in Papers of a Miscellaneous Kind, containing Scraps of Poetry, History, Trials of Highwaymen, Pickpockets, and many other Subjects, that tend to debauch the Morals of the Commonalty, for which they insist by *Law* that no *Duty* is payable either as *News-Papers* or *Pamphlets:* so that in reality there is scarce *one Paper* in ten that are daily dispers'd as *News Papers* pay any Duty, and these not one in *five* pay according to the Intention of the *Legislature*."[54] The writer went on to estimate that there were at least thirty different types of such papers published in London.

The difficulty of enforcing the Stamp Act contributed to the appearance from the mid-1730s of several halfpenny and farthing papers which, evading the tax altogether, relied largely on their obscurity for survival. Evidence for the form and character of the halfpenny posts is very limited but if, as the Audit Office records suggest, the *Original London Post* was a halfpenny paper,[55] it seems possible that they generally appeared as thrice-weekly, four-page publications laid out in two columns. On the other hand the farthing papers, for which more information is available, were usually single-leaf dailies with a three-column division for the first page, devoted largely or entirely to serializations, and a two-column layout for the second.[56] A certain amount of use seems to have been made, in this section of the press, of decorated titles, and both the *Original London Post* and the *London Farthing Post* carried large pictorial headings using newspaper hawkers as the motif. This may only have been an occasional device and while the farthing paper dropped the feature before the end of the short surviving run,[57] none of its rivals or successors seem to have incorporated a similar illustration.

By the end of the decade a substantial member of such cut-price papers were circulating in the London area. In 1738 the author of the *Craftsman* claimed that he had "lately seen no less than six *half-penny-Papers* besides an Advertisement of another, which was to come out on *Monday* last; and I am told that there are almost as many *Farthing Papers*."[58] On the same day it was stated in the *London Evening Post* that ten of those unstamped papers were published in the capital, of which 50,000 copies were sold each week.[59] On the following Monday a similar paragraph in the *Daily Post* included unstamped penny papers in the total of ten definite titles and raised the number of copies in weekly circulation to 80,000.[60] Whether these hostile estimates were realistic remains unclear, although they were given some ambiguous support five years later by the printer Daniel Pratt. In a petition to the Duke of Newcastle, Pratt pointed out the prevalence of tax evasion and claimed that there were "Several printers, who print Ten or twelve thousand farthing papers and others Daily and Weekly."[61] He concluded by specifying eight regularly unstamped papers, of which at least four were farthing dailies,[62] and if, as seems likely, his printing figure referred to a daily output, this would have implied a total in line with the earlier estimates.

The build-up in unfair competition from the unstamped papers provoked a good deal of comment in the upper reaches of the press and a clamor for more effective tax enforcement. The call for action was more strident in the opposition papers, which suggested that official quiescence was deliberate policy aimed at undermining their circulation.[63] In 1738 an editorial in the *Craftsman* combined some ironic asides on the ministry's political prosecutions with a typical attack on the production of unstamped papers:

> Now as this is a bare-faced Breach of the *Law,* defrauding the *Publick Revenue,* and there is a large Penalty upon every Paper sold *unstamp'd,* I should be glad to know why the offenders are not brought to Justice.—If the *Commissioners of the Stamp Office,* whose Business it is, neglected their Duty, why is not the *Messenger of the Press* despatch'd to ferret Them out of their Lurking-holes and the *Solicitor of the Treasury* order'd to prosecute Them?—Why does not his *Worship of Sohoe* apprehend some of the Hawkers, who hawk *these Papers* every Morning, in Droves, before his Door?[64]

Such criticism was at least partly justified, and it was perhaps an indication of the security of the unstamped papers from prosecution that the *London*

Farthing Post carried the name of either its printer or publisher openly on the imprint.[65]

While agreeing that action was necessary, the author of the ministerial *Daily Gazetteer* emphasized the difficulties facing the Stamp Office. As well as the ambiguities in the law, the problems of tracking down the personnel engaged in production and distribution were often insurmountable. Most halfpenny and farthing papers appeared with a humorous or uninformative imprint, while at least one printer seems to have attempted to confuse the authorities by using a garbled and meaningless title.[66] At the same time the distributors were often very elusive. As the author of the *Gazetteer* pointed out after stressing the obscurity of the printers, "their Hawkers or Carriers are no less adroit in evading Justice: To avoid being caught in selling or dispersing unstampt News Papers, they shall throw them in at the Doors or Windows of their Customers, and reckon with them at leisure. Thus like the Thief and Receiver, are the Creditors of the Government pillag'd and cheated by the joint Craft of the Publisher and Reader."[67] Even after arrest the degree of personal loyalty that seems to have existed between the printers and the hawkers probably made the discovery of sources of supply extremely difficult. According to the imprint of the farthing *London Evening Advertiser,* the paper was sold "only by such Hawkers as have *True Hearts and sound Bottoms,*"[68] and the printer Daniel Pratt claimed, in 1743, that the printers of the unstamped papers "keep up a Bank, to maintain such of their hawkers that are or may be putt in prison for selling the same."[69]

Magistrates seem to have taken sporadic action during the late 1730s against the printers and publishers of unstamped papers,[70] but it was not apparently until the end of the decade that the authorities began to organize a concerted drive against the unstamped press. In June 1740 the *London Evening Post* reported that "the several Printers and Publishers of the Half-penny and Farthing Posts are all under Prosecutions by Order of the Commissioners of the Stamp-Office, who are determined to punish them with the utmost Severity of the Law, for daring to sell unstamp'd Papers, and suppress so notorious an Imposition as the Crown as well as so great a Hardship on those who justly pay the Stamp-Duty to his Majesty for several Daily and other Papers."[71] Subsequent action may occasionally have been taken against such printers as Robert Walker,[72] but the real weight of Stamp Office intervention continued to be levelled at the more accessible hawkers. In December 1740 the Attorney General, Sir Dudley Ryder, in a detailed report citing the Acts for licencing hawkers and pedlars (9 and 10 William III c. 27), ruled that newspaper sellers were "obliged to take out a License and liable to be seized and detained as other Hawkers are for not having it and subject to the like Penalties."[73] Subsequently, the legitimately stamped papers carried an increasing number of paragraphs recording their arrest, and between January and October 1742 the *London Evening Post* reported twenty-three such prosecutions. Nonetheless, the Stamp Office commissioners complained that Justices were often unwilling to convict under the existing regulations and a request was made for the insertion of a suitable clause in the pending Vagrancy Bill.[74] Consequently, with the passage of the Act (16 George II c. 2) in May 1743, the hawkers of unstamped papers became liable to a maximum penalty of three months hard labor, and a reward of twenty shillings was offered for information leading to a conviction.

The newspaper clause in the new Act introduced no extension to the tax but, by boosting administrative efficiency, had a considerable impact on the press. The hawkers seem to have been hounded with renewed energy and a large number of committals were regularly recorded in the London papers. In February 1744, for example, it was reported that "Last Thursday Ann Mahoney, otherwise Irish Nan, was committed to Clarkenwell Bridewell, for three Months to hard Labour, by James Fraser, Esq: for selling unstamp'd News-Papers. This is the seventh Time of her being committed for Offences of the like Nature."[75] The clamp down on distribution, which resulted in the prosecution of at least one printer, John Nicholson,[76] led to the complete disappearance of the halfpenny and farthing papers and there does not appear to have been any attempt to resurrect this sort of popular publication for the rest of the century. Some publishers of penny newspapers, including those of the *British Intelligencer* and the *Penny London Morning Advertiser,* continued to evade the tax,[77] but the tightening up of the law resulted in a generally more scrupulous use of stamps. The national revenue from the tax for 1743 was nearly double that of the previous year and the increase in the amount of business done by the Stamp Office obliged the commissioners to rent new premises in Lincoln's Inn and provide a further press.[78]

The expansion of the London newspaper output represented by new titles was irregular and is to some extent obscured by a general lack of detailed information as well as by the multiplicity of forms. Among the full-priced papers a good deal of the hectic activity was offset by cannibalistic competition. A pamphlet published in 1729, answering complaints about the growing number of London papers, pointed out that "as one makes its Way, another declines or goes off the Stage; and thus as they push one another out, the Number of Papers is not likely to be much increased."[79] Overall growth was also curbed by the restrictive practices put into effect by vested commercial interests, which saw an increase in the number of papers as a threat to their livelihood. The most important of these groups was composed of the bookseller proprietors of established London newspapers, whose activities were both far-reaching and effective in suppressing potential rivals.[80] However, similar external pressure was also exerted from an entirely different direction. The London coffee-men, whose houses provided an important outlet for papers of all types, particularly the full-priced dailies, engaged in a long-term struggle to check the rise in the number of London papers. Action of some sort was evidently taken in the early 1720s[81] and the potential influence of the coffee-men was clearly demonstrated in the swift and effective campaign in 1728 to reverse the *Daily Journal* price increase. At the end of the decade a head-on clash between the two interests developed, accompanied by a revealing pamphlet controversy.[82] The coffee-men's principal complaint concerned the expense involved in taking in the proliferating London papers. It was claimed that these cost the proprietors of the various houses "most of 'em Ten, many Fifteen and some Twenty Pounds a Year, and upwards,"[83] which was "more than the Trade and Profits of one half of the Coffee-Men will allow."[84] The Pamphlet on their behalf, which contained a series of complaints on the advantage taken by the newspapers of coffee-house facilities, ended with a reprint of a circular letter from a committee of eleven coffee-house proprietors sent to the principal London houses. Dated 6 November 1728, it outlined the plan, put forward at various assemblies and meetings of coffee-men, of themselves producing two half-sheet papers at 1½d. to be published every morning and evening, thus cornering the market.[85] The newspaper proprietors in a detailed attack on every aspect of this case ridiculed the scheme and ironically proposed setting up half a dozen coffee-houses since, they claimed, the newspapers formed the basis of coffee-house appeal.[86] Although no copies seem to have survived, the coffee-men's scheme was put into a least partial effect, as a curious, occasional publication in opposition indicates.[87] However, early in 1730 this rather eccentric enterprise collapsed with the demise of their morning paper,[88] and there is no evidence that similar attempts were ever made. It is perhaps significant that the *Daily Advertiser,* aiming for a similar sort of monopoly in advertising, carried an increasing and very unusual number of coffee-houses on the imprint of the early issues, and this may reflect a return of some of the original hopes. The coffee-men continued to grumble at the volume of London newspapers and to wield an influence over them,[89] but they were unable ultimately to exercise any direct control.

As a result of a variety of such pressures, the growth in the total number of full-priced papers published in London at any one time was undramatic, although the balance between the different forms varied. Between 1726 and 1736 the number of four-page weeklies and single-leaf essay-sheets rose from about six to thirteen, while all the surviving thrice-weekly morning-posts ceased publication and the number of thrice-weekly evening papers remained static at about four. In the same period the number of dailies published in London increased from about three to six. The outbreak of war at the end of the 1730s, the subsequent suppression of the cheap publications, and the Jacobite crisis in 1745 gave an important boost to circulation and prompted a good deal of activity in the press, but led to no overall increase in the sum of full-priced newspapers in publication. By 1746 the number of weeklies and essay-sheets had fallen back to about six, while the number of thrice-weeklies and dailies remained constant also at about six in each case.

Although the suppression of the halfpenny and farthing papers in 1743 put an end to the period of unrestricted growth in the cheap press, extended weeklies and cut-price thrice-weeklies, operating generally within the limits of the law, continued to appear. But while the number of such papers is difficult to pin down, it does seem that following the dramatic boom that began in the mid 1730s there was some run-down in the overall total published by the middle of the following decade. By this time two of the leading entrepreneurs in this area of output had abandoned the London press, while no more than two or three penny thrice-weeklies were appearing on the market.

2

The Distribution of the London Newspapers

Although London with its massive population, high level of literacy, and sophisticated commercial structure formed the hub of the newspaper business, provincial distribution was crucial to a large section of the London press. From the 1690s the principal London papers picked up and extended the distribution pattern of the long-established, manuscript newsletters, which themselves continued in circulation well beyond the middle of the eighteenth century. Whatever the striking popularity of such essay-sheets as the *Tatler, Spectator,* and *Examiner* during Queen Ann's reign, the most successful periodical publications in the long run were such prosaic London newspapers as the *Post Man, Post Boy,* and *Flying Post.* These were specifically oriented toward the provinces. Invariably published on Tuesday, Thursday, and Saturday to coincide with the timing of the mails out of London and sometimes with a section of paper left blank for correspondence, their titles alone suggest their symbiotic relationship with the Post Office. The build-up in the output of this form of newspaper was hardly checked by the Stamp Act. In an ironic aside in the first issue of a new essay-sheet published in 1715, the author remarked that "the Words; *Flying-Post, Post-Man, Post-Master, Post-Boy, London Post,* and *St. James's Post* are already taken up; so that there is no Post left for me but the Penny-Post."[1]

The level of competition for provincial sales suggested by this sort of comment was expressed most sharply in a shift in the timing of distribution. From the second decade of the century a new range of thrice-weekly papers began to challenge the established morning posts through the exploitation of evening publication. By appearing at 4:00 or 5:00 P.M. on the same days, the new evening posts were able to offer material from the latest foreign mails, sometimes added in a last-minute postscript, as well as items copied from their morning rivals. Consequently, when sent into the country the same night, they provided the most up-to-date reports available outside London. After the *Gazette* the thrice-weekly evening papers continued to be the most regularly used source of news of the expanding provincial press.[2] At the same time, in spite of their clear dependence on country distribution, the evening posts could also, as the author of the *Grub Street Journal* remarked in 1737, achieve a good rate of sale in the capital.[3] The untypical *Champion* was said to have been greatly in demand in the city,[4] while surviving issues of both the *General Evening Post* and the *Englishman's Evening Post* carry "London" in their title area, possibly suggesting special publication.

The impact of evening sale on the original thrice-weeklies was soon clear enough. In 1717 John Toland, in a complaint to the ministry, claimed that the circulation of the three long-established morning-posts, the *Post-Man*, the *Flying-Post*, and the *Post-Boy*, as well as that of the *Daily Courant*, had been severely curtailed, "for whereas before People us'd to send all or most of the four papers aforesaid to their friends and correspondents in the country every post-night, now the sale of them is almost confin'd to this town. Nay the vent of them is even much lessen'd here, many persons contenting themselves to read over the same evening posts, which they send to their friends at night."[5] The position of the morning-posts was clearly vulnerable, and during the 1720s they all seem to have gone into a protracted decline. Stephen Whatley, proprietor of the *Flying-Post*, stated that his paper had been a "Great Loss and Discouragement" since 1720,[6] while the *Post-Man* was described in the late 1720s as "so decrepid with Age and Infirmity, that he can scarce creep upon All-fours."[7] The hopeless position of the morning-posts seems to have been recognized by the new proprietors of the *Post-Boy* who, in 1728, switched to daily publication and in this form the paper outlived its contemporaries by several years.[8] A similar shift in publication was forced on the proprietors of the *Champion* which appeared for the first sixty-five issues on the post-day mornings. It was only after the adoption of the publication time and format of the conventional evening-posts that the paper began to achieve any degree of commercial success. An attempt to give a new twist to morning publication occurred in 1746 when a bid was made to by-pass the evening papers by using the extended postal service that had begun to operate daily between London and major eastern and western centers.[9] The *Extraordinary Gazetteer* was published on Monday, Wednesday, and Friday mornings so that "the News of the Gazette etc. may be convey'd into the Country by the Extraordinary Post, and by the News-Carriers, almost two Days sooner than by the Evening Papers."[10] In spite of this apparently attractive offer, there are no indications that the venture, which was more of a bastard evening paper than an old-style morning-post, lasted the year. The provincial success of the evening-posts was reflected in the overall increase in their number during this period from four to six, and by 1750 the most popular of the locally distributed London newspapers was the politically notorious *London Evening Post*.[11] The strength of this opposition paper in comparison with competitors in other forms seems to have been considerable and, whereas in 1746 the important *Daily Post* and weekly *Universal Spectator*, also under the management of the printer John Meres, were both dropped, the *London Evening Post* continued in production for the rest of the century.

The provincial readership that underpinned the development of the thrice-weekly London newspapers was equally important to the journal-form weeklies that appeared after 1712. From the first the proprietors of the full-priced papers were concerned with establishing a foothold in the provincial market. In 1715 the author of the *British Mercury* announced that among the advantages of advertising in his paper was *"its spreading so far, there being near 4,000 printed every Time, and those carefully distributed into all Parts, not only of the City, but of the whole Nation."*[12] By 1720 such weeklies as *Applebee's, Read's,* and *Mist's* had achieved a national reputation,[13] while early in the decade the *London Journal's* campaign against the administration stirred up local feeling throughout the country.[14] Such provincial distribution was of increasing importance to papers of this type, which were basing their appeal largely on a leading essay, usually designed for the upper levels of newspaper readership. Between April and November each year, a large proportion of polite society, together with their households, left the capital, and the general decline in newspaper circulation that resulted would have threatened the survival of any journal relying too heavily on a London distribution. The extent of this potential setback was suggested by the struggles of the weekly and twice-weekly essay-sheets. These papers, which consisted of a single leaf containing no news and minimal advertising and which retailed at 2d., can have had little general appeal to country readers. Consequently they were extremely vulnerable to the summer drop in sales and during these months many either collapsed or suspended publication.[15] The prospect of this inescapable slump seems to have influenced the proprietors of the *Craftsman* to abandon the single-leaf form in May 1727 and to produce the paper as a conventional weekly with the additional subtitle of the *Country Journal.* In an editorial to the new-style paper it was stated that the change, which was to be maintained only during the summer, had been carried out to facilitate postage to readers, many of whom had left town at the parliamentary recess.[16]

The journals were usually published in London on one of the three post days and, while the majority were issued on Saturday in order to include the week's news, a number appeared on Thursday, perhaps primarily to allow copies to reach provincial centers by the weekend. The proprietors of several Saturday weeklies attempted to get the best of both worlds by issuing their papers for provincial distribution the previous Thursday. The author of the largely unsuccessful *Weekly Miscellany* took special pains in the late 1730s to advertise this service. He was particularly indignant at malicious rumors that his paper was not available on Thursday night *"till tis too late to be put up in any Parcel, and sent to the Inns, to be taken next Morning by the Coaches, Carriers, etc.,"* when in fact it could be obtained from the printer at 6:00 P.M.[17] In 1737 the *Craftsman* carried an apology to country readers for an edition completed too late for provincial distribution, and five years later a correspondent claimed to have stopped an issue passing through the Post Office "upon the *Thursday* before the usual day of Publication."[18] Similarly, in the mid-1740s the author of the *Westminster Journal,* in a notice to a contributor, stated that "ATTICUS' *Letter came too late, this Journal being always at Press on* Thursday *Morning, by reason many are sent into the Country by Post, Coaches, Waggons, and reach 50 or 60 Miles by the same Morning they are published here.*"[19] The occasional use of the word London in the title area of such papers as the *Weekly Register* and the *Englishman* may also imply dual publication, although this needs further detailed investigation.[20] Pressure of competition within the capital itself caused most of the variations in the timing of London publication and several of the less popular weeklies, such as the *Weekly Register,* the *What-D'Ye-Call-It* and the *Weekly Miscellany* were obliged to switch from a Saturday to a Thursday or even a Friday issue, apparently without much success.[21]

The primary importance of country distribution to the full-priced London weeklies made them particularly vulnerable to the build-up in competition outside London. Between 1740 and 1746 the number of provincial weeklies in production rose from thirty-one to forty-two,[22] and their influence was gradually extended to London itself. By 1743 the *Reading Mercury* was regularly filed at two public houses in the capital[23] and seven years later the *Western Flying Post* could be read at fifteen such centers.[24] From the late 1730s the proprietors of a growing number of provincial papers established agencies in the capital where advertisements were taken in and where their papers, if not always available for purchase, could at least be read.[25] On the other hand, competition in the provinces was also provided by a spate of weekly and monthly magazines published in London from the 1730s and usually offering local readers a cheap synopsis of the journals' essay content. Consequently, although the more violently anti-ministerial journals, such as *Old England,* were apparently able to maintain their position in the provinces, the general decline in the London weekly press was probably a direct result of the loss of this important sector of the market.

The London dailies were in a rather different position and during the first half of the eighteenth century circulated mainly in London and its environs. Their reliance on income from advertising rather than sales enabled them to survive and flourish within a more restricted geographical area. Even so, the *Daily Courant* and its later and more successful rivals were sometimes regularly sent out of London and the attraction of a wide-ranging readership occasionally drew their proprietors into attempts at extending distribution. One of the reasons given in the *Daily Journal* for its change to a quarto format was that it was designed to *"oblige several of our Correspondents in the Country, and divers* Port-Towns, *who have wish'd to see it in so commodious a Form, as to be sent them by the Post."*[26] In the late 1730s the *Daily Gazetteer* was produced in a special double issue of four pages for country distribution, but this was for political rather than commercial reasons. In the end the expense involved and the restricted number of posts made it impossible for the London dailies to compete seriously with the evening papers in the area during the 1720s and 1730s. Even the extension of the postal service in 1741 does not seem to have provided an immediate stimulus to their country sales, although it is possible that the large increase in circulation of the mid-1740s, was partially the result of a wider dispersal.

The distribution pattern of the cheap London newspapers was more ambiguous, although to some extent it coincided with that of the full-priced forms. The extended weeklies of the 1730s, for example, were sometimes intended for local distribution and Robert Walker published his *London and Country Journal* on Tuesday for provincial readers and on Thursday for readers in the London area.[27] Walker also extended his interest in the provincial market by pioneering the London production of a series of specifically local papers that were offered with his polyglot part publications.[28] Although this sort of preoccupation was probably widespread among the printers of the ambiguous weeklies, there is very little indication that the penny thrice-weeklies or the unstamped halfpenny and farthing thrice-weeklies and dailies were aimed at a provincial readership. The frequent and general use of post in the titles of these papers and the recurrence of the words Oxford and Country[29] seem to indicate some effort in this direction. Against this the cheap thrice-weeklies were invariably published between post days, on Monday, Wednesday, and Friday, and the difficulty and expense of provincial distribution probably prevented any large scale attempts to exploit this market; there is no evidence to show that the cheapest London papers reached any provincial center in quantity. There was, however, a steady extension of their distribution area and it is probable that the geographical gap between the adjacent towns and the central districts of London came to provide their principal market.

The supply of purchasers within these broadly overlapping areas of dispersal extending through London into the English provinces and beyond was a very complex process involving a series of commercial, as well as a number of political, interests. The printing office remained an important center for distribution and while all forms of paper carried requests for regular orders, individual subscribers in London and adjacent areas could usually obtain their copies through a free delivery service. Names and addresses could either be supplied directly to the printer himself or could be passed on by way of a variety of agents identified on the imprints or in advertisements.[30] Readers of the newly established *Daily Advertiser,* for example, were urged to *"Book the same, as they usually do other Papers,"*[31] giving notice either to the printer or to the person carrying out the initial *gratis* delivery.[32] Early in the century the printers and proprietors of a variety of London papers employed men to serve their regular customers in the central area,[33] and occasional comment that continued to appear in the press suggests that subscribers to most forms of newspaper could be supplied in this way.[34]

The printers themselves sometimes offered their papers for casual sale through shops linked directly with the printing office and within the organization of the full-priced papers, shadowed by the risk of political prosecution, the initial publication for resale was often handled by the printer or one of his employees. Mist's warehouseman, John Brett, and Standen's "servant," Edward Pickard, for example, were responsible for publishing and organizing the finances of *Mist's Weekly Journal* and the *Original Craftsman* respectively.[35] However, increasingly in the less-risky ventures, distribution to the retailers was handled by a professional "publisher" who also assumed extensive responsibility for the paper's finances. The term was itself rather ambiguous but, while in law it continued to be used to describe any distributive agent, by the 1730s it was also being applied specifically to wholesale dealers in pamphlets and newspapers.[36] John Peele, in a memorandum to Walpole, stated that his "proper business is that of a Publisher,"[37] in a direct reference to his position as middleman between the printer and the retailer. A number of such prominent wholesalers as Thomas Warner, James Roberts, and Thomas Cooper apparently operated on a very large scale in this area, often acting for several papers at the same time. Peele himself simultaneously handled the *Daily Post*, the *London Journal*, and the *Free Briton*[38] and his name appeared on the imprints of a wide range of London newspapers throughout the 1720s and 1730s. The professional expertise and personal influence of the publisher were probably of considerable value in extending the range of available retail outlets and by the mid-1740s most full-priced London newspapers were handled by such intermediaries.[39]

The bulk of these papers apparently reached their final purchasers through the pamphlet shops, whose proprietors bought copies at a discount from the printer or publisher.[40] The "mercuries," who were often the wives or widows of printers, managed shops that were scattered through the major centers of commercial and social activity but concentrated around the Royal Exchange,[41] Temple Bar, and Charing Cross. The close personal links that often existed between the printing trade and the mercuries appears clearly in the case of Elizabeth Nutt, the widow of the printer John Nutt and the proprietor of one of the cluster of shops at the Royal Exchange. Mrs. Nutt apparently took over the running of her husband's printing office in the Savoy, although by the mid 1720s she had probably handed over control to her son Richard.[42] At about the same time, Richard Nutt inherited a second office in the Old Bailey from his father-in-law, Hugh Meere,[43] where by 1730 he was printing the *Daily Post,* the *London Evening Post,* and the *Universal Spectator.* Consequently, Mrs. Nutt's shop at the Exchange formed a useful adjunct to this extensive printing business, and similar links can be established for most of the London mercuries who sometimes, as in the case of Mrs. Anne Dodd at

Temple Bar, continued to be involved in the production as well as the distribution of printed material. The number of pamphlet shops established in the London area and the scale of their newspaper business are difficult to establish. However, while it appears that the two most important outlets were the shops run by Mrs. Nutt and Mrs. Dodd, who often supplied subsidiary dealers,[44] some fragmented information on the scale of the newspaper intake of a number of mercuries emerges from the frequent political prosecutions that were leveled at the retail distributors. Mrs. Dodd, whose name cropped up on newspaper warrants with monotonous regularity, seems to have had a substantial turnover of opposition weeklies over a long period. In 1721 she took in about 2,700 *London Journals* out of an extended edition of 10,000 copies,[45] and she was apparently a major distributor of the *Craftsman* from its first appearance.[46] By 1731 she was receiving a weekly order of about 1,500 copies[47] and at the end of the decade was still taking in about 1,200.[48] In spite of this long-term association, she was also receiving in 1739 about 300 copies of the spurious *Original Craftsman*,[49] as well as about 750 copies a week of *Common Sense*.[50] These substantial figures reflected the popularity of the papers concerned, and Mrs. Dodd was far more cautious in handling a new and highly speculative venture such as the *Alchymist*. During February 1737 she received about 150 copies of this journal, of which about 100 remained unsold and were returned to the printer.[51] Mrs. Nutt's intake is less well documented and, although she apparently sold the *Craftsman* from 1726 at least until the late 1730s,[52] there is no clear indication of the numbers involved. However, in 1739 a prosecution directed against the *London Evening Post* indicated that her shop was taking in over 350 copies of each issue of this publication,[53] a number that suggests a considerable newspaper interest. The scattered figures available for the other London mercuries also reflect the variations in both the popularity of the opposition papers and their scale of business. In 1731, a Mrs. Pierce was shown to be regularly taking in about 1,250 copies of the *Craftsman*,[54] while in 1739 John Brett received nearly 600 copies of *Common Sense* every week.[55] On the other hand, references to an intake of a handful of copies suggest that the smaller mercuries at least offered their customers a cross section of the principal London papers.

Customers were also supplied with the London newspapers by the semi-destitute, self-employed hawkers who purchased copies at a discount from the printers and mercuries and offered them for sale in the streets of the capital. The hawkers seem to have carried all forms of full-priced paper, providing, for example, a useful London outlet for the principal weeklies. In 1739 the author of *Common Sense*, attacking the *Daily Post* for a pre-publication piracy, explained that "The *Craftsman* and *Common Sense* are delivered out on *Friday* Nights late, for the Conveniency of those poor People who got their Living by hawking them about the Town and Country adjacent; and the Printers of that Paper found Means of getting one of these on *Friday* Night."[56] The commercial importance of the casual sales structure of the conventionally priced weeklies was underlined by a notice published the same year in the *Original Craftsman*. It was stated "THAT for the *Conveniency* of the *Mercuries* and *Hawkers,* and *other Sellers* of *News Papers* and *Pamphlets,* Mr. J. STANDEN, Publisher of this Paper; is remov'd from his late House, D'ANVERS'S HEAD in CHANCERY LANE, to D'AN-VERS'S HEAD in the OLD BAILY, being within a *few Doors* of the PRINTER of the *DAILY POST* and *LONDON EVENING POST;* where the *CRAFTSMAN* will be PRINTED and PUBLISHED for the future."[57] However, the majority of the freelance hawkers seem to have dealt in the cut-price papers, which required minimal investment and which were principally distributed through street sales.[58] The extent to which the hawkers relied on these newspapers was indicated by George Parker in his petition of 1725. One of his major points was that the suppression of the halfpenny posts would ruin "the indigent *Poor* and miserable *Blind Hawkers,* whose deplorable Circumstances greatly deserve Compassion."[59] He went on to point out that "divers of them, who are Industrious, and have but a Penny or Three Half-Pence, for a Stock to begin with in a Morning, will before Night advance it to *Eighteen Pence* or *Two Shillings,* which greatly tends to the comfortable Support of such miserable Poor and Blind Creatures, who sell them about the Streets."[60] The volume of street sales in London remains largely obscure, although reports of the arrests that followed the clampdown on tax evasion in 1743 suggest that some of the hawkers of illegal publications were operating on quite a large scale. In August, for example, Ann Mahoney was arrested in possession of "upwards of 400" unstamped papers,[61] and the following October it was reported that "two Officers belonging to the Stamp Duties, seiz'd Susannah Wilcox in Ratcliff-Highway, with near 300 unstamp'd News-Papers upon her."[62]

The supply of subscribers outside the central areas of London was organized through a complex network of channels and, although problems of time and cost remained largely insuperable, subscribers throughout the country apparently had little difficulty in obtaining copies of the London papers. In the immediate vicinity of the capital the printers of the cut-price and unstamped publications established the sort of interlocking system of newsmen and agents that characterized provincial distribution.[63] In 1740 Sir Dudley Ryder, in his report on the unstamped press, stated that some of the proprietors "by their Mercuries and Hawkers not only dispose of them in great Numbers in the Streets of London and Westm^r. but in all the Contiguous Counties and have lately taken up a Practice and have found means to disperse them 50 or 60 Miles from London by their Agents and Hawkers some Travelling on Horses and others on foot going from Town to Town and House to House to the very great Prejudice of the Revenue as well as of the fair Trader who grievously complain thereof."[64] Five years later it was claimed in the *Penny London Post* that the paper was "chiefly dispers'd in the City and Suburbs of London etc. and within Thirty Miles around the same,"[65] a radius extended in subsequent notices to forty miles.[66] These distances suggest similar stages to those used in the provinces,[67] although the absence of any direct comment on suburban distribution in the cheap papers themselves obscures the details of the process. It seems likely that "Puff" Moore, committed in June 1743 for selling unstamped papers "about the Towns of Deptford, Greenwich, Lewisham, Dartford, etc.,"[68] was one of the London newsmen. The fragmentary evidence of links between the distributors of the legitimate weeklies and major centers not too far from London perhaps suggests a more widespread use of specially supplied agents than can at present be shown. The imprint of the *Weekly Oracle* indicated that in 1735 the printer had established poste-restante facilities with the Theater coffee-house at Cambridge and Harding's coffee-house in Greenwich,[69] while in the same year it was announced in the *Weekly Miscellany* that Cambridge subscribers could be supplied with the paper every Saturday *"at Mr. Crow's Bookbinder, by St. Mary's Church."*[70]

The same ambiguity surrounds the comparable links that occasionally existed between the London distributors and dealers in more distant provincial towns. In 1721 a report to the Secretary of State's office stated that the opposition *London Journal* was distributed to the Birmingham hawkers "by one Pasham a bookseller of Northampton" and was offered for casual sale within a radius of thirty or forty miles of the city.[71] The nature of Pasham's association with the printer or publisher of the *London Journal* can only be guessed at but it seems likely that a number of London weeklies were redistributed from major provincial centers in this way. This was the case with the *Universal Spy*, first published in London in 1732. In the third issue the imprint, which had previously stated that the paper was printed for W. Hinton near Serjeants-Inn-Gate, was extended to include the words "and Sold by T. HINTON Printer in *Bath:* At both which Places *Advertisements* are taken in."[72] Among the most comprehensive use of such contacts was that made by Robert Walker. His advertisements of the late 1730s all implied that the wide range of printed material that he produced in London, including the *London and Country Journal*, were available through local agencies. Although he invariably used a blanket formula to refer to his distributors, it seems possible that the thirteen booksellers and others who acted as agents for his patent medicines in towns as far apart as Bristol, Birmingham, and Ipswich also handled his newspaper.[73] The broad range of items supplied by Walker perhaps made it economic for him to arrange a special delivery of his weekly paper to dealers within this very extensive area. In most cases the problem of regular supply probably discouraged the establishment of far-flung agencies which, if receiving copies through the regular channels, could offer neither a cheaper nor speedier service than could be obtained from the London distributors themselves. It seems that while a few local booksellers, such as John Clay of Northampton,[74] occasionally offered London papers to their customers, they bought their copies casually from London dealers and seldom acted as agents for particular publications.

Provincial distribution was therefore for the most part organized directly from London. Orders continued to be handled by the printers, and perhaps the publishers, as well as by a variety of commercial and private contacts. Although the identity of these distributors is extremely difficult to pin down, it seems likely that the London booksellers were among the most important. During the 1720s and 1730s Benjamin Motte and Robert Gosling both supplied their provincial clients with a substantial number of London papers,[75] and it seems likely that this was a conventional practice. Although such agents continued to handle orders, the expense of distribution inevitably restricted the scale of activity. Costs could be kept to a minimum by making use of the network of carriers who operated between the capital and most provincial centers. The copies could be delivered to the inns that served as departure points and then deposited for collection along the routes. Notices in the *Weekly Miscellany* suggest that its distribution was frequently carried out through such channels while the supply of the *Craftsman,* faced with regular official obstruction, could be organized through a variety of low-cost intermediaries. In November 1728 customers *"in almost all Parts of the Kingdom,"* who had complained of irregular supply through *"the* General *and* Penny Post," were urged to employ *"Coachman, Carriers, Watermen etc. as best suits their Convenience."*[76] The four undated subscription lists, seized from the printer in 1730, suggest that Francklin himself was supplying at least some of his political customers in this way.[77] A large proportion of the orders were not linked with delivery instructions and, in a number of cases, they were simply directed to the subscriber's townhouse or to an agent or personal contact in London. However, Sir William Wyndham received his forty and forty-eight copies by way of the Frome carrier, while Sir Edward Stanley and Henry Fleetwood both received the same bulk orders of ten and twelve copies by way of "the Lancashire Carrier at the two Swans in Lad Lane." The cost to subscribers of papers sent out of London by these means was clearly less than if they had passed through the more rapid official channels. In 1791 it was stated that the "Customary charge" for sending a newspaper by coach was ¼d,[78] and it seems probable that this sort of very low rate obtained in the earlier period. The scale of the newspaper activity of these free-lance distributors is impossible to assess, although the proposed prosecution in 1746 of the Cambridge University "News Carriers" may conceivably reflect some Post Office concern with the extent of this side of their business.

Whatever the alternatives, the Post Office was able to provide the most rapid and reliable means of access to the provinces. The main problem it presented was one of expense and the high cost of general postage, worked out on a complex scale of weights and distances, could effectively have blocked its use for large-scale newspaper distribution.[79] That this inherent difficulty was overcome was the result of the intervention of groups who had privileged access to the system. By using their right to frank material through the post free of charge, members of these groups were able to cheapen the cost of London newspapers to provincial subscribers and in so doing became crucial intermediaries in the process of supply. The most important of these groups under the Walpole administration were the six clerks-of-the-road who as Post Office employees were responsible for overseeing the despatch of the mails to areas lying along the principal routes out of London. By the mid-1720s the clerks had established a substantial newspaper interest on their own behalf and in 1728 were disparagingly described by the author of the *Craftsman* as "a sort of *licensed Hawkers* over the whole Kingdom."[80] Subscribers from all over the country placed orders with the clerks,[81] who were supplied with copies by an intermediate Post Office official dealing directly with the printers. From about 1739 this was undertaken by the ex-diplomat Isaac Jamineau and during the review of Post Office procedure in 1788 he gave an account of his role in handling the initial stages of newspaper distribution.[82] Jamineau stated that since succeeding to the position he had "continued to supply the Office upon the terms settled by the Postmaster General, which are three halfpence a dozen profit upon what he pays to the Printer, who also allows him one paper in every Quire of twenty-four. He collects all the Papers at his Office near the Post Office, where the Clerks of the Roads receive them."[83] Copies were then parcelled up by area and sent down to the postmasters, who provided a ready made network of local agents. It seems possible that some of the local officials chose to remain aloof from this extensive but informal process. By the 1740s a number of postmasters were acting independently on behalf of local printers,[84] and some competition for their services may already have begun to develop by mid-century.[85] In spite of the advantages of receiving copies from the clerks, the service to subscribers was not altogether reliable. By the mid-1750s an unspecified number of the Post Office officials held shares in both the *General Evening Post* and the *Whitehall Evening Post*[86] and personal interest seems to have resulted in some degree of informal censorship at a much earlier period. In 1731, advertisements for the *Grub Street Journal* carried an "N.B." that stated that the paper was published "early every Thursday Morning, and may conveniently go by the Carriers into the Country: which is mentioned because the Conveyance of it by the Post has been interrupted by Persons concerned in another Journal, which has been frequently sent by them into the Country, instead of the Grub-street contrary to the Direction."[87] The following year the author of the same paper complained that newspapers were often obstructed by Post Office employees "who either, contrary to their superiors injunctions, hold shares themselves in news-papers, or have been prevailed upon by proper application, to promote the ruin, and to hinder that of others."[88] These latter remarks were probably aimed at the printer Edward Cave who, as the proprietor of the *Gentleman's Magazine*, was regularly charged with abusing his place in the Post Office. Among a variety of malpractices, he was accused of touting for provincial custom by way of "scandalous and scurrilous advertisements," while he in turn accused the proprietors of the *London Magazine* of making "mean application to post-boys and carriers" to promote their sales at his expense.[89] It seems possible that such devices were also employed by the clerks on behalf of the weekly and thrice-weekly papers in which they had a commercial interest. More seriously the clerks, as government employees, were not only subject to direct political control[90] but also appear to have had a personal incentive to encourage the distribution of writings on behalf of the administration. According to Horatio Walpole, in a rather obscure comment on policy, the usual way of encouraging the authors of proministerial papers was to give a gratuity, while "the Clerks of the Post Office have their petty fees which the Government does not take from them when they circulate such papers."[91]

The clerks' role in the postal distribution of the London newspapers was to some extent paralleled by that of the employees of other government departments who also held franking privileges. War Office and Admiralty personnel had the right to send letters through the post free of charge and, although it was stated in 1764 that this was not understood to extend to newspapers,[92] it seems likely that a few provincial orders at least were handled at these centers. However, the most important subsidiary Post Office distributors were the officials of the Secretary of State's Office, who had been involved in the provision of news since the seventeenth century.

This obscure line of newspaper distribution has been brought into clearer focus through the discovery of a ledger kept during the last four years of Queen Anne's reign by Charles Delafaye, a senior clerk at the office.[93] In it he outlined what was clearly an extensive business in newspapers, and although Delafaye may have had a special interest in the press (he worked for a time as compiler of the *London Gazette*), it suggests the way in which government officials could become deeply involved in the process of supply. The material is not always clear or consistent, but it seems that he was involved in dealings with at least seventy-two individuals scattered through the English counties or in Ireland, with two customers in Scotland and one in Guernsey. He also acted as supplier to eighteen London coffee-houses. The papers in which he dealt were of two sorts. First, those published in London, which included a manuscript "Letter" probably produced at the office, the parliamentary *Votes,* and the English and French versions of the *London Gazette,* as well as a cross section of the main commercial thrice-weeklies and essay-sheets. Precise numbers in this setting are elusive, but it appears that at peak periods Delafaye was sending out between four- and five-hundred copies per week. The second group consisted of papers published on the Continent, including the *Paris-à-la-Main* and a variety of foreign gazettes, most of which were supplied to his coffee-house customers. The organization underpinning the business was complicated and far reaching. Delafaye, whose Huguenot background gave him a personal link with an international newspaper interest,[94] seems to have employed an agent to obtain the gazettes in Holland, while he used others to act as redistributors of copies of the London papers from several provincial centers, the most important being Dublin. All the papers he supplied were franked through the Post Office or sent by way of the Penny Post.

Delafaye was a major distributor of London newspapers and it may be that the subsequent build-up in the involvement of the Post Office clerks superseded such large-scale activity based on a government office. Nonetheless, the arrangements revealed by the ledger seem to have remained in use. Subscribers continued to place orders for specific papers with office personnel who were supplied with copies by one of the Charing Cross mercuries.[95] In 1728, for example, a correspondent of the undersecretary, James Payzant, asked for the supply of the *Whitehall Evening Post* in place of the *London Journal,* offering half-yearly payments through a London agent.[96] The following year another requested "every post a written English letter and your *St. James's Evening Post,*" the cover being marked "begin on the 27th to Send the *St. James's Evening Post* and the Circular."[97] In spite of the subsequent mass distribution of free newspapers by the Walpole administration, the Office seems to have retained its distributive role and a letter to Newcastle in 1738, requesting the London papers as usual, specified "an Evening Post, the *Daily Gazetteer,* the *Weekly London Journal.*"[98] Political circumstances inevitably curtailed the range of papers available through this channel and the service was perhaps as often personal as commercial in character. Individual M.P.'s also had Post Office franking rights but, although there is evidence that some were willing to provide franks for their personal contacts on quite a large scale, there is no clear indication of the sort of combination with the commercial dealers that developed following the extension in franking rights of 1764.[99]

Although provincial subscribers were able to evade the full cost of postage by placing orders with privileged officials, the charges made for the service pushed the price of copies well above the London retail rate, providing a commercial opportunity for the development of the provincial papers. This was partly the result of overheads which, in the Post Office at least, were substantial. The clerks were obliged to pay Jamineau's commission,[100] and the profits, which may have had to cover a fee for the local postmaster,[101] were required to supplement both their own salary and that of a whole range of subsidiary officials. In 1779 the clerk of the Kent road felt obliged to inform one of his customers, who was threatening to cancel his order, "that our Salary as Clerks of the Roads is confined by the legislature to the bare perquisite arising from the Sale of Newspapers in the Country which we are privileged to send free from Duty of Postage. Out of this perquisite we pay upwards of eleven hundred pounds per annum towards the Salary of Other Officers in the Department."[102] At the same time, possession of a monopoly inevitably encouraged some commercial exploitation. In a subsequent Post Office memorandum it was stated that, were the dealers enabled to establish a similar monopoly, they would find it as much to their advantage "as it was that of the Clerks under Government to sell a less number at an advanced price," since "the capital employed would not be so large nor the trouble nor risk so great."[103] The committee of 1764 estimated that between them the clerks were earning £3,000 or £4,000 per annum from newspapers, although this was probably the gross rather than the net profit.[104] The usual charge to subscribers, who bore the weight of these expenses, is difficult to pin down and was apparently subject to some local variation. However, the papers supplied by the Post Office clerks seem usually to have cost an extra 2d. per copy, with an additional delivery charge if not collected from the posthouse.[105] The only detailed accounts for papers distributed in the provinces by personnel at the Secretary's Office under the Walpole administration are those for copies of the official newsletter and the subsidized *London Journal* sent out on behalf of the Duke of Newcastle.[106] These accounts may have been settled by the Duke himself as part of a personal propaganda effort, but the costs entered are high. The thrice-weekly newsletter was charged at over 9d. an issue, while each copy of the *London Journal* cost about 6d. A similar very high rate appeared in the account of an Irish subscriber who was charged £2. 8s. 9d. (Irish) for a nine-month supply of the *St. James Evening Post* and the *London Journal*.[107]

Of the growing number of newspapers produced in London, a large proportion were sent out of town by way of the Post Office, and it is likely that a majority of these were sent under frank. Unfortunately, it is not possible to quantify this process very accurately. Figures are available for the massive political use of the post during the 1720s and 1730s[108] but it is mainly through parliamentary investigations into the abuse of franking privileges that some limited information on the general scale of Post Office distribution becomes available.[109] A report of 1734 made no specific mention of newspapers but identified a steady rise in the amount of material sent through the post free of charge.[110] Thirty years later a similar investigation focused on the newspapers, which must have formed the bulk of the problem, but even here there are ambiguities.[111] The report of 1764 specified the amounts lost to the revenue through the activities of the privileged groups in a single week in March of that year. This provides a view of their relative involvement in newspaper distribution, although there is no reason to suppose that the relationship was stable through the first half of the century. In the report, the Post Office clerks were debited with £1,055.10s.8d. for the week, other government officials with £310.15s.4d., and individual M.P.'s with £465.5s.8d. No figures for the number of newspapers were given, and because the costs were so variable no direct extrapolation is possible. Later in the century it was claimed in a Post Office assessment that by the mid-1760s the clerks alone were handling about 21,000 copies per week.[112] Using this total with the proportions given in the report, a weekly figure of something over 35,000 papers franked through the post can be suggested.

Within this framework of distribution, copies of the London papers were also made widely available to readers at less than full cost or entirely free of charge. Group purchase and personal loan were organized at all levels, while by the mid 1720s a semi-legitimate hire service seems to have been established by the hawkers of several full-priced London essay-papers. In 1723, for example, the author of *Mist's Weekly Journal* complained of a "Combination betwixt some of my gentle Readers and my ungentle Hawkers," whereby his paper was borrowed for ½d. and subsequently "returned upon his Hands all damaged, without the least Consideration for all his Labour and Study, and with the entire Loss of what is laid out for Paper and Print."[113] The following year it was announced in Mist's paper that no refund would be allowed to hawkers for returns.[114] Fresh complaints appeared in the twice-weekly essay-sheet *Pasquin*. The author in this case blamed his low financial ebb partly on the prevalence of borrowing, asking rhetorically "Why are Five Hundred of these Papers *Extraordinary* demanded every Day, and for what? Not to be sold, no; but to be distributed round St. *James's* Parish, read at *Half-pence* each, or so much a Quarter, and return'd."[115] Access to nonpurchasers was most fully developed in the capital through the distribution of copies to centers of social and commercial activity. London contained a striking concentration of public houses. It was estimated in 1739 that there were totals of 551 coffee-houses, 207 inns, and 447 taverns, as well as a vast number of beer and brandy shops in the central area.[116] Few coffee-houses can have afforded to ignore the press and in 1728 it was stated that the proprietors of the leading establishments were spending up to £20 a year on newspapers[117] and were taking in "some two, some three, some four of a Sort of the leading Papers, every Day, besides Duplicates of most of the others."[118] A few even seem to have offered loan facilities and in a popular guidebook of the 1720s the author described the scene at a *"Three-half-Penny-Library"* where "Numbers of bedridden Ladies and Gentlemen were continually sending hither their Servants for *Intelligence,* each leaving the full Value of every Paper as a Hostage for the safe Return of it."[119] The scale of this gratis readership in the capital was suggested by an apparently accepted claim that in the coffee-houses alone an edition of a single paper could pass through 20,000 hands in a day.[120] A comparable service was apparently provided by a large proportion of the inns and taverns in the London area and although most of the small alehouses and brandy shops were probably outside the orbit of the press, it seems likely that some at least took in one or two papers.[121] A variety of tradesmen such as barbers and chandlers also provided copies for their customers[122] and at the lowest level the London papers were often available at second hand after their disposal to miscellaneous shopkeepers as packaging. Even the newspaper proprietors themselves occasionally conspired to extend this free access and in 1742 the methodist printer John Lewis announced in his penny *Weekly History* that "those who can neither afford to buy them, nor have an Opportunity to borrow them, shall be welcome to repair to the Printer's House, to read 'em *gratis*."[123]

The prevalence of this sort of secondary distribution in both town and country meant that a single copy of a London newspaper was likely to reach a very large audience. In 1711 it was estimated that each issue of the *Spectator,* a daily essay-sheet circulating largely in the London area, passed through about twenty hands.[124] In 1732 the author of an attack on the *Craftsman,* a weekly journal with a national distribution, claimed that it was read "by no less than four hundred thousand of the good People of *Great Britain,* allowing no more than 40 Readers to a Paper."[125] These assessments were inevitably speculative but they at least indicate that the widespread availability of the London newspapers makes nonsense of any attempt to link circulation figures with total readership.

Within concentric areas of distribution the various forms of London newspaper continued to dominate the national scene, extending their influence to Ireland and beyond. In the capital itself and adjacent districts the combination of the full-priced and cheap papers provided what amounted to saturation coverage. Despite the suppression of the cheapest unstamped publications in 1743, the cut-price thrice-weeklies remained widely available, and within a large area around London very few attempts were made to establish a local newspaper. At the same time the volume of full-priced London papers passing into the country through the Post Office and other channels continued to rise sharply. The emergence of the local weeklies clearly played a part in undermining the provincial position of the London journals. However, no attempt was made locally to challenge the authority of the evening-posts and, in some respects, the role of the provincial newspaper continued to parallel that of the cut-price publications distributed in the London area.

3

The Finances of the London Press

Much of the evidence concerning the details of costs and profits of London newspapers in this period is fragmentary and oblique, and the situation is complicated by important variations in the financing of the different forms. However, an increasing amount of material is coming to light that makes it possible to arrive at some general assessments and to suggest the sort of financial return that the weekly, thrice-weekly, and daily papers could produce.

The establishment of any form of paper in the increasingly crowded London market required a certain amount of capital investment. In the case of the full-priced forms, this was increasingly provided by a variable number of shareholders,[1] who seem, in most cases, to have put up an initial stake of £200. This was the amount established as common fund by the twenty shareholders of the daily *London Gazetteer* in 1748,[2] and three years later Bubb Doddington stated that a new political weekly was to be "supported by about twenty of us at 10 guineas each, and what else we can get."[3] Although £200 may have been adequate to launch a new venture, the backer or backers seem generally to have found it necessary to provide further financial support for a new paper during the early stages of publication. Following the appearance of the *Grub Street Journal* in 1730, the proprietors were faced with at least three calls of seven guineas and a further three of one guinea for each share on top of any original investment,[4] and the need for substantially higher stake was clearly indicated by the printer of the *Alchymist* later in the decade. Set up in 1737 by Dennis de Coetlogan, the paper seems to have had no real financial support and to have had increasing difficulty in surviving public indifference and the attacks of competitors. De Coetlogan's attempts to find suitable backers were completely unsuccessful and his printer, Walter Baker, rejecting the offer of a share, wrote, "I was not at the first Projecting of the Paper, for if I had, I am conscious to myself that I shou'd have had no Concern at all in it, for as I have formerly observed, there should have been, at least, £500 employ'd to the forview of the Paper," and went on to remark, "If a share in the Paper was ever so advantageous to me I cou'd not accept, because at present, I am not able to support it."[5] The sort of difficulty that could arise in a jointly owned paper from an underestimate of the initial expense was suggested much later in the century at the setting up of the thrice-weekly *London Packet*. The proprietors seem initially to have put up £200 but in January 1770, two days after a call for five guineas a share, a further demand for £25 led to the instant resignation of three of the partners.[6]

One of the immediate, if subsidiary, uses to which invested capital was put was to bring the paper to the attention of the public by means of a variety of advertising techniques. These continued to be employed by most papers, particularly to boost flagging sales or to announce important changes of policy, but the most consistent use of advertising was made during the early stages of publication. Among the cheapest and most popular methods, employed primarily by the weeklies, was the distribution of handbills announcing the paper's aims and content.[7] The proprieters of both the *Grub Street Journal* and the *Alchymist* employed this form of advertisement, the printing cost of the bills being only 5/- and 7/- per thousand respectively.[8] The *Grub Street Journal* ledger does not indicate the issues that the bills were designed to announce, but simply gives a block entry of 4,000 for the first 30 issues and a further 2,000 for the remaining 34.[9] The *Alchymist* account was more specific. It shows that between 17 February and 30 April 1737 Baker printed an almost continuous weekly number, generally 500, charged at 5/-.[10] The use of this form of advertisement for such a financially moribund venture indicates the extent to which it was considered a useful and necessary expense.[11] The weeklies also made greater use of press advertising than the other forms during the early stages of publication. The proprietors of the *Grub Street Journal* entered three 3/6 advertisements a week in London papers during its first six weeks of publication.[12] This was subsequently reduced to one a week during the next month and thereafter was used only occasionally.[13] The method of advertising that probably represented the greatest expense was the free distribution of the first and sometimes subsequent issues, although the gratis copies could remain legitimately unstamped. During its first six months of publication 1,876 copies of the *Grub Street Journal* were "given away," a number roughly equivalent to the whole printing of three issues of the paper.[14]

New full-priced papers in other forms were also circulated free of charge and, while the first issue of the *Champion* was offered gratis,[15] special efforts seem to have been made to push the *Daily Advertiser* in this way. A title-notice in the first issue announced that the paper would be "*given* Gratis *to all Coffee-Houses Four Days successively,*"[16] apparently before becoming available for public sale, and following the introduction of a news section it was stated that "*for the better Dispersing and Publishing the Usefulness of this Undertaking, This* Paper *will be left* Gratis *for some Days at most of the Houses of the Nobility and Gentry, and the Coffee-Houses.*"[17] Allied with this approach was the widespread posting of copies, which was introduced not only to make the papers generally known but to encourage advertisers by offering extended coverage. Special efforts were again made in this direction on behalf of the *Daily Advertiser* and in the first issue it was also announced that *"in order to make the Publication as known and general as possible, it is intended that Copies of the Paper shall be every Day fix'd up at the* Royal Exchange, *the* Customs-House, Excise Office, Bank of England, *the* India-House, South-Sea House, Temple-Bar, Westminister Hall, *and all other the most publick Places of the Town."*[18] The papers' format was specially adapted to facilitate posting by the addition of a second title on page two,[19] and the continued use of this method by the London dailies was indicated in 1746 by a notice in the *London Courant* announcing to potential advertisers that it would be posted in *"the most frequented Parts of this City and suburbs."*[20] Posting also represented a way of sidestepping some of the restrictive practices used against new papers in this period[21] and a surviving one-page copy of the *Englishman's Evening Post* of 1740, containing an affirmation of publication and the day's leading essay, was clearly intended for this purpose.[22]

Although advertising a new paper was of considerable importance, the total expense involved was comparatively slight. The bulk of the capital investment was needed initially to support the basic costs of production, made up of printing and paper, editorial work, and publication. Printing costs, based on the workmen's wages bill, were the most liable to fluctuate according to the paper's size and column space, although by 1746 the general uniformity of layout must have minimized these distinctions. *Mists* and the *Craftsman,* as four-page journals, were set by two compositors,[23] and it seems likely that this was usual for papers of the size as well as for the complex single-leaf dailies.[24] Copies were then worked off at the press by a combination of miscellaneous employees.[25] There is no evidence for the payment of special rates and since the newspaper formed only part of the printers' work-flow, it is impossible to deduce the payments to individual workmen.[26]

Nonetheless, newspaper printing costs followed a regular pattern and the few surviving accounts indicate the level of outlay necessary in this period for the production of the principal forms. The cost of printing a single-leaf, two-column essay-sheet appeared from the records of the early issues of the *Craftsman.* These indicate that a basic edition of up to 500 copies cost about 15/-, while editions of up to 1,500 copies were priced at 19/-.[27] The way in which these modest printing costs rose progressively with the more complex newspaper layouts, appears clearly from the accounts of the four-page *Grub Street Journal.* In its initial small-size, two-column form an edition of 500 copies cost £1. 16s. to produce. However, with the increase in page size and the addition of a third column, the cost for the same number of copies rose sharply to £2. 10s., subsequently increasing by 3/- for every extra token of 250 copies.[28] The terms accepted by John Huggonson in 1733 laid down the established rate of £2. 10s. per thousand copies.[29] That these prices represented the conventional cost of printing a weekly journal is supported by the account for the *Alchymist* compiled in 1737.[30] Walter Baker charged the proprietor £2. 12s. 6d. a week for printing this paper, and although the number is not specified it seems likely that it referred to a basic edition of 500 copies.[31] These figures represent the amounts paid for the whole printing process, but a clue to the make-up of the detailed scale of costs appeared later in the century in the records of the *General Evening Post*. In 1779 a sharp rise in circulation led the proprietors to consider a second setting of the last page to allow the paper to be worked off at two presses.[32] In a report on the extra expense that would be involved, it was claimed that the process would add an extra half guinea to the production costs of each issue.[33]

In the long run the greatest expense in newspaper production lay in the cost of the paper itself and, more significantly, of the stamp that it carried. As has been described, the Act of 1725 fixed the tax on all forms of London Newspaper and this automatic cost represented a considerable financial burden. The only qualifying clause in the Act of 1712, also contained in that of 1725, ordered repayment by the Stamp Office of the cost of the stamps cut from unsold papers.[34] This represented quite a substantial saving since, in the case of the *Craftsman* in 1727, about 20 percent of the month's printing figures were shown as returns and a similar proportion appeared in the account for the first six months of the *Grub Street Journal*.[35] However, this money does not always appear to have been refunded. According to the petition of Daniel Pratt in 1743 "if any Countrey Dealer or Printer, return any Stamps the least Sullied, they are return'd on their Hand, to the great Damage and Hurt of the King and the fair Trader,"[36] and the same practice may have affected the London printers.[37] Following the doubling of the tax in 1757 a discount of one penny stamp in fifty was allowed,[38] and a similar arrangement may have existed earlier in the century.

The quality of paper used provided one of the sharpest divisions between the upper and lower levels of the press. The full-priced papers seem to have found it commercially desirable to maintain a reasonably high standard. James Read was obliged to abandon the attempt to peg the price of his weekly journal by using poor quality paper,[39] while in 1727 the proprietors of the *London Journal* thought it advisable to ask their readers to "excuse the Badness of the Paper for a Week or Two, being disappointed of our usual Sort, and there being but one Paper-Mill in *England* that can now make the same."[40] Similarly, the supposed success of *Old England* in 1746 was claimed to have led its proprietors not only to enlarge the page size but to raise the quality of its paper.[41] A precise breakdown of paper costs, which appears in two of the surviving account, indicates incidentally the way in which the size of the sheet was extended to evade the full force of the tax. The paper used by the two-page *Craftsman* appears at 6/6d. per ream[42] and the four-page *Grub Street Journal* at 14/6d. and 15/- per ream.[43] This increase in price for the *Grub Street Journal* was simply the result of the enlargement of the sheet so that it was still, as in the case of the *Craftsman*, adequate for two copies of the paper, which therefore remained technically a half-sheet. The relative cost per copy underlines the real similarity, the paper of the single-leaf *Craftsman* costing roughly ⅑d. and of the four-page *Grub Street Journal* ⅕d. and this sort of cost was probably shared by all forms of full-priced newspaper.[44] A modest return from this outlay on paper could be obtained by disposing of unsold copies as waste. About 1712 the author of a petition to parliament on behalf of the newspaper printers remarked that "there are few Printers in this Town, who have not many Thousand Copies by them, which they daily sell for waste Paper,"[45] while, in the 1760s, Henry Woodfall regularly received 5/- a thousand for back numbers of the *Public Advertiser*.[46] The publisher of the *Gazetteer* subsequently received comparable amounts.[47]

In the lower reaches of the press attempts were made to economize as far as possible on materials, particularly the paper, and it was the coarse texture of the halfpenny posts that Parker stated put them beneath the notice of "the generality of Gentlemen."[48] Parker also claimed that a specialized industry had grown up, "employing an abundance of Hands" and paying valuable duty, to supply the printers of the cheap papers with the annual 20,000 reams used in their production.[49] The doubling of the price following the Stamp Act of 1725 did not allow for any increase in production costs and if subsequently some of the more successful penny newspapers improved the quality as well as increased the size of their sheets, the paper used by the penny and unstamped newspapers remained generally poor. No information is available on the sort of prices involved, but they were probably well below those paid by the proprietors of the full-priced publications.

To the cost of printing and paper were added the often extensive editorial expenses. In this area the cut-price papers, relying largely on second-hand material, were able to practice economies that their full-priced counterparts, struggling for survival at the top of the market, could seldom afford. At the same time the expenses probably varied a good deal between the principal forms, which emphasised different areas of content. The number of those employed by the proprietors of individual papers on a regular and free-lance basis is impossible to pin down in detail although they often included journalists, the suppliers of foreign and home news, and translators.[50] As well as the outlay on wages and fees from an indeterminate number of such personnel, some subsidiary expense was also generally involved in the purchase of printed material, either for republication or reference.[51] The earliest indication of total expenditure on the content of a full-priced London newspaper appears in the accounts of the daily *Public Advertiser* that survive for the period 1765 to 1771.[52] There is no breakdown of individual items, but a regular monthly entry for "News etc."

shows a payment, fluctuating from year to year, of between £54 and £76. 10s., giving a rough average of between £2 and £3 an issue. These sums may have included payment of an "editor" and are perhaps rather higher than the amounts paid out during the earlier period. However, they do suggest the relative importance and possible extent of the common outlay on news content.

The compilation of the advertising section also involved a certain amount of expense and a quite substantial sum was probably required from the proprietors of the *London Daily Post* for its major advertising concession with the London theaters. The paper's first issue in 1734 announced that the managers of the five principal houses had, for convenience, decided to advertise in one publication, and a notice in each advertisement showed that the paper was to be used exclusively for performances at Drury Lane, Covent Garden, and Goodman's Fields, and regularly for those at the Haymarket.[53] During the 1760s the ledger of the *Public Advertiser,* the amended title of the same paper, showed payments to the London theaters of up to £200 per anum,[54] and the valuable monopoly was probably from the start based on a comparable financial agreement.[55] For the most part the outlay on advertising was limited to payment for bringing in or collecting notices. In the provinces 2d. was sometimes paid to the newsmen for this service,[56] while the proposals for the coffee-house papers in 1729 provided "that every Coffee-Man concerned taking in an Advertisement, to be published in the said Papers, shall be allowed Sixpence for the same."[57] By the 1750s the *Gazetteer* was employing "a proper Person" to collect the advertisements handed in to specified booksellers and coffeehouses,[58] and it is possible that the employment of a collector added to the wages bill of principal dailies prior to this time.

A final and important drain on the finances of all forms of London newspaper lay in the cost of distribution. This was largely composed of the discount allowed on the cost of each copy, ½d. in the case of the full-priced publications ¼d. in that of the penny papers.[59] This was passed on to the mercuries and hawkers as well, perhaps, as to other secondary distributors such as the booksellers or Isaac Jamineau at the Post Office. Even when these retailers were by-passed, the discount sometimes continued to operate to the advantage of the customer. In 1746 it was announced in the *General Advertiser* that while the paper could be bought from the mercuries and hawkers at the usual price of 1½d., the printer would sell or deliver the paper at 1d. a copy.[60] Besides the discount, a large number of London papers had the added expense of a publisher's fee, which would yield a useful return to large-scale operators. In the early 1730s Peele reckoned that, if he had acted simultaneously as publisher of the *Daily Post,* the *Daily Post Boy,* the *Whitehall Evening Post,* and the monthly *Political State of Great Britain,* he would have earned £115 per annum.[61] However, the cost to the newspaper was slight. The proprietors of the twice-weekly *Craftsman* paid a publication fee of 2s. for every thousand copies distributed,[62] while

Roberts, as publisher of the *Grub Street Journal,* received between 4s. and 5s. a thousand.[63] A peripheral addition to publication costs may have been the small sums paid for porterage, which appeared in both the *Craftsman* and the *Grub Street Journal* accounts.

To offset the expenses of production and distribution and provide a viable profit margin, the London press relied on the income derived from a variable combination of sales and advertising. Commercial pressures prevented any increase in the standard retail prices,[64] and consequently the importance of sales revenue in covering production costs and producing a profit was closely linked with the degree of internal complexity. The single-leaf essay-sheets selling at 2d. were financed entirely by the return from sales. The monthly accounts of the *Craftsman,* when appearing in this form,[65] indicate that an average circulation of between 250 and 300 copies was sufficient to break even,[66] while an average of 1,000 copies brought in about £1. 16s. per issue. It seems unlikely that any paper of this type achieved a much higher sale. On the other hand the complex six- and, from 1725 four-page journals, with subsidiary advertising content, needed a substantially higher circulation to recoup production costs. In 1735, after the withdrawal of the shareholding proprietors, William Webster reckoned he could support the *Weekly Miscellany* with three or four hundred "fixed customers," several of those he had already approached having offered to subscribe for six papers a week.[67] This would probably have guaranteed a sale of something over 1,000 copies but it seems unlikely that he could have done more than cover his basic costs at such a level. This is borne out by the accounts of the *Grub Street Journal.* Between August 1730 and March 1731 the number of papers printed rose steadily, averaging 1,600 copies a week for the eight-month period. The gross receipts were entered at £394. 4s. 2d., the outgoings on general expenses at £386. 1s. 7d. and, if this statement for the 34 issues is complete, the total profit to the proprietors amounted to only £8. 2s. 1d.[68] In 1739 Henry Haines, printer of the *Craftsman,* put the minimum circulation rather higher in claiming that a weekly issue of 2,000 copies had proved inadequate to support his paper.[69] On the other hand, access to the national market and weekly publication allowed for considerable expansion, and during the 1720s and early 1730s the *London Journal, Mist's Weekly Journal,* and the *Craftsman* all achieved a sale of 10,000 copies or more.[70] Once the cost of the basic edition had been met, the return per copy, assessed by one contemporary as high as ¾d.,[71] rose sharply. The potential extent of this sales-based income is indicated most clearly in the generalized records of the *Craftsman* for the thirty-four months following the switch to journal form.[72] These show a rise in the total profit from an average of 2 guineas a week in May 1727 to an average of £21. 14s. 1d. a week in February 1730. The latter figure, indicating an income of over £1,000 per annum, was apparently still rising. Although this return was exceptional, the possibility of such a striking income must have stimulated interest in this form of paper.

Sales income also provided the main support of such thrice-weeklies and dailies as the *Post Master,* the *Whitehall Evening Post,* and the *Daily Courant,* which continued to appear in a simple format at 1½ᵈ· No accounts for a paper of this type have turned up, but a sale of about 500 or 600 copies was probably adequate to finance production, while the profit margin was apparently sufficient to produce a handsome income early in the century. In 1705 de Fonvive reckoned that the *Post Man,* then with an average sale of about 4,000 copies per issue, produced a return of £600 a year.[73] However, papers of this type, particularly the morning posts, were in decline by the 1720s, and it seems unlikely that any established a regular sale of more than 1,000 copies.[74] In contrast, the complex thrice-weeklies and dailies, which apparently achieved the most consistent circulation growth, could scarcely have produced an adequate return from sales alone. In one of his periodic breakdowns of expense the printer of the *Daily Journal* pointed out the deficiency of the return from the usual retail price, "*for as* One *Half-penny in* Three *is paid for the* Stamp, *and* Another *is allowed to the Retailers: there is but* One *left to defray all the Expenses of* Foreign, Domestick, *and* Ship Intelligence; *as also that of the* Paper, Printing, Publishing, Postage, and other chargeable *Incidents.*"[75] From the early 1730s such full-priced thrice-weeklies as the *London Evening Post* and the *General Evening Post* probably cost at least as much as the journals to produce, and from the mid-1740s this outlay was increased. Consequently, it seems likely that a circulation of about 2,000 or 2,500 copies per issue would have been necessary before any return was obtained from sales. The almost complete absence of figures makes it difficult to assess how far this sort of circulation was achieved, but some oblique speculation on the very successful *London Evening Post* can perhaps suggest the potential level of sales toward the middle of the century. In 1744 the extension in the size of the paper was accompanied by a radical alteration in layout. For the first time a London paper appeared with advertising on the two inner and news on the two outer pages, a move clearly intended to facilitate rapid printing. Twenty-seven years later the daily *Gazetteer* carried through a similar change, transferring the main news from page two to page four,[76] and in 1779 a similar move was considered by the proprietors of the *General Evening Post.*[77] The circulation of the *Gazetteer* at the time of the change was about 5,000 a day and of the *General Evening Post* about 4,500 per issue. If the same pressure was influencing the proprietors of the *London Evening Post,* a regular sale of about 5,000 copies seems possible. Few of the complex thrice-weeklies can have achieved this sort of circulation and even at this level the sales return was probably little more than £3 per issue.

The finances of the cut-price thrice-weeklies and the unstamped halfpenny and farthing posts rested almost entirely on sales revenue. However, the absence of any detailed accounts makes it impossible to assess the sums that they produced for their proprietors. The only direct evidence for the circulation of a legitimate paper in this section of the press is provided by a claim made in the successful *Penny London Post* in 1745. It was stated that "the Number printed each Time of Publication is upward of Seven Thousand, (a far greater Number than any other Paper printed in England)."[78] Although this sounds an inflated estimate, demand at this level was considerable and it seems likely that papers of this type could be very profitable.

The full-priced dailies such as the *Daily Advertiser* and the *London Daily Post,* with a restricted area of distribution and an increasingly extended form, owed neither their survival nor their level of profits directly to sales income, although a reasonable circulation was necessary to attract advertisers. During the 1720s and 1730s the London dailies seldom achieved a circulation of over 1,000 copies per issue.[79] That even this modest circulation was above the general level is suggested by the only known run of printing figures for a London daily paper that survives in a set of marked copies of the *London Daily Post and General Advertiser.* The manuscript entries, possibly made by the printer Henry Woodfall, appear in isolated copies at the end of 1741 and are complete for the years 1743 to 1746. They show not only the number of copies of the paper printed each day, but also the return from each advertisement and other paid entries. During the last three months of 1741 the number printed ranged between 600 and 730, and this sort of figure was still being recorded in 1743 when the lowest number for any issue was 500 copies in August, and the highest 740 for issues in February and March. Subsequently the printing figures show a continuous overall increase, with the maximum daily issue rising each year, reaching 1,250 in March 1744, 1,350 in December 1745, and taking a considerable leap forward to 2,300 in December 1746. The impact of the Jacobite crisis is clearly reflected in the circulation, and with the start of the London season in November 1746, the paper maintained a continuous daily sale of 2,000 or more copies to the end of the year. Such an expansion in sales for a daily, and by this time continuously four-folio-page paper, probably created important production problems and resulted in greatly increased costs through the employment of additional personnel and perhaps the purchase, or use, of an extra press.[80] However, it seems that there was no real dislocation in the production of the *General Advertiser,* whose printer simply announced in February 1746 that "having lately met with uncommon Encouragement, the Sale of this Paper being now more than Double what it was Six Months ago, the Proprietors find themselves under a Necessity of making a second Publication, which will be done at Nine o'Clock every Morning."[81] The apparent ease with which the paper met these growing demands, involving capital outlay that could not be recouped by profit from sales, underlines the primary importance of advertising revenue to this type of paper and the close link between the two sources of income was indicated by their parallel fluctuations during the year. The sales of the *London Daily Post* generally reached their peak in February and March, while income from advertisements was at its height in March and April; similarly, both were at their lowest point during August.

While sales revenue continued to be the main prop of sections of the London press and to provide some substantial short-term profits, the most consistent signs of financial growth appeared in those papers deriving their income from advertisements.[82] Since Queen Anne's reign, advertising had provided a useful adjunct to sales revenue and by the mid-1720s the amount of space devoted to this material was provoking some vigorous criticism. In 1725, for example, the author of James Read's *Weekly Journal* indicted the principal London papers of being "cramm'd with Advertisements" and self-righteously convicted them.[83] The following year Thomas Robe, in a scheme to control the press, described advertisements as "the great support of the proprietors, Writers and Printers of News Papers," going on to outline his plan to drastically reduce the number of papers by depriving them of this source of income.[84] Whatever the reservations of some contemporaries, the number of advertisements published in the London press continued to increase. In 1729 the shilling duty yielded £1,795 to the government and by 1750 this had risen to £4,951.[85] The development of advertising as a source of income was most marked in the full-priced thrice-weekly and daily papers, and the publication during the 1730s of the *Daily Advertiser* and the *London Daily Post, and General Advertiser* reflected in their titles the shifting financial emphasis. The other forms of London paper took variable advantage of this source of income. Both James Read and Thomas Robe included the weekly press in their strictures and such papers as the *London Journal* and *Mist's Weekly Journal* carried a substantial number of advertisements before and after the curtailment of 1725. Subsequently, the proprietors of the weeklies often used any increase in the size of the sheet to extend this form of content. In its first issue in journal form the *Craftsman* carried only 12 advertisements,[86] but by 1730 the number published in a single issue had been raised to 55.[87] In spite of this sort of increase, advertisements provided only a subsidiary source of income.[88] In his attack on the *Craftsman* in 1731 the author of the *D'Anverian History* stated that the paper's advertisements produced a sufficient return to pay for half the cost of the paper and printing of an impression of about 12,000 copies.[89] This apparently realistic assessment suggests an income of about £5 a week, and it seems unlikely that space allowed any scope to achieve a higher figure. While a number of full-priced weeklies such as *Read's Weekly Journal* continued to carry a minimal number of advertisements, the cheap newspapers only obliquely reflected the advertising boom. The successful *Rayner's Morning Advertiser* owed its title more to prevailing fashion than to weight of advertisements[90] and the farthing "Advertisers" were also apparently attempting to cash in on a current catch phrase.[91]

The charge for placing advertisements in an individual paper varied with its form and relative popularity and was seldom regularly specified,[92] although after 1712 the cost of a basic unit of ten or twelve lines never seems to have risen above 3/6 or to have fallen below 1/6. Even when the basic advertising rate is established, an accurate assessment of income from this source remains virtually impossible without direct evidence. This is inevitably rare. However, in the case of two major London papers, extended runs of copies marked up with the charge for each advertisement have survived. The first of these is of the *General Evening Post* for 1736[93] and the second the run of the *London Daily Post and General Advertiser* already referred to. Nonetheless, although they provide a valuable insight into the finances of each of these forms, they also underline the difficulties involved in estimating advertising revenue generally. In the first place, even where basic costs are clearly stated, the way in which they were increased must remain to some extent a matter of guesswork. The marked copies show a large proportion of the advertisements to have been charged at a standard rate, but there are also a considerable number of unusual length or form for which the charges were variable. Reduction for repeated entries, as well as some inexplicable fluctuations, make the establishment of hard-and-fast rules on the cost of advertisements extremely difficult, even in the case of the marked copies.

A second problem raised by the marked papers concerns the extent to which advertising revenue was supplemented by income from the manipulation of other sections. It was the practice during this period to place some advertisements among the news paragraphs, with no differentiation, and this practice appears in both sets of marked papers, the charge being similar to the rate for conventional advertisements.[94] It also appears that similar payment was made for the entry of certain news paragraphs, as well as for the omission of others. A number of copies of the *General Evening Post* contain an entry for "leaving out," while the *London Daily Post* specified the subject of the items omitted, which concern bankrupts, trials, marriages, deaths and other miscellaneous topics. The yield from such paragraphs was slight, but added to it was the income from the publication of letters and similar entries which produced a useful, if variable, sum. In 1745 one copy of the *General Advertiser* contained five paid contributions relating to the Jacobite crisis on pages one and two, which brought in £1. 18s. 6d.

The greatest problem to be faced in attempting an assessment of advertising revenue is presented by the general publication of cut-price advertisements. This was sometimes done to attract advertisers and in 1729 the *Daily Post-Boy* was accused, in an ironic advertisement, of not only "dunning and working under Ground for Advertisements," but also of "The Modern Practice of inserting *Puff* Advertisements, and Advertisements only for the Duty . . . to draw others in."[95] Far more often, cut-price advertising was the product of the system of group ownership since it became a general practice for the partners in a London paper to enter their advertisements at the cost only of the duty of 1s. Here again, even if the identity of the proprietors is known, the agreements reached seem to have been subject to important variations and to have been altered according to the situation of the paper. At the projecting of the *Grub Street Journal* the partners seem to have agreed that they should be allowed to insert a twelve-line advertisement for 1s., paying 1d. for each extra line, but this applied only if there was room, and insistence would mean payment at the full rate.[96] In April 1731, at the beginning of the difficult summer period, the paper's financial condition seems to have led to a change in policy indicated by the order for the partners to enter one advertisement a week for each share held, on pain of a fine.[97] The ledger contains an account of two subsequent changes, the withdrawal of the fine in 1735[98] and its replacement at the end of the following year.[99] No similar agreements for this period have been discovered but if, as seems likely, such variations were usual, the considerable difference between the number of cut-price advertisements in the two runs of marked papers can be explained.

The *General Evening Post*, first published in October 1733, carries a very large proportion of 1s. advertisements placed by booksellers who were probably partners in the paper.[100] This ranges between 21 percent and 44 percent of the total monthly number published and includes issues in which 10 out of 14 and 8 out of 11 advertisements were entered at the cut-price rate. The *Grub Street Journal* ledger shows a preference given to outside advertisers and this seems to have been a general rule among jointly owned papers.[101] Consequently, it may be that the paper was unable to attract sufficient advertising and was being maintained by the efforts of its proprietors. On the other hand, the bookseller shareholders may have been content to use it simply as a vehicle for their own advertisements, excluding those of trade rivals, even at the price of a low financial return. The situation is quite different with the *London Daily Post*. From the marked copies it appears that 1s. bookseller advertisements were published only during the slack months of July, August, and September, while the same advertisers, who may also have been shareholders,[102] were charged a higher, if not the full rate, at other times of the year. This points to a healthy financial situation confirmed by the paper's general development.

Such wide variation in the publishing of cut-price advertisements underlines the impossibility of making even a general assessment of a paper's prosperity from the extent of its advertising section. The way in which this could even confuse contemporaries was illustrated in the coffee-house controversy. Complaining about the number of advertisements appearing in the London press, the spokesman for the coffee-men picked on the *Daily Post* as guilty of the abuse and claimed that it was "often equipped with Thirty; which yield *Three Pounds Fifteen Shillings* that Day to the Proprietors, for the least: And sometimes that Paper has more. Well may they divide Twelve Hundred Pounds a Year and upwards."[103] To this it was answered, probably with some justification, that "that Paper has often eight or ten Partners to fill up the large Size, which that, as also the *Daily Journal* affords to the Publick, in 3 large Columns, at the common Price, and which, by the Duty, are a Charge, and no Benefit at all to the Paper."[104]

The only detailed account of advertising income is therefore provided by the statements in the marked papers, although the question remains of how far they are useful in illuminating the general position. The run of the *London Daily Post* is the most satisfactory since it covers a period of years and the advertising content is predominantly charged at the full rate. The shorter run of the *General Evening Post* is more ambiguous since, although the paper appears as the type of a successful thrice-weekly, the extent of its cut-price advertising meant that the paper's income from this source was surprisingly low. Absolute precision in the calculation of financial totals, even in these cases, is impossible since the physical condition of the papers alone makes some omissions inevitable. In the totals I have not attempted to assess which of the items embedded in the text paid tax and have included returns from all types of paid entries.

In 1736 the *General Evening Post* published 2,435 advertisements, of which 790 were charged at 1s. and which after tax brought a clear profit of £156. 12s. 6d. This could have given the paper an average income for each issue throughout the year of just under £1. There was some variation in the monthly level and the profit for March of £15. 0s. 6d. was the highest total for the early part of the year, while for the month of September the profit fell to a low of £8. 17s. In November and December there are signs of an upward trend, and the number of cut-price advertisements was lower than at any previous time, the December profits mounting to £18. 8s. 6d. On only one occasion did the total income before tax of a single issue reach £3.,[105] while during August and September this figure was quite often well below £1.

The marked copies of the *London Daily Post* reveal an entirely different state of affairs. In 1746, with the return from advertising at its highest point, the paper published 12,254 advertisements which, after tax, yielded £753. 10s. The average income throughout the year for each issue of the paper would therefore have been £2. 7s. 6d. From 1743 the annual income from advertisements rose steadily, if undramatically, and this growth was reflected in the number of four-page issues published during the year. The practice of extending the paper when the demand for space was at its greatest was well established by 1743 and the paper's income early and late in the year remained fairly constant. In March 1743 the paper earned £70. 12s. 6d. after tax from 963 advertisements, while three years later the income from 1,319 advertisements was £82. 3s. 6d. The gradual extension of the number of four-page issues with their higher rate of return[106] throughout the year, culminating in 1746 with the abandonment of the single-leaf format, meant that the greatest increase in profits occurred during the summer months. In September 1743, 407 advertisements brought in £29 after tax, while in September 1746, 869 advertisements yielded £60. 8s.

These returns were probably in part needed to cover production costs and do not therefore necessarily represent a net profit. At the same time, it

Page four of the *General Evening Post* 427, Thursday 29 July 1736. Each advertisement is priced in manuscript and the total income from all forms of advertising in this issue is shown below the third column.

seems possible that throughout the press the full income from sales and advertising was seldom realised. The proprietors of all forms of London paper were obliged, like their provincial counterparts, to operate a system of credit, which, as well as tying up capital, multiplied the difficulties of obtaining payment. Although the secondary London distributors handling bulk orders of the full-priced papers were accessible and seldom appear to have evaded or delayed settlement, some problems arose even in this area. This appears from the dealings between the proprietors of the principal evening papers and Isaac Jamineau at the Post Office. In 1788 Jamineau claimed that he was "obliged to give the Clerks a month's credit" and that this period was frequently extended,[107] a process that inevitably delayed his payment of the printers. The effect on the finances of papers passing through the Office in increasingly large numbers was probably serious, and during the mid-1750s the proprietors of the *General Evening Post* and the *Whitehall Evening Post* took recurrent and concerted action to try to enforce a regular monthly settlement.[108] The hawkers also seem to have given some trouble by hiring out rather than selling full-priced papers, but the main problem was invariably with the individual subscribers dealing directly with the printers and perhaps the publishers. All forms of London paper were apparently available on subscription, and although very little evidence is available on this side of newspaper finance, the experiences of the booksellers may reflect some general difficulties and variations. Although Robert Gosling assessed his clients' newspaper accounts on a monthly basis, settlement was sometimes considerably delayed. Richard Reynall, for example, was supplied with the *Whitehall Evening Post*, the *St. James's Evening Post*, and the *Universal Spectator* for nearly three-and-a-half years without settling up, and the final entry in his news account stated ruefully, "This Debt not paid, lost for not applying soon enough."[109] This sort of difficulty was probably well known to all the primary newspaper publishers and the records of Charles Delafaye suggest another way in which the cash income from sales could be curtailed. As well as providing eight of his customers with free copies, a further six appeared with the note "No Agreement." This may suggest a negotiated fee or perhaps some sort of payment in kind. This latter suggestion is supported by the entry against John Traile of Worcestershire, who apparently received a newsletter, the *Gazette*, the *Votes*, and three conventional newspapers in return for a hogshead of cider or perry. Such arrangements probably became increasingly unusual, but it seems possible that a cash return was not the invariable form of payment for copies.

Similar problems probably arose over the payment for advertisements, although the two runs of marked copies contain no indication of delays or evasions. The *Grub Street Journal* proprietors showed some concern with the collection of outstanding sums and the stress placed on the printer's responsibility in this direction perhaps reflects a general difficulty. He was ordered to present at the end of each month an account of all advertisements, with details of how much was owed by whom "on the penalty of paying two shillings and sixpence For every default & Sixpence per day for every day after That he shall Neglect the same & that he shall go to The persons Indebted and Endeavour to Collect the Same And deliver to the Treasurer an Acct of the persons Indebted before he is paid the said Month's printing."[110] There even seems to have been some awkwardness in collecting the money for advertisements placed by the proprietors themselves.[111] The government was not exempt from the problem and sums due to the Stamp Office for advertisement duty, sometimes reaching well over £100, suggesting both a lax system of collection and a possible inability on the part of the papers to meet the demands promptly.

Newspaper production involved a number of financial fringe benefits, of which one of the most profitable was the republication of material in an alternative form. However, the total yield to the proprietors from a combination of all sources very seldom reached £20 a week during the Walpole period and the massive growth in profits that took place through advertising later in the century was only tentatively prefigured. The financial motives behind the establishment of a London newspaper were mixed. On one hand the regularity of the income may often have weighed more heavily with projectors than its scale, while on the the other the efficacy of the papers as vehicles for house advertisements could more than offset a limited return. Consequently, in order to place the finances of an individual paper in its correct commercial perspective, it is necessary to obtain a clear view of its internal organization.

4
The Booksellers and Group Ownership

No other intervention of the eighteenth century had such a far-reaching impact on the press as that of the groups of London booksellers. The build-up in their involvement, running parallel to an existing range of political interests, provided the newspapers with a commercial structure that was both durable and restrictive, and it was within the framework that they established that most of the changes in physical form, distribution, and finance were worked out. This intervention of the booksellers was entirely a London-based phenomenon. Nowhere else was there such a concentration of resources or potential for investment. At the same time, their takeover of a large section of the press was helped by the long-standing experience of joint action that existed within the London trade at large.[1] By 1700 the London booksellers had already begun to combine to distribute the costs of book production and to protect their interests in copyrights.[2] The lapse of the Licensing Act in 1695 had removed all legal restraint and although the Act of 1710 provided for tenure of up to 28 years, this was seen as a totally inadequate security. Consequently, both before and after the Act the principal owners of copyright, wholesale booksellers who numbered less than one hundred at the beginning of the century, created a variety of informal associations to defend their investment against all forms of encroachment. Out of these defensive alliances emerged the important groups known to the booksellers themselves as "Congers." The first major partnership formed in the 1690s and dissolved shortly after 1719[3] was one of a number of such organizations established during the early eighteenth century,[4] the members holding shares in a very variable property. During the second decade transactions in copyright shares[5] increased in volume, becoming centered in the trade sales at which booksellers as individuals as well as members of the "Congers" competed for a variety of holdings.[6]

The stages by which the booksellers gained a dominant financial interest in the upper reaches of the London press remain largely concealed. Since Queen Anne's reign, individual members of the trade, such as Abel Roper, had owned newspapers, while it seems possible that simple combinations of proprietors had also existed from the early years of the century.[7] A nudge towards the development of the group ownership of newspapers may also have come from outside the trade altogether. From 1710 the *British Mercury* was under the management of the twenty-four variable shareholders of the Sun Insurance Office, including Matthew Jenour and Hugh Meere, the consecutive printers of the paper, as well as a third printer, a stationer, a bookbinder, and a bookseller.[8]

In spite of these early developments the London press does not appear to have attracted large-scale bookseller investment until late in the second decade, when activity in conventional share dealing was becoming both more widespread and more formalized.[9] By 1720 a substantial cross section of full-priced London newspapers was owned by groups of shareholding booksellers. These papers included the *Daily Courant,* the *Whitehall Evening Post,* the *St. James's Post,* the *St. James's Evening Post,* the newly established *Daily Post,* and almost certainly its immediate rival, the *Daily Journal.*[10] This newspaper interest seems to have broadened out during the late 1720s when a number of full-priced weeklies were set up, apparently under group ownership. The *Universal Spectator,* the *Knight Errant* and its successors, and later the *Grub Street Journal* were all controlled by members of the trade. Consequently, by 1730 a large proportion of the principal London newspapers was in the hands of the booksellers, and although a few printer-owned journals continued on the market, it appears that at the death or retirement of the proprietors they were either abandoned, as in the case of *Applebees Original Weekly Journal,* or, like *Read's Weekly Journal,* reorganized under group ownership. Only the cut-price papers, like the provincial weeklies, remained consistently in the hands of the printers.

The stimulus behind this rapid and comprehensive extension in bookseller ownership was provided by two commercial considerations. In the first place newspaper investment, involving only a moderate outlay, could provide a regular and potentially long-term income. The financial demands made at the setting-up of a new paper and the subsequent calls on shareholders have already been described.[11] However many of the bookseller proprietors bought into an established venture and the very variable level of payments necessary to obtain a share in the different forms are indicated in the few surviving trade-sale transactions. The highest recorded price for a share in a weekly journal was £23 for 1/12 of the *Universal Spectator,*[12] while shares in the thrice-weeklies and dailies tended to be proportionately more expensive. In 1750, for example, 1/26 of the *General Evening Post* was sold for £56. 10s,[13] and in 1734 1/20 of the *Daily Post* fetched £80.[14] It was often possible to obtain shares at well below these rates and the same proportion of the *Daily Post* in the early 1740s only cost £7. 10s.[15] Later in the century the share value of the thrice-weekly *St. James's Chronicle* was regularly fixed at the proprietors' general meeting at sums that rose by stages from 25 guineas to £300.[16] The return that could be expected from this sort of investment was itself very variable and depended on the commercial success of individual publications. No fortunes were made but a useful profit could be hoped for. Direct evidence on the level of dividends is very fragmented, but it certainly appears that the proprietors of the weekly *Grub Street Journal* had to be satisfied during the 1730s with a modest income. The payments crop up erratically in the records and indicate monthly dividends of between 10s. 6d. and £1. 10s. 6d.[17] During the 1750s and 1760s a share in the *General Evening Post* or the *St. James's Chronicle,* after an initial hiatus, would have produced somewhere between £50 and £100 *per annum,* a respectable sum that increased through time.[18]

Although income was of importance, the principal spur to investment probably lay in the booksellers' appreciation of the value of the newspaper as an advertising medium. As John Henley pointed out in the *Hyp-Doctor,* "One Consideration which forc'd *the Trade* to start and multiply such Papers was to contract the Expense of advertising their own Books by Partnership in public Papers of their own Property and Management where they might the most freely, commodiously, and cheaply insert their own Advertisements, and command those of the Town."[19] The cut-price publication of their own advertisements was probably the main incentive. However, as Henley suggested, the potential negative influence of newspaper ownership was an equally important consideration. The frequency of complaints about the suppression of advertisements suggests that self-interested censorship soon became a characteristic feature of bookseller control. During the early 1730s the proprietors of one translation of Bayle's *Dictionary* found their advertisements refused by the *Daily Courant,* the *Daily Journal,* the *Daily Post,* the *Daily Post-Boy,* the *London Evening Post,* and the *Whitehall Evening Post,* apparently as a result of pressure from the more influential owners of a rival translation.[20] Similarly, Edward Cave had the greatest difficulty in placing advertisements for the *Gentlemans Magazine.*[21] Both the range of this sort of commercial control and the value to advertisers of an alternative outlet through the cut-price papers was suggested in 1742 by an advertisement appearing in *Rayner's London Morning Advertiser.* "We are credibly informed," it stated, "that a certain Body of Men are in a Combination to oblige the inquisitive and studious Part of Mankind to purchase every Book they read, nay before they read it by depriving those, who *lend Books,* of the Benefit of advertising their Design in the Publick News Papers: And that Mr. *Fancourt,* who has opened an UNIVERSAL CIRCULATING LIBRARY, next Door to the *Royal Society House,* in *Crane-Court, Fleet-street,* has been actually deny'd this Privilege by the *Daily* and *General Advertisers,* thro' the instigation of those that seem to be in Pain, that his Subscribers should have the agreeable Entertainment, as well as the Advantage, of looking into such a great Variety of Subjects, for so small an Expence."[22]

Ownership of the leading papers also gave the booksellers the capacity to take similar action against rival publications, and their developing control of the London press was perhaps most clearly suggested by the complaints of potential competitors. In 1733 the author of the weekly *London Cryer* was quoted as complaining that the booksellers owned all the London papers, except perhaps the *Craftsman,* and were adopting sinister restrictive practices.[23] In 1740 both the *Champion* and the *Englishman's Evening Post* ran into trouble through the opposition of the bookseller shareholders of established papers[24] and by mid-century a virtual monopoly in the market seems to have been established. The author of the thrice-weekly *National Journal* claimed in 1746 that "*as there seems* to *be a Combination among the* Proprietors *of* all *the* daily Papers *but one, not to suffer any* News-Paper *to be set up, in which they have* no Concern; *and as most of the* Pamphlet Shops, *etc. are by Necessity or Choice become* such Slaves *to them, as to* deny selling *any Paper which has not the good Fortune to be* licensed *by these Demagogues: it has prevented the first* two or three Numbers *of this Paper, from coming to the Hands of many* Gentlemen."[25] The general operation of this sort of pressure also appeared from a title-notice run in the ministerial *True Patriot* stating that

> *whereas we have been informed by several Persons, that they have not been able to procure the* True Patriot *at any Rate: And we have great Reason to believe that many malicious and base Endeavours have been used to suppress the Sale of this Paper, by some who are concerned in imposing on the Public, by propagating Lies and Nonsense, which we have endeavoured to detect and expose. If any Hawkers, or others, will acquaint* Mr. A. Millar, *Bookseller, opposite* Katherine-Street *in the* Strand, *with the Name of any Person who had bribed, or offered to bribe them to refuse delivering out the* True Patriot *to their Customers, they shall be well rewarded, and their Names, if they desire it, concealed.*[26]

The extent of bookseller interest in the press was reflected in the steady if elusive dealing in newspaper shares that was carried on during the 1720s and 1730s. In 1732 Henley claimed that "to live on the Sale of these Papers, Advertisements, and Shares, is above half the modern Trade of *Grub* Bookselling; they are transferr'd, and sold over and over in the Manner of Stock jobbing, to a 16th Share, if not less, at their Meetings in Pater Noster Row, and other Places."[27] Henley was referring to the trade sales, and was certainly exaggerating when he described the dealers as "Grubs," since among the purchasers of newspaper shares were Bernard Lintot, Samuel Birt, Robert Gosling, Thomas Woodward and Joseph Davidson, five of the most substantial booksellers of the day. In substance, as was often the case, the basis of Henley's claim seems to have been correct. The extent of dealing was to some degree reflected in the small fractions into which newspaper shares were sometimes divided and which went well beyond Henley's estimate. In 1736, for example, Theophilus Cibber disposed of $\frac{1}{3}$ of $\frac{1}{10}$ of a share in the *Daily Post* for £28.[28] The *Grub Street Journal* records indicate that sale of a moiety of a personal holding did not necessarily involve loss of managerial status[29] and comparable rulings may have encouraged this sort of transaction. The number of partners in a conventional jointly-owned paper was variable but, taking the share divisions as a very rough guide, it appears that the weeklies generally had six to ten shareholders, thrice-weeklies ten to fifteen, and the dailies offering the greatest advertising space, twenty.[30] Consequently, a large number of book-sellers and others held shares in the London press and there was probably a regular turnover of peripheral personnel. Although the number of pro-prietors of the *Grub Street Journal* at any one time does not seem to have risen above nine, and toward the end of the paper's career fell to six, at least twenty-three booksellers and printers held some share in the property during its seven-year existence.

In practice the nature of the booksellers' interest in the press led the proprietors to take steps to ensure that these sales should not undermine their collective position and there were a number of internal restraints on the movement of shares. An attempt at least to keep a close check on transactions appeared from an early ruling in the *Grub Street Journal* min-utes that "every Partner, who shall for the Future dispose of his Share, shall give Notice to the Treasurer for the Time being with the Name of the Persons he sold to within 15 Days after such Sale, and that the Treasurer communicate the same at the next Meeting to be enter'd in the Book."[31] A more formal oversight was subsequently established in the *Gazetteer* agree-ment of 1748 and also between the shareholders in the *General Evening Post*, in both cases permission from a general meeting of the partners being necessary before a sale could take place.[32] Comparable regulations may have accounted for the comparatively small number of shares that were offered for casual sale at the trade-sale auctions.[33] A further restriction on investment was usually imposed on the newspaper proprietors by the general ruling against holdings in similar papers. This was not apparently written into the original agreement of the *Grub Street Journal* proprietors, as was subsequently the case with the *Gazetteer*, but in 1732 it was agreed that "no person shall hold a share in the Grub-street Journal, who holds a share in any other weekly Journal whatsoever."[34] There does not seem to have been any attempt to prevent holdings in alternative forms, and an interest in a combination of a weekly, thrice-weekly and daily paper became charac-teristic of leading newspaper printers.[35]

Identification of booksellers with a special interest in the press or who acted jointly in controlling more than one newspaper is extremely difficult to establish without direct evidence. Attempts to pin down the proprietors of individual papers through an exhaustive analysis of advertising content inevitably remain inconclusive without a certain amount of background information. Similarly, newspaper imprints are of little value in this highly problematical area, although the lists of names associated with editions of collected essays can provide some useful pointers. In certain instances it is possible to detect some overlap in ownership and to make some tentative remarks about one or two groups of shareholders in the full-priced London newspapers. A link between the proprietors of the *Daily Post* and the *London Evening Post,* which were both under the management of the printer Richard Nutt, was constantly asserted by contemporaries.[36] In the *London Evening Post* itself such a link was categorically denied and, in reply to an attack in the *Daily Journal,* it was stated that "If the most *Active* and *Vindictive Proprietors* of this Paper were *Proprietors* of the *Daily Post,* That we hope would be greatly in its Favour, and add much lustre to it: But its false in Fact."[37] The parallel advertising content of the two papers suggests that this may have been a considerable overstatement and that at least some of the shares were held in common.[38] There is also fragmentary evidence linking the principal proprietors of the short-lived *Knight Errant,* the *Weekly Register,* and the monthly *London Magazine,*[39] although the complexities involved in establishing the ownership of these publications and others related to them are considerable.

The only group of shareholders whose varied newspaper holdings can be identified with any semblance of accuracy are found in the generally untypical area of the political press. The major opposition weeklies remained largely outside the sphere of bookseller control, as their characteristic volume of medical rather than literary advertising suggests, although in some instances, notably those of the *Craftsman* and *Old England,* a group of politicians filled much the same role as the booksellers. At the same time, *de facto* ownership of the *Craftsman* remained in the hands of two shareholding proprietors, the bookseller Richard Francklin and the author Nicholas Amhurst, and the same arrangement probably obtained for many of the other principal opposition papers. In the same way, the property of the ministerially subsidized essay-papers remained throughout in private hands and the evidence suggests that those involved formed a quite small closed group composed of a printer, a publisher, and a small number of booksellers. Some, perhaps all, of this group had other newspaper interests, but their association becomes most clear in relation to the five papers circulated by the Walpole ministry.

Initially, the printer associated with this group was William Wilkins who produced and part-owned the *London Journal* as well as, for a time, the *Daily Courant.*[40] Nichols described Wilkins as "the favourite printer of the Whig party," and claimed in a note to the Negus list of 1724 that he produced five newspapers,[41] which may have included some other of those receiving ministerial support for which no printer is known. However, in the mid-1730s there are indications of some political strains and, after being obliged to give up his share in the *Daily Courant,* Wilkins seems to have broken altogether with his fellow proprietors.[42] His place was taken by Samuel Richardson, who was already associated with other members of the group as printer of the *Daily Journal*[43] and who printed and held a share in the *Daily Gazetteer* from its first appearance. He also, at about the same time, replaced Wilkins in the *London Journal,* which continued to appear for some years after the withdrawal of the government subsidy. Richardson's interest in this paper appears principally through its obvious links with the *Daily*

Gazetteer, sometimes having the same contributors and also appearing in joint advertisements.[44] In 1736 Aaron Hill wrote to Richardson referring to two newspapers in which he and John Peele had an interest and, although he specified only the *Daily Gazetteer,* it seems almost certain that the other was the *London Journal.*[45] Peele, a leading newspaper publisher, was a central figure in this group of proprietors holding a major share in the *London Journal,* a 50 percent interest in the *Free Briton* and, subsequently, part ownership in the *Daily Gazetteer.*[46] Only three other booksellers emerge as shareholders in these papers. Thomas Woodward, who held a minority 1/10 share in the *London Journal,* a joint interest in the *Free Briton* with Peele and perhaps a share in the *Daily Gazetteer*;[47] John Walthoe, who received the subsidy for, and was probably therefore a leading shareholder in, the *Daily Courant,* the *Corn Cutters Journal,* and the *Daily Gazetteer*;[48] and a "Mr. Tovey," who appears briefly as a principal shareholder in the *London Journal.*[49] Consequently, in 1735 it seems that Samuel Richardson, John Peele, Thomas Woodward, and John Walthoe formed at least the nucleus of a group that controlled a number of important, if politically one-sided, London newspapers. A glimpse of this group in action perhaps emerges in the case of the *Daily Post Boy.* This paper, directed by the printer George James, had been in trouble with the authorities several times during the early 1730s for its hostile reports on foreign affairs. In 1735 a sudden reversal of its political attitude took place and in November the *London Evening Post,* attacking several false news items, stated that deliberate errors were not surprising, "for since the Death of Mr. James the Printer, the *Post Boy* is fallen into the same Hands as carry on the *Gazetteer,* is printed by the same Person, and of equal Credit in their Domestick Intelligences with *that Paper.*"[50] The paper did not survive this apparent change of ownership for long and its disappearance suggests that any takeover by this politically oriented group was a straightforward commercial exercise that was not underwritten by the ministry.

The great majority of shareholding proprietors were booksellers and printers and very few individuals outside the trade seem to have held an interest in the London newspapers in this period. The self-contained ventures of the politicians and the coffee-men were exceptional in this respect, although the *Weekly Miscellany* seems to have been set up with some official Church of England backing.[51] Its proprietor, William Webster, subsequently attempted on at least one occasion to get the Bishops to boost its circulation by encouraging the clergy to subscribe.[52] In the main it was only on the periphery of the full-priced press that individuals with varied backgrounds acted as backers and shareholders. Projectors who could not attract investment from the trade were obliged of necessity to look elsewhere and the priorities in this area were suggested in the offer of a share in the *British Oracle* or some related publication to "any Bookseller, Printer, or other willing to run some Hazard for some advantage . . ."[53] In the 1730s de Coetlogan offered a share in the moribund *Alchymist* to a change broker and another unspecified businessman,[54] but this seems to have been rejected, and there are no other indications that capital from such a source was used to keep any London paper afloat. The restriction on the sale of shares in established papers probably itself limited the extent of outside investment. However, exceptions to this general rule appeared in the case of the leading dailies. In the first place, Hugh Meere, under examination for printing number 44 of the *Daily Post,* stated that "as he has heard some of the Play-house are concerned therein."[55] The identity of these supposed shareholders remains obscure, but the link between the theatrical profession and the London dailies reappeared fifteen years later. At this point the actors Theophilus Cibber, Benjamin Griffin, and John Mills held between them ⅓ of ¹⁄₁₀ of the *London Daily Post,*[56] and it seems likely that they were among its original proprietors.[57] The names of other individuals from outside the book trade crop up sporadically in relation to the London newspapers. Henry Vander Esch, deputy master-worker of the Mint, for example, was credited with being the "original proprietor" of the *Daily Advertiser,* a paper that appeared to have strong coffee-house connections. Later in the century the proprietors of the *St. James's Chronicle* were permitted under their agreement to hold more than one share in trust, and five of the original twenty were held in this way.[58] It is possible that this sort of arrangement existed in the earlier period and therefore that some of the booksellers' holdings were in fact partly the property of individuals not concerned in this area of trade. There is no direct evidence for this, and the *Chronicle* arrangements may simply indicate a later tendency to diversify shareholding. In the mid-1770s the eighteen proprietors of the *Gazetteer* included a ship broker, a merchant, and two "gentlemen" as well as an Oxford bookseller.[59]

Whatever minor variations existed, it was the book trade shareholders who dominated the newspaper business from the 1720s. Political groups followed a similar organizational line, but their activities were less far-reaching and, in some ways, less interventionist than those of their commercial counterparts. The booksellers seeking to use the press for a variety of purposes developed a sophisticated management system to support their supervision of every stage in the process of production and distribution. Information about this system and its development has gradually built up as a series of important but scattered records have been discovered, often in unexpected locations. The first collection of materials was found by R. L. Haig among the voluminous papers of the Court of Chancery and used in his comprehensive study of the *Gazetteer.* Through the proprietors' agreements of 1748 and 1753 and a mass of accounts and papers largely dating from the 1780s and 1790s, he was able to sketch in some of the elements of group management. Subsequently, three sets of the minutes kept by groups of newspaper shareholders at their regular meetings have surfaced and, in conjunction with the fragments of material that were already known to exist, have made possible a fuller although still incomplete analysis.

Two of these items relate to the second half of the eighteenth century and are concerned with the management of successful thrice-weeklies. The records of the *St. James's Chronicle* covering the years 1763 to 1808 have been described in useful detail by Richmond and Marjorie Bond. A parallel but as yet unpublished series of minutes held in the W. S. Lewis collection are those of the shareholders in the *General Evening Post* beginning in 1754, over twenty years after the paper was set up, and running through to 1786. The third set of records is concerned with the management of the weekly *Grub Street Journal*, covering the period from its first appearance in 1731 to the winding up of the venture in 1739. This important material has been printed in full in the journal *Publishing History*. Each of these documents has a variety of shortcomings. The original agreements, for example, are missing from the records of the *General Evening Post* and the *Grub Street Journal*, and while there are some large gaps, the entries are often brief and repetitive. At the same time, each contains a view of a working newspaper that cannot be found elsewhere, and by using the *Grub Street Journal* records as a focus it is possible to fill out the shadowy picture of newspaper management in the first half of the eighteenth century.

The content of the *Grub Street Journal* suggests that the main lines of management practice, in use throughout the century, were already established by the 1730s. However, there are some oblique indications that the proprietors' approach to problems was rather more pragmatic than appeared with the other papers, perhaps reflecting a general lack of experience in some aspects of this sort of organizations.[60] Each of the three sets of minutes indicates the adoption of a two-tier structure. General meetings of all the partners were established to take the major financial and policy decisions and to exercise a broad oversight of the business. These were held quarterly or twice-yearly. Unfortunately the records of neither the *Journal* nor the *Post* contain regular minutes of the general sessions, although in the *Chronicle* books the record is full and often runs to two or three pages.[61] This may imply that in the case of the older papers a separate record was kept, possibly with the financial accounts. Henry Woodfall's monthly balance-sheets of the *Public Advertiser* in the 1760s were totaled and signed under the December entry, the pages usually being torn out and perhaps filed in this form,[62] and it seems likely that the general accounts and minutes of the other papers were sometimes combined in this way. A feature of these meetings, which does emerge clearly from the records, is the way in which managerial business was frequently combined with pleasure. By the 1730s the summer meeting seems to have taken on the character of a country jaunt, and in June 1734 the proprietors of the *Grub Street Journal* agreed that the next general session would be "at the Green man Black-heath by ten in the morning in order to which those who think fit may meet at the Gun-tavern in Billings-gate by eight."[63] The proprietors of the *Chronicle* seem to have favored Hampstead, and although the shareholders in the *Post* gave up their regular out-of-town dinner they allowed themselves additional expenses of up to £3 at their general meetings to be held in future at a tavern rather than a coffee-house.[64] Such junketings at Midsummer and Christmas were a familiar feature of the business and political life of eighteenth-century London and in this case must have helped to emphasize the element of group solidarity among the freely associating newspaper shareholders.

The infrequent general meetings would hardly have been adequate to organize the conduct of a weekly or thrice-weekly newspaper, and the routine business of management was invariably delegated to a committee that, after 1750, usually consisted of about half the partners. This meant ten nominees for the *Gazetteer,* six for the *Post,* and five for the *Chronicle.* Initially all the proprietors of the *Journal* seem to have been expected to attend the executive sessions, an expectation that was seldom, if ever, met. In each case the regularity of committee meetings is hard to assess. Some of the gaps in the *Grub Street Journal* records were probably the result of the proprietors' failure to meet but at the same time scrappy and haphazard entries in the ledger suggest that a proportion resulted from secretarial defects. The number of meetings recorded during full years of the *Grub Street Journal*'s publication ranged from thirteen in 1731 to five in 1734 and 1735, and these were not evenly spaced throughout the year. Similarly, the *General Evening Post* ledger prior to 1779 frequently contained entries for only two or three meetings a year, although at this point the management of the paper seems to have undergone something of a shake-up and for the rest of the period the number recorded in a full year ranged between thirteen and nineteen. All the records indicate problems with attendance and in each case there was an attempt to enforce promptness and regularity through a system of graded fines. The first indication of efforts of this sort appeared in the *Grub Street Journal* ledger in January 1731, when it was agreed "that cach Partner that does not come to a Meeting appointed by the Treasurer within an Hour after the time mention'd in the Summons, to be reckon'd of Saint Paul's Clock, shall forfeit 2s. 6d."[65] It became the usual practice to exact 2s. for nonattendance and 1s. for lateness, lists of absentees and the fines being sometimes included in the minutes. In spite of this the numbers attending seldom rose about five and often dropped to three toward the end of the paper's existence. A similar system of fines was written into both the *Gazetteer* and *Chronicle* agreements. Following a long period of scanty minutes, usually signed by two or three partners, the proprietors of the *General Evening Post* made a new effort to stimulate punctual attendance, "for the want of which great inconveniences have arisen to the Interest of the Paper,"[66] by introducing the apparently standard payment of 5s. for attendance as well as a fine of 5s. for absence.[67] The monthly sessions were all held at a coffee-house or tavern specified at the preceding meeting, the Treasurer, printer, or publisher sending out reminders to the partners. During the first two years of publication the proprietors of the *Grub Street Journal* met at a variety of establishments largely in the neighborhood of Temple Bar and St. Paul's,[68] although from 1732 the usual meeting place became successively the Oxford Arms in Ludgate Street and the Salutation Tavern in Newgate Street.[69] The proprietors of the *General Evening Post,* meeting in the same area, also patronized a variety of public houses with a series of regular locations, including the Horn and Globe Taverns in Fleet Street, the Bedford Coffeehouse and the Shakespeare Tavern. The fact that the *Chronicle* shareholders also patronized the Globe and the Bedford may indicate that some of the public houses were specially identified for use by those engaged in the newspaper business. The level of entertainment laid on seems to have varied, but in the case of the *Grub Street Journal* does not appear to have been very lavish.. The only references to this in the ledger appeared in November 1731, when the expenses at the Oxford Arms were shown to amount to 9s. and it was ruled "that at every monthly meeting, after 10 of the clock, every partner shall pay his club, for whatever is called for after that time."[70] Later in the century the partners of the *Gazetteer* and the *General Evening Post* were supplied with a dinner, and John Nichols may have been referring to the latter paper when he remarked that he and Ralph Griffiths "were partners with several others, men of superior abilities, in an Evening Paper, and for 16 or 17 years successively we dined together at least eight or ten times in a year."[71]

A review of newspaper finances probably took up a good deal of time at the proprietors' meetings and the minutes contain a large number of recurrent entries concerned with the consideration of accounts. In all the jointly-owned papers a treasurer was chosen from among the partners to handle some aspects of the accounting process, although the basis of selection and the nature of the responsibilities involved seem to have varied. In the case of the *Grub Street Journal* the position was elective and held for three months. However, in 1734, after some discord over the choice of the printer John Huggonson,[72] a firm ruling was made on subsequent practice. It was agreed "that the Treasureship for the future shall be according to the priority of shares as following,

Mr. Russell	Mr. Wilde
Mr. Gilliver	Mr. Clarke
Mr. Brotherton	Mr. Wilford
Mr. Ratley	Mr. Huggonson

and that if any person shall decline it in his turn, he shall forfeit one guinea; and the next in order shall take it, or forfeit the same."[73] By 1731 the treasurer of the *Grub Street Journal* was responsible for compiling monthly accounts based on material supplied by the printer[74] and publisher. These included a separate list of proprietors' advertisements, apparently paid for at the meetings,[75] and a statement of any balance that provided the proprietors with their short-term dividends. The early entries in the ledger indicate that the treasurer also compiled a quarterly account at the end of the three-month term that was audited by two fellow proprietors and presented for signature at the next general meeting.[76] This arrangement, which was closely paralleled in the *Gazetteer* agreement of 1748, indicates the nature of the Treasurer's position as business representative of the proprietors. Even prior to the 1720s responsibility for the immediate handling of newspaper finance was occasionally passed to the publisher.[77] The records of the dailies and thrice-weeklies issued during the second half of the century suggest a frequent merger of the two roles, with the publisher either acting as Treasurer himself or with the Treasurer as a shadowy and inconsequential figure in the background.

While financial administration was the proprietors' main concern, they also exercised a comprehensive oversight of management generally, and the surviving minutes provide a good deal of information on the range of the shareholders' direct interest in the production and content of their newspapers. The printers of the jointly owned papers usually had solid security of tenure, but when changes were made, the hiring and firing was organized at the proprietors' meetings and, although no agreements are available for the Walpole period,[78] the process of selection was illustrated in the early 1730s by a series of decisions of the *Grub Street Journal*'s partners. In June 1732, probably following the death of Samuel Palmer, it was agreed that the principal shareholders, Richard Russel and Lawton Gilliver, should "look out for a Printer to print the Grub-street Journal, who is fixed as near as may be to Temple Bar."[79] The following month Gilliver, Brotherton, and Russel were empowered to make an agreement with "Mr. Bowyer Printer in White-Friers," to produce the paper "at a rate not exceeding the price which has been hitherto payed for it."[80] In the event, satisfactory terms could not be obtained and in August Gilliver and Russel were nominated to contract with "Mr. Aris, Watson, or Gover,"[81] Samual Aris being the final choice. A year later, perhaps at the end of the term of this agreement, new problems seem to have croppped up and it was decided that all the proprietors "shall meet Mr. Aris, and discourse fully with him about the present price and inconveniences of printing the Grub-street Journal, and propose some better way of printing the same."[82] Aris's suggestions, considered two weeks later, do not appear to have been acceptable, and the printing was placed in the hands of Palmer's ex-partner, the proprietor John Huggonson, whose terms were specified in the minutes.[83] Although the *Grub Street Journal* ledger does not contain any explicit decision on either the layout of the paper or the quality of the printing, both these aspects of production were probably dealt with as they were by the committee of the *General Evening Post*. In 1766, for example, the enlargement of the evening paper with the adoption of a four-column page division, and the use of clearer type were ordered by the proprietors,[84] and lapses in the standard of printing continued to be the cause of exchanges between the committee and the printer.[85] The supply of paper was the responsibility of the proprietors and was paid for directly by the treasurer, while in the case of the *Grub Street Journal* the proprietors actually owned the molds used in the paper-making process.[86] Business concerning this aspect of production was frequently on the agenda and in 1732 it was agreed by the *Grub Street Journal* proprietors that "Mr. Russel and Mr. Huggonson shall go down and settle the dispute about paper with Mr. Johanett and that one Guinea be allowed for their expenses."[87] Later in the century the *General Evening Post* committee was frequently concerned with such matters as the quality and color of the paper supplied.[88] The publication of the newspapers also came under regular review at the meetings and during the 1730s a certain amount of friction seems to have developed between the proprietors of the *Grub Street Journal* and the major publisher, James Roberts. This first emerged when in 1732 the proprietors resolved to oblige Roberts to put his name on the imprint.[89] However, the main dispute arose over the number of returns Roberts was making each week. In September 1734 the proprietors resolved to allow no returns at all,[90] although this was clearly impracticable. No further comment appeared until the following February, when it was agreed to notify Roberts that a hundred returns a week were too many.[91] The publisher seems to have been unable or unwilling to comply with the proprietors' demands and in July 1735 he was replaced by the shareholder John Wilford with the proviso that "no more returns shall be allowed than fivety per week: of which the Treasurer is to give him notice."[92] The problem of returns was also considered at the *General Evening Post* meetings nearly fifty years later and, while the publisher John Bew was directed to check the rate allowed by the proprietors of other evening papers,[93] a ruling was made shortly afterward that no hawkers' returns would be accepted after the night of publication.[94]

The part played by the shareholders in the direction of editorial policy is difficult to establish with any accuracy, although the minutes suggest that their influence was rather greater than is usually assumed. The literary content of the *Grub Street Journal* was probably during the first years of publication left largely in the hands of the major shareholder and literary editor, Richard Russel. However, his relations with his fellow proprietors seem to have become increasingly uneasy.[95] This was probably a side effect of his long-running editorial dispute with the printer Huggonson.[96] At all events, in 1736 the partners took the very unusual step of initiating supplementary weekly meetings at which the paper's content was regularly reviewed. There is no indication of the sort of decisions taken on these occasions, although when the Journal's affairs were being wound up, nine parcels of unspecified books were divided among the proprietors on the basis of their shareholdings,[97] and discussion of their relative merits probably formed part of the agenda. This seems to be supported by the *General Evening Post* minutes following the build-up in the use of various forms of supplementary content in the late 1740s. In September 1754, for example, it was agreed to buy a copy of "Mr. Postlethwayte's Dictionary of Trade and

Commerce" out of the common fund,[98] and the following month it was resolved to remind the printer to use material from this source as well as to include pieces from the *World* and the *Connoisseur*.[99] The committee, which took a number of decisions on the inclusion of new material,[100] also kept a careful check on the quality of news contributions,[101] the members themselves providing material for the paper's important *Postscript*.[102] One major decision on content that could crop up was whether the proprietors should allow their paper to become involved in political controversy. This seems to have been a matter for careful consideration and could lead to serious disagreements among shareholders. In a statement on behalf of the active ministerial publisher, John Peele, it was claimed that "He threw up the Publication of the *Daily Post* (after having published it thirteen years) because he could not prevail upon the Proprietors to continue it a neutral Paper, as it always had been."[103] The only direct evidence of the way such decisions were reached appeared in 1785 following an approach to the editor of the *General Evening Post* by representatives of both the opposition and the ministry. The requests for support were laid before the proprietors and unanimously rejected, a note of thanks being passed to the editor "for his Conduct and integrity upon the occasion,"[104] perhaps an indication that some unobtrusive bias could have been introduced without notice.

The responsibility of the shareholders for the content of their newspapers also appeared obliquely in the handling of the frequent public and private prosecutions that resulted from the publication of all types of material. The printers and publishers bore the brunt of these actions but, in most cases, the backers seem to have accepted joint financial responsibility for the expenses incurred. In this area the role of the politicians with an interest in the press was of particular importance and paralleled that of the shareholding booksellers. This emerges most clearly in the case of the *Craftsman*, which was under considerable legal pressure from its first appearance. Writing in 1740, the author of *An Historical View* stated that a subscription had been set up by the backers "by which they obliged themselves to indemnify the Author and Printer from all Charges of Prosecution upon what should be inserted in the *Craftsman*, to the value of three thousand Pounds."[105] That the existence of such a fund was at least rumored following the first prosecution of the paper early in 1727 was suggested by an ironic notice in the pro-ministerial *Weekly Journal*, which stated that among some papers found between Covent Garden and St. James's there was "a Draught of an Advertisement, showing, where any enterprising Bookseller, Printer, or Author, may be assured of finding sufficient Bail upon any Exigency, at the first Notice."[106] The promise of this sort of help was apparently held out to the printer Haines in 1732 as an added inducement to allow his name to appear on the imprint, and he was assured "that there was a SET OF GENTLEMEN of GREAT FORTUNES, AS HE (Francklin) WAS PLEASED TO EXPRESS HIMSELF, who supported the Paper, and defended all Prosecutions at their own Expence, and who could make him a suitable Present, in case any corporal Punishment should be inflicted on him."[107] How this worked in practice is not clear, and there is no direct evidence available to show either the extent or the reliability of this support. In 1743 William Pulteney, then Lord Bath, was ridiculed in the opposition press on the grounds of his previous activity in this direction. "Did you not, Sir, even get the better of that *sordid Avarice,* which so universally characterises you and subscribe 100 Guineas to defend the Paper which the Government, who was not then pursuing Schemes or Measures near so disgraceful or destructive as these you are now enjoining, thought to be *libellous?* Did you not upon a deficiency advance 100 more?"[108] Amhurst claimed that Haines's defense in 1737 had been entirely at the proprietors' personal expense,[109] while it was subsequently stated that Francklin's losses in law suits had amount to over £1,000.[110]

The booksellers, on the other hand, while accepting liability and providing similar protection for their personnel, did their best to keep to a minimum the expenses arising from prosecutions. The *Grub Street Journal* minutes suggest that some attempt was made to ensure that outside contributors of potentially inflamatory material secured the partners. In April 1735 it was agreed "that a proper security should be taken from J. C. to indemnifie them from any action already brought, or which may be brought against them, their publisher or printer on the account of any Case relating to Ward's pill, communicated by the said J. C. and inserted in the Grub-street Journals to this time."[111] That such efforts were not always effective was indicated two years later when Lawton Gilliver was deputed "to represent in the strongest terms, to the Gentleman who encouraged the publishing of the Advertisements against Jeremy More Smith the expences of the Law-suit occasioned thereby."[112] An interesting external view of the practical way in which the proprietors attempted to minimize the legal risks was also provided by Lady Hertford in her journal for 1742.[113] On Monday 1 March a paragraph was sent to the *Daily Advertiser* announcing the dismissal of the Earl of Hertford from his military appointments. This appeared the following day with "the words turned out changed to that of resigned" on which one of the proprietors was directed to rectify the error and prevent republication in the evening papers. No satisfaction was made in the Wednesday issue of the *Advertiser* and a renewed demand for correction was answered by a request for £500 as security. At this point a friend of Lord Hertford visited the bookseller proprietor, Samuel Harding, "to assure him that my Lord would bring them before the House of Lords if they would not retract the falsehood they had published." On Thursday the paper again appeared without reference to the paragraph and a stormy interview between Lord Hertford, Harding, and Henry Vander Esch resulted in the insertion of a cautious correction including the words "(we insert this by his Lordship's direction)." As Lady Hertford remarked, "This parenthesis was awkward enough, and plainly inserted for fear the ministers should be angry that they had a last told truth." Whatever the motives involved, this account clearly indicated the proprietors' concern with the content of their paper and active intervention over material likely to result in prosecution. In 1753 the proprietors of the *Gazetteer* established an internal safeguard by making the printer responsible for half the costs of a prosecution directed at any item not signed by two of the committee. However, there is no evidence to indicate whether this was a conventional practice during the earlier period.[114]

A subsidiary commercial interest of the newspaper proprietors, which linked their concern with finance and content and which coincided most closely with their conventional book-trade activities, was the republication of collections of leading essays in book or pamphlet form. This method of supplementing the income derived from the press enabled the proprietors to cash in on public demand or recoup a financial loss,[115] and prior to the abandonment of the *Grub Street Journal* the partners were mainly concerned with the production of the two volumes that finally appeared in 1737 under the title of *Memoirs of the Society of Grub Street*. The first mention of a collection was made in November 1731. In spite of the emphasis on production with "all the expedition imaginable,"[116] nothing seems to have been done and the following March it was agreed that the volume, to be corrected by Russel at 12s. a sheet, should be sent to press the next week.[117] The thousand copies ordered at this time were increased in September 1734 to twelve hundred and fifty,[118] but still no publication took place and in July the following year volume two and two frontispieces were ordered to be printed before either was released.[119] In October the sum of twenty guineas from the stock was voted to cover printing expenses, but it was not until December 1736 that details of publication were finally settled. It was agreed that

> the price of the *Memoirs of the Society of Grub-street*, in 2 Vol. to be published next month shall be £3. 15s. per 25 Setts to the Partners in sheets; that the price to the Trade, for the same number, shall be £4. 1s. and that they shall be kept strictly at 4s. per single Sett. That the Books shall be delivered to the respective Partners on the 4th day of January next, and that at the monthly meeting on the 6th following, Notes shall be given by each Partner for £6 per share, payable one month after date, for defraying the expences in printing etc. the say'd Book.[120]

In April the publisher, Wilford, was ordered to account each week with Huggonson, who in turn was to spend at least two guineas on advertising the volumes, producing a financial statement for the proprietors at the May session.[121] This revealed that a call of £4. 4s. 6d. per share was necessary and also that a dispute with Wilford's assignees had led to the repossession of his share.[122] Subsequently a good deal of discussion took place on the handling of publication, which remained in Wilford's hands, as well as the division of sets, the remaining copies of the impression of 1,000 being divided among the proprietors in August 1737.[123]

Very little information is available on the process of winding up a jointly owned paper and the *Grub Street Journal* ledger is disappointingly oblique. No direct mention, for example, was made of the reshuffle that led to the publication of the *Literary Courier of Grub Street*, although as early as November 1736 it was agreed that "on a Proposal made for the setting up of some other Paper or Pamphlet, monthly or oftener, every Partner is at free liberty to be concerned in any such Pamphlet or Paper, independently of this Society."[124] The sharing out of books took place in August 1737 and the resolution to discontinue the paper was made at a general meeting in December.[125] Although recurrent references were made to the settling of the accounts, which was not completed until March 1739,[126] no details of the financial or other arrangements involved appear in the ledger.[127]

The practice of group management revealed through the minute books indicates the pervasive character of bookseller involvement in the London press. The system of internal control was probably in the process of consolidation during the 1720s and 1730s and it appears, for example, that the *Gazetteer* agreements were altogether more comprehensive and detailed than anything drawn up between the partners in the *Grub Street Journal* twenty years before. Nonetheless, the experience of concerted action, which the booksellers transferred to the London press, meant that they were soon exercising an effective oversight of all areas of the business. Even if the practice of control sometimes fell short of the theory, the standing arrangements could always be reactivated if this was seen to be desirable or necessary. The newspapers were important to the booksellers in a variety of pragmatic ways and by mid-century the London press had been subsumed into the commercial structure of the book trade.

5

The Newspaper Printers

The shifting pattern of newspaper management that accompanied the takeover of the London press by the booksellers involved all the personnel engaged in the business. Changes in status and function varied in timing as well as between commercial levels and were not at all clear-cut. The London newspapers never represented more than a strand of commercial interest in the careers of most of those individuals concerned and consequently it is usually hard to identify with any precision the way in which relationships extending beyond the newspaper press were mediated within it. Even so, it is worth attempting to establish some of the variables in the day-to-day processes of production and distribution, and of these the most important related to the pioneers of newspaper development, the London printers.

There has been a tendency to suggest that as increasing specialization was introduced, the printer was deprived of most of his former independence. This view clearly contains an element of truth, but it on the one hand underestimates the often vital role of the printer in the management of a paper under group ownership, and on the other ignores the emergence of the printer entrepreneur as a key figure in the boom in cheap papers during the 1730s and early 1740s.[1] The number of printers at work in London had increased rapidly with the lapse in formal control that occurred in 1695 and less than twenty years later one of the many petitioners to parliament, urging the reimposition of some effective restraint, claimed "that there are near Seventy Printing Houses, and One hundred and fifty Apprentices at this time, besides a very great Number of Journey-men, and more daily coming in: Some of the Masters, who are but Yeomen of their Company, having Five Apprentices, many Four and almost all an Irregular Number."[2] To this estimate the petitioner added "several Booksellers who have taken upon them to set up Printing-Houses, and Use and Exercise the Art of Printing (*How*, a Bookseller, being the Printer of the *Observator*) and they also have a Train of Apprentices and are daily adding to the Number." Although the rate of increase slowed under the considerable pressure of

A satirical view of newspaper printing published in the *Grub Street Journal* 147, Thursday 26 October 1732.

competition, the number of printers continued to rise. In 1723 Samuel Negus compiled a probably incomplete list of seventy-five masters at work in London and Westminster,[3] while forty years later William Strahan estimated that there were about 150 presses in the same area.[4] One of the main characteristics of this expanding trade was the distinction, reflected in the existence of the full-priced and cheap press, between the important master printer, operating on an increasingly large scale,[5] and those on the fringes of the trade with little or no formal training working at an altogether lower level. The newspapers represented one of the few areas, of which the related production of books in parts was another, in which the output of all sections of the printing trade overlapped.

The number of printers who were engaged in newspaper production from the mid-1720s is impossible to estimate accurately, but it does appear that an important proportion had an interest in the press at some stage in their careers. It is also clear that there was some concentration of newspaper production in individual printing offices. The usual limit in the upper reaches of the trade seems to have been three, often composed of one weekly, one thrice-weekly, and one daily paper. Such an output could only have been undertaken by quite large-scale businesses or by those accepting some degree of specialization, since it would have required the constant use of two presses and probably the employment of eight or more workmen and assistants. The variety of papers printed in a single office resulted not only from the obvious value of diversification but, sometimes at least, from the stipulations of the joint proprietors against the production of rival ventures. This is not only suggested by the usual restrictions on share holdings in the same form of paper but also by the earliest known contract, that between Mary Say and the proprietors of the *Gazetteer* in 1775. It stipulated that while she continued to print the daily paper, only the weekly *Craftsman* and thrice-weekly *General Evening Post* should be produced at her office.[6]

A number of printers stand out as having had unusually wide interests in the full-priced press, perhaps the most important being Samuel Richardson, who ran an increasingly substantial business in Salisbury Court and who was already employing twenty compositors and pressmen in 1734.[7] Two years later, when his newpaper interest seems to have been at its height, Richardson was apparently printing two weekly papers, the *Weekly Miscellany* and the *London Journal,* and two daily papers, the *Daily Journal* and the *Daily Gazetteer,* as well perhaps as the *Daily Post Boy.* William Wilkins of Little Britain, who printed five newspapers, including some taken over by Richardson, seems to have had a comparable interest during the early 1730s. However, Richard Nutt produced one of the most interesting concentration of newspapers at his printing office in the Old Bailey. Nutt had inherited the office itself, together with the printing of the *Daily Post,* from his father-in-law in 1725,[8] and it seems that it became a specialized center for the production of periodicals.[9] The *London Evening Post* was printed here from its first appearance in 1727 as was the *Universal Spectator,* and these papers, together with the *Daily Post,* continued to be printed at his office until the 1740s. All three were conventional, group-owned publications, and it seems possible that Nutt's other commitments restricted further expansion in newspaper production. If so, they did not place a bar on other forms of periodical output and Nutt also produced the quarterly *Historical Register* at his office until its demise in 1738.

The advantage to the printer of such multiple holdings probably extended beyond the immediate financial benefit, and association with groups of booksellers and politicians probably had an important incidental value. This was clearly indicated in the case of Richard Francklin who, though not a printer himself, was responsible for organizing the production of the *Craftsman.* He had, it was claimed, been raised from "very low circumstances"[10] to comparative affluence through his political connections, and his success story seems to have become part of the folklore of the trade. In 1729 an opposition pamphleteer, attempting to persuade Robert Walker to print one of his pamphlets, was said to have proposed a meeting with a group of leading politicians who "would make as great a man of him as they had done of Francklyn."[11] The combination of advantages that newspaper production could provide was clearly laid out during partnership negotiations between the printers Emmonson, Spens, and Bowyer in 1759. In a letter to Bowyer it was stated that Emmonson proposed to keep production of an unspecified newpaper at his own office because it would not take up three hours in a day and because "it will be £50 a Year clear Money, and a constant Introduction to the Booksellers."[12]

The status of the printer within the framework of group ownership is usually very difficult to pin down since the circumstances surrounding the establishment and conduct of individual newspapers remain largely unknown. Although printers continued to act as the projectors of full-priced papers, obtaining outside support and becoming from the first major shareholders, the extent of any such holdings and their influence on the business structure are highly speculative.[13] The surviving records do suggest that the printers of the jointly owned papers generally held some share in the property, although Walter Baker wisely refused to accept an interest in the financially moribund *Alchymist.* However, while such holdings did not in themselves guarantee security of tenure, the printers became in some cases unshakably entrenched. Although John Huggonson seems to have been involved in a certain amount of bickering with at least one of the *Grub Street Journal* proprietors, he continued to print the paper and by 1737 had increased his holding from one to three shares.[14] Similarly, three members of the Say family continued successively to print the *Gazetteer* and the *General Evening Post* for nearly fifty years, in spite of major upheavals and recurrent complaints.[15]

Whatever the printer's technical status, his immediate control of production gave him a useful lever in any business dispute that might arise. The scope for individual action was well illustrated during the late 1730s by the organizational breakdowns that took place in three of the major political weeklies. In each case this resulted from unilateral action taken by the printers in response to a variable challenge to their position. The causes of the split that developed between William Wilkins and his fellow proprietors of the *London Journal* are not altogether clear. Trouble had already arisen over his disposal of the ministerial subsidy and, although this seems to have been settled satisfactorily,[16] the ministerial reshuffle of papers that took place in 1735 prompted further bad feeling. Richardson was appointed printer of the *Daily Gazetteer,* and also ousted Wilkins as printer of the *London Journal,* provoking him into direct opposition to his former associates. On Saturday 19 July 1735 the first issue of a new journal was published under a title notice stating that "The *London Journal* being dropt, in a manner very prejudicial to the *Proprietors* of the *principal Shares;* the Publick is obliged with this New Paper, entitled, *The Independent London Journalist;* which shall inviolably preserve the *Character* the *Title* bears."[17] In fact, the *London Journal* had not been dropped, as an indignant advertisement in Monday's *Daily Journal* pointed out. This asserted that the paper would continue to be published by John Peele "By whom ONLY advertisements are taken in; the Person who has hitherto Printed the Paper for the Proprietors having dropt it in a very extraordinary Manner, in order to impose a New Paper on the Town."[18] Whether Wilkins's challenge was at all successful is dubious, and although some sort of financial accomodation may have been reached, there is no evidence that his journal continued to appear.

The second split in a major London paper, resulting from the action of its printer, divided the opposition journal, *Common Sense,* the following year. The immediate cause was the attempt, probably on the intiative of the projector and author Charles Molloy, to transfer the printing from the office of James Purser in Bartholomew Close to that of John Purser in White Friars. Molloy and John Purser had formerly been associated in *Fog's Weekly Journal* which, after a brief revival in political extremism, had collapsed, leaving its printer free to take up the production of *Common Sense,* which was transferred to his office. The family relationship between the two Pursers, if any, has not been discovered,[19] but on this occasion, at least, commercial considerations were uppermost and James Purser refused to accept the alteration, continuing to produce the paper under the slightly amended title of *Old Common Sense.*[20] Molloy and his associates claimed that John Purser's was the authentic paper and that "what is now published by JAMES *Purser* of *Bartholomew Close* is spurious, and an Imposition upon the *Publick* as well as an Injury to the *Authors* and *Proprietors of that Journal.*"[21] James Purser was apparently unmoved by such comments and a protracted wrangle in the press ensued. The substance of James's case was that only one of the authors, against the "particular Customs" of the trade, had removed the paper solely for motives of self-interest, "which he should therefore not complain of in the conduct of his original printer."[22] On the other hand it was claimed that all the original authors wrote for John Purser's paper and that "if an *Author* or *Bookseller,* cannot trust his *Title* or his *Copy* to a *Printer,* without having it *pyrated,* it must as effectually put an End to the *Liberty of the Press* as any Law for that Purpose."[23] The division continued beyond James Purser's death at the beginning of 1738,[24] and it seems possible that William Rayner, who also had a hand in the subsequent split in the *Craftsman,* was for a time involved with *Old Common Sense.*[25]

The division between the journeyman printer Henry Haines and the joint proprietors of the *Craftsman* was to some extent the result of Haines's ambiguous position within the organization of the paper. His own statement of the case appeared, following his imprisonment in 1738, in a pamphlet entitled *Treachery Baseness and Cruelty Displayed to the Full in the Hardships and Sufferings of Mr. Henry Haines, Late Printer of the Country Journal, or Craftsman,* and was also published in two installments in the *Daily Gazetteer.*[26] In reply, Nicholas Amhurst, author and co-proprietor, wrote a vigorous defense in the *Craftsman* against what he described as "this filthy jakes of *personal Slander,* and villainous *Forgeries,*"[27] and these sources provide a full, if rather ambiguous account of the dispute. During his early months in the King's Bench prison, Haines continued to direct the production of the *Craftsman* at his Hart Street printing office through his sister Margaret.[28] However, toward the end of the year, negotiations over the handling of the paper's finances and the extent of the support that Haines was to receive while in prison broke down for reasons obscured by the welter of counter accusations. Haines claimed that a series of promises of assistance had been made by Francklin and Amhurst, all of which had been broken, and that their bad faith had culminated in the violent repossession of the printing equipment and other goods that he had looked on as personal security. Amhurst, on the other hand, stated that Haines had held back a large proportion of the profits since the beginning of the year, amounting to about £400, and "that the Sweets of the *Paper* had so intoxicated his Brains, that He would never part with it again without *Compulsion.*" The final offer, appearing in a letter from Amhurst and printed in both accounts, guaranteed Haines, should he decide to give up printing the paper, the journeyman's wage of one guinea a week and all possible help in obtaining the "rules" of the prison. This would have enabled him to set up a printing office in the neighborhood of the Kings Bench and run it on his own account. At this point Haines, whatever his motive, attempted to remove the *Craftsman* altogether from the control of the original proprietors, entering into some sort of agreement with the notorious entrepreneur and his fellow prisoner, William Rayner, by which it was to be printed at the Hart Street office apparently for their mutual benefit.[29] In response, Francklin and Amhurst employed Henry Goreham of Fleet Street to produce the *Craftsman,*[30] and the two virtually identical journals met in a head-on clash. In the ensuing struggle neither side seems to have gained the commercial advantage and after three months Haines and his former employers again opened negotiations. Although some progress was made on the basis of Haines's agreement to drop his paper, his position was entirely undermined by Rayner, who refused to abandon his share, transferring the printing to Chancery Lane and perpetuating the schism, leaving Haines to fend for himself.[31]

The printer's negative recourse of producing an alternative paper suggests his importance within the business structure as well as his capacity for maneuver under pressure.[32] The proprietors had no legal protection against such action, which continued to affect papers of all types well beyond mid-century.[33] The contract between the proprietors of the *Daily Gazetteer* and Mary Say indicates their particular concern to avoid the sort of division that had dislocated the management a few years before. The clause stating that she "shall not nor will during the time aforesaid assign or make over the profits of printing the said *Gazetteer* or Print the same in the Name of any Person or Persons but by Consent of a Majority of the Proprietors . . . ,"[34] and the demand for the substantial security of £2,000, probably represent an attempt to keep a firm hold on production.

The printer's *de facto* control of this process was paralleled by an immediate concern with newspaper content. While the compilation of the news section was often left largely in his hands, this activity was probably extended in a few cases to include an oversight of the other forms of content. The printers were often responsible for hiring and paying the regular contributors, and Mary Say's contract stipulated that she should enter into the account book "the true Names Places of abode and Professions of all and every such Person and Persons as she shall employ to write for the said *Gazetteer* . . . ."[35] Although it is very difficult to identify any instance in which the policy of a jointly owned newspaper was directly influenced by the printer, it seems possible that the political stance of the *Daily Post* and the *London Evening Post,* reflected through correspondence and news paragraphs respectively, was partly induced by the printer Richard Nutt. Nutt's father-in-law was listed by Negus among the "High Flyers," and he himself was a Tory, being elected to the anti-Walpole Common Council in 1736.[36] Similarly, John Meres, who printed his papers from 1737, was described in the *Daily Gazetteer* as an Irish Catholic, although this was vigorously denied,[37] and it is conceivable that it was Nutt's political attitudes that were decisive in the decision to include opposition material in these papers, as well as in the news section of the *Universal Spectator,* in the early 1740s.

In the politically backed essay-papers, editorial policy was clearly established and the printers seems generally to have been sympathetic to the party line. On the other hand the possibility of conflict always existed and on at least one occasion disagreement with official policy may have resulted in a change of printer. On Friday 12 April 1733 the *Daily Post* carried a paragraph expressing surprise that the printer of two ministerial papers, the *London Journal* and the *Daily Courant,* had taken part in the massive anti-excise demonstration of the previous Tuesday. Far from denying the report, Wilkins published a lengthy and prominent notice in the next day's *Daily Journal* in which he stated

> *the Printer of those Papers chuses this Occasion to assure the Merchants and Traders, and all whom it may concern, That from the first Opening of the late Project about Excises, he at all Times, and in all Companies, gave his Opinion freely against it; that he voted in Common Council both for the Application to our Representatives, and for the Petition to Parliament; and that tho' he prints the said Papers, he is no way the Author or Director of either; always disapprov'd every Thing unbecoming in them; and consequently, ought no more justly to be charg'd with Blame in this Case, than he ought to have had the Merit given him of Writing the Learned and Ingenious Mr. Bayle's Works, if he should have happened to be the Printer thereof.*[38]

Such a categorical rejection of the ministry's measures seems to have had repercussions, and six months later, perhaps following a proprietors' meeting or directly through political pressure, a notice appeared in the *Daily Journal* stating: "THE PRINTING OF THE *DAILY COURANT* being remov'd from Mr. Wilkins, several Shares of the said Paper are to be sold. Enquire of Mr. Wilkins, at his House in Lombard-street."[39] It seems possible that Wilkins's position in the *London Journal* was more secure and that, as a leading proprietor of long standing, he was able to resist any attempt to dislodge him at this stage.

A number of London printers continued to exercise personal control over full-priced newspapers. The weekly journals established after 1712 remained, like the cut-price publications, in the hands of a single proprietor, at least until his death or retirement. The title alterations of *Applebees Original Weekly Journal*,[40] *Mist's Weekly Journal*,[41] and *Read's Weekly Journal*[42] to include the name of the printer as well as each paper's lack of characteristic book-trade advertising emphasized their independence from the booksellers. The weekly newspaper remained the principal sphere of the printer even under the conditions of group ownership. Later in the century Henry Baldwin and Charles Say, printers respectively of the *St. James's Chronicle* and the *Gazetteer,* each established a sole interest in a weekly newspaper that they ran independently of their other commitments.[43] At the same time, even the printer-owned papers were occasionally organized in a way that reflected the complex pattern of group ownership. This appeared clearly in the case of Nathaniel Mist's *Weekly Journal.* Following an official prosecution in 1722, Mist's apprentice, Doctor Gaylard, who had been tried and convicted for publication, petitioned the authorities to defer judgment, providing a full account of his role in conducting the paper. In it he stated that he had been in charge of production for three months and that Mist had allowed him "to buy one half of his printing Materials, that your Pet[r] might be better Enabled to serve him in his absence, in Consideration whereof your Pet[r]. was to have one half of the profitts of printing the Journal, but had no Share in the Property or Profitts of the said Paper."[44] Such an arrangement was perhaps unusual but it indicates a degree of specialization within the larger printing houses which may have complicated the internal organization of a number of London papers.

Most printers tended to operate exclusively at one or other of the differing levels of newspaper production, but certain individuals had links with both the full-priced and the cheap press. James Read, who was described by Thomas Gent as "a worthy master printer"[45] and who achieved considerable standing in the trade, printed three unusually varied papers, his own full-priced weekly journal, the jointly owned St. James's Evening Post, and the cut-price Penny Post. Both he and John Applebee had close personal connections with the printers of cheap newspapers and this was reflected in the appearance and content of their important weeklies. Read's son Thomas had very wide interests in this area, while members of Applebee's family were associated with the printer-entrepreneur William Rayner. However, in the lower reaches of newspaper production, the majority of printers formed a heterogenous group with little or no status, often working outside the law.

Most members of the London printing trade in this period operated on a small scale, usually with a single press and perhaps two or three employees.[46] The distinction between the small master and the journeyman, like Thomas Gent who doubled as master and employee in one of the "great houses,"[47] was negligible, while a number of those who set up as printers came from outside the trade altogether.[48] At this level the printer still carried out all the functions that had become specialized activities farther up the scale, purchasing copy direct from the author or writing himself, carrying out the printing, and subsequently organizing distribution. To such printers the newspaper provided a valuable means of keeping the press employed at minimal expense and individuals in the humblest circumstances were sometimes involved in newspaper production. Gent's employer, for example, the catholic Francis Clifton, who was not apparently a trained printer, began to produce the cut-price Oxford Post as soon as he had set up a press.[49] The scale of Clifton's business, which after a prosecution for debt was moved within the rules of the Fleet prison,[50] appeared from Gent's account of his working conditions. "Some time, in extreme weather, have I worked under a mean shed, adjoining to the prison wall, when snow and rain have fallen alternately on the cases; yet the number of wide-mouthed stentorian hawkers, brisk trade, and very often a glass of good ale, revived the drooping spirits of me and other workmen."[51] Nearly twenty years later the author of the Craftsman, in attacking the printers of the unstamped papers, drew a comparable picture, claiming that "the Persons concern'd in these Papers are poor low Wretches, who either live within the Rules of the Fleet and other Prisons, or Conceal themselves in the most obscure Corners of the Town."[52] The small-scale printers sometimes relied largely on the cheap newspaper for their livelihood and

George Parker's petition of 1725 stated that the halfpenny publications were the principal source of income for the five London printers engaged in their production.[53]

Among the printers operating at this level, one of the most interesting and important was the ubiquitous William Rayner, whose name is constantly cropping up in association with publications of all kinds and in particular with the variable forms of London newspaper. Carried on in the more obscure areas of the trade, Rayner's career emphasizes the possibilities open to an opportunist with an eye for the market and throws a good deal of light on the organization of production among the small printers as well as on their relationship to their more prosperous counterparts. Some aspects of Rayner's career, which was given an unduly tragic cast by Wiles,[54] remain hidden but it is possible to distinguish three separate phases characterized by differing circumstances and output. The first ended with his imprisonment in 1733, the second, and apparently most fruitful, with his release from the King's Bench in 1741, and the third with his death twenty years later.

Rayner apparently had formal links with the printing trade and was bound apprentice in 1714, although not made free of the Stationers' Company until twenty-three years later.[55] His early circumstances are very obscure and it is tempting, in the light of his subsequent medical interests, to suggest some sort of the connection with the surgeon W. Rayner who advertised widely in the London press in the late 1720s. But although the "Speedy and Safe Cure for the Pox or Clap," would have been in Rayner's line, the surgeon's Tower Hill address does not tally with any of Rayner's known locations.[56] By 1728, he seems to have established an ill-defined business relationship with the printer Robert Walker, who also pioneered the cheap newspaper and who came to have a unique holding in the provincial press.[57] Both Rayner and Walker were apparently the sons of gentlemen, Rayner migrating to London from Charlton in Worcestershire.[58] Their early business association, suggested by the imprints of a variety of publications,[59] was confirmed in 1731 when Rayner acted as witness to a notice played by Walker in the *Daily Journal*.[60] There continued to be some remarkable similarities in their subsequent careers, but while there is no direct evidence that this association lasted beyond the early 1730s, it would be surprising if their activity in nearly identical spheres of production did not lead to some competition or cooperation, or at least to a degree of mutual influence. Rayner may already have had his own premises in the parish of St. Andrews Holborn[61] when he opened "A new Pamphlet Shop next Door to the George Tavern at Charing Cross,"[62] evidently run by his wife. It is not clear when he began operating the printing office at Marigold Court off the Strand,[63] but it seems conceivable that, for a time at least, he worked either with or for Walker at his Devereux Court premises near Temple Bar. The scale of their business activities at this stage is hard to assess, although both seem to have acted as middlemen employing authors and subcontracting various jobs to small printers. Neither Rayner nor Walker was involved in the production of any London newspaper at this stage, although they specialized in the sort of cheap opposition pamphlets that were aimed at the market developed and exploited by the *Craftsman*.[64] In 1731 the author of the *Daily Courant*, in listing the forces of the opposition, referred to the "Infinite Number of *Banditti* and *Marauders*, sent forth from the fruitful presses of Messieurs *Walker* and *Rainer*."[65] Such material was potentially profitable but it also carried considerable risks. Both Rayner and Walker were involved in official libel actions at the end of 1729[66] and, more seriously, were taken up for "Robins Reign, *or Sevens the Main*," a publication made up of the frontispieces to the collected essays of the *Craftsman* linked with a virulent commentary.[67] No case seems to have been brought against Walker and the whole weight of the prosecution was directed against Rayner as publisher. After several delays and a trial arousing a good deal of public interest,[68] he was sentenced to two years' imprisonment with a fine of £50 and ordered to give security for his good behavior for seven years.[69]

Rayner's imprisonment in the King's Bench from the summer of 1733, far from acting as a check on his output, seems to have stimulated him to diversify and extend the range of his activities. During the early stages of his sentence the Marigold Court printing office and the pamphlet shop were kept in operation by E. Rayner, whose name appeared on the imprints of the full range of output.[70] After a short period, this arrangement seems to have lapsed and before the end of 1733 William Rayner had shifted his business within the rules of the King's Bench, where he joined a number of other low-key speculators.[71] This concentration of activity was already causing some political concern. In 1734 John Lyons complained to Walpole that "in this large Extent of the Rules there is a great Number of People, many of whom are of the most prolifick, and projecting Heads, and restless Spirits nor are there a few of great Wit Capacity and address, and some live in a plentiful manner, here are Libels and Ballads made, and here was much of the Management of the late Election concerted. . . ."[72] Rayner can have had little difficulty in establishing himself in such an environment after he opened his office in Angel Court opposite the prison. The journeyman printer, Doctor Gaylard, claimed to have started work here in September 1734,[73] and it seems possible that the overseer of the press, Abraham Ilive, and the workman and servant who were listed in 1736 as Rayner's employees[74] also joined him at about this time. Although he probably met with some initial difficulties, it appears that Rayner's business prospered. By 1739 he owned a house in Falcon Court[75] and it is tempting to suppose that the advertisement, which appeared in his paper following his removal across the river, referred to his own property. It offered "a freehold Estate near St. Georges Church in the Borough of Southwark in the County of Surrey, consisting of two strong-built Timber Houses, in good Repair, and well tenanted, at Five Pounds per Annum for

Robin's Reign or Seven's The Main. William Rayner was arrested and convicted for publishing this broadsheet composed of the frontispieces from the first collected edition of essays from the *Craftsman.*

each House. . . ."[76] This is speculation, and to set against it is the petition from William Rayner to the Treasury claiming after eight years' confinement, to be in no position to pay his fine and begging for release.[77] It is impossible to gauge the sincerity of such a document but in the light of his extensive publishing and medical ventures and his purchase of the freedom of the Stationers Company in 1737, it seems probable that it was no more than a financial device.[78]

The basis of any success that Rayner achieved during this period must have been centered around his prolific newspaper output, which was developed from the earliest period of his imprisonment. Perhaps finding it advisable to drop his former political interests, Rayner was quick to see the commercial possibilities of the sort of extended low-price paper offered by Thomas Read, whose *Penny London Post* had just started to appear with a supplementary folio sheet, containing serialized material, at no extra cost.[79] On 13 September 1733 Rayner advertised the second issue of the thrice-weekly, two-sheet paper, the *Compleat Historian, or the Oxford Penny Post,* and announced the forthcoming appearance of the three-sheet *British Mercury, or Weekly Pacquet,* selling at two pence.[80] Both papers, which were explicitly aimed at the provincial as well as the London market, did not perhaps achieve much success. However, from this point Rayner seems to have concentrated his attention on the newspaper press and, in spite of Wiles's poor opinion, his activity at the lower levels was both widespread and influential. It is not possible to establish accurately the number of newspapers produced at his Southwark printing office. Only the ambiguous Audit Office returns give some idea of the extent of Rayner's interests as printer and projector of the various forms of paper combining news and serialization.

Between 1734 and 1741 he was debited with advertisement duty from three weekly and four thrice-weekly London newspapers. Several of these appear to have been very short-lived and the records suggest that the *St. James's Weekly Pacquet, Rayner's Penny Post,* and the *London Tatler* did not survive a year and that *Rayner's Halfpenny Post* ceased publication within two. On the other hand he produced three papers that had quite substantial runs. The two weeklies, the *Royal Oak Journal; or, Rayners General Magazine* and the *Universal Weekly Journal,* which appeared in 1736 and 1737 respectively,[81] seem from the Audit Office records to have survived into the early 1740s. Rayner's most successful venture in cheap newspapers combining news and serialization was his *Morning Advertiser* which, first published in December 1735[82] and selling at one penny, continued to appear with various alterations in title and form at least until 1743.

The number of papers set up by Rayner during this period was, as in the case of Robert Walker, higher than the Audit Office records suggest, and he probably produced newspapers of all types that either through some form of tax evasion or through rapid collapse were not included in their lists. One such paper was his *Lady's Curiosity; Or Weekly Apollo,* which appeared in 1738 "covered with a Wrapper, giving the Week's News."[83] It may not have carried advertisements but would in any case, on account of its ambiguous form, have probably been claimed to be exempt from the duty. Similarly, in 1737 Rayner seems to have projected a new thrice-weekly penny paper of which the only record is the notices appearing prior to publication. Announced initially as the *General Advertiser* "Printed for Edward Applebee, near St. Georges Church, Southwark,"[84] its publication was delayed and in subsequent advertisements a number of changes appeared. The title was altered to the *London Post Boy, and General Advertiser,* the original serial was dropped, and Applebee's name was replaced by the perhaps deliberately falsified "William Reynallds."[85] It is not clear when or even if this paper came on the market, but the attempt that seems to have been made to obscure its source is itself revealing.

A further complication in attempting to assess the range of Rayner's newspaper interests in the 1730s, which the Audit Office records do little to clarify, arises from his consistent association with and employment of outside printers. It seems possible that in some cases cheap newspapers debited by the Audit Office to printers with no established link with Rayner were in fact produced on his behalf. It is tempting to see, for example, the *Kings Bench Halfpenny Post* debited to George Parker in 1735 as such a venture. This is little more than guesswork and all the evidence for his involvement with unstamped papers is oblique, a fact that may reflect his skill at sidestepping the investigations of the Stamp Office. However, a link between Rayner and the illegal press can perhaps be made through his business connections with Jacob Ilive. He had been employed by Rayner in 1729[86] and, while his brother Abraham was overseer of the Southwark press, Jacob's advertisements appeared consistently in the *Morning Advertiser,* sometimes in conjunction with Rayner. Whether this association was extended into the area of newspaper production remains, along with much of the detail at this level of activity, highly problematic, and although it seems possible that Ilive printed the *Monthly Oracle, or Gentlemans Magazine* for Rayner, it is difficult to go much farther.[87] Mr. Wiles, in some interesting if necessarily devious conjecture, suggested that the title of the farthing daily *All Alive and Merry* contained a punning allusion to A. Ilive, and that the paper was produced at the Aldersgate Street office.[88] If this is in any way correct, it could imply an oblique association between Rayner and the illegal press that is not indicated elsewhere. Similarly, Jacob Ilive's apparent interest in printing a Maidstone paper in 1737[89] could indicate that Rayner was still loosely connected with the sort of provincial venture that was beginning to interest Robert Walker.[90]

The only direct evidence for Rayner's employment of other printers on newspaper work crops up during his foray into the political press in the mid- to late 1730s. In this important move, several of the shady features that characterized Rayner's output were combined. Prior to his imprisonment he had achieved a reputation for his unscrupulous attitude toward other people's literary property. In an advertisement exposing his spurious edition of Fielding's *Welch Opera,* the public were urged to reject "the intolerable and scandalous Nonsense of this notorious Paper Pyrate,"[91] and his activities in this area, in which Robert Walker was also involved, seem to have continued unchecked. In 1734, following breach of his Shakespeare copyright, Jacob Tonson was informed that inquiries into an edition of the *Merry Wives of Windsor* had revealed "that Mr. Gardner of Bartholomew Close who reprints for that scandalous Fellow Rayner in the Kings Bench gives great Encouragement to the said Pyratical Edition, and that a greater Number of those are reprinted than by Walker. . . ."[92]

By the middle of the decade Rayner was also again involved in the production of various sorts of dubious political material. Much of this output was very low-key and so is hard to identify, but there are indications that it was at least tinged with extremism. Two of his employees, Abraham Ilive and Doctor Gaylard, had Jacobite sympathies[93] and Rayner's office seems to have become a focus for some fairly seditious and eccentric individuals. The unbalanced nonjuror Robert Nixon was a case in point. His bizarre plot to explode a package of hand-bills in the House of Commons, which he carried out in 1736, was hatched in the immediate neighborhood of Rayner's office, with Gaylard employed to print the material attacking various Acts of Parliament. The extent of Rayner's personal involvement, if any, is far from clear. Gaylard had traveled across the river with a portable press to carry out the printing on Nixon's premises, and although Rayner's name cropped up as Gaylard's employer, he was not directly implicated. However, in May 1737, not long after Nixon had been committed, Rayner and Ilive were both brought before the House of Commons for publishing the text of the violently unpopular Gin Act, which had figured in Nixon's bomb. Ilive claimed that he was entirely responsible, having permission from Rayner to print any small pamphlet he chose without informing him of the content.[94] Although Rayner also testified to this, in what must have been a fairly routine defense, the evidence was conflicting and both were ordered into the custody of the Sergeant-at-Arms. Whether any mention was made of the Nixon case is not clear but it seems that, as usual, Rayner was sailing very close to the wind.

It was against this background that he began to explore what was probably even for him a novel area of newspaper publication. During the late 1730s he became involved in the production of several full-price political papers in which he combined a commercial interest in opposition politics with an almost total disregard of the niceties of trade practice. Rayner had a sharp eye for the main chance and his involvement in this section of the political press suggests both its popularity and vulnerability. There is some indication that he had attempted to break into this area of the market prior to his attack on the *Craftsman* in 1738.[95] The previous year Charles Bennet, the nominal printer of the *Alchymist,* testified that it was in fact printed by Walter Baker "in the upper part, of his, the examinant's, Dwelling House, which he let to William Rayner at Lady Day Last."[96] This implied connection is strengthened by the subsequent employment of the paper's author, Dennis de Coetlogan, to write for Rayner's *Craftsman* and it is conceivable that failure in this case may have prompted him to attempt to cash in on somebody else's established reputation.

In spite of an unusual amount of documentation resulting from a prosecution in 1739, the details of the business organization of Rayner's *Craftsman* remain somewhat obscured by conflicting testimony. Production of the paper following the abandonment of Haines was, to all appearances, shifted to John Standen's printing office first in Chancery Lane and subsequently in the Old Bailey. However, at his examination in 1739, Standen claimed that he had no part in the production, receiving money from an unknown source for allowing his name to appear on the imprint,[97] and this claim was supported by the author Norton Defoe.[98] On the other hand, Doctor Gaylard, who composed the paper, and Edward Pickard, who stated that he was entirely responsible for the paper's finances, both claimed to be employed by Standen at the Old Bailey office.[99] This conflicting evidence can be resolved by assuming that Standen's position was similar to that of Bennet in the case of the *Alchymist* and that, although his premises were used for the printing, it was in fact carried out by Rayner's personnel.[100] Standen seems to have used the head of Caleb Danvers, fictional author of the *Craftsman,* on the sign of his printing office,[101] while Defoe stated that he accepted nominal responsibility for the paper to ensure his employment by Rayner in another printing job. It seems certain that their association was closer than Standen himself stated and the Audit Office returns debited him from 1739 with several of Rayner's newspapers. Rayner seems to have remained the sole proprietor of his *Original Craftsman,*[102] while apparently having an interest in two comparable ventures, *Old Common Sense* and the *New London Evening Post,* both debited to Standen in 1739.[103] Besides organizing production, Rayner also arranged for the supply of contributions to the political papers under his control. Both Defoe and de Coetlogan, who wrote for the *Original Craftsman,* were hired and paid by Rayner, who received the copy at his house in Southwark.[104] During this period the range of Rayner's newspaper projects was therefore exceptionally wide and only Robert Walker, who had an interest in at least eight periodical publications between 1735 and 1738[105] rivaled the scale of his output. Rayner, like Walker and a substantial proportion of the small-scale printers and booksellers in London, had also established a flourishing trade in quack medicines. In 1738, for example, he offered the famous *Daffy's Elixir Salutus* and *Soughtons Drops,* which could be obtained from "the Men that carry the News" or from "Mr. RAYNER'S Elixir Warehouse Southwark."[106]

The circumstances of Rayner's career following his removal from the vicinity of the King's Bench prison to a printing office in Wine Office Court, Fleet Street, are very obscure. His name does not appear on the imprint of any material published after 1740 held by the British Library and he seems increasingly to have subcontracted the production of any newspapers in which he had an interest. Consequently, his role in the publication of new ventures is extremely difficult to pin down. He appears to have been behind the publication of the *British Champion; or, Admiral Vernon's Weekly Journal*,[107] while the inclusion of the *British Intelligencer, Or Universal Advertiser* among Rayner's papers, debited by the Audit Office to Elizabeth and George Applebee from 1743, may suggest his interest.[108] According to John Nichols, Rayner married a rich widow at about this time.[109] However, he seems to have continued in the printing trade, at least during the early 1740s, and the character of his output was suggested by a notice appearing in the *London Morning Advertiser* in 1743 that announced "Stolen from the House of Mr. William Rayner, Printer, in Wine-Office-Court, Fleet-street, at sundry Times, several Volumes of Thomas A Kempis, Sherlock on Death, and the Preperation of the Sacrament, all bound; and on Monday Night or Tuesday Morning the 11th Inst. Two Volumes of the Holy Bible by Way of Question and Answer, Printed in Folio on a large Crown Paper with Cuts, and bound in plain Calf Letter'd, and when stole was without Titles."[110] He certainly continued to maintain some links with the press, holding at his death in 1761 1/20th shares in *Read's Weekly Journal* and the *St. James's Evening Post*.[111] It was these newspaper holdings that were purchased by Henry Baldwin and used in the establishment of the *St. James's Chronicle* and the related publications.[112]

Although the printers were overtaken by the development of group-ownership, they were able within this framework to maintain a good deal of independence. The newspaper business remained firmly rooted in the printing office and the essential routines of sales, distribution, and finance were all organized around the process of production. The printer assumed responsibility for any additional newspaper personnel paid for by the shareholders, and continued as a key figure in the conduct and management of the London press. Nonetheless, final control rested with the partners, and the printer, even as a major shareholder, was obliged to conform to the standards and directives of the bookseller-dominated committees. At the lower levels of output the printer/entrepreneur was very active during the 1720s and 1730s. However, as the arteries of the trade hardened, the independent operator was squeezed out of newspaper production. Neither William Rayner nor Robert Walker was able to maintain the momentum of publication through the 1740s,[113] and the pincer movement of trade restraint and tax regulation effectively prevented any serious challenge from this direction to the established commercial interests.

6
The Journalists

The professional writers employed in the compilation of the London news-papers are often the most elusive of the personnel. Many were only casually associated with the press, drifting from one form of literary output to another, and the comprehensive anonymity that cloaked all forms of content still obscures the position of a large porportion of even the most notable contributors. Nonetheless it is possible to suggest the way in which a profession of journalism was beginning to develop in this period and to define a little more closely the position of the writer in the structure of the London press. The term *journalist* was already in use during Queen Anne's reign, and from the early years of the century a small number of sometimes notorious individuals had contrived to earn a living either as editors of the thrice-weeklies or as authors of the variable essay-sheets.[1] During the second decade writers continued to work on the established forms, Stephen Whatley, for example, remaining in sole charge of the *Flying Post*,[2] while Daniel Defoe, the archetype of the professional newsman, managed and held a share in *Dormer's News Letter*, edited the *Whitehall Evening Post*, and collaborated on the *Manufacturer*, a standard twice-weekly essay-sheet.[3] However, the new and increasingly successful weeklies were by 1720 becoming the principal focus for the activity of professional authors, and it was the writers at work on these papers who came to form the nucleus of an emerging profession.

The commercial status of the weekly journalists, like that of other news-paper personnel, was subject to major variations. Initially the writers on the new-style journals all seem to have held a subordinate position as employees of the printer. Neither Daniel Defoe nor Richard Burridge, for example, as principal authors of Mist's and Read's journals respectively, seem to have had any financial interest in the ventures,[4] and during the 1720s and 1730s, journalists working on papers controlled by their printers remained in a state of dependence. James Pitt, though a prominent government controversialist, continued as an employee of the printer William Wilkins, while John Kelly, author of the highly inflammatory revival of *Fog's Weekly*

Journal, was paid by the week by John Purser. At the lower levels the writers working on the semi-piratical ventures of William Rayner did so on a very casual and subordinate basis. Dennis de Coetlogan, for example, was employed "to write upon political Subjects to be inserted in such printed papers as the said Wm. Rayner should think fit."[5] This dependence was dictated to some extent by the prohibitive cost of setting up a new journal and during the 1730s attempts by authors to establish this type of paper under their sole ownership ended in uniform disaster.[6] De Coetlogan himself experienced the worst effects of underfinancing as he attempted to support the *Alchemyst* on the basis of sales alone. His efforts to stimulate interest through the adoption of a strong opposition line led directly to his confinement in Newgate, where he lost an eye, providing a particularly striking example of the pitfalls of an individual initiative.

The intervention of the booksellers in the London press offered a new line of opportunity for the professional author. By obtaining financial backing from the trade, it became possible for the writer to project a new paper and avoid the extravagant risks and expense of sole ownership. Consequently, from the late 1720s most of the full-priced journals were apparently projected by the authors within the framework of group ownership. In some cases the author took the lead and kept a major holding in the property. The joint authors of the *Grub Street Journal,* for example, Richard Russel and John Martyn, initially held at least five of the twelve shares, and although Martyn soon disposed of his interest, and presumably ceased to contribute, Russell continued in possession of a major holding of three until the journal ceased publication in 1737. On the other hand Henry Fielding's minor $2/16$ share in the *Champion,* which he is assumed to have projected after his career in the theater collapsed, probably reflects his financial inability to support a larger element and perhaps tougher negotiations with the backers.[7] Fielding's share was reassigned after some delay to his successor, James Ralph, and an interest in the property may not have been an automatic perquisite of the principal author of a jointly owned paper. Besides the leading author, additional writers were sometimes taken on as regular contributors, although they remained in a subordinate financial position.[8] At the same time, the status of the author within an individual paper was liable to fluctuate. This appeared clearly in the case of William Webster, author-projector of the religious *Weekly Miscellany,* who accepted a series of alterations in his financial status in an attempt to secure the paper's continued existence. Webster, a clergyman in the Church of England, began to write the *Miscellany* in 1732 after a period of unemployment when, in his own words, he "must have died like a poisoned rat in a hole" without the intervention of some friendly creditors. In 1741, at his retirement from the venture, Webster gave readers an outline account of his experiences. He stated that

At first setting out I engag'd several Booksellers as Proprietors in the Paper, hoping that, out of the Prospect of Gain, they would be industrious to propogate it. But, partly thro' Negligence and Ill-Management, and partly thro' the Corruption of the Age, the Design not answering their expectations, they left me and the Paper to shift for our selves.—I then went upon my own single Bottom, till upon making up Accounts with my Printer, I found myself considerably in his Debt. I was still unwilling that the Design should sink, and agreed with another Printer, who was more at leisure vigorously to pursue the Interest of it; by which Agreement he was to be entitled to the whole Profits arising from the Sale of the Paper, (if he could make any) and I to furnish him with the Letter gratis.[9]

The commercial opportunities created by book-trade investment ran parallel to those already available to the professional author through political intervention. From the 1690s the involvement of politicians as backers and sponsors of London newspapers had created a potentially valuable means of support for the writer. Whether in power or out, politicians saw the press as a crucial instrument, and those willing to act as intermediaries in the propaganda process could hope to benefit from the setting up of new papers or the buying in of established publications. Throughout the first half of the eighteenth century a coherent group of more or less talented essayists, working on a variety of sponsored papers, formed an identifiable subgroup within the organization of the London press.

Like the printer, the author was obliged to pay for increased financial security by giving up some degree of independence. In the bookseller-owned newspapers, both were likely to be subject to the more or less irritating and regular oversight of the partners. Friction arising from the circumstances of group management seems to have accounted for Henry Fielding's departure from the *Champion* in 1741 and probably contributed to the difficulties experienced in the *Grub Street Journal*. However, the constraints placed on the authors working regularly in the London press fell most heavily and obviously in the context of essay-papers sponsored by political groupings. The relationships that existed between the authors working in the London press and their political backers are hard to pin down and probably involved some very variable forms of personal contact. Before the build-up in political tension in the 1720s, a more relaxed approach to oversight may have been adopted, as appears in the case of Ambrose Phillips, who was employed in 1718 to write the *Freethinker*. In a letter requesting a contribution to the paper, Thomas Burnet, an active literary supporter of the ministry, stated that "though I am not the Author, yet I am one of a Club that revise every one before they go to the Press. And sometimes we quite work up a new Paper, when we do not like what is brought to us. The government have sett the Author upon it, and know that we are assisting to him, so that a Paper now and then would be a kindness to me."[10] Such arrangements must have been close to those used to compile the nonpolitical *Universal Spectator* in the late 1720s as well as a variety of other papers put together by an author working with an established circle of contributors.[11] This rather low-key approach would have been entirely unsuitable for the conduct of the fierce and protracted disputes generated under the Walpole adminsitration, and from the mid-1720s a number of professional authors came to act more directly and consistently as intermediaries between the leading politicians and the sponsored newspapers, assuming in some cases an important semi-official status.

On the opposition side the writers, who usually held a major share in the property of their papers, seem to have taken some pains to obscure any direct links. Nicholas Amhurst, as principal author and joint proprietor of the *Craftsman*, was a key figure in this area although there is little evidence to suggest the precise nature of his position in conducting the paper. His association with Bolingbroke, Pultney, and other leading members of the opposition was regularly stressed by his political opponents, even if they varied in their estimates of the extent of his dependence. A conventional view of his authorial role was put forward in 1732 in a pamphlet underlining the *Craftsman's* political bias. The author claimed that the paper was given credit by readers "because it is wrote under the Patronage of Gentlemen of Distinction, whose Understandings they cannot doubt, and whose Fortunes set them above writing for Gain; which is indeed true: But the People are not aware that the Gentlemen trouble themselves very little with putting Things in Form, though they may often furnish Materials and Protection to the Writer. But the Course of the Paper is perform'd by an Hireling, who does it for Gain and a Livelihood; and it is he we mean when we mention the Secretary or the Author."[12] Such hostile comment seems to contain an element of truth. However, the precise extent to which Amhurst was subject to direction and oversight at different times during his journalistic career remains largely concealed.[13] Similarly, the links between the other major opposition journalists, Charles Molloy and William Guthrie and their political sponsors, are only obliquely evident. It seems possible that such writers come under only sporadic political control and the very flexible terms offered to James Ralph and David Mallet in the early 1750s may reflect the literary independence of an earlier period.[14]

On the ministerial side of the press the political journalists came under a much more formal and consistent oversight. None of the principal writers for the Walpole administration held any share in the papers that they wrote, remaining, with the exception of James Pitt, employees of the government. The generally subordinate condition of service was suggested by the offer made in 1733 to Richard Venn, who was promised "his own terms, if he would write for the Government, but he was told he must at the same time go thorough stitch, and do as directed, which he with scorn refused."[15] The journalists employed on this sort of basis sometimes came under the direct oversight of Walpole himself, and the degree of personal supervision to which they were subjected appears clearly in the brief career of William Arnall, whose professional relationship with Sir Robert Walpole is comparatively well documented by items preserved among the minister's private papers. Arnall seems to have been recruited by Walpole himself sometime in 1728 when still under twenty[16] and, until his premature death in 1736,[17] was employed in writing a series of newspapers as well as a number of political pamphlets. After initially contributing to the *British Journal*,[18] the bulk of Arnall's ouput appeared in the *Free Briton*, which may have been established specifically as a vehicle for his essays, and his special responsibilities in the ministerial press were emphasized by his subsequent precedence over the heterogeneous group of journalists writing for the *Daily Gazetteer*. During most of his career Arnall seems to have had regular meetings with Walpole, at which he received variably detailed instructions on the conduct of the political campaigns. According to Lord Egmont, Arnall's essays were dictated by Walpole "on extraordinary occasions,"[19] and he seems to have been kept under particularly close surveillance during newspaper debates on major economic issues. Following the abandonment of the Excise scheme, for example, Arnall, in an equivocal letter to Walpole, replied that he had either been instructed not to write on the subject or that he had kept out of the way to avoid being ordered to deal with such a controversial matter. "I have," he wrote, "forborne troubling You with my Attendance during the last Fortnight eagerly sollicitous as I have been to engage in the late Debates and indeed the greater the Clamour hath been against your late Propositions in Parliament the more passionately desirous have I been of an Opportunity to confute that Clamour";[20] he went on to ask permission "with a warm and with a full Heart" to write in its defense. Arnall's enthusiasms occasionally caused Walpole some concern and the close check kept on his writing appeared two years later when the Bank Contract became a matter of controversy. Arnall seems to have entered the dispute precipitately and to have been obliged to promise to print nothing more on the subject until it had been scrutinized by Walpole. In a letter referring to this agreement, Arnall enclosed an issue of the *Craftsman* dealing with the contract, and asked to be allowed to continue the controversy with the assistance of "such short Hearings as may not be troublesome or inconvenient to you."[21] Walpole's fear that Arnall was again going to exceed his instructions appeared in a note from Nicholas Paxton assuring him that "nothing will be published till Mr. Arnall has the Honour to wait upon you on Tuesday Morning."[22] Arnall himself wrote confirming this, and on Tuesday received a series of "Rules" for handling the issue.[23] Subsequently, Arnall wrote to Walpole in Norfolk asking for further directions,[24] and the close political oversight of his work seems to have continued until his death.

Neither of the other principal opposition journalists, James Pitt, who wrote for the *London Journal*, and Ralph Courteville, who took over from Arnall, seems to have had such close personal links with the prime minister.[25] In general, the work of the ministerial writers seems to have been coordinated by the Treasury Solicitor, Nicholas Paxton, whose rather shadowy role in this area also reflects the degree of dependence of journalists on this side of the press. Paxton, as his note on Arnall suggests, acted as

Walpole's go-between with the journalists, perhaps dealing largely with the subsidiary writers who worked on the *Daily Courant* and the *Daily Gazeteer*. Neither James Ralph in his history of the Walpole administration nor the author of *An Historical View* mentions Paxton's supervisory function and both assert that Thomas Gordon, who had been taken over with the *London Journal* in the early 1720s and who was given a place in the Wine Office, exercised a general control.[26] There is no documentary confirmation of these often-repeated claims, although they are given some contemporary substance in a virulent attack on Gordon that appeared in the *Universal Spy* in 1732.[27] "Don Gordonio" was described by the author as "*General Master of the Hacks in and about* Arlington-street" and addressed in scathing terms on this basis. "When you presided over *Tacitus*, you spoke big, and dictated like a *Cato*, but all your Patriotism dwindled to the little Post of correcting *Walsingham*, giving a Dash to the *London Journal* and a wipe to the *Courant*." The author, probably the eccentric Matthias Earbery, went on to remark that "as you guide the Pen in Mr. *Walsingham*'s Hand, and a great Man guides it in yours, that Man must share the Rebukes I give to you." Gordon was frequently identified as a contributor to the ministerial press,[28] and it seems probable that he exercised a literary oversight, in the early 1730s at least, while Paxton was concerned with the practical aspects of recruitment, the passing on of policy and the making of payments to the minor journalists not included in the Treasury accounts. Paxton's functions in this area, which complemented his extensive responsibilities in the attempt to control opposition comment,[29] emerge most clearly from the literary products of his opponents. In 1742, following his imprisonment, a pamphlet containing a dying peroration to his former employees indicated the popular view of his position. In it he was made to ask "How often have I regaled you with *Porter* and *Gin* when I have paid you your *monthly* Appointment, or have assembled you to give you proper *Instructions* for your Conduct? To how many of you that could not stay a Month for his Money, have I readily *advanced* it, without the least Consideration?"[30] How far such an ironic attack contains an element of truth is uncertain, but it does coincide with the view expressed ten years earlier in the satirical peom *Verres and his Scribblers*.[31] This contains a mock-heroic account of the character and activities of Walpole's journalists and it seems possible that "the ready lawyer," Phormio, who appears as chief legal adviser to Verres and employer of his writers is Paxton. In the poem Verres, after deciding to launch a campaign, gives directions to Phormio, who sends his clerk to assemble the writers at his rooms in the Temple where he passes on individual instructions. Though such meetings may be pure fantasy, there is enough evidence to suggest at least a degree of underlying reality, and it seems likely that the organizational reshuffle that led up to the establishment of the *Daily Gazetteer* was carried out by Paxton under Walpole's direction, as the author of the *Craftsman* suggested.[32] Journalists writing on behalf of subsequent administrations do not appear to have come under any closer supervision than their opposition counterparts, and there is no evidence that Henry Fielding, for example, in writing the *True Patriot*, received more than occasional literary support.

While the principal author was subject to variable oversight by the controllers of the London press, whether commercial or political, his editorial position was also far from clear-cut. The news and advertising sections of the newspapers were traditionally the province of the printer, and the gathering and sorting out of this material remained his responsibility. The essay section, on the other hand, itself made up of a variety of miscellaneous contributions, was usually under the control of the principal author. There was no clear line of demarcation and while the printer-proprietors of the original weekly journals seem to have exercised a total editorial supervision, the principal author could become involved in the preparation of material for the printer's section. This was particularly evident in the leading opposition papers in which the news, and to a limited extent the advertising, formed a consistent element in the propaganda campaigns. Even here there were ambiguities of practice. Nathaniel Mist's editorial role, for example, seems to have extended to the shaping of the news section for propaganda purposes. This emerged obliquely following Mist's flight to France in 1728. He left the management of his paper in the hands of "Mr. Bingley," probably the replacement printer, and Bingley's political involvement with the news section was spelled out by a ministerial informer.

> as Mr. Mist has left him in chief Trust of his Affairs, and he may be properly call'd the Author of the Paper, excepting the Political Essay in the Beginning, (which I know to be done by another) it may be convenient to ask him who the Authors were of some Paragraphs that have been lately publish'd in Mists Journal, such as The Pun upon my Lord Townshend's Name in relation to Mr. Bernard's being chosen Alderman, which I know to be his own Writing; and of another since that in the Paper of Saturday [was] sevennight about the contemptuous Rejection of the City Petition; for which last I know he was under some Apprehensions of being call'd to Account.[33]

Such subsidiary news editing seems occasionally, as in the case of James Ralph on the *Champion*, to have been handled by a writer hired exclusively for the purpose. More often the principal authors themselves wrote up their paper's news content. It seems likely, for example, that Nicholas Amhurst was at least partly responsible for the "Chain of News" developed in the *Craftsman*,[34] and that Henry Fielding wrote a good deal of the news-narrative published in the *True Patriot*.[35] The principal authors' participation and supply of news appeared directly from items surviving in Charles Molloy's papers.[36] Among the material that he passed on the printer of

Common Sense were a variety of politically angled paragraphs frequently accompanied with instructions for their placement in the home news section.[37]

Given the overlapping responsibilities of author and printer in the area of editorial oversight, it is not surprising to find that a certain amount of friction could be generated. This problem seems to have been behind the difficulties experienced in the *Grub Street Journal*. Although the details are not spelled out in the ledger, it appears that the principal author, Richard Russel, and the printer, John Huggonson, were at odds early in the life of the paper over the selection of correspondence. A minute scrawled across the page in Russel's own hand in April 1732 recorded the agreement "that no Letter directed to Mr. Bavius or Author of the *Grub Street Journal*, shall be broke open by any other Person under the Forfeiture of one Shilling for each Letter."[38] No further reference was made in the minutes to this evident disagreement, but it may be that the unusual decision of the partners to assume collective control of the paper's essay content was an attempt to mediate in an editorial conflict between two leading shareholders. In January 1736 the proprietors agreed to meet "at the Falcon in Falcon Court, every Thursday evening at 6 precisely, by St. Dunstan's clock; where, at a quarter after that hour, the Letters from our Correspondents shall be broken open, and read, in order to determine what is proper to be printed the ensuing week."[39] The confusion that could arise over editorial practice was sometimes evident in the printing office itself, where a pragmatic response to deadlines could overule any formal arrangements. A long notice in *Mist's Journal* in 1724 indicated some of the realities of content selection. The author described how a letter, containing remarks on Bishop Burnet's *Travels,* had arrived through the penny-post on 11 December with a request for insertion in the journal the same week. However, "the Director of this Paper having perused its Contents ordered that it should be deferr'd to the Week following, intending, in the mean Time, to inform himself, in the best Manner he could, of the Authorities therein mentioned; two or three Days he endeavoured to get Bishop *Burnet's* Travels, and enquired of several Gentlemen what they remember'd of that Matter, but met with nothing to convince him, one Way or other; after this, other Affairs happening, it went out of his Head. In the mean time the Letter lay in the Drawer where such Things as come in for the Use of the Paper are always deposited, till the end of the following week, when that Part of the Paper which is reserv'd for domestick News, not being full, the Men search'd this Drawer, to see what Materials were come in, and meeting with this Letter, they put it in without more ado, being press'd in Time to get out the Paper."[40]

The most successful London newspapers of the mid-eighteenth century were the dailies and thrice-weeklies, largely made up of news and advertising in which *de facto* management and editorial oversight were fixed in the printing office. The evidence suggests that when the *Daily Gazetteer* ceased to be a consistent vehicle for political comment, editorial control passed from an author, perhaps the elusive Stephen Whatley, to the printer. This arrangement seems to have remained in operation and in 1769 management of the *Gazetteer* as well as that of the *General Evening Post* and the *Craftsman* was in the hands of the ex-compositor Roger Thompson. He became the first individual to be referred to, initially in the printing office and subsequently in the *Gazetteer* itself, as "the editor."[41] This development, which emphasized the pragmatic and nonliterary basis of journalism, had long-term implications for the character of the profession.

The earnings of the majority of journalists in this period were very limited but, while no fortunes were made through the London press, the highly desirable element of regular employment must have more than offset the generally modest returns. The writers contributing to the printer-owned wecklies seem usually to have received about one guinea a week, the amount paid to John Kelly and Norton Defoe in the late 1730s as the authors of *Fog's Weekly Journal* and the *Original Craftsman* respectively.[42] However, while Daniel Defoe's wages were soon boosted by Mist from twenty to forty shillings,[43] journalists in this subsidiary position were equally vulnerable to exploitation. Dennis de Coetlogan, describing his dealings with William Rayner, claimed that "the said Rayner promised to pay him a Guinea a Week for his trouble, and accordingly paid him four Guineas for four Weeks, and afterwards half a Guinea a week, for three weeks to the best of the Examinants Remembrance, who complaining that he could not live upon that, the said Wm Rayner allowed him afterwards Sixteen Shillings a Week."[44] The income of the journalists who were also proprietors of their papers was probably very variable, depending both on the extent of their interest and the success of the venture, and there is no clear evidence of the financial position of most shareholding authors. The only estimates that throw any light on this area concern Nicholas Amhurst, whose status as joint owner of the *Craftsman* placed him in a somewhat untypical position. Contemporary accounts usually credited him with an income of five guineas a week,[45] and it was claimed that during the negotiations with Haines he had offered to write the paper for six of the total ten guineas profit, although he vigorously denied ever receiving this much.[46] It seems unlikely that any of the journalist-proprietors were able to earn much more than £5 a week out of their papers and probably often received a good deal less.

The only journalists to receive a striking financial return for their work in the London press during this period did so as a result of direct payment from the major political groupings. On the opposition side the evidence is as usual oblique, but it appears that the generally erratic contacts between the writers and their sponsors were complemented by a certain amount of financial disappointment. Amhurst was said to have boasted during the late 1730s of a proposed pension of £200 per annum,[47] and some confirmation of this as well as a further indication of its nonpayment cropped up in a newspaper attack on William Pulteney the year after Amhurst's death in 1742. In a series of rhetorical attacks on Pulteney the author of *Old England* asked "Did you not saddle your Estate with a Rent-Charge (to be paid indeed *after your Death*) of £200 to an Author, whose Character, as such, was more emminent for his *Talents of Abuse,* than for his *Abilities* in *Reasoning?*"[48] Subsequently Amhurst was usually described as a victim of the unfeeling conduct of his political patrons.[49] Similarly, Thomas Carte implied that although Molloy had actually received a pension from the Pretender, this had been cut off when he ceased to give political satisfaction,[50] and he appears ultimately to have had to secure his own financial position.[51] It seems likely that for the most part the opposition journalists were obliged to depend on the commercial income from their papers, although the substantial offers to Ralph and Mallet in 1753 may suggest that more money was circulating in this area of the press than the limited evidence suggests.

On the other hand, the cash returns of Walpole's journalists, a subject of bitter and usually exaggerated comment in the opposition papers, were apparently higher and certainly more regular than those of their political opponents. It is possible to get some idea of the extent of individual incomes from the Treasury accounts although external sources suggest that these have important shortcomings. The entries against the *London Journal,* for example, contain a £200 a year payment for writing, indicating that Pitt's regular income was in the region of £5 a week. However, Peele's memorandum of 1734 pointed out that the printer Wilkins had held on to most of this money and until recently had allowed Pitt only a guinea a week for providing the paper's leading essay. Arnall, on the other hand, through his close relationship with Walpole and also because he received the subsidy for the *Free Briton* himself, was in a much stronger position. The Treasury accounts, which seem to include the writing fees, suggest that his initial payments were moderate and perhaps little more than a guinea a week. In March 1730 Arnall wrote to Walpole asking for £30 to defray his living expenses in town,[52] implying a comparatively low status. It appears that shortly after this his financial position was revolutionised. A detailed account, printed by Hanson, shows that by October 1731 he was receiving quarterly payments of £100 for writing the paper together with additional fees. These amounted to £60 for writing three important issues against the Common Council and £50, perhaps the standard rate,[53] for a ministerial pamphlet.[54] Only one payment of Arnall's total salary was entered in the Treasury accounts, where it appeared as "Royal Bounty"[55] and in 1736 the well-informed *London Evening Post* announced that, with his death, "a Pension of about £400 per annum (*which convinced him of the Goodness of the Cause he wrote in*) reverted to the Government."[56] The payments as well as the variable extras paid officially or embezzled by Arnall made him by far the most highly paid of the London journalists, and the extravagant style of life he adopted was the constant subject of comment by his political opponents. Whether similar sums were passed on to Ralph Courteville when he became principal author of the *Daily Gazetteer* is doubtful and the Treasury accounts give no indication of any payment made for writing. However, it seems likely that his financial rewards were still above the average and in 1740 the *Champion,* in an ironic proposal for the publication of his "Life,"[57] purported to show "How he set up a splendid Equipage, in Imitation of his late renowned Predecessor *Francis Walsingham,* Esq; and made no small Figure at the *Prime-Minister's* Levee, as well as at *Court,* upon *Birth Days,* and other *public Solemnities.*" Although William Webster subsequently claimed to have been offered a pension of £300 a year to turn the *Weekly Miscellany* into a pro-ministerial paper,[58] the only other journalist who received payment directly through the Treasury in this period was Stephen Whatley who was credited annually with about £50 "Royal Bounty." Whether this was a fee for contributions to the ministerial press is not altogether clear. Evidence that it was appeared in the late 1720s when Whatley, as author of the ministerial *Flying Post,* petitioned the King "to support him in the continuance of the said Paper which Encouragement will enable your Petitioner to render it as Serviceable to the Public as to his Family,"[59] and payments began to be made at the beginning of 1729.[60] They continued until the summer of 1741 and, as Haig has pointed out, there is some indication that Whatley was working on the *Daily Gazetteer* and that this was therefore a journalist's fee.[61]

The rewards of political journalism occasionally included the receipt of lucrative sinecures although, in spite of violent opposition denunciations, there is no evidence of prolific, ministerial handouts of this sort.[62] Only James Pitt, who does not appear to have received any considerable cash payment, was given an ample recompense in the form of two quite profitable posts. In 1729 he was given a place in the customs at Portsmouth, which it was widely rumored he later sold for £1,100,[63] while in 1731 the *London Evening Post* announced "James Pitt, Esq; (who is said to write the *London Journal*) is appointed, by the Lords of the Treasury, Surveyor of Tobacco, in the room of Mr. Evans lately deceased; a Warrant Officer in the Port of London, whose salary is £200 per Annum."[64] Pitt may have been granted these favors in view of the reliability of his character, while Arnall was not trusted with such independence. That Arnall hoped for some security of this kind is indicated by his appeal to Walpole to guard him against the possibility of what he described as a "grovelling revenge" by granting him the position of Clerk of the Pipe in the Exchequer Court or, failing this, of an auditorship.[65] He seems to have received neither, and was apparently still unprovided for in this way at the time of his death.[66] Similarly, Courteville wrote to Walpole asking him to use his influence to secure him a place,[67] but while in 1739 the *Craftsman* was ironically encouraging such application,[68] he also seems to have been ultimately unsuccessful. Even Walpole's belated attempts to have him nominated in 1744 as a Justice of the Peace for Westminster on the grounds of his past services came to nothing.[69] The only other ministerial journalist known to have received a place was the Irishman Matthew Concanen, who became Attorney General and Advocate General of Jamaica in 1732.[70] In this case the reward marked the end of a writing career and was probably for more general services than his newspaper contributions.

The hope of ministerial support with the prospect of considerable personal gain and a guaranteed newspaper circulation prompted a number of applications from the author-projectors of unpublished essay sheets, three of which have survived among Sir Robert Walpole's private papers. The Reverend Samuel Madden sent thirteen issues of his proposed paper, none of which have survived, outlining his plan to undermine the *Craftsman* by ridicule,[71] a scheme adopted by John Henley in the *Hyp Doctor* and later in the ministerially subsidized *Corn Cutters Journal*. Madden concluded rather lamely that such a paper could not fail, given the support of "Doddington, Sir Wm. Young, Mr. Littleton, Dr. Young" and others. The two manuscript papers that do survive in the collection were also intended as adjuncts to the ministerial press. The first written by the Spanish Protestant Anthony Gavin, under the title "The Protestant Journal," by Thomas Plain-truth Gentleman was sent to Walpole in September 1734 as "a specimen of my Endeavour to serve you. If you should approve of it, or think, it may be of some use, I shall wait upon you to receive your Commands. In my humble oppinion, this new way of hammering Caleb D'anvers will be more agreeable to the Generality of People, and will teaze that Champion."[72] The second, undated and with no attribution, was entitled "The Moderate Man or The Citizen's Journal," by Sir Charles Freeport of Charter House Square, and was dedicated to a discussion of trade matters.[73] Neither seems to have appeared in print but it is possible that the authors later contributed to existing ministerial papers.

The security offered by ministerial employment also resulted in a flow of applications from individual journalists, many of whom had either written for the opposition or were subsequently obliged to look for work on this side of the press. Ralph Courteville may have contributed to the *Craftsman* before doing some probationary work on the *Daily Courant*,[74] while Amhurst seems to have attempted to find employment with the ministry before entering on his career with the *Craftsman*.[75] Among the subsidiary figures, most of the prolific hack journalists, including some of Rayner's employees, were in touch with Walpole. Norton Defoe, who was involved with the *London Journal* in the early 1720s,[76] was particularly persistent in his requests for financial support, which he seems occasionally to have received.[77] In the late 1730s his position according to his own account was desperate, partly, he claimed, as a result of giving away two hundred copies of a shilling pamphlet that had met with Walpole's approval.[78] His unsolicited services do not seem to have been rewarded on this occasion and, following his arrest in 1739 for writing in Rayner's paper, he wrote to Lord Harington that, having been let down by Walpole, "I took refuge in the

Craftsman printed by J. Standen: My Lord, I could have starved Myself; but it was for the bread of my Children I took refuge in that paper, when I had no other refuge."[79]

During this period the extended opportunities in journalism attracted a very wide range of authors to the London press. The principal journalists were usually professional writers with experience in other literary fields, or members of the professions, generally the law or the church, who had already appeared in print. The principal variations on these conventional backgrounds appeared in the case of Walpole's closely supervised journalists whose formal educational and literary qualifications were negligible. Arnall, who had apparently had a very limited schooling[80] and who continued to display a notorious weakness in spelling, had previously worked as an attorney's clerk, while Pitt had been employed as a schoolmaster in Norwich and Courteville as a church organist. The sort of background from which the ministerial writers were sometimes drawn was perhaps suggested by a surviving application for work from John Gordon. Writing to Walpole in 1736, he stated that he had

> often intended to communicate my designs to you, but hitherto declin'd, imagining some abler hands wou'd offer their Service, and make it their only Study, strenuously to oppose, those who place their pleasure in entertaining dissention, and lay hold of every triffle to cry down your just Administration. But now since Mr. Arnall is dead, and Mr. Pitts as I am informed writtes no more, I hope, in offering my Service, I shall not be so unfortunate to incurr your displeasure. I cou'd with ease write a weekly paper or two. My Education has been pretty liberal, having been brought up in University's and gon through regular Courses of Philosophy etc, I am no Stranger to Forreign Countries, having liv'd Several years abroad especially in France. My present Employment is Teaching Languages in Gentlemens Families.[81]

Although the unusual character of the ministerial authors was a constant theme in the opposition press,[82] it is difficult not to give a broader application to Walpole's own comment on behalf of Courteville that "if his Genius did not appear in the first light, it was not inferior to others who have found their account on the contrary side."[83]

The practice of journalism, particularly in politics, continued to be regarded as one of the least respectable forms of literary activity. In a perhaps exaggerated rejection of the handsome opposition offer of 1753, Mallet directed the intermediary to inform his potential sponsors that, although flattered by their opinion of him as a writer, he was "more mortified by their bad opinion of him as a man. They are probably utter strangers to me; as I am entirely unacquainted either with the justice or nature of their complaints: and yet they are in hopes of being able to retain me as a party-writer, under their management, for hire only. This character is, I believe, not very uncommon: but it does not, therefore, cease to be both contemptible and iniquitous. In one word, Sir; I never was, and I never will be an organ of scandal and defamation, an author or spreader of libels, on any consideration whatever."[84] This view, emphasizing the author's dependence as intermediary between the politicians and the press, could have been extended to take in his position in the commercial publications. While the nonpolitical essay papers were briefly attracting bookseller investment, the professional author was in a position to establish some independence of action. However, trade finance was increasingly focused in the major news-carrying papers, in which the role of the author was restricted largely to the menial tasks of translating and newsgathering. As the range of content of the dailies and thrice-weeklies broadened out from mid-century, some new opportunities of a limited sort opened up. Nonetheless the professional author remained uneasily poised between the dominant booksellers or politicians and the printers, working on the margins of the London press and seldom establishing an independent status within it.

7
The Press and Politics

The rapid expansion of the London press during the early years of the eighteenth century coincided with the build-up in party conflict, and comment on politics continued to provide a common denominator between the content of all forms of newspaper, most at some point adopting an identifiable political stance. The specialist essay-papers supplied the framework of argument within which thrice-weekly and daily newspapers engaged in vigorous conflict. The vitality and popularity of this political material varied widely. Periods of comparative inertia, when the sponsored papers continued to tick over following routine lines of argument, were interspersed with others of great activity as the politicians grouped and re-grouped and issues of national concern were identified and pursued. The timing of this process, which touched all forms of newspaper whatever their organizational base, provides one of the most important chronologies in the development of the London press.

By the time Walpole had maneuvered himself into the position of prime minister, the London press had long been accepted as an important and legitimate component of the political system. No other medium offered such ease of dispersal and range of regular access to the nation at large and these advantages, which also gave the London papers their force as an advertising medium, was from the 1690s exploited by most leading politicians. Robert Harley was the first to attempt a comprehensive use of the press to secure as well as to gain access to power and in so doing he constructed a complex organization concerned with production and distribution as much as with oversight of his opponent's output.[1] As his influence declined prior to 1714, the structure he had created lost its shape and was not fully reconstructed until Walpole found it necessary to become involved in the same area of propaganda. His apparently reluctant decision to move in this direction was itself largely a response to opposition material published in the London press, which had been growing in volume for several years.

Although the death of Queen Anne was followed by the eclipse of the

113

Tory party, its supporters, both Hanoverians and Jacobites, continued to provide a low-key focus for political opposition.[2] This rather fragmented grouping was represented in the London press through the most popular of the new weekly journals run by the printer Nathaniel Mist. Mist was himself a Jacobite who had regular contact with leading members of the party on both sides of the channel, and his paper, which first appeared in 1716 as the *Weekly Journal; or, Saturday's Post,* provided for almost ten years the main line of opposition comment within the London press.[3] However, by the early 1720s the broadening opposition was receiving support in a variety of London newspapers that increasingly directed their attacks at Walpole personally. Until it was bought up by the administration the *London Journal* achieved a substantial national success through its leading essays subsequently republished in several editions as *Cato's Letters.* Similarly, the inflammatory essay-sheet the *True Briton* hovered on the brink of what could be called sedition, and seems to have established an extensive readership before being forced out of publication in 1724.[4]

Consequently, the major impact of the *Craftsman,* first published as a twice weekly essay-sheet at the end of 1726, was not the result of novelty in either form or content. Appearing as one of a series of variably successful opposition papers in this format, it was itself apparently based on Erasmus Philipps's moribund *Country Gentleman,* in which its putative author, Caleb D'Anvers, first made an appearance.[5] The originality of the *Craftsman* lay primarily in its links with a powerful and extended opposition centered around Lord Bolingbroke and the Pulteneys and its influence as a political catalyst within the London press arose from its status as the semi-official vehicle for "legitimate" attacks on the administration. Like other political papers, the *Craftsman* offered its sponsors a variety of benefits, among which the creation of an illusion of group solidarity was perhaps one of the most useful. The presentation of argument and comment through the single fictional author helped, however superficially, to conceal the fissures within the heterogeneous opposition. The unusual range of the paper's political support was reflected in the identity of the subscribers whose names appeared in the four lists confiscated from Richard Francklin in 1730. They included such extreme Tories as Sir William Wyndham, Henry Fleetwood, and Sir John Hinde Cotton, moderate Whigs such as Samuel Sandys, Lord Morpeth, and Sir John Rushout, and even such uncommitted politicians as Arthur Onslow, Speaker of the House of Commons, and Sir Joseph Jekyll, Master of the Rolls.[6] In spite of its comprehensive appeal, the *Craftsman* was never an exclusive medium for consistent anti-ministerial comment. *Mist's Weekly Journal,* with its established and perhaps socially broader readership, continued to follow an opposition line and, with the *Craftsman's* adoption of journal form in 1727,[7] the two papers offered a complementary commentary on national politics. Their usually friendly rivalry was continued following the metamorphosis of *Mist's* into *Fog's* in 1728, when the printer Mist overstepped the line of acceptable comment and was forced into exile. The change of title was a modest and ironic concession to authority, and the paper continued to carry sharp attacks on the government that were at least as effective as those carried in the *Craftsman.*

The relative success of the major opposition papers during the late 1720s varied a good deal. Initially it seems likely that Mist's paper, with its erratic but inflammatory comment and journal form, was far more popular than the *Craftsman.* According to a writer in the *Daily Gazetteer,* "*Mist's* treasonable Papers were sold sometimes for Half a Guinea a-piece,"[8] and the author of the *Senator* was probably correct when he remarked ironically that "in the demand for their Writings also, there is or has been, a little Disproportion, *D'Anvers* has vented his Thousands *Mist* his Ten Thousands."[9] However, as *Fog's* the paper seems to have lost ground. In 1729 the author of *Read's Weekly Journal,* in an ironic aside, remarked that "You, Mr. Fog, are more than a little displeased that Caleb tops you in the Sale of his Papers,"[10] and the following year it was stated in a ministerial pamphlet that, while the *Craftsman* brought in an annual income of £1,000, *Fog's* only produced £500 or £600.[11] In 1732 the same author provided a further assessment of the decline in the position of *Mist's* now *Fog's,* stating that "it may now, indeed, bring in not above Four or Five Hundred Pounds a Year instead of Eighteen Hundred or more, which it once did."[12]

The corresponding success of the *Craftsman* and the process by which it rose to preeminence can be seen in some detail from the surviving accounts.[13] In its twice-weekly, single-leaf form the number printed rose steadily during the first four weeks of publication from 250 to 500 copies per issue and in number nine it was claimed that "*great demand for several of the first Numbers of the Paper*" had led to the essays being reprinted in pamphlet form.[14] Five collections were published but, although selling quite well, demand for this sort of secondary output seems to have declined. The first passed through three editions and sold 2,500 copies in all; the second achieved two editions of 1,000 copies; and the last three were printed in only one edition of 1,250 copies. This pattern was to some extent reflected in the sales of the paper itself. At first the number printed continued to rise, reaching the thousand mark in mid-January 1727 and a ceiling of 1,500 in February, following the opening of the ministry's campaign of prosecutions. However, the growth rate was not maintained and a leveling out at between 850 and 900 copies had begun by March. The switch to journal form in May seems to have resulted in a much more favorable public response and the paper's circulation again began to rise steadily, reflected in the growth of the four-weekly profits from an initial £8 8s.[15] The first £50 figure was reached in February 1728 and it is perhaps significant that the first £70 profit appeared at the end of this year following the partial breakdown of *Mist's Weekly Journal.* Profits continued to rise and the last entry, against issues that appeared in February and March 1730, showed the highest income to date of £86.16s.4d. If it can be assumed that Haines was accurate in estimating that the *Craftsman's* weekly printing of 4,500 copies produced a clear profit of 10 guineas,[16] then the average weekly income from the last issues mentioned in the accounts of something over £21 suggests a regular printing of about 10,000 copies.[17] An apparently authentic support for these estimates appeared in 1732 when the hostile author of the *D'Anverian History* provided a detailed breakdown of the *Craftsman's* circulation figures at the beginning of the decade. After estimating the income from the paper on the basis of "a round Computation of 10,000 in Number Weekly," the author went on to remark,

> but their usual Number was not less than 12,000 or 13,000 for a long Time, even till since May 22, 1731, when in a Course of Disputation with the Author of the *Free Briton,* and Others, his Patrons were detected in so many Falsities in Facts, as well in his Journal as other Pamphlets, that his Paper lost a great deal of its Credit, sinking in a short Time near 4,000 in Number; that is from 13,000 to less than 9,000: About the Time of his (Francklin's) Tryal it rose a little again, but, notwithstanding this Prosecution, the Paper is still carry'd on in its utmost Malignancy, thus profitable and thus popular.[18]

The broadening of the opposition challenge through the London press evoked a series of variable responses from those in power. Prior to the publication of the *Craftsman* the Walpole administration had few serious problems with the newspapers. The most popular attacks on the ministry from a moderate political standpoint had appeared at the beginning of the decade in the *London Journal* and in this case prompt financial action immediately transformed the paper into a vehicle for ministerial propaganda.[19] On the other hand the ministry did not lack defenders. The essay sheet *Pasquin,* also printed and published by Wilkins and Peele, supplemented the reformed *London Journal* and opposed Wharton's *True Briton,* while a number of uncommitted London newspapers carried occasional support for the administration. During the mid-1720s divisions within the ministry itself and the establishment of the *Craftsman* created an entirely new situation evoking two distinct forms of response.

Initially a consistent attempt was made to use the law to suppress publication.[20] This was only partially successful and from the late 1720s a more coherent policy of rebuttal began to emerge, aimed at discrediting or at least answering opposition newspaper attacks. A certain amount of apparently spontaneous pro-ministerial writing had continued to surface in the press and James Read's *Weekly Journal* became the vehicle for regular essays in support of the administration. At the same time, a number of new essay-sheets, the *Plain Man,* the *Citizen,* and the *Senator* were published in defense of Walpole and his policies, although invariably with marked lack of commercial success.[21] The position of such papers was neatly summed up in the last issue of the moribund *Senator,* where it was pointed out that "as to the Success of these Papers, it is evident I presume from the first that appeared under this Title, that I did not mistake the way to popularity, but purposely declin'd it. No one is so ignorant as not to know that the Temple of Fame, according to the modern Structure of it, has but two Gates, which are *Faction* and *Infidelity*."[22]

It may have been the failure of the independent pro-ministerial papers to establish a secure foothold in the market as well as the clear success of the *Craftsman* that prompted Walpole to extend the ministry's interest in the press beyond the already subsidized *London Journal*. The new ministerial campaign seems to have been initiated in 1728, when the *British Journal*, appearing under the added subtitle of the *Censor*, became a vehicle for William Arnall's closely supervised essays.[23] However, at the end of the year, perhaps because of a commercial clash with the *London Journal*, the *Free Briton*, a Thursday essay-sheet, was set up as a more suitable alternative.[24] In 1730 the range of officially sponsored papers was further extended by the development of a direct link with the *Daily Courant*. It seems just possible that at some earlier time, negotiations had been opened with the proprietors of the more successful *Daily Journal*.[25] There is only circumstantial evidence for this and the *Courant*, oldest of the London daily papers, was already closely associated with the authorities through its personnel. Its leading proprietor, Samuel Buckley, as Gazetteer for life[26] was active in the Secretary of State's office on press affairs, while the *Courant's* successive printers, Samuel Gray and Edward Owen, were appointed respectively Messenger of the Press[27] and printer of the *London Gazette*. The paper's position during the 1720s had been in decline, particularly, it seems, as a result of competition from the newer and apparently more successful *Daily Post* and *Daily Journal*. This was reflected in the price that the *Courant* shares were fetching during these years. In 1719 a ¹⁄₂₀th share cost Bernard Lintot £51 5s. Od.,[28] while six years later a similar holding was sold for £22,[29] and Lintot later stated that he gave up his share to Buckley "when the Sale of the Paper did not pay the Expenses."[30] Consequently, the *Courant* seems to have been ripe for a ministerial takeover. The fourth essay-paper for which there is direct evidence of ministerial sponsorship was the *Corn Cutters Journal*, perhaps written by John Henley[31] and receiving government support from its first appearance in 1733.[32] The popularity of these ministerial papers as reflected in their circulation figures was well below that of their opposition rivals. In 1730 it was claimed that while the *Craftsman* sold 10,000 or 12,000 copies a week, the *London Journal*, perhaps the most popular of the subsidized papers, sold 2,000 or 3,000 copies.[33] Although no detailed sales figures are available, it seems that this sort of discrepancy underlay the recurrent ministerial attacks on the view that popularity and merit were in any way allied.

Any commercial disadvantage was at least partly offset by ministerial control of the Post Office. On one hand official influence could be used to obstruct the passage of leading opposition papers. On the other the prin-

A clear Stage and no Favour.

CRAFTSMAN, *Saturday, December* 12, 1730.

THE PERSONS, whom you threaten, SIR, neither value your Favour, nor fear your Anger. Whenever you attempt any ACT OF POWER against any of them, you shall find that you have to do with Men, who know they have not offended the LAW; and therefore trust They have not offended the KING; who know They are safe, as long as the LAWS and LIBERTIES of their Country are so; and who are so little desirous of being safe any longer, that they would be the first to bury themselves in the Ruins of the BRITISH Constitution, if You or any M——R, as desperate as You, should be able to destroy it. But let us ask, on this Occasion, what You are, who thus presume to threaten?——Are you not ONE, whose Measure of FOLLY and INIQUITY is full; who can neither hold, nor quit his Power with Impunity; and over whose Head the long-gathering Cloud of national Vengeance is ready to burst?——Is it not Time for You, Sir, instead of threatening to attack OTHERS, to consider how soon you may be attacked YOURSELF?—— How many Crimes may be charged upon You and YOURS, which almost every Man can prove; and how many more are ready to start into Light, as soon as the Power, by which you now conceal them, shall determine?—— When next you meditate Revenge on your ADVERSARIES, remember this Truth. *The LAWS must be destroy'd, before* THEY *can suffer, or* YOU *escape.*

DAILY COURANT, *Monday, December* 21, 1730.

To the AUTHORS *of the* CRAFTSMAN.

GENTLEMEN,

THE Person whom you threaten, neither desires your Assistance, nor fears your Opposition. You have to do with a Man who knows he hath not offended the Law, who knows himself a faithful Servant to his PRINCE, and to his Country; and therefore he knows he is safe, as long as the *Laws* and *Liberties* of his Country are so: If you are come to such a Height of desperate Wickedness as to attempt to destroy your Country, because the Publick Affairs are not under your Direction, he trusts that by the Wisdom of the KING, and the Loyalty of his People, all your wicked Devices will be confounded, and all your vain Imaginations disappointed. But were it possible the vile Arts you make use of could prevail upon your Fellow Subjects to work their own Destruction, he would then think it the greatest Glory to fall by his MASTER's Side, and be buried in the Ruins of the present Establishment. Let me ask, on this Occasion, who you are, who thus presume to threaten? Are you not those whom Disappointment has fill'd with Rage, and Vanity and Ambition depriv'd of Reason? Is it not time for you, instead of threatning to attack others, to reflect upon your own Guilt, who have made it your Business, by scandalous Parallels, and malicious Insinuations, to render his Majesty's Person and Government odious and contemptible to his People? This is a Crime, which every Man who reads your Papers can witness you are justly charged with. When next you meditate Mischief against the Person whom you injure because you envy, and hate because you have injur'd, remember this Truth, While the Laws have their due Force, and a just PRINCE fills the Throne, you cannot ruin an innocent Man, and cloath yourselves with his Spoils.

LONDON: Printed for Messieurs FIGG and SUTTON. MDCCXXXI. [Price 6 d.]

A clear Stage and no Favour; **political confrontation through the London press. Henry St. John, Viscount Bolingbroke appears on the left and Sir Robert Walpole on the right. The fictitious imprint refers to two noted prize fighters.**

cipal value of Post Office control lay in the scope it offered for the bulk distribution of the sponsored essay-papers. Both political sides seem to have attempted a general dispersal of copies of their main publications, although the members of the opposition groupings were obliged to look for alternative channels to the post. "Orator" Henley, in the first number of his pro-ministerial *Hyp-Doctor*, ironically claimed that if he were not supported by the public he would be obliged to become a pensionary writer for the opposition and as a slave to the party leaders, "get my *ministerial Papers* subscrib'd off at 50 a Head by each of them; and pack them *like B-ds, in Carts and Caravans to debauch the Country*."[34] Henley was more accurately informed than his style of writing suggests, and country distribution of the *Craftsman* seems to have been partly handled in this way.[35] Nonetheless, the highest total of copies appearing on any of the confiscated subscription lists was 766, and while there is no evidence to suggest the consistency or general application of such opposition activity, it seems likely that it was entirely swamped by the scale of the ministry's circulation of free newspapers through the Post Office.

The development of this ministerial propaganda effort is comparatively well documented. A record of the official payments made for copies to proprietors and others appears in the Treasury accounts as well as in a number of scattered items largely preserved among the Walpole papers and consequently it is possible to suggest both the timing and scale of the gratis distribution. Following the takeover of the *London Journal* in 1722, 650 copies were ordered to be sent ot the Post Office every week,[36] and the Treasury accounts indicate that until the end of the decade this modest total was not extended.[37] However, from 1729, 800 of the newly established *Free Briton* also began to be sent through the post, while the official circulation of important issues was occasionally boosted as high as 5,000 copies.[38] The problems of distribution posed by the *Daily Courant* were solved by its production in "double" form and its free circulation as a thrice-weekly paper, 750 copies of each edition being initially sent out each post day.[39] Consequently, by 1731 about 3,700 copies of the sponsored essay-papers were being distributed weekly at a cost to the Treasury of £30 15s. Although a steady rise in numbers continued to take place, the rate of increase was not accelerated until the striking build-up in political tension in 1733. By the end of the year 2,000 copies of each of the *London Journal*,[40] the *Free Briton*,[41] and the newly established *Corn Cutters Journal*[42] were regularly distributed through the Post Office, while the same number of "double Courants" was also sent out every Tuesday, Thursday, and Saturday. In each case the official circulation apparently continued to rise to a ceiling of 2,200,[43] and at the beginning of 1734 some 12,500 copies of the four subsidized essay-papers were reaching provincial readers every week at a cost to the ministry of about £104.

Whether this represented the administration's total newspaper interest during the late 1720s and early 1730s, either through subsidized distribution or payment of personnel, remains obscure and is only partially indicated by the Treasury accounts. The first newspaper entries appeared in 1729, although the *London Journal* had been officially circulated since 1722, and the extent of the omissions in other areas is considerable.[44] Consequently, it seems likely that papers that were not included, either before of after this date, received some sort of encouragement. The extension of the ministry's financial involvement in the London press was constantly denounced in the opposition papers, which tended to ascribe the publication of any pro-Walpole essay material to a supply of public money. It was frequently stated that among the London essay-papers of this period the *British Journal, Read's Journal,* the *Weekly Register,* and the *Hyp Doctor* were all supported by the administration.[45] But in spite of various contemporary claims,[46] there is no direct evidence of any such involvement.[47] It is also far from clear whether the ministry had a financial concern in any of the full-priced thrice-weeklies and dailies. Eustace Budgell asserted in 1730 that the *St. James's Evening Post* was supported by a subsidy of £200 a year and was distributed gratis throughout the country.[48] But here again there is no evidence to show that this was more than a shot in the dark, suggested perhaps by the paper's regular distribution through the Secretary of State's Office. On the other hand both Stephen Whatley and Henry Vander Esch, proprietors of the *Flying Post* and *Daily Advertiser* respectively, were receiving payment from public funds, and the latter paper seems to have been used occasionally as an outlet for semi-official political comment.[49] It seems possible that during the early 1730s the ministry's financial stake in the London press extended very widely, although the ambiguous nature of the payments has obscured the details.

The Post Office provided the main channel for the dispersal of government propaganda, whether in newspapers or in specially written pamphlets. Among the Walpole manuscripts are a series of accounts for the distribution of five pamphlets published in the 1730s.[50] These indicate that a total of about 10,000 copies of each was disposed of and that a substantial proportion passed through the post to be redirected by locally based government officials. These arrangements, which probably also applied to the newspapers, required the comprehensive involvement of the Post Office employees. Referring to publications defending the ministerial position on the excise, a pamphleteer ironically claimed that such numbers had been sent out that

> *The poor hackney beasts of the* Post Office *have couched under their Bruthen.* Circular Letters have been sent in the name of Mr. JOS. BELL to all the *Post-masters* in the Kingdom, with Orders *to make* these Papers *as public as they can;* to send up the Names of all Persons within their Delivery, who keep Coffee-houses, where Gentlemen resort to read the NEWS, that They may likewise be furnished with them GRATIS, and even most private families have them crouded in upon Them by the same Hands.[51]

Local redistribution was also organized through the Collectors of the Customs and of the Excise, a strikingly unpopular but geographically effective group of intermediaries. The pamphlet accounts also reveal the involvement of the personnel of the main government departments who received copies in bulk, and few of those in office or with any sort of political interest were left off the list of those identified for individual supply. Whether the distribution of London newspapers was handled in such a detailed way or not, the effort of dispersing the large number of copies suggests the value placed on printed propaganda as well as the level of activity that was thought to be necessary to combat the superior selling power and general appeal of the opposition publications.

Among the London papers apparently acting independently the polarization of political views based on a variety of obscure and probably mixed motives was increasingly evident from the mid-1720s. This was most clear in the case of immediate commercial rivals that tended to hold opposed political attitudes. Of the essay-carrying papers, the *Weekly Register* and the *Grub Street Journal*, and the *Weekly Miscellany* and the *Old Whig*, although not primarily concerned with politics, came down for and against the ministry, while the same pattern emerged among the primarily news-carrying publications. The consistency and intensity of the political support given by the thrice-weeklies and dailies varied considerably and found fullest expression in a small group of politically orientated newspapers under joint ownership. On the more popular opposition side, the *London Evening Post* and the *Daily Post*, printed by Richard Nutt, became the most outspoken critics of the administration. Both had contained occasional anti-ministerial items since the 1720s, but hostility to the excise scheme and official efforts to obstruct their circulation through the Post Office prior to the election of 1734[52] was followed by the adoption of a vigorous political line. The *London Evening Post,* in particular, subsequently provided important backing for the opposition campaigns. On the other side, defense of ministerial policy and attacks on the opposition appeared in the *General Evening Post,* first published a few days before the *London Evening Post* began to complain about ministerial interference,[53] while Samuel Richardson's *Daily Journal,* which had appeared in support of the administration since the 1720s, paralleled the role of the *Daily Post.*[54] In the commercial and political struggle between these papers, the advantage clearly lay with the opposition and, while the *General Evening Post* had largely abandoned its partisan approach by the end of the decade and the *Daily Journal* collapsed in 1737, both the opposition papers continued to appear, apparently with a good deal of success. The evident imbalance in political appeal that this suggests may also have been a factor in the disappearance of the *Daily Post Boy,* which collapsed almost immediately after the adoption of a pro-ministerial line following the 1735 takeover. Although most full-priced thrice-weeklies and dailies carried occasional comment on politics, they sometimes maintained an aggressive neutrality. John Peele claimed that he "refused to publish the *Whitehall Evening Post* because they occasionally inserted Letters and Paragraphs against the Administration, though more frequently for it."[55] However, this kind of political impartiality was unusual and not apparently very successful, and the cheap London papers almost invariably came down against the government, attempting to cash in on the anti-ministerial and anti-Hanoverian sentiments that existed at the lower social levels. Rayner's *Morning Advertiser,* for example, ran a highly inflammatory political dialogue on loss of liberty during 1736,[56] while more oblique political comment appeared in such items as the historical justifications of the Stuarts, which were serialized in a number of papers, including Walker's *Weekly Tatler.*[57] The recurrent use of the word *Oxford* in the titles of the cut-price London papers may itself have had a more directly political than geographical connotation.

The propaganda deployed through the sponsored essay papers worked at a variety of intellectual levels, with the opposition making most of the running. The campaigns of the Queen Anne period had been vigorous but fragmented. During Walpole's term in office the consistent and long-drawn-out confrontation between politicians in and out of power allowed for the development of a more sophisticated debate. On both political sides the newspapers offered the most fully worked out statement of ideology available to contemporaries, and the elaborate critiques of national history and politics helped to conceptualize the opposition and ministry divisions and provided the setting for the more detailed and parliament-centered strategy.[58] At this second level the opposition press focused on issues that linked their general programme with the deep-rooted concerns of the nation at large. During the late 1720s the *Craftsman* continuously hammered away at the supposed betrayal of national interest displayed in the administration's conduct of foreign affairs, a line that led to the successful prosecution of Francklin in 1731. Subsequently, the Excise crisis and the Spanish Convention stimulated a high level of activity in the sponsored papers, particularly since a general election was not far off in either case. The rise and fall of political involvement in the London press was directly related to these external issues and, as in the early 1730s there was a great deal of sporadic activity, so in the mid-1730s something of a decline set in.

Walpole's abandonment of the Excise scheme and his success in the general election of 1734 was followed by a slackening of political tension and the leading political essay-papers on both sides seem to have experienced a fall in status and popularity. Lord Bolingbroke's departure for France in May 1735 deprived the *Craftsman* of its most important contributor, whose essays had been largely responsible for the paper's dramatic success. This had been clearly demonstrated earlier in the decade when between July 1731 and September 1732 Bolingbroke apparently contributed only one item. According to Arnall, writing in October 1731, the *Craftsman* had "lessened in its Sale above TWO THOUSAND Papers a

Week, in no longer Space of Time than these last *three Months*,"[59] while the following year a ministerial informer also stressed the paper's decline, which he attributed to its being left almost entirely in the hands of its "Author in Ordinary," Nicholas Amhurst. "Formerly He received great Assistance from Other Hands as well as those of the Chiefs in the Party as those who wrote as Candidates for its Favor but of late both those Helps have failed pretty much the first through the Indolence of his Patrons and the latter through the Discouragement he has given to such Attempts for fear of being Supplanted by some brighter and more Assiduous Writer of Fortune which was indeed a just Caution in respect to Himself tho' a manifest injury to the interest of the Paper which for some Months has been declining in its Sale tho' I am told Measures are now concerting to bring it into greater Reputation than ever."[60] After 1735 the amount of such assistance probably declined sharply and, while the falling off in the quality of the *Craftsman's* essays became a constant theme in the *Daily Gazetteer*,[61] the paper's weekly printing had dropped by 1738 to 4,500 copies.[62] The malaise was evident elsewhere in the opposition press. In 1736 the *London Evening Post* announced that "Mr. Nathaniel Mist the Printer, who has resided some years at Bollogne in France, is expected here in a few Days, having obtained a *Noli Prosequi*, and a Warrant under his Majesty's Sign Manual to return."[63] Mist kept up his Jacobite associations in England,[64] but a condition of his return seems to have been the neutralizing of *Fog's Weekly Journal* which, although it continued to appear, did so in an emasculated form.[65] As the author of *Common Sense* remarked, the paper that had passed "by a natural Progression from *Mist* to *Fog*, is now condensed into a Cloud, and only used by way of wet brown Paper, in case of Falls and Contusions."[66]

The consolidation of the ministry's newspaper interests in 1735 may also have been influenced by the new political atmosphere. However, it seems likely that it was partly an attempt to tighten up control of the Treasury payments that had begun to cause trouble the previous year. The first sign of dislocation appeared in a memorandum from John Peele, as publisher and part-owner of the *London Journal* and the *Free Briton*.[67] He claimed that both the printer Wilkins and the journalist Arnall who received the payments had been guilty of some sharp practice in their redistribution of the money. Wilkins, he stated, not only kept most of the writing fee for the *London Journal*, but also "all the Profits that arise from sending the Post Office 2000 of the Paper weekly." An investigation of the journal's finances by the Secretary of the Treasury followed and his report, probably made toward the end of 1734,[68] seems to have confirmed the substance of Peele's charges. Wilkins was shown to have kept the halfpenny per copy traditionally allowed to the publisher without reference to his fellow proprietors, although their acceptance of his accounts up to the time of Peele's complaints ruled out any question of retrospective compensation. Arnall, on the other hand seems to have failed to pass on the Treasury payments at all and was said to owe Peele nearly £900 on account of the *Free Briton* while also, like Wilkins, attempting to undermine his position as publisher. The presence among Walpole's papers of Peele's detailed accounts for both the *London Journal* and the *Free Briton* itself suggests that at this stage some attempt was being made to tighten up the organization of payment. If so this may also account for the unusual character of the Treasury payments for the *Free Briton* between 4 July and 26 September 1734, which appear to have been only for the paper itself, with no indication of the substantial fee usually paid to Arnall, whose affairs were in serious disorder.[69]

The creation of the *Daily Gazetteer* in 1735 was therefore probably as much part of a drive for administrative efficiency as for economy. Although both the *London Journal* and the *Corn Cutters Journal* continued in subsidized publication,[70] the principal ministerial journalists were amalgamated on the *Gazetteer,*[71] which, from its first appearance seems to have become the only officially distributed London newspaper.[72] Issued in the same "double" form as the *Daily Courant,*[73] it was circulated free of charge for the rest of the decade on a very large scale. The Treasury accounts suggest that 2,600 copies of each thrice-weekly edition was initially sent into the provinces.[74] By 1741 this number had risen to 3,600, giving a total weekly distribution of 10,800 copies at a cost of £90.[75] The new venture was greeted with ironic contempt in the opposition press and the *London Evening Post* at the end of its first week announced,

> The *Daily Courant* which was so justly thrown out of most of the Coffee-Houses in Town for grossly abusing the Merchants, etc. about the *Excise,* is laid down under that Title, as is the *Free Briton;* and *Mother Osborne* writes no more political Letters in the *London Journal;* but all three are revived, in *Principle and Defamation,* in a new Paper, called the *Daily Gazetteer:* In this Paper the *modest* Mr. *Walsingham, Mother Osborne, Britannus, Carus* and the whole Crew of hir'd Mercenaries, are to appear; if they were to be supported *only* by the *common Sale* of the Paper, what a starving Condition would they soon be reduced to? for the *Daily Courant, Free Briton* and *London Journal* were grown so contemptible that scarce anybody in Town would *buy* them, nay few even of those to whom they were sent down in the Country Ministerially (i.e. *gratis,* Paper and Postage paid) wou'd read them; so these *heavy Authors* have now join'd all their Forces together, and are to cram into one Paper what they retailed before in three.[76]

The absence of major political issues and the retraction in volume and decline in quality of political writing in the London press was apparently quite marked. A pamphleteer commented with satisfaction on the decline in "Party Spirit," and after describing *Fog's* change of policy, went on to state that "as to the *Craftsman* and *Gazetteer,* their Disputes rather concern themselves than their Readers; if the one can preserve its Advertisements and the other conserve their Paper, it is as much as they can reasonably expect. As for the *London Journal* it is just where it was many years ago, so little devoted to either Party, that it is disliked by both."[77] This period of political stasis in the London press was quite short-lived. In 1737 De Coetlogan attempted to cash in on the vacuum created by *Fog's* political defection, advertising his short-lived journal the *Alchymist* as "*The Spirit of* Fog *Reviv'd; or, an Atonement for the Loss of that late Hero.*"[78] His intervention was premature. In May 1737, following Mist's retirement from newspaper ownership, an attempt was made to resurrect *Fog's* itself through the publication of a series of astringent attacks on the ministry written by John Kelly.[79] However, both papers were severely upstaged by a major, new opposition journal that began to appear on 5 February 1737 under the title *Common Sense*. Initially at least, the paper provided a point of contact for the whole spectrum of opposition groupings. With the evident decline in the political impact of *Fog's*, the Jacobites were left without a direct line into the London press and during 1736 Charles Molloy, a long-term associate of Mist and projector of the new paper, held an extended correspondence with the Pretender and his agents.[80] James himself gave some encouragement to the new publication on the grounds that "such sort of things do good more or less with the public"[81] and Molloy's rumored pension may have been connected with this project. On the other hand the setting up of *Common Sense* coincided with the formation of a new opposition group revolving around the Prince of Wales. During his negotiations with the Pretender, Molloy claimed that he had a promise of assistance from Alexander Pope, Lord Chesterfield and his friends and Lord Grange.[82] In the event, several of the politicians and at least one of the professional writers who had previously contributed to the *Craftsman* and *Fog's* provided essays for the new paper. Lord Chesterfield, George Lyttelton, and Henry Fielding can all be identified,[83] although the extent of their involvement and the relationship between the paper and the reconstituted opposition is, as usual, largely a matter of speculation. *Common Sense* achieved a good deal of instant notoriety, the sure mark of commercial success. According to one of its own contributors it "happened to take so well with the Public, that when it grew scarce, a great many single Copies were sold for Twelve Pence a Piece."[84] The flurry of opposition activity in the London press at the beginning of 1737 was sufficiently marked to stir the ministry into taking some quite far-reaching legal action, which hastened the end of some papers and contributed to serious divisions in the management of both the *Craftsman* and *Common Sense*.[85]

Toward the end of the decade the increase in international tension, culminating in the outbreak of war with Spain, revitalized political issues and led to renewed public interest in the struggle between the opposition and the ministry. Newspaper support for the administration was, by 1740, at a very low ebb. The *Daily Gazetteer,* though still widely circulated through the Post Office, had sunk in prestige since Arnall and Pitt had ceased to contribute. The estimate in *Old Common Sense* that not more than 250 copies of the *Gazetteer* were sold direct to the public, though it was to be found "almost in every petty Ale-House in the Kingdom," was probably not far from the truth.[86] The growing unpopularity of the Walpole administration was also reflected in the very limited amount of essay material published elsewhere in its defense; only the derelict *Hyp Doctor* and perhaps the *Corn Cutters Journal* continued to carry pro-ministerial comment into the 1740s. Similarly, most of the thrice-weeklies or dailies that had previously acted as open or tacit advocates had either collapsed or ceased to have a political slant, although some erratic support was still provided by the *Daily Advertiser*.

On the other hand there was a steady rise in the number of new essay-papers carrying opposition comment and supplementing the established journals. Publication of the *Champion* and the *Englishman's Evening Post* shortly after the outbreak of war, both as vehicles for original essay material, added significantly to the volume of opposition comment. In 1740 the author of the *Gazetteer* was provoked into remarking that "of all the Scribbling Insects that nibble at the Root of the Nation's Repose and Happiness this Season, I think the two Mushroom Writers lately sprung up of the Papers call'd the *Champion* and the *Englishman's Evening Post,* the most incorrigible, crude, and inconsistent."[87] Although it is possible that the latter had some links with members of the opposition through William Guthrie, the *Champion,* initially appearing as a morning paper, gave some early indications of being a largely uncommitted paper of the *Spectator* type.[88] However, the swing to politics was soon evident and it seems possible that this was first emphasized as a stimulus to sales when the paper was threatened with financial disaster.[89] The commercial possibilities in the public demand for opposition material, further stimulated by the general election of 1741 and its aftermath, seem to have encouraged other previously uncommitted essay-papers to adopt an opposition line.

At the beginning of 1742 Richard Nutt's *Universal Spectator* announced the abandonment of its already crumbling neutrality, and began to include in its news section the sort of politically loaded paragraphs appearing in the related *London Evening Post*.[90] The pressure to take up an opposition stance appeared most clearly in the metamorphosis of the *Weekly Miscellany* into the politically active *Westminster Journal*. Three weeks after the collapse of William Webster's original paper,[91] a nearly identical publication with a more varied, though still nonpolitical, form of content appeared under the title of *New Weekly Miscellany*. It seems likely that the property was taken over by a new set of proprietors, although the content links between the two papers were stressed.[92] In November, however, during the vigorously contested Westminster election, the paper appeared with new numbering under the amended title of *The Westminster Journal, Or, The New Weekly Miscellany* by Thomas Touchit, of Spring Garden, Esq.[93] The first number, distributed free of charge by the proprietors, appeared under a large title picture of Westminster, and although the essays contained a good deal of miscellaneous material, the tendency toward a predominantly political tone was soon clear.

Walpole's resignation at the beginning of 1742 caused a considerable hiatus among the political newspapers, and was accompanied by the prompt abandonment of the system of state-subsidized propaganda. The change of attitude on the part of the reconstructed administration appeared in the rapid and public downfall of Nicholas Paxton and Joseph Bell, who had been most directly responsible for the organization and distribution of newspapers and pamphlets as well as for the execution of the spasmodic policy of restraint. Both refused to give evidence before the parliamentary committee set up to enquire into Walpole's disposal of public funds and were ordered into custody.[94] Although they were released at the end of the session, Paxton had already been replaced as Treasury Solicitor while, later in the year, Bell was found guilty of fraud and dismissed from his position of Comptroller of the Post Office.[95] Paxton seems to have remained in touch with the Duke of Newcastle on press affairs,[96] but the functions that had accrued to their respective positions as a result of Walpole's concern with newspaper propaganda were not resurrected by subsequent ministries. The new administration's change of policy fundamentally altered the position of the *Daily Gazetteer*, and the immediate impact on the authors under Paxton's supervision, as well as on the paper's artificially boosted circulation, must have been considerable. Walpole's resignation was announced on the 11th February and on the 20th the *London Evening Post* opened its news section with a paragraph stating, "We hear *the Gazetteer Legion* are disbanded, and those Wretches that have prostituted the *Honour* and *Interest* of the Nation to the vilest Purposes, publickly defended *Bribery* and *Corruption*, and *ridiculed* and *despised* the Merchants and Traders of the City, *are turn'd adrift*, to live in that Obscurity, whence they were brought, *for such dirty Purposes*."[97] The following Monday, at the head of its own London news section, the *Gazetteer* carried a defiant answer to these remarks, stating that "As the *Gazetteer-Legion* never had any other Existence than in the *Imagination* of some of our *Brother News-Writers*, so they had certainly a Right to *disband* the *Troops* they had *rais'd* whenever they saw fit."[98] This was received ironically in the other opposition papers, and the *Craftsman* at the end of the week reported of the *Gazetteer's* authors "that their Muster-Master-General N— P— has been *order'd* to disband them,"[99] and subsequently devoted a derisively sympathetic essay to their hard lot.[100] The last payment for officially distributed copies of the *Gazetteer* appears from the Treasury accounts to have been made on 25 March 1741. Even so, it seems likely that the subsidy continued beyond this point, as was suggested by the *Champion's* report at the beginning of March 1742 that "A stop has been put to the *Gratis Circulation of Gazetteers* thro' the Post Office conduit, etc. by special Order from above."[101]

In spite of its changed position, the *Daily Gazetteer* continued publication,

The Solicitor Committed, or the Dumb Screen. Nicholas Paxton in Newgate after Walpole's resignation.

immediately adopting a modified policy that emphasized the nonpolitical side of the paper's content. After denying the existence of the Gazetteer-legion, the author went on to point out that "with respect to the other *Reflections* upon this Paper, we must take the Liberty of saying that they are very *ill founded,* our Pains and our Expense in procuring *Intelligence* useful to the *Mercantile* part of the World having been much greater than that of our Neighbours; and as to the conduct of the *Gazetteer* for the future, we hope, that if we deserve *better* of the Publick than *most* of our *Brethren,* we shall not be *worse* received; and in a just Confidence of this, we shall continue to use our utmost Intelligence and best Endeavours to *please all Parties* and to *offend none.*"[102] The paper continued to carry page-one essays and, although during the early Summer of 1742 it remained politically quiescent, Haig is wrong to suggest that the "writers of the time were content to allow the *Gazetteer* to proceed unmolested in its reformed state."[103] By the end of the year the paper had to some extent readopted its former pro-ministerial position, coming under increasingly hostile attacks from its opposition rivals. As early as July the *Champion's* news section contained a rumor of the reestablishment of the Gazetteer-Legion,[104] which was also ironically asserted in the *Westminster Journal* later in the year.[105] In November a letter in the *Craftsman* asserted that the previous Saturday "that Channel of Filth, the *Gazetteer,* which had been for some time, damm'd up, was again open'd; and in it a ridiculous Attempt was made, by one of the Corps of political *Whitsters,* to blanch those he had formerly help'd to blacken, with all the Grime of Styx itself."[106] This sort of comment was also linked with occasional attacks on the *Gazetteer's* principal political author. In December 1742 a letter was published in the *Westminster Journal* purporting to be from "Ralph Courtevil," in which the journal's author was asked to transfer his allegiance to the recently formed ministry, for which he would be "amply rewarded by the new *Muster-Master General* who is raising a new Corps of Political Hussars."[107] This may have been no more than a reflection of Courteville's former reputation. However, his continued association with the *Gazetteer* also appeared in a letter that he sent to the Secretary of the Treasury, James West, in 1747.[108] Courteville's position does not emerge clearly from his comments but it seems that he was still exercising some sort of oversight of the *Gazetteer's* essay content. After complaining of the seditious tendency of William Horsley's contributions,[109] he went on to remark that he had "lately intercepted two virulent Papers sent for Publication which would have been Prejudicial to your Hon.^r and given some Uneasiness." There is no direct evidence of continued financial support, but while Courteville assumed that Horsley might have been acting under West's orders, his request for patronage may itself suggest the continued existence of some official links. Although the *Gazetteer* continued to carry pro-ministerial essays, the volume of this material underwent a steady decline. Similarly, although the *Daily Advertiser* came under constant attack, particularly from commercial rivals, for supporting the new administration, it seems generally to have been accepted that this was more the result of a mistaken sympathy than of financial backing.[110]

The realignment of the remaining pro-Walpole papers behind the new ministry was paralleled by the action of their former opponents. A brief period of euphoria in the opposition press following Walpole's resignation was succeeded by an increasing disillusion with what was stated to be the rather shady compromise between the leading politicians. Consequently, by the end of 1742, all the papers that had opposed Walpole had taken up an equally hostile attitude toward the new administration. As in 1726 the reconstructed parliamentary opposition seems to have been aware of the value of a stake in the London press, although it does not appear that any consistent effort was made to use the established weekly papers that had anyway lost a good deal of their original prestige and bite. The *Craftsman* was still suffering from the results of the split in management of the late 1730s, William Rayner's rival paper seems to have continued to appear until 1746,[111] while Amhurst's retirement and death[112] had deprived the paper of its most experienced author.[113] *Common Sense* was in a similar position. Although no longer faced by its fratricidal competitor, *Old Common Sense*, the paper had been abandoned by its projector and principal author, Charles Molloy, and its former Jacobite connections may have made it seem a dubious vehicle for the sort of vigorous anti-Hanoverian attacks that formed the basis of the campaigns of the reestablished opposition.

Consequently, a new weekly paper entitled *Old England; or, the Constitutional Journal* by "Jeffrey Broadbottom" was set up, the first issue appearing early in the parliamentary session in 1743.[114] There is no evidence to suggest the steps by which it came into existence, although it seems likely that there was an organizational link with *Common Sense*. Two weeks after initial publication, the proprietors of *Common Sense* felt obliged to deny a rumor that they were abandoning their paper in favor of *Old England*, stating categorically "that we have no Interest, directly or indirectly, in *Old England* Journal and that we are absolutely strangers to the Author and Proprietors of the said Paper."[115] That this was at least partly untrue was indicated in March, when William Guthrie was arrested for essays appearing on the same day in *Common Sense* and *Old England*.[116] At the same time, both papers were printed by John Purser at his Fleet Street office[117] and, although he gave up nominal responsibility for *Old England* in November 1743, he continued as its *de facto* printer.[118] The disappearance of *Common Sense* at the end of 1743[119] may therefore have resulted from the sort of agreement rumored earlier rather than from commercial pressure from a more successful competitor. The links between *Old England* and the political opponents of the new administration can only be tentatively deduced. The title alone gave the paper an opposition flavor while the views it expressed were closely in line with those of the parliamentary opposition. Perhaps in an attempt to emphasize the connection, it was claimed in the first issue that publication would cease as soon as government was purged of its faults and opposition itself became unnecessary. Whether or not this traditional line was seen as realistic in parliamentary terms, in *Old England* the prospect of an end to publication continued to be put up as a real possibility. Following Lord Carteret's resignation it was suggested that Jeffrey Broadbottom was shortly going into retirement,[120] a claim that appeared more likely when Guthrie accepted a place from the new administration.[121] However, given the realities of political life, as well as those of the newspaper business, such comments were at best overoptimistic. It was soon found to be necessary to caution readers in a sequence of six title notices that "whereas some imagine that this Journal is now drop't; the Authors hereby beg leave to inform the Public, that the Week previous to the Publication of the final Paper, publick Notice will be given in this, and the other Papers."[122] The subsequent reestablishment of the political *status quo* led to the publication of a new announcement in which the author, "having now no Prospect of any Alteration but for the worse," stated that the paper would continue to appear.[123]

The publication of the vigorously anti-Hanoverian *Old England* early in 1743, possibly with political backing, may have prompted new moves among Jacobite supporters to reestablish a foothold in the London press. In May Thomas Carte wrote to the Pretender stressing the value of "a paper in which one might from time to time be sure of inserting anything proper to be drawn up and published for your M's service; the despair of getting such writings inserted hindering their being drawn on several very proper occasions that have been offered."[124] Carte put forward George Gordon's name as a potential projector and, while himself offering to obtain contributions, asked for a pension to be paid to Gordon when he had set up his paper. Nothing seems to have been done at this point, and although similar ideas continued to be put forward,[125] there is no clear indication that the *National Journal,* set up by Gordon in 1746 and rapidly suppressed, had any Jacobite support.

Both *Old England* and the *Westminster Journal* achieved a good deal of popularity in the early 1740s based on the quality of their political essay content. *Old England* maintained an unusual degree of virulence in its attacks on Lord Carteret's administration and the Hanoverian connection and Sir Charles Hanbury Williams, writing of an issue at the end of 1743, remarked that it spoke out "more than any other Paper that has been published in that Journal or indeed any other Paper I have read. I think the stile good and very inflammatory."[126] The *Westminster Journal,* as its subtitle of the *New Weekly Miscellany* suggested, based its appeal on a more flexible approach, including, for example, a large number of satirical dialogues between political characters, and, in the case of both papers, some use was made of illustrated material.[127] No circulation figures are available to suggest the extent of their popularity, although the immediate republication of a large number of their essays in pamphlet form is perhaps indicative of a good rate of sale.[128] The claims for remarkable demand in the advertisements for the *Old England* reprints are plausible if only in the light of the ministry's response to the paper.[129] The continued existence of both, itself suggests their success, and "Jeffrey Broadbottom" may not have been exaggerating when he stated at the time of his proposed retirement that "the Income, which from the single Success of the Paper with the Public, I am to sacrifice, by dropping it, would be no inconsiderable Addition to the Fortune of any private Person."[130]

However even before the rebellion with its attendant pressures, the commercial position of the opposition essay-papers had begun to crumble. The reconstruction of the ministry following Carteret's resignation deprived the parliamentary opposition of a good deal of its credibility, and the newspaper campaigns, still hammering at issues raised in the early days of the *Craftsman,* had an increasing air of unreality. The enforced modification in tone was therefore combined with growing public indifference and a general retrenchment seems to have taken place by the end of 1746. While the *Champion,* after a period of some obscurity, had collapsed the previous year,[131] the *Craftsman* itself was at a very low ebb. An epigram in the hostile *Gentleman's Magazine* headed "On the Cr——n, and its present Author, Not applicable to this Paper only," summed up the authors' position.

> C——he toils with malice from a wretched head,
> To animate a paper long since dead.
> So silly imps (we're told) their pranks exhibit
> In some dead body borro'd from a gibbet.[132]

The last copy of the main run in the Burney Collection is number 964 Saturday 22 December 1744 and, while only two further copies of this paper appear in the collection up to 1750, other surviving issues are isolated and hard to find.[133] At the same time, although apparently in a state of almost total commercial collapse, the paper survived, attracting some official attention,[134] and in one form or another it continued in publication to the end of the century. Both the *Westminster Journal* and *Old England* seem to have held their own, the former being recommended to readers of the abandoned *Universal Spectator*[135] and the latter increasing in size as a result, it was claimed, of an increased sale.[136] However, even these papers had lost a good deal of their original impact and it was subsequently asserted that both were written in the late 1740s by John Banks "without offence to any party."[137] In these circumstances the opposition essay-papers posed no real problems for the administration, and from the middle of the decade the authorities were able to rely largely on financial persuasion to combat any challenge in the London press. Those journalists who did not apply for support became the focus of a series of undignified auctions, which usually, as in the case of William Guthrie, James Ralph, and David Mallet, ended in favor of the government.

It was perhaps partly a symptom of the decline in the political temperature that the long-established dailies that still identified closely with political groups also lost ground. The *Daily Post* ceased publication in 1746, while the *Daily Gazetteer,* abandoned by Richardson in the same year, remained virtually moribund until the commercial take over of 1748. However, the established anti-ministerial bias remained in evidence among the full-priced London papers. The most successful was the *London Evening Post,* which continued to follow a consistently astringent opposition line and in 1747 Courteville claimed that he had written a political piece "which with a Guinea I sent to every Daily Paper, But as it was in favour of the Minister and Administration they one and all refus'd it."[138]

8
Political Control of the Press

The intricate relationship that developed at the beginning of the century between national politics and the London newspapers was not viewed with any enthusiasm by those holding office. The two centuries of state control over all forms of printed material that ended in 1695 were not forgotten by successive governments, and the idea of reintroducing some kind of pre-publication censorship lingered on.[1] However, in spite of recurrent efforts in parliament the dual interests of commerce and politics were unable to turn back the clock. The idea of a "free press" had taken root, and whatever the sharp and divergent views of Whigs and Tories on the practical limits of its use, a degree of consensus had been reached on the need for its existence. Even so, the position was never very clear-cut and fears of the introduction of a new system of licensing were still being widely expressed in the opposition papers of the late 1730s. Whether the Walpole administration had any such designs in view is not clear but the introduction of the Stage Licensing Act in 1737, accompanied by the vigorous legal action against the opposition press and remarks in the *Gazetteer* in favour of regulation,[2] combined to promote an air of perhaps artificially stimulated foreboding that lingered until Walpole's resignation. In 1742 the *Champion* contained a paragraph that summed up these fears. Its author stated that he had been "credibly informed, that if his late Honour had not *fallen*, the *Liberty* of the *Press*, till then the only remaining *Bulwark* of the *Liberties* of the People, could not have been preserv'd; a Bill, as 'tis said, having been actually prepared for subjecting it to the *Tyranny* of a *Licensor,* as *foretold* when the *like Restraint* was laid up on the *Stage*."[3]

If a general control of this kind became increasingly inappropriate and hard to justify, the government still had an armory of weapons at its disposal that could be deployed against the newspaper press. In the petitions submitted by members of the printing trade in favor of restraint, the relationship between commercial and political interests was regularly stressed. According to the author of one such appeal, the journeymen who were setting up in business in quite large numbers were obliged to "fall into the sad necessity of either Libelling or Invading Property, or else must subject themselves to Beggary and Starving."[4] The evident relationship between some anti-ministerial comment and commercial expediency may have influenced the authorities to focus on financial pressure as a means of suppressing or containing political activity in the London newspapers. The Stamp Act of 1712 in this context, combining a range of duties with some limited machinery for the regulation of printed material, can be seen as part of a general attempt to exert financial pressure on the press, although even at the time not everyone agreed that such legislation would work. The author of another petition to parliament claimed that "with all submission, nothing will contribute more to the *Spreading* and *Publishing Seditious Libels,* than the said Tax; because, it is to be fear'd that many of the *poorer Printers,* to prevent their Families from Starving, will be tempted to Print whatsoever shall be offer'd them, by any Person who will be at the Charge of the Impression, tho' at never so great a Hazard."[5] In the event, the Stamp Act did nothing to check the spread of opposition writing, although the prospect of imposing an overall political restraint on the press through oblique financial measures lingered, at least into the mid-1720s. Preserved among Walpole's private papers are two nearly identical schemes, submitted at this time by Thomas Robe, which made the familiar identification between the number of papers and the volume of opposition comment and which were designed to bring financial pressure to bear on the press generally.[6] Robe, who had himself written the *St. James's Journal* and was appointed Clerk of the Market in 1726, proposed "Means to reduce if not entirely destroy the Weekly Journals, Daily and Evening News Papers etc being all of them expensive, some useless, and others even pernicious to the Subject without the least Imputation of restraining the liberty of the press." He recommended that a government paper should be established to corner the market in advertisements and hence deprive the London papers of their chief source of revenue. As he stated in his second application, "these News-mongers with their abominable Moral and Political Letters, would soon be undone and rendered incapable to abuse daily and weekly the Liberty of the Press," pointing out as a particular advantage the possible extent of the *Craftsman's* losses.[7]

The growing financial strength of the London press, particularly with the intervention of the booksellers, must have made this sort of strategy appear increasingly eccentric.[8] At the same time piecemeal financial pressure continued to form an important element in the application of the law, the most powerful and adaptable instrument of political restraint available to successive governments. In private hands the law of libel was a constant problem to the proprietors of London newspapers whose publications with their extended, miscellaneous content and rapid production schedules were regularly involved in private libel actions. In the hands of government the legal process represented a serious threat to a large section of the London press. The publication of false news or of a wide and ambiguous range of political libels could be held to contravene existing legislation and throughout the Walpole period erratic attempts were made to check news-paper criticism by official prosecutions. Two studies of the law and its applications to the press in the first half of the eighteenth century have been made; Laurence Hanson's useful *Government and the Press, 1695–1763* and Frederick Siebert's less satisfactory *Freedom of the Press in England, 1476–1776*. Mr. Hanson's clear outline of the subject, based largely on material in the State Papers, includes the only detailed account of the administration of the law during the first half of the century. However, the picture he provides is incomplete and in some respects oversimplified, partly through lack of information on subsidiary figures on both political sides and partly through an underestimate of the short-term impact of the legal processes on the opposition press generally.

The responsibility for launching an official prosecution rested with the Secretaries of State, who took a very variable interest in press affairs. During Queen Anne's reign both Robert Harley and Lord Bolingbroke had been closely concerned in press control and subsequently Lord Townshend and the Duke of Newcastle were particularly active in such matters as the issue of warrants against newspaper personnel. There is no clear evidence of a coordinated policy toward the press or of the existence of special responsibilities in this area and to some extent at least, newspaper prosecu-tions were the result of an individual reaction by the Secretaries to political comment. Nonetheless, formal machinery was soon established at a lower level that was designed to facilitate official action. Harley had recognized the need early in the century for a reliable and comprehensive intelligence service and had himself established a network of agents, including the Queen's Messengers, who supplied him with regular reports on the press and copies of new publications appearing in England and Scotland.[9]

A very similar system of oversight was developed during the 1720s, although how far it was based on Harley's organization and how far Wal-pole himself was involved in its construction is not clear. The first moves coincided with Walpole's takeover at the Treasury and subsequently he was closely if inconsistently concerned in its direction. In 1721 a parliamentary committee was set up to investigate ways of achieving more effective re-straint,[10] and from 1722 Nicholas Paxton, assistant to the Treasury Solic-itor, was employed at a salary of £200 a year to check the content of all papers and pamphlets appearing in the British Isles.[11] He received copies of items published within the Bills of Mortality from the Messenger of the Press and of those published elsewhere from the Comptroller of the Post Office, reporting to the Secretaries of State on the presence of any seditious material. Paxton thus became a key figure as intermediary between the authorities and the press, a role that underwent a gradual extension, particularly after his promotion in 1730 to the position of Treasury Solic-itor. The practical importance and regularity of his supervisory respon-sibilities probably varied a good deal. Early in 1726 a Treasury memorandum stated that Paxton's services were an unnecessary expense and should be dropped,[12] and on the strength of this comment Hanson suggested that although payment of his extra salary continued, the function lapsed.[13] This was far from the case and while the galvanizing effect of the *Craftsman,* published at the end of the same year, probably reemphasized the need for some form of political scanning, Paxton continued to exercise an oversight of the London press that paralleled his supervision of the ministerial newspapers. A number of reports from both Paxton and Anthony Cracherode, who preceded him as treasury solicitor, were passed on to the Secretaries indicating items in the London papers that appeared to merit prosecution.[14] Paxton himself as Solicitor initiated proceedings on the basis of newspaper material[15] and his continued receipt of copies for scrutiny was indicated by the complaint of the Comptroller of the Post Office that at his death in 1744 Paxton still owed him £72 "for the Country newspapers paid for out of my pocket for the Government Service."[16] Paxton's role as quasi-licensor was also reflected in a wide range of personal allusions in contemporary literature,[17] and even after his arrest and dismissal he remained in touch with the authorities, recommending action against John Henley and the personnel of *Old England* shortly before his death.[18] There is no evidence that his successor, John Sharpe, maintained a comparable surveillance over political publications, and the failure to renew Paxton's role was a further indication of the new ministry's change of attitude toward the press.

Any formal supervision that existed during this period was supplemented by the employment of a variety of semi-official informers who, in liaison with the Secretary of State's office and the Treasury Solicitor, gave notice of the preparation of attacks on the ministry and accounts of the personnel engaged in their production. The number and identity of such informants remains largely obscure.[19] However, in the case of the professionally anonymous John Smith, correspondence dating from the early 1730s and surviving in Newcastle and State Papers help to illuminate the sort of relationship established between such shady characters and the authorities.[20] Smith addressed himself directly to the Duke of Newcastle and offered information on all subsidiary opposition writers. He initially claimed that "knowing the Character, Capacities, Stile, Persons and Interests of these Authors perfectly I will undertake (if your Grace comply with my Proposal) to give you proper intelligence of every thing they do— distinguishing to you those who spread Sedition for Bread and those who are the real Engines of the Anti-ministerial Party and accompany my Accounts with such Circumstances as shall prevent equivocating in Examinations."[21] Smith's terms were laid out at the end of the letter and probably conformed to the usual pattern of such arrangements.

1. That my letters be concealed and no attempts ever made to bring me as a Witness.

2. That I may be allowed to remain undiscovered and to carry on All by a Litteral Correspondence.

3. That once a Month your Grace will allow me what your Grace shall think my Services Deserve. I put myself into your Graces Hands and devote myself to your peculiar Service if you incline to grant these proposals be so good as to send an Advertisement to the Daily Journal in these Words Mr. Smith is desired to do as he proposes and what He desires shal be complied with."

This notice appeared at the head of column two on page two of the paper on Tuesday 19 September and Smith began to send Newcastle a series of letters containing a certain amount of trivia on press and other matters that he himself acknowledged to be unimportant, blaming this on "the Dead Season of the Year."[22] As a result he seems to have experienced considerable difficulty in getting paid, his last letter in October consisting of a short request for money.[23] The following April Smith again wrote to Newcastle warning of the probable activity of opposition writers at the close of the parliamentary session and offering weekly reports on every paper and pamphlet attacking the ministry in return for his bare expenses.[24] His renewed approaches were not greeted enthusiastically. An abbreviated note on the back of the offer stated "His letter received and former one which not answered it not offering any more—when his further correspondence shall prove so he will have suitable encouragement." There is no evidence of further contact.

Smith was apparently operating on the fringes of the newspaper world, but there are oblique indications that members of the personnel of some of the main opposition papers were in pay as informants.[25] The only evidence pointing directly to the activity of an individual in this risky area concerns the jobbing printer Doctor Gaylard who, besides running his own paper that was rapidly suppressed in the early 1720s, had worked on *Mist's Weekly Journal* and in the 1730s was employed on William Rayner's multifarious opposition projects.[26] In 1738 Gaylard received a £200 reward, authorized by Paxton, for his part in obtaining the conviction of the deranged Robert Nixon[27] and, in the following year, Dennis de Coetlogan was almost certainly referring to Gaylard when he described the activities of "a certain Compositor noted for having been an informer" and who was "suspected to follow the same vile practice."[28] Some support for this view appears in the mid-1740s, when Gaylard's wife was regularly employed by the Secretary of State's Office to supply information on seditious publications,[29] and it seems possible that Gaylard himself had established this link possibly under duress, sometime previously.[30] Rumors of minor personnel employed by the government were occasionally aired in contemporary literature,[31] and in view of the prominent part played by printers' men in the few successful prosecutions, it is possible that some financial links were established at this level.

A number of subsidiary sources also provided information on which legal action against the opposition papers was occasionally based. The check on material passing through the Post Office sometimes yielded results, particularly since the Saturday journals were sent into the provinces the previous Thursday, allowing prompt preventive action. The author of a letter published in the *Craftsman,* purporting to be an apology to Caleb D'Anvers from a Post Office employee, stated "I cannot help reflecting on my officious Behaviour in an Office which gave Me Power to open all suspicious Packets or Letters; by these Means I made Myself Master of the inclosed upon the *Thursday* before the usual Day of Publication, and immediately carry'd it to the *Secretary's Office,* from whence a Warrant issued, the Effects of which I fear both You and your Printer have too severely felt, though no Prosecution was ever commenced against that Paper."[32] Similarly, the official complaints lodged by the public figures, including diplomatic representatives, or contained in the presentments of the Middlesex Grant Jury occasionally prompted or justified the prosecution of the opposition papers.[33]

While the application of the law was assisted by an irregular flow of information from a variety of sources, the strength of the government's position in a newspaper prosecution lay in its control of the administrative processes applied through the Secretary of State's Office. The Secretaries themselves continued throughout this period to exercise the power of initiating proceedings on the basis of an *ex officio* information, a right that was regularly challenged in the principal opposition papers. However, the weight of newspaper criticism was leveled at the sequence of general warrants[34] and, although Hanson suggested that orders for the arrest of unnamed personnel were rare by the late 1730s,[35] such warrants were clearly among the government's principal instruments of restraint. An incomplete list prepared for use in the Wilkes case indicated that between 1725 and 1746 twenty-five were issued, of which twelve were directed at London newspapers, and the Secretaries' warrant books contain at least another four aimed at unspecified newspaper personnel.[36] Hardly any of the warrants of the period indicated the materials to be seized, using in each case a general formula that allowed very wide discretion. The Secretaries' warrants, sometimes originating at a lower level,[37] were put into effect by the King's Messengers who were attached to the office and who, during the 1730s, were often under the immediate direction of the Treasury Solicitor, Nicholas Paxton.[38] The Secretaries also occasionally examined prisoners and set bail. However, the routine administration of this type was usually left to subordinate officials, and although there was no clear division of duties in the office, experience as Gazetteer probably encouraged the assumption of a good deal of responsibility for such matters. The undersecretary, Charles Delafaye, who had held the position during Queen Anne's reign, and Samuel Buckley, Gazetteer for life from 1717 and a J.P. for Westminster, were often concerned in tracking down seditious publications,[39] as well as being regularly, although not exclusively, concerned in handling the minor administrative processes.[40]

Although the principal law officers were almost invariably consulted prior to the issue of a warrant and were usually responsible for the conduct of the ministry's case in court,[41] the Treasury Solicitor was the linchpin of the legal administration. Paxton, in particular, who by 1730 had already been concerned in the prosecution of at least twenty printers, booksellers, and authors,[42] was closely involved at every stage. In liaison with the Secretary's office, he was responsible for compiling the documents to be used in court, including detailed accounts of the crown witnesses,[43] and also for reporting to the Treasury on the progress of cases under consideration.[44] Paxton's belated accounts indicate that he was also responsible for organizing payment of the principal council and for payment and direction of the messengers in carrying out such minor functions as buying copies, checking bail, and entertaining witnesses.

A small number of government employees with specialist knowledge of the press were therefore in control of legal powers that themselves represented the principal threat to the personnel of the opposition papers. Arrest, seizure of property, confinement, payment of bail, and delay before trial hit all those concerned in newspaper production and distribution and even in the case of an eventual acquittal there was no prospect of recouping the often considerable costs involved.[45] The journalists of this period were as vulnerable to arbitrary harassment as other newspaper employees, and Hanson in his account considerably overemphasized the security of the author, failing to distinguish between the casual correspondent and the professional writer.[46] The loyalty of the printer or publisher under examination seems to have depended to some extent on the journalist's status in the paper and, while the identity of an employee was seldom withheld, that of a leading proprietor was as seldom supplied. This distinction seems to be reflected in John Purser's willingness to supply evidence against John Kelly as author of *Fog's* but flat refusal to answer questions on the authorship of *Common Sense* projected by the journalist Charles Molloy.[47] The author's position sometimes depended on an established agreement with the printer or publisher by which he was made liable for his work. In 1722 John Peele was authorized by Norton Defoe to identify him in case of prosecution, a guarantee that Robert Walker also obtained from the authors of some of his inflammatory pamphlets, while Francklin, on at least one occasion, was authorized by Amhurst to supply his name in self-defence.[48]

In most cases the authorities seem to have had little difficulty in establishing the identity of the essayists, who suffered a good deal of incidental hardship as a result of their activities. This was grimly reflected in the vagaries of Dennis de Coetlogan's career in journalism during the late 1730s. In 1737 official action against the *Alchymist* led to the seizure of his papers and his committal to Newgate where, according to his own unpublished account entitled "The Secrets of the English Inquisition Revealed," he remained without trial for six months, losing an eye in the process.[49] Two years later, after joining Rayner's staff, de Coetlogan was again arrested and, like his co-author Norton Defoe, apparently held in custody for a further three months before being released under the substantial bail of £100 with sureties.[50] The more important opposition journalists could also come under considerable pressure and William Guthrie, arrested in 1743 for writing both *Common Sense* and *Old England,* was committed to Newgate and placed under the exceptional bail of £1,000 with sureties.[51]

Although no London journalists seem to have been tried and convicted in this period, suspended action following release on bail probably imposed a real check on their political activity. John Kelly, after his release from Newgate, was obliged to attend the King's Bench for four consecutive terms,[52] while Matthias Earbery, arrested for writing the *Universal Spy* in 1733, was still receiving notice of trial in 1738.[53] Nonetheless, the real security of the journalist rested in the virtual impossibility of establishing a watertight case. These difficulties appeared most clearly in the failure of the authorities to obtain a verdict against Nicholas Amhurst as author of the *Craftsman,* or even to bring him to trial, in spite of the fact that he was first examined during action against the sixteenth issue.[54] Ten years later, in July 1737, a special effort was made to pin a charge on him. Following the initial examinations of the *Craftsman's* personnel, Lord Chancellor Yorke wrote to Newcastle recommending Amhurst's arrest as a printer's workman named Perry was prepared to testify that the copy of the material under prosecution was in his hand.[55] He went on to suggest that the arrest be deferred "till after Haines hath been examined; because, as Haines appears to be most trusted, if Amhurst should be taken up immediately upon his being examined, he may suspect that Haines has made some discovery and be the more ready to speak." Amhurst was arrested and held in custody for ten days before being released on a writ of Habeas Corpus. However, the case against him had to be dropped—Haines by his own admission having "grossly prevaricated" during his examination at Hampton Court,[56] while the material witness, Perry, died in custody the following February.[57] Consequently, Amhurst remained beyond the reach of the law, as did the equally notorious Charles Molloy, who does not appear to have been arrested at any time during this period, although the seizure of his papers in 1739 suggests that he also suffered some harassment.[58]

By comparison, the printers were both easier to get at and more vulnerable to legal action. Identification could often be made through the paper's imprint and, although there was no legal obligation to supply any information concerning the printer and publisher,[59] the business side of the organization required the use of an accurate and generally known name and address. However, while the risks involved led Francklin, Nutt, and Purser to have their names replaced on the principal opposition weeklies by subsidiary personnel, there remained a good deal of ambiguity over the printer's identity. In 1737 Charles Bennet admitted allowing Walter Baker to use his name on the imprint of the *Alchymist* "as being a Freeman of the City of London which Baker is not."[60] The prevalence of piracy also complicated the issue. In 1718, for example, Francis Clifton warned readers of his *Oxford Post* against possible sharp practice by James Read. "I'm credibly inform'd," he announced, "this Grand Pirate Printer designs to invade my Right, by Printing and publishing a Paper by the Name of the Oxford Post, as also that he'l put at least the two First Letters of my Name to it, and get the same Figure at the Frontispiece; I have therefore only this to beg that my Readers will give themselves the trouble of looking that my Name be Right Spelled and at full length, at the Bottom of the first and last Page, for if one Letter thereof differs from this Present Paper, you may assure your selves the whole is spurious."[61] Later, Richard Francklin claimed that Robert Walker had put his name "to some pamphlets or papers as the printer and publisher thereof; but he has not thought it worth while to go to the law with him on that account."[62] Such practices gave at least superficial conviction to the printers' claims under examination that papers carrying their names were not in fact their work. Francklin regularly denied his association with the *Craftsman* and Meres, on at least one occasion, claimed to have nothing to do with the *London Evening Post* while under prosecution.[63]

Government action, though comprehensive in its effect, was focused on the printers of the principal opposition papers, and the most consistent and vigorous measures were aimed at dislocating the business of newspaper production. During the early 1720s Nathaniel Mist was one of the principal sufferers at the hands of the authorities, although a perhaps even more concentrated series of legal measures were taken against Thomas Payne as printer of the *True Briton*.[64] It was remarked with some justice in 1725 that the authorities intended to keep him in a state of poverty by "perpetual Indictments, Informations, Fines, Imprisonments etc."[65] With the publication of the *Craftsman*, Richard Francklin also became a regular target for legal action and the sort of pressures that could be, and were, brought to bear were clearly demonstrated in the case of his employee, Henry Haines, who in 1737 was at the center of two major prosecutions. According to an account published in the *Craftsman* itself, the initial arrest in July under a general warrant was carried out with the utmost violence. Seven unidentified persons entered the Bow Street office at about 10 o'clock on Wednesday night and, after ordering Haines to stop work began to search the premises,

> leaving *Haines* and *one of the Workmen* in his *composing Room* by themselves; upon which *Haines* desired the *Workman* to shut Them out, imagining them to be either *Bailiffs*, or *Thieves*; but upon This, Mr. *Cowell*, one of the Messengers, burst open the Door with such Violence, that it knock'd the Man down that had bolted it, then enter'd the Room with a PISTOL

in his Hand, and swore by God he would shoot the said *Haines* and *Workman* through the Head, if they offer'd to make the least Resistance; and then said, and not till then, they were *King's Messengers*, and had Authority from *his Majesty* for what they did.[66]

The messengers and their assistants seized the forms of type in which the *Craftsman* had been composed,[67] as well as Haines's business records, including "the *Shop-Book, Advertisement Book*, and other *Books of Account*," taking Haines himself and his workman into custody. The same account claimed that Haines was confined for two weeks before examination and for a further two weeks afterwards, the Messenger submitting him to a certain amount of dubious treatment. Even after examination it was claimed he was "not suffer'd to come out of the room, in which he was confined, but once for a Fortnight; and the *Messenger*, under Pretence of securing him the better, though lock'd up in his *strong Room*, lay in the Bed with Him during the whole Time, except three Nights." Haines was finally bailed at £300 with two sureties, a sum that it was later claimed was "*two hundred* more than has usually been ask'd in the same Case, and from Persons in much better Circumstances."[68] Even before his case came to trial, further action was launched by the authorities, and in December the Bow Street office was again raided and the entire impression of the *Craftsman*, ready for London publication the following day, was seized and a number of workmen arrested.[69] The question of surety for good behavior being *sub judice*, Haines was released without further bail and although apparently urged by Francklin to renege,[70] surrendered himself for sentence.

Haines's treatment at the hands of the authorities does not appear to have been unusually severe. In 1721 Francis Clifton, in appealing to Delafaye for relief, claimed that "The Misery and Poverty the Committm[t] to Newgate and the Removal from thence, the Spoiling of that little Letter I had by kicking it out and battering the Forms is almost inexpressible."[71] The printers of a number of papers under prosecution, such as John Meres, who was more than once confined in Newgate,[72] or John Purser, who was obliged to find more substantial bail,[73] had at least as much cause for complaint as Haines. Very few of the printers seem to have been taken to court, partly perhaps because of the difficulty of obtaining a conviction.[74] However, when the case was carried through, the printer could face substantial penalties to add to the expense, and with the creation of the Special Jury in 1730, the prospects of a conviction were considerably increased. Francklin, after at least two previous trials,[75] was sentenced in 1731 to a year's imprisonment and £100 fine, and Haines in 1737 to double the amount in each respect, while both were placed under a substantial bond for seven years' good behavior.

If the printer was the main target of government action and under the law was held to be responsible for the content of any of his publications, action, particularly under a general warrant, also tended to implicate subsidiary personnel. The workmen shared the printer's legal responsibility and were therefore liable to the same rigors of prosecution. The author of the *Craftsman* strongly condemned this position, pointing out how unreasonable it was:

> that the *common Labourers of the Press* who get an hard Livelyhood by the Sweat of their Brows, without any other View, should be liable to the same strict Inquisition, Expenses and Penalties. The *Compositors* themselves whose Business it is to put the Letters together, which they pick out of different Cases, one by one, have often the Copy deliver'd to them by Peacemeal, and in disjointed Fragments, without any Coherence or Connection, one Part of it being given to one Compositor, and another to another for the sake of Expedition; especially in periodical writings; so that they have seldom any Opportunity to read or judge of what they were composing. The Press-men are still more in the Dark; for as soon as they have receiv'd the Frames ready set from the *Compositors* They have nothing to do but work them off as fast as They can; and the Devil, as he is call'd, is only the Servant of the rest, whom they hire to run upon Errands, and do all their Drudgery. Many of *these poor Creatures* cannot so much as read; or if they can, is it to be supposed that They are able to judge what is strictly speaking a Libel, or not a Libel, which is so far from being any easy Point to determine, that it often puzzles the *nicest Splitters of Cases*?[76]

Such arguments received no support from the courts[77] and, during proceedings against Mist's paper in 1728, his entire staff as well as that of the neighboring printer William Burton, whose press had been used to work off part of the edition, were taken up.[78] In July 1737 similar action taken against Haines was accompanied by the arrest of six of his workmen, while in December at least another five of his employees were arrested.[79]

The legal processes, which imposed a considerable strain on the principals, had a proportionately greater impact on the minor personnel. Mist's employees, who were left to bear the brunt of government action, were placed under exceptionally high bail after being committed to Newgate.[80] His housekeeper and the two compositors were expected to find £400 each with sureties, and the pressmen and two apprentices £300 each also with sureties. Although these substantial sums may not have been enforced, Haines's employees, arrested in 1737, were less fortunate. Those taken up in July were expected to find what was described as "*extraordinary Bail*"[81] and in October the author of the *Craftsman* stated that "several of the *Workmen* are still in *Custody* and God knows when any of Them will be discharged without an *Habeas Corpus* for every one of Them, as well as *Bail*, which must be very *expensive* as well as *troublesome*."[82] In December they were still in custody and, while Perry died in the hands of the Messengers over six months after being taken up, it is not clear when the others were released or on what terms. The situation of the workmen arrested in

December was equally hopeless. The two journeymen, Henry Stapleton and Charles Robinson, petitioned the Secretary's office for release in February, claiming that by that time they had been "obliged to make away with what small Matters we had in the World," and that their families were starving.[83] A month later a third employee, Robert Wilson, sent in a desperate petition claiming that as a "foreigner" he was completely unable to find the necessary bail.[84] However, they all remained in custody until April and May 1738, when they were released under their own recognizances of £50.[85]

The occasional mass arrests of subsidiary personnel were perhaps prompted by the need for material proof to support the crown case and the petitions from the workmen each contained fulsome offers of evidence. Their potential value to the authorities was reflected in the important part played by the printers' devils in securing the few convictions of this period. Thomas Randal was described on the list of Mist's personnel as "a good one who gave us the clue to printing and publishing," and subsequently the second devil, James Ford, claimed responsibility for the convictions obtained the following year.[86] Haines, in 1738, also seems to have been convicted largely on evidence supplied by his devil Samuel Griffin.[87] Such complicity with the authorities suggest the pressure that could be exerted through application of the law since, as Hanson has pointed out, a strict code of personal loyalty existed within the printing trade.[88] In their petition Robinson and Stapleton stated that Haines had reported "that we were the two Persons that were the Cause of the Paper being stopp'd before publish'd, so that no One of the Trade will care to employ us if the Matter be not clear'd up," while Griffin claimed that he was "in a starving condition" as a result of being blacklisted.[89] Ford was apparently secured by a place in the customs but, as Griffin's petition suggests, such treatment could not always be relied on. It was clearly not worth the authorities' while to follow up action against most subsidiary personnel. although the exceptional circumstances of the Mist case in 1728 led to charges being pressed against his employees, who received a series of harsh sentences. The *London Evening Post*, which regularly emphasized this sort of material, gave the result in full, reporting that "John Clarke, the Press-man, for printing and publishing, was sentenced to stand three Times in the Pillory, viz. at Charing Cross, Temple Bar, and the Royal Exchange, and to suffer six Months Imprisonment; Robert Knell the Compositor, to stand twice in the Pillory, once at Charing Cross, and once at the Royal Exchange, and also to suffer six Months Imprisonment; Joseph Carter (the Apprentice, and a Press man) to walk round the four Courts in Westminster-Hall, with a Paper on his Forehead, denoting his Offence, and to suffer one Months Imprisonment; Amy Walker (Mist's Maid) for publishing the said Paper, to be sent to the House of Correction for six Months, there to be kept to hard Labour, and to be stript down to her Waist, and receive the Correction of the House."[90]

The crown's case against the printers of opposition papers often rested heavily on evidence of publication and during the initial stages of a prosecution the Messengers brought up copies, sometimes from the printer himself, but also from a variety of distribution centers, for use in court. Consequently, although major publishers were seldom taken up, the pamphlet sellers were regularly implicated and newspaper warrants usually named two or three of the London mercuries. Mrs. Dodd and Mrs. Nutt, as major newspaper distributors,[91] were under recurrent attack in this way, although both also appeared on the imprint of pro-ministerial publications[92] and to some extent their links with the opposition press were dictated by the exigencies of the trade. Mrs. Dodd summed up the mercuries' dilemma in this respect when she stated in a petition to Newcastle in 1731 that "the business sometimes compels me to sell Papers that give Offence, but I must beg leave to Declare Sincerely that what Papers I sell in just Praise of our Happy Government, far exceed the other in Number. Hard Case! that I must either offend where I am shure I would not, or else starve my Poor Babes."[93] Such pleas were largely ineffective and the mercuries continued to be unfairly subjected to the same administrative pressures as the newspaper personnel. In 1728, for example, in spite of a claim of serious illness, Mrs. Dodd was committed to Newgate,[94] while Mrs. Nutt was more than once during the 1730s placed under bail of £200.[95] The seizure of material under attack could also be financially damaging,[96] and in the cases that were followed up, the mercuries became little more than pawns in the game, facing prosecution or acting as witnesses according to council's opinion.[97] Although there is no clear evidence of a conviction, Mrs. Nutt was unsuccessfully taken to court at the age of nearly seventy and prosecuted for publishing Mist's Jacobite paper of 1728.[98]

The impact of the legal processes on individuals working within the organization of the London press was often considerable, but their effect on the structure and content of the newspapers themselves was rather more complex. Government prosecutions within these twenty years were focused in three main periods, although sporadic action continued to be taken in the interim against items judged to be unusually flagrant. The first and most protracted legal campaign followed publication of the *Craftsman* in 1726. Prior to the successful prosecution of Francklin five years later, ten issues of the paper were acted against,[99] and at least another two were given official consideration.[100] A parallel series of actions continued to be leveled at Mist's paper, which had been under attack since its first appearance. During 1728 four issues were prosecuted between July and September,[101] although attention was focused on number 175, which contained the Duke of Wharton's treasonable attack on the Royal Family. In spite of some modification in tone, four further issues of the paper under its amended title of *Fog's* were prosecuted in the period up to 1732.[102] These concentrated proceedings sometimes involved entirely unrelated papers in which, either by accident or design, material under attack was reprinted. A number of provincial papers were implicated in the major prosecutions of *Mist's* and the *Craftsman*,[103] and the sort of chain reaction that could occur in London itself was indicated by the handling of a fictional speech by the Alciade of Seville in 1729. This item formed the basis of a prosecution of the *Craftsman*, the *London Evening Post*, the *St. James's Evening Post*, and the *Evening Post*, regardless of their variable political sympathies.[104]

Following Francklin's conviction and sentence for printing and publishing Bolingbroke's *Hague Letter*, the application of consistent legal pressure was abandoned and it seems possible that a deliberate decision was taken to step up the distribution of ministerial papers as a viable alternative. Between 1732 and 1737 neither the *Craftsman* nor *Fog's* was prosecuted, although at least three issues of the *Craftsman* were considered,[105] and the most regular attacks were focused on the *Daily Post Boy* for its foreign news reports. However, in 1737 a sudden and comprehensive series of actions were launched against the opposition journals. These followed the passage of the Stage Licensing Bill and were heralded by a presentment of the Middlesex Grand Jury which, after reflecting on "the Impunity with which the most vile and infamous Libels have been published against the Administration," stated that "in order therefore to put a Stop, as far as it is in our Power, to that unexampled Licentiousness of the Press which has of late years prevailed, and to deter others, by so just and necessary a Prosecution, from committing Crimes of the like Kind we present the Authors, Printers, and Publishers of a most Scandalous, Seditious and Treasonable Libel intitled, the *Alchymist; or, Weekly Laboratory*."[106] Almost simultaneous action was taken against this paper, the *Craftsman*, and the newly revitalized *Fog's*, while at the end of the year further measures were taken against both the *Craftsman* and *Old Common Sense*.[107] The flurry of prosecution did not continue beyond the end of the year and although *Common Sense*, *Old Common Sense*, Rayner's *Craftsman*, the *London Evening Post*, and the *Daily Post* all subsequently came under attack, the increasingly unfavorable political atmosphere probably influenced officials to relax the use of legal pressure still further. During the last two years of the Walpole administration no London newspaper, even the active and virulent *Champion*, was prosecuted.

While the reconstructed ministry of 1742 displayed a new indifference toward the press, the continued presence of the Duke of Newcastle, Lord Hardwicke, and Sir Dudley Ryder made it unlikely that the opposition papers would continue to escape prosecution. In an interview with the King in 1742, Hardwicke urged that the time was ripe for a general repression of opposition publications since "those, who, perhaps, used to patronize and support them, will turn against them, and juries will be found now ready to convict them."[108] Perhaps because public opinion was less favorable than anticipated, no action was taken by the authorities until 1743, when the publication of *Old England* evoked an immediate response.

The sixth issue was prosecuted together with *Common Sense* and an attempt made to suppress the seventh[109] while, prior to the rebellion, three further issues came under vigorous attack.[110]

The concentrated application of the law against opposition essay-papers seems to some extent, to have been aimed at achieving a total suppression and, in the case of the mushroom growth of publications relying entirely on sales revenue, the authorities achieved a good deal of success. The *Universal Spy* in 1732, the *Alchymist* in 1737, and the *National Journal* in 1746, all papers lacking financial stability, went out of business as a direct result of official prosecutions. The principal opposition papers, on the other hand, underpinned by a variable combination of backing and popular success, survived recurrent attack with the loss only of isolated issues. However, their continued survival has obscured the substantial modifications in organization and content that were imposed by the law and the authorities could also have claimed an at least partial success in this area. The business side of Mist's paper was entirely dislocated by the continuous pressure of the law and the principals were one after another harried out of the country. Mist himself, after a period of imprisonment in 1727, during which he escaped briefly from the King's Bench, withdrew to the Jacobite community in France. He was joined the following year by his manager, Mr. Bingley, who had been on the run during most of the early part of 1728,[111] and following the prosecution of number 175, his printer, John Wolfe, reneged on his sureties and also fled to France. Consequently, the failure of the authorities to obtain a satisfactory conviction was largely offset by the managerial upheavals that permanently removed the most extreme element. Mist's paper lacked substantial political backing, but even in the case of the more securely established *Craftsman* legal action had an immediate impact on the diffuse business structure. The first signs of strain appeared in the failure to establish an accessible address for the paper's correspondents. In the third issue readers were invited to write to Caleb D'Anvers at Ballards Coffee house in Albermarle Street,[112] and in number six this was altered to the Cocoa Tree Chocolate house in Bridges Street, Covent Garden.[113] In number sixteen, the first issue to be officially acted against, a notice was published stating that *"the Master of the* Cocoa-Tree *Chocolate house having, for certain Reasons, published an advertisement in the Courant of Wednesday last, that he will receive no more letters directed to the author of this paper, we desire our Correspondents for the future, to direct them to* T. Warner *in Pater-Noster-Row; and if they have favoured us with any letter within these five days past, they are desired to signify the same, we having received none within that Time."*[114] Much more serious was the apparent upheaval that followed the initial legal action. Both the printer Samuel Aris and the publisher Thomas Warner seem to have precipitately dropped the *Craftsman*, and the convulsion that occurred at this point was indicated by the four-day delay in the publication of number 18. It was probably this official action that obliged Francklin to open the printing office at his shop in

Covent Garden and to take over publication of the paper himself, providing the authorities with a clearly identifiable target for future attack. It also seems likely that the legal measures acted as a deterrent to the mercuries who, although unwilling or financially unable to drop the *Craftsman*, were perhaps less inclined to circulate it freely. The way this form of discouragement worked in practice appeared after Francklin's sentence in 1732, when it was stated in the paper that "last *Saturday* a Report was industriously spread about the Royal Exchange that the Printer of *this Paper* was taken up that Morning, with a Design, as we apprehend of intimidating the Publishers and Hawkers from selling it; but as the Report was soon discover'd to be groundless, it dy'd away, like other mean Artifices of the same Kind, without any Effect."[115] Legal pressure continued to impose a considerable strain on the organization of the principal opposition papers and the prosecutions of 1737 contributed a good deal to the damaging splits in management that took place in both the *Craftsman* and *Common Sense*. This was most clear in the case of the *Craftsman*, which broke up as a direct result of Haines's imprisonment.[116]

Although application of the law did not put a stop to political criticism, it did impose some curbs on the content of the leading opposition essay-papers. The sort of attack contained in number 175 of Mist's paper was clearly well beyond the accepted limit and the indications are that its appearance was a deliberate provocation, perhaps a last fling by the Jacobites in the face of the journal's declining usefulness as a vehicle of extremist propaganda. The special printing arrangement, the doubts of the workmen, and the unusually large edition all suggest premeditated action, while it was rumored that Wolfe received a sizable indemnity for inserting the copy.[117] In its new form the paper was generally recognized as more cautious in tone,[118] and although *Fog's* continued to give vigorous support to the legitimate opposition, the law can be said to have blunted its extremist edge. It was a further application of the law that subsequently obliged Mist to remove the paper from the political struggle altogether. Similarly, the attacks on the *Craftsman* clearly imposed some restraints on its political content, and such a dramatic ministerial success as the conviction of Francklin in 1731 seems to have cast a shadow over the paper and the publication of opposition material generally. According to the informer Smith, this event "was of infinite Service" and he assured Newcastle that "the Press is not likely to prove troublesome to the Government as it has been heretofore. Francklyn's Prosecution has made him very wary as your Grace may perceive by the few Pamphlets he has published since."[119]

To some extent the impact of the law depended on random political circumstances and the period of its greatest influence as a curb on opposition writing occurred in the mid-1740s with the emergence of the Jacobite threat. The swing in public opinion behind the ministry and the repeals of the Habeas Corpus Act both made the opposition press more vulnerable to attack. In March 1744 Paxton wrote to Newcastle advising immediate action against the personnel of *Old England* as "if there be any body to be try'd for Libels, I think, according to the present Disposition of the people, they may be convicted in London, or any where else."[120] The effects of the more protracted repeal of Habeas Corpus the following year were subsequently outlined by the author of *Old England* in a rather wild essay describing Jeffrey's escape from "a terrible State Bull" with the help of his "faithful Bull-Dog Habeas." "But alack-a-day!" he wrote,

> there is no contending with Power supported by Numbers. The Coalition frightened by a few ragged Highlanders call'd in the House of Mono-syllabae to their Assistance, who laying hold of poor Habeas, muffled up his Chops and put him under such an Inchantment and suspended all his Faculties and Virtues for Six Months; and thereupon issued out divers State-Bulls with broad Philactories in their Front, direfully inscrib'd *Treasonable Practices*; which had such a terrible effect upon the useful Part of his Majesty's good Subjects inhabiting the Garrets of Grubstreet, that they became speechless in their political Capacity, or were so taken with Cramp in their Fingers, that they could hardly hold a Pen between them ever since, and to this Misfortune most of the wrong Measures taken since at C—t are suppos'd to be owing, and these political Writers were restrain'd from their weekly Lucubrations in aid of the State: Even Jeffrey himself became cautious and consequently dull, so that the People did not so much follow after him, whereas he was much follow'd and esteem'd among the Populace as Dr. Rock or Orator H—y.[121]

Although prosecution could therefore have a considerable impact on the leading opposition papers, their capacity for survival under pressure emphasized the unsatisfactory side effects of legal action that discouraged its regular use. The considerable boost to the notoriety, and hence the sales, of a paper that resulted from legal action was generally accepted. In 1730 it was claimed to be a usual device on the part of the proprietors of the *Craftsman* "to write something every now and then for which they hope to be sent for by a Messenger, otherwise the Paper is supposed to have lost its Poignancy,"[122] while in reply to Francklin's complaints on the expense of the prosecution the author stated that this was ludicrous since "the very Papers on this Account will be reprinted (at least 'tis usual to reprint them on such Occasions, or, which is the same thing, to print at first a more than usual Number) and he may get twenty or thirty pounds by them." The shortcomings of Francklin's sentence as a financial curb on the production of the *Craftsman* were even more fully described by the same author two years later. After assessing the annual income from the paper at be-tween£1,600 and £1,800, he went on to remark "Here has been now one Prosecution against him, I admit it a chargeable one too, on which he is fin'd £100 and a Year's Imprisonment, which (by the Way) is in the *King's-Bench*, where he has the Liberty of the *Rules*, I say, *all this chargeable Prosecution, cannot amount to above a Quarter of a Year's Gain of the Paper.*"[123] On the other hand, the legal attacks invariably provoked a response in the press where each stage of the process was fully reported and where, particularly in the *Craftsman* and *Old England*, defiance of the authorities was intermingled with protracted condemnation of the illegality of such measures.[124] These defects were clearly understood by the authorities' advisers, and in 1734 the Attorney General, urging Newcastle not to take action against the *Craftsman*, pointed out that "Prosecutions of this sort ought to be avoided as much as possible; For papers of this kind, If not taken notice of, seldom survive the week, and fall into very few hands; But when a Prosecution is commenced Every body is enquiring after them, or they are read by thousands, who otherwise would never have heard of them. Besides upon Tryals of this sort, His Majesty's Enemies always take an opportunity of writing up the mob against the Government, and let the Success be one way or the other, It always affords a Handle for Complaint."[125]

The government's attempts to control the production and content of the opposition newspapers by prosecution were paralleled by the efforts to impose a check on distribution. In London itself the coffee-houses, as a principal outlet for the press, were apparently subject to some forms of pressure, but although plans were put forward prior to 1725 to withhold the licenses of houses displaying papers under prosecution, they were not followed up.[126] In this area the opposition were able to exert at least reciprocal pressure. In 1733, for example, the author of the *Free Briton* claimed that "It is not many Months since a great deal of Application was used, and the Point was at last effected, in compelling some *Coffee-houses about the Royal Exchange* to exclude certain *Papers on the side of the Administration*. What Triumph, what Joy had the *Craftsman* and his Friends, in the Success of this *Low Jobb!*"[127] However, if the coffee-houses remained largely independent, the Post Office as a government agency was used consistently, under the Walpole administration at least, to restrict the national circulation of the opposition papers. The controller of the Inland Office, Joseph Bell, who was a staunch political supporter of Walpole, and who was closely involved in the distribution of subsidized papers, played an important supervisory role in this area of restraint. The Post Office was one of the earliest targets of the *Craftsman's* campaigns, and it seems possible that some attempt was made initially to oversee the private correspondence directed to the paper. According to the author, the regulations regarding the opening of letters were being evaded "by leaving a *Blank dormant Warrant* at the Office, to be fill'd up at the Discretion of the *Postmaster general*, by the Direction and for the service of his Principles, as occasion requires."[128] These remarks were probably stimulated by the paper's own experiences and Post Office action may account for the notice appearing shortly after the first prosecution, which stated that correspondents "*who have anything curious to communicate, are desir'd, for a particular Reason, to send by a* special *Messenger*."[129] It does not appear that official checks on newspaper correspondence were widely used, but they were certainly attempted in special cases. In 1735 George James and John Wilford were arrested for printing and publishing the *Daily Post Boy* of 30 May containing an inflammatory letter from the Hague.[130] Neither would or perhaps could identify the source of the material,[131] and shortly after this examination Newcastle authorized Edward Carteret, Post Master General, "to stop, open, and send to me all Letters, that shall come to your office by the Mails from Holland, directed to George James of London Printer, to T. Woodward in Fleet street Bookseller, and to John Wilford near St. Pauls Stationer."[132] Such action does not seem to have represented a real threat, and much more concern was expressed over the tampering with private letters and packets that contained copies of suspect or proscribed newspapers. In the late 1720s it was stated that it was difficult to send the *Craftsman* even ten miles without interception.[133] Similar problems were claimed in the late 1730s by *Common Sense*,[134] while the author of the *Champion* in 1740 hoped that subscribers would take care in forwarding the paper, "scarce four Champions in Twelve having at present the good Fortune to find their Way by the Post tho' the Superscriptions are written ever so legible."[135]

The interception of private correspondence was linked with efforts to check the activities of the clerks, whose indiscriminate attitude toward political papers caused some concern in the late 1720s. Action was ordered by the Lords of the Treasury to prevent the distribution of opposition material,[136] and the steps taken at this point seem to have had an immediate effect on the *Craftsman*. In January 1728 a notice appeared in the paper stating that the proprietors had "received complaints from our Readers in all parts of the Kingdom that the usual Conveyance of our Paper the Clerks of the Post Office has been lately interrupted; on which Occasion they received the following letter. 'Sir, the *CRAFTSMAN is to be sent* no longer. Be pleased to order *what Paper* you would have in the *Room of it*.' But as we intend to continue this Paper, we hope some other Method of Conveyance will be found out, in which we shall assist them to the utmost of our Power."[137] Whether the ban on the *Craftsman*, extended in 1728 to include *Mist's Weekly Journal*,[138] was subsequently maintained and enforced is not clear. However, at the time of heightened political activity following the Excise crisis, the ministry seems to have attempted to tighten up its control over the passage of opposition papers through the office. The ministry's pragmatic intentions were indicated by an unsigned note among Walpole's papers that almost certainly belongs to this period and that simply stated "Memorandum. To put a stop at the Secretary's Office and at the Post Office to the Circulation of the *Craftsman, Fog's Journal, The London Evening Post* and *Daily Post*."[139] The first two were already perhaps under some sort of proscription, while the *Daily Post* probably had a very small country sale and consequently the order made in October 1733 seems to have been principally directed at the *London Evening Post*, which reacted sharply. On October 13 it appeared with a title notice stating that the clerks had been ordered not to send the paper to their customers as a result of the Excise comments, ending with the hope that readers would *"either have the Said Paper sent to them by their Friends, or some other Way convey'd to them, and not suffer a* Court Paper *to be forc'd upon them."*[140] Shortly after the publication of Bell's orders on the distribution of ministerial papers, the *London Evening Post* contained the circular letter sent out by the clerks, which stated, "Sir Being Order'd the 11th Instant to omit sending *London Evening Posts* is the Occasion of my sending you others; and shall continue to do until I receive your Direction therein."[141] The ministry's action was advertised in the leading opposition weeklies, readers being recommended to deal direct with their booksellers or Samuel Neville, the paper's printer.[142] To some extent action of this kind by the ministry may have stimulated sales in the same way as prosecutions and the proprietors announced in November that "Since the late Attempt to restrain the Liberty of the Press the Sale of this Paper is considerably increased" and that consequently it would be enlarged at no extra charge to the public.[143] Even so, any form of circulation restraint was potentially damaging to a paper of this type and while the increase in space may have reflected the need for greater advertising revenue, the price increase to 2d. in April could also have been a sign of financial pressure exacerbated by the Post Office squeeze.[144] Instructions continued to be given to the clerks throughout the period, Bell apparently exercising a general supervision,[145] and the circulation of *Common Sense* in 1739 and the *Champion* in 1740 seems to have been forbidden, the author of the latter remarking "The Clerks of the Road not relishing a certain News-Paper called the *Champion*, it is not permitted to visit the Country by the Post, for fear, perhaps, it shall quarrel with the *Gazetteer* upon the Road."[146]

During the first half of the eighteenth century, government controls formed an important part of the framework within which the development of the London press took place. To some extent the lapse of the license in 1695 was the first of the false dawns that recurred in the history of the English newspaper. To contemporaries the "free press" that emerged was defined only by the absence of state intervention through prepublication censorship. In practice, within the sphere of politics, the pragmatic controls that were applied were firm enough. Whatever the shortcomings of the system of oversight, the difficulty of obtaining a conviction, and the inevitable increase in public interest that accompanied an official prosecution, the law of libel was a powerful instrument. By limiting the range of political comment and effectively preventing the appearance of material that could be described as extremist, it fixed the boundaries of political debate. At the same time, application of the law ensured that only those papers with sound financial backing, whether provided by booksellers or politicians, could survive. The legal process bore heavily on a wide range of committed and uncommitted newspaper personnel, providing a continuous check on the level of political conformity. In this way the law and the political system helped to reinforce the process by which the booksellers were consolidating ownership of the newspaper press in their own hands. Both interests took active steps against maverick individuals and groups who were likely to attempt to use political comment for commercial purposes. Neither was prepared to see an unchecked growth of newspaper publication. The politicians, particularly those involved in successive administrations, probably saw the increasing "commercialization"[147] of the London press with some satisfaction.

9

The Content of the London Newspapers

Part 1: News and Information

The material offered through the London newspapers published during the first half of the eighteenth century was in many respects more complex than is generally allowed by historians. The most satisfactory account of comparable material had been made by Cranfield in his graphic and important study of the provincial press.[1] However, in quite rightly stressing the pioneering role of the country newspapers, he tended implicitly to underplay their dependence on the London press for all forms of content. A good deal of the material he cites as characteristic of changes and developments in the local papers had its origin in the capital, where a much greater flexibility of approach was possible. Consequently, although many of Cranfield's remarks apply with equal force to the content of sections of the London press, they can only provide an oblique and partial view of the range and quality of material that was offered to readers in the capital.

The dramatic expansion in production that followed the lapse of the Licensing Act was based largely on the voracious and growing demand for news that developed both in London and in the provinces. In 1712 the author of the *British Mercury* referred disparagingly to the "furious Itch of Novelty" and the "immoderate Appetite of Intelligence," which existed at all social levels and which had led to "*that inundation of* Post-Men, Post-Boys, Evening Posts, Supplements, Daily Courants and Protestant Post-Boys, *amounting to twenty-one every Week, besides many more which have not survived to this Time.*"[2] The subsequent expansion of the London press was based largely on this insatiable "appetite" and the papers providing the fullest and most up-to-date news coverage achieved the greatest long-term success.

The sources of information exploited in compiling the individual London papers were complex and are often hard to identify. Nonetheless, it is possible to outline the way in which the raw material was accumulated by the London news compilers. Those in the best position to obtain early and authentic information were concerned in the papers with direct political connections. The *Daily Courant's* preoccupation with foreign news and its initial reputation for accuracy reflected Samuel Buckley's access to the extensive news sources of the Secretary of State's office.[3] Following the organizational changes of the late 1720s, Buckley's interest in the paper seems to have lapsed but, in 1733, it was requested "that the Publisher of the *Daily Courant* may receive from the Secretary of States Office such foreign News as is proper to be printed; this Indulgence would add much to the Circulation of a Paper calculated and carried on entirely for publick benefit, and is a favour which was formerly granted to the Proprietor of that Paper. The Clerk who has the Trouble of sending this News shall be paid by the Proprietors to his Content."[4] Although it is not clear whether this request was granted, the politicians on the opposition side often supplied their sponsored papers with News material that could be integrated with the main themes of their propaganda campaigns. In 1732 it was claimed that the *Craftsman* regularly contained items supplied by its political backers, which they had "Information of by Correspondents Abroad and Whisperers at Home, which the lower Stations and Fortunes of the Proprietors of other News-Papers cannot procure."[5] The offers made to potential opposition journalists also suggest that the provision of current information was a regular adjunct of political support. In 1743 Thomas Carte undertook to supply Gordon with copies of all the papers laid before Parliament,[6] while Mallet was offered "the earliest and the most useful Notices of all Transactions foreign and domestick."[7] News supplied by political backers was an important feature of Fielding's *True Patriot*, and in advertisements for the paper it was explicitly stated that the quality of the news would be unusually high, "The Undertakers being Gentlemen, who have much better Opportunities of receiving Information than the common News-Writers."[8]

Although such sources of inside information were not generally available, most full-priced papers claimed their own exclusive channels of information. Much of the material quoted from correspondence in the press was probably obtained in an *ad hoc* way from private letters widely available through London's unique social and economic position, as well as through the established contacts of the bookseller proprietors. However special arrangements were increasingly made by the proprietors of the leading papers although in most cases the nature and extent of any such links are not easy to get at.[9] In 1717 Mist announced an established correspondence with "*the* Hague, France, *the* North, Italy, Germany, *and even into* Hungary, Turkey *and* Russia,"[10] a claim that was probably based largely on the random supply of information from these areas.[11] During the 1720s and 1730s the leading dailies at least usually claimed a *"particular Correspondent"* at Paris and the Hague,[12] and sometimes at other European centers. In 1733, for example, with the arrival of a French mail, the editor of the *Daily Journal* remarked that "the following Advices from different Parts, will shew the Extensiveness, as the agreeable Manner of Narration will the

Peculiarity, of our foreign Correspondence," printing a series of items headed from Rome, Compiègne, Brest, Dunkirk, and Paris.[13] Even if the organization of such correspondence was based on the casual activity of men primarily involved in commercial or other activity, it seems likely that some financial outlay was involved and by mid-century the first tentative steps had been taken toward establishing a regular international intelligence network.

In spite of the fact that the evidence is again tantalisingly oblique, it seems that direct links between the principal papers and major centers of the British Isles, particularly the ports, were firmly established, and the same sort of claims for exclusive contacts were also made in this area. The initial advertisements for the *London Evening Post* regularly stressed the extent of its local contacts,[14] and at the end of 1728 the proprietors announced that *"having settled such a large Correspondence . . . they find it impracticable to furnish the Town with all the Advices they receive, unless they enlarge the Size of their Paper, and the Measure of the Print."*[15] During the early 1720s both the *London Journal* and the *British Journal* ran a "Portsmouth Letter" as a regular feature, the author in the latter describing himself specifically as a "News-Writer,"[16] and it seems likely that correspondents in other provincial towns were employed by a number of the full-priced London papers.[17] Direct evidence of this sort of organization is provided in the later records of the *General Evening Post*. In 1756 the printer was negotiating for a correspondent, again in Portsmouth,[18] while subsequently regular reports were obtained from Weymouth, the Isle of Wight, and Gosport for a very variable outlay ranging from the payment of a quarterly salary to the simple supply of the paper itself.[19]

From the beginning of the century the compilers or editors of the London papers continued themselves to double as news gatherers.[20] However, the miscellaneous items printed in the "London" section, particularly the domestic paragraphs, were often supplied by subsidiaries, sometimes apparently acting as wage-earning employees.[21] In 1728 it was claimed that one or two news gatherers were employed on each daily paper,[22] and ten years later a correspondent of the *Weekly Miscellany* remarked that "The Writers of other Papers can afford to keep various Emissaries in Pay, all of whom bring in the foreign and domestic Advices they collect to the Printing House."[23] This may suggest in a few cases coverage of the principal news centers by regular employees,[24] although any such organization is only obliquely reflected in the hostile comments of commercial rivals. In 1728, for example, the author of the *Flying Post* stated that the proprietors of the *Universal Spectator* had resolved above all "to top their Bretheren in *Domestick News* (An Article that requires a most profound Judgment, as well as great Reading) and for that purpose have setled fix'd *Salaries* of two-pence *per diem,* on a considerable Number of antiquated *Herb Women,* to whom they have appointed their Rounds, in the same Manner as the *Watchmen,* to collect all the Occurences of the Week."[25] The author of a paragraph in

Read's Journal, attacking a "club" responsible for compiling the news published in *Mist's,* was more specific. "One of their Agents," he stated,

> has a Commission for scraping the Jails in Middlesex and Surrey of their Committments; another has a Warrant for scouring the Ale-houses and Gin-shops for such as dye of excessive Drinking: A Person is posted at the Savoy to take up Deserters; and another in the Park to watch the Motions of the Guards, and their military Punishments; a Third lends a kind Hand in Reverend Matters; and the more important Affairs, as Armaments, Invasions, Presents to the Chevalier, etc. are committed to the Care of a very *able* Person; Deaths, Marriages, Births and Miscarriages, are all under proper Care and Order for the more expeditious dispatch of so *laudable* an Undertaking.[26]

A similar ironic picture of regular routine emerged four years later from the coffee-men's attack on the reporters attached to the leading dailies. According to the author, they would "hang and loiter about the Publick Offices, like House-breakers, waiting for an Interview with some little Clerk, or a Conference with a Door-keeper, in order to come at a little News, or an Account of Transactions; for which the Fee is a Shilling or a Pint of wine." They were also, he claimed, in regular touch with the "*Death-Hunters*" employed in drumming up business for the undertakers who "for a Treat and a little Money tell them what they hear: And by this Means the Publick is informed of the Progress of Death and Distemper among People of Condition."[27] Such remarks are at best inadequate,, but they do perhaps suggest that the evolution of the specialist reporter was already underway in sections of the London press.

Original news items were also supplied to the papers by a variety of casual contributors. In 1725 it was ironically claimed that half the united parishes of St. Annes Blackfriars and St. Andrew by the Wardrobe, in the heart of the newspaper district, were "employ'd in collecting furniture for these Papers, as Births, Marriages, Deaths, Miscarriages etc. and have their Shares and Perquisites in proportion to their respective Services."[28] Readers themselves also sent in a good many paragraphs. According to Doctor Gaylard's petition of 1721 the domestic news in Mist's *Weekly Journal* was partly compiled from material "sent in by Correspondents thro' the Penny Post,"[29] and a number of papers carried sporadic notices rejecting unsuitable items received from an unknown source.[30] Toward the end of this period some attempts were apparently made to develop the use of this occasional supply. In 1746 the imprints of the newly established *London Courant* and the *Mercurius Latinus* both announced that news as well as advertisements would be taken in at the specified centers.

All the London papers drew extensively on secondary news material, although this was often unacknowledged and is therefore impossible to identify in detail. A wide range of continental papers provided a substantial proportion of the foreign news and in 1712 the author of the *British*

Mercury, listing the papers ransacked for intelligence, included "the Gazettes *or* Courantes *of* Paris, Brussels, Antwerp, Amsterdam, Hague, Rotter-
dam, Leyden, *and some others not so common, besides the* French *and* Holland
Gazettes a-la-main."[31] This ties in with the supply organized by Charles
Delafaye for the eighteen London coffee-houses[32] and material from the
Continental publications was only gradually superseded as the main source
of foreign news.[33] The process by which information was transferred from
the Continental to the London press could have its political uses. According
to John Oldmixon, the Tory ministers in Queen Anne's reign "had a trick of
sending Paragraphs to the News-Papers in *Holland,* to be taken thence, and
inserted in their infamous Paper the *Post-Boy.*"[34] This device seems to have
continued in use[35] and the circumstances surrounding the prosecution of a
group of newspapers in 1729 indicates the way in which news material was
circulated over a wide area and through a large number of papers, sometimes at least in the service of party propaganda. A report first published in
the *Craftsman* on 12 July was subsequently reprinted in the *Utrecht Gazette,*
from which it was copied on the 17th by the *Daily Post.* reappearing the
same day in the *London Evening Post,* the *St. James's Evening Post,*[36] All the
papers were prosecuted. The Dutch news reports on English affairs were
often very comprehensive since the freedom from oversight allowed the
sort of reporting that was too risky for most London papers. In 1737 the
London Evening Post stated in one of its angled news paragraphs "We hear
the Dutch News Writer has not only been severely reprimanded in Holland,
on the complaint of the British Minister, for inserting the Account of the
Proceedings, etc. of the British Parliament, but order'd never to mention
Sir Robert's *Bounties* to his Friends."[37] Most of the full-priced dailies and
thrice-weeklies seem to have employed a translator to handle material
arriving from the Continent,[38] and although his work may have involved
translating original correspondence, the bulk of the duties were probably
made up of handling items from the foreign press.

Increasing use was also made of a number of American papers, particularly the *Boston* and *Maryland Gazettes,* which figured prominently in the
mid-century London press. However, the principal published source of
both foreign and home news remained the constantly plagiarized *London
Gazette.* Its reports were given special emphasis in time of war, and during
the mid-1740s the major thrice-weeklies sometimes opened their news
sections with large-titled quotations from this paper.[39] News material was
also occasionally extracted from the provincial press. Nichols claimed that
during the 1720s Edward Cave, by using his Post Office contacts, "procured
country newspapers, and sold their intelligence to a journalist of London
for a guinea a week."[40] The lack of attributions in the paper themselves
makes it extremely difficult to pin down the extent of any such borrowing,
although it seems likely that the evening posts in particular made use of
provincial reports. On the rare occasions when the London papers were
scooped by their local competitors on news of national interest, the material

was quickly republished in the capital, although again not always with full acknowledgment. During 1740 and 1741, for example, the printer of the *Newcastle Journal* received a series of eye-witness accounts of British naval action in the West Indies.[41] A few days after the publication of these strikingly original and topical items, containing a number of plans, they were prominently republished in the jointly managed *Daily Post* and *London Evening Post* as well as the *General Evening Post* without direct reference to the original paper.[42] Similarly, following the outbreak of the Jacobite rebellion in 1745 in Scotland, several London papers published extracts from such on-the-spot sources as the *Caledonian Mercury* and the *Derby Mercury*. However, the general absence of hard local news in the provincial press[43] did not encourage plagiarism, and although the number of occasional items taken explicitly from such local publications as the *Gloucester Journal* was apparently increasing,[44] the traffic between papers was still largely one way.

News items were to some extent a common property and the symbiotic relationship between the London papers was particularly clear in the process of semi-legitimate news sharing. A circular movement of reports took place between the different forms of full-priced papers. Prior to 1725 the six-page London journals usually carried a substantial number of paragraphs copied directly from the other forms,[45] and after the curtailment of space several of the new weeklies abandoned any attempt at originality. This approach was given an original twist in the *Grub Street Journal*.[46] The paper's news section was made up entirely of second-hand news items, with the source of each clearly indicated and with conflicting reports ironically juxtaposed. The initial advertisements for the paper offered "A large and most authentic Account of all the News Both DOMESTICK and FOREIGN; collected in a new Method from all the Papers of the preceding Week; with short Remarks Serious and Comical, shewing the BEAUTIES, the DIFFERENCES, and the MISTAKES which occur in them."[47] A more serious attempt at providing a news compilation was made in the rival *Weekly Register*, and the advantages of this approach, which predated and almost certainly prompted the emergence of the fully fledged magazine, were emphasized in the early issues. It was stated that through this "Collection" readers could be fully informed of "what is transacting in the World without Expense of such a Multiplicity of Papers as are necessary to pick out piece meal the Occurences here to be met with," while those who read the news daily could obtain "the Marrow of the whole Week's Occurences, as well Foreign as Domestick, on one succinct methodical View."[48] The offer of this sort of news service does not appear to have been altogether successful in the long run. One of the reasons given for the collapse of the *Grub Street Journal* in 1737 was its reliance on stale reports and such papers, lacking the immediacy of the thrice-weeklies and dailies and the comprehensiveness of the magazines, were under constant pressure. The weeklies inevitably contained a mass of plagiarised news,[49] but this was often combined with a certain amount of original coverage. The editors of the journals produced in conjunction with other forms of newspapers had access to original sources and were consequently able to offer a good deal of unpublished material. Advertisements for the *Universal Spectator,* printed at the same office as the *Daily Post* and *London Evening Post,* stated that "this Journal (besides the Letter of Entertainment) contains about six Times more Domestick News than the Common Journals; with several material Paragraphs of fresh News, not in any other Paper,"[50] and throughout its long existence the paper's "London" news section was unusually comprehensive and up-to-date. Later in the century the position of the weekly newspaper as a digest of material appearing in the other forms of output was sometimes formalized within the structure of group ownership. The printers involved in the production of the standard combination of newspapers would often use the thrice-weekly or daily in the group as the main source of material for their own weekly publications. Henry Baldwin, for example, set out to use the content of the *St. James's Chronicle* as the basis for his *London Journal,* while Charles Say compiled the news section of his *Craftsman* from the *Gazetteer.*[51]

The thrice-weekly evening posts in their turn leaned heavily on material taken from the dailies. As John Meres, printer of the *London Evening Post* pointed out under examination, "every Post we copy the principal Paragraphs from the Morning Papers (without which our Evening Paper would be of no Service to the Country)."[52] The balance between second-hand and original material in such papers is also difficult to assess and probably varied widely. In an attack on the *St. James's Evening Post* in 1728 for using nothing but "copy'd stale News," the editor of the *London Evening Post* claimed that one issue of his own paper had contained as many as eighteen original paragraphs, and this probably represented something approaching an upper limit for fresh domestic items.[53] On the other hand, the dailies and dwindling morning posts also took a certain amount of news from the alternative forms as well as from each other. In 1746 the printer of the *Daily Post,* in an apparently unsuccessful attempt to stabilise the paper's position, announced that publication would be switched from the morning to 4:00 in the afternoon, because "it affords me a better Opportunity to procure you *all the material News* in the Morning Papers, as well as the *freshest Advices* both *Foreign* and *Domestick,* of the current Day."[54] The plagiarism of the dailies was occasionally noted in the evening papers as a recommendation to the public and in 1746 an advertisement for the *Extraordinary Gazette* claimed that the quality of its news content was proved by "the Decision of the Daily Papers, who already do us the Honour frequently to insert our Paragraphs sometimes one and sometimes two Days after us."[55] While a section explicitly composed of reports from rival papers was subsequently introduced into the *Gazetteer,* publication of borrowed news apparently continued to represent a useful means of cutting costs. In 1769 Charlotte Foreman remarked that she had probably been laid off as translator on the *Gazetteer* because the printer intended "to take the news from the evening papers as he used to do, to save expenses."[56]

The process came full circle with the occasional republication of items originally appearing in the weeklies. During the late 1730s, for example, the author of *Common Sense* was moved to compose a vigorous attack on the recurrent plagiarism of material featured in his paper. He stated that the contributors

> now and then make some little Remarks upon Events that happen in the World, which they chuse to throw out by Way of Paragraphs rather than introduce them into their Essay; and which they observe are constantly stolen by the *London Evening Post*, without any acknowledgement from whence he has them;—We hereby order the said *London Evening Post* to keep to his own province of stealing silly paragraphs of Domestick Newes Wherever he can pick them up, not meddle upon any pretence whatever with Things which are onely designed for *Common Sense*. — If they goe on to commit these Depredations they shall hear of It in a Manner that wil doe them no Service.[57]

The news sections of the cut-price London papers, while sometimes containing original paragraphs concerned with the realities of low life,[58] were very largely made up of miscellaneous items extracted from their full-priced competitors.

The sharing round of news emphasized the high level of uniformity in the content of the London papers and contributed to the ironing out of variations between individual publications. On the other hand, although the incidence of news borrowing could help to perpetuate mistakes, it also provided a rough-and-ready check on the accuracy of reports that were inevitably sifted by the process of selection. Repetition also guaranteed the widest coverage for items that passed through the circle of London papers into the provinces and beyond. As the author of the *Free Briton* ironically remarked, "Our Economy of Intelligence is also most wonderful. In foreign Kingdoms, a Man may hang or drown himself with all desirable Silence and Security: but here, if a Lover is seen pendent on a Willow-Tree, it is known in a Week, from the Land's End to *Berwick* upon *Tweed*, and thence it runs over all *Europe*.[59]

The balance between material obtained from these primary and secondary sources probably varied a good deal according to the financial circumstances of individual papers. At the same time this balance, as well as the quality of reports, also depended on the rigor of selection. The dailies were in the most difficult position, because there was so little opportunity for checking the accuracy or authenticity of reports before publication. In the leading papers at least a positive effort was apparently made to strike a reasonable balance between novelty and truth. In 1729 the proprietors of the *Daily Courant*, announcing the introduction of home news, stated that *as the Reason for omitting Domestic Occurences hitherto, has been purely to avoid the Errors almost inseparable from the Papers which aim at hasty or too early Intelligence, it shall be the constant Care of the Managers of the Daily Courant rather to be Exact than Early and that their Home Articles shall rather be Important than Numerous. . . .* We shall only add, That as we pretend not to Infallibility: *if by Mistake or Misinformation any thing should escape us that recquires it, we shall think we owe it to the Reputation we aim to preserve, and to Ingenuity, to take notice of it as soon as possible.*[60]

Such rigorous caution may not have been commercially stimulating, but the evidence indicates that consistent efforts were made in the full-priced dailies and thrice-weeklies to make sense out of the prolix material with which they were supplied. The correction of mistakes in subsequent issues, the occasional inclusion of comments linking news items or providing a short commentary on their significance, the rejection of material sent in by readers—all suggest a fairly thorough process. The same sort of editorial activity seems to have taken place in the cut-price papers and the few surviving runs contain indications of careful selection. In 1725, for example, George Parker, after including a false report about the Turks in his halfpenny *London News,* published a vigorous denunciation of his casual supplier and a humble apology for the mistake.[61] A few weeks later he again felt obliged to apologize to readers as "Being absent from home last Tuesday my *Collector* of News for the next Morning's Paper, thro' Inadvertency transcrib'd an absurd and ridiculous Paragraph from *Monday's Daily Journal.*"[62] In the full-priced papers the selection of reports was sometimes made a matter of particular emphasis. In the first issue of the *Weekly Miscellany* an introduction to the paper's domestic news stated that "our Intention is under this Article to insert such Things principally as may deserve the Perusal of an intelligent Reader, avoiding as much as possible, such trifling Particulars as are unworthy of the Attention of a Person of Sense."[63] In a similar piece introducing the foreign news it was claimed that only such material would be included "as may render this Article fit to be referr'd to as Occasions shall happen, as a brief History of Foreign Affairs," while the offer of "an Index of the principal Matters" was made to those who "think fit to keep Sets of these Papers." A program of careful selection with an eye to the future was also presented in advertisements for the short-lived *National Journal* in 1746. Besides the occasional essay, it was stated, the paper would include "a regular and true Account of all Occurrences foreign and domestic, so as to serve by way of a History of the present Times; for which Reason it is printed with such a Margin as to admit of being bound up in a Volume annually; and to make it useful to Posterity as well as the present Generation, our Customers shall at the end of every year have an Index Gratis."[64]

While some editorial concern with the quality of news was evident throughout the press, few attempts were made to diversify its presentation.

The layout followed routine lines and the pattern established early in the century was only slightly modified before 1750. News was divided between the foreign reports, usually drawn from secondary sources and given precedence,[65] and locally gathered material appearing in a highly miscellaneous "London" section. This was centered on socially graded domestic items but also included correspondence and paragraphs relating to other areas. Although some attempts were made across the press to improve the layout of news, often by the introduction of geographical subheadings, the material continued to appear in a very stereotyped form.[66] The unwillingness to tamper with an established formula may also have played a part in the general reluctance to diversify news content by the inclusion of illustrations. Problems of production and expense were clearly key factors in this area,[67] although the publication of pictorial items seems almost invariably to have stimulated considerable public interest. Prior to the mid-1720s Mist's *Weekly Journal,* and more particularly James Read's rival paper, had contained occasional maps, cartoons, and other illustrations,[68] and such items continued to appear sporadically in the London press with some success. In 1727, for example, the inclusion of a plan of Gibraltar in the *Original Weekly Journal* led to the paper's reissue,[69] while in 1730, in anticipation of exceptional demand, seven thousand of an issue of the *Grub Street Journal* containing a portrait of the Lord Mayor were printed, over three times the number of any unillustrated edition.[70] A scurrilous political cartoon attacking Walpole's use of corruption, which was published in the *Champion* in 1740, was also reprinted,[71] and seems to have given an important boost to the paper's notoriety, and hence to its popularity at a critical point. Nonetheless, such items were rare and, although the outbreak of war and the onset of the forty-five stimulated the appearance of a number of simple plans linked with reports of naval or military action[72] and at least one anti-Jacobite cartoon,[73] illustrated material continued to be limited very largely to the blocks used in the advertising section.

The conservative approach to news content was also reflected in the absence of any attempt to highlight major news stories under a separate headline. Italic print continued to be used to differentiate subheadings, editorial comment, and occasionally original contributions, as well as for general emphasis. However, while no use was made of a distinctive type face to point up individual reports, neither was the increased use of ruled divisions and large headings developed for this purpose. Only occasional indications appeared of a more positive approach.[74] During Queen Anne's reign a number of essay-sheets carried the main points under discussion in the title area[75] and in 1728 advertisements for the modified *Post Boy* suggested an application of the same principle to news content. It was stated that the first daily issue would include, for example, comment on ". . . What is doing at Soissons. . . . The Emperor's Journey to Trieste, while the King of Spain keeps his Bed. . . . Count Coningsele interposes in the

Affairs of East Friesland; how received.—"[76] There was apparently no follow-up in the paper itself, and the nearest approach to the use of headlines only came in the mid-1740s. At this point several of the leading dailies introduced prominent marginal slogans that underlined the paper's attitude to important current issues.[77] In March 1745 the margins of the *Daily Advertiser* carried for a week the cry of "No French Cambricks, No Smugglers,"[78] and following the outbreak of the forty-five, the *General Advertiser* printed up each side the words "No Pretenders. No Popery. No Slavery." and across the top and bottom "No Wooden Shoes. No Arbitrary Power,"[79] slogans taken up by the *Penny London Post* and at least one provincial paper.[80] Subsequently, when the question of returning Cape Breton to France arose, the words "Cape Breton for Ever" began to appear in the margins of the *General Advertiser*. But although giving rise to some caustic comment on possible developments,[81] such marginalia were not adapted to apply to individual news stories. It was characteristic of the generally cautious approach to presentation that the most important development in the layout of news was an extension in the use of the long-established "Postscript" in the leading thrice-weeklies. At the beginning of the century, late news had been offered by the proprietors of the morning posts and other London papers on a separately printed or manuscript sheet, supplementing the material already in circulation.[82] Although this cumbersome and expensive practice continued in occasional use, the successful development of the evening posts soon made such additional publications virtually obsolete and a late news section became an irregular feature of the papers themselves. During most of this period a "Postscript" continued to be squeezed into spaces left blank for the purpose, usually below the imprint on page four. However, with the general increase in page size that took place among the principal evening posts in the mid-1740s, the role of the "Postscript" was extended. In most of these papers the news came to be regularly divided into two sections.[83] The first contained the news that could be set in advance, while the second, sometimes also divided into the same categories, contained the most recent reports from all sources. The subsequent importance of the "Postscript" was clearly reflected in the concern of the proprietors of the *General Evening Post* to obtain suitable material for this section of their paper.[84]

The pattern of news coverage offered through the London papers remained in some respects as static as the layout. The publication of any form of content was determined by the complex interaction of readership interest, management structure, external constraints, and national circumstances. However, within this shifting vortex of pressures the London newspapers were consistently directed toward the upper and middling social levels and more particularly to those engaged in areas of commerce and politics. Even the cheap newspapers, while to some extent pushing back the social frontiers, identified the London tradesmen as an important element in their readership.[85] As a result, the areas of news and information that were given the greatest emphasis were those which served to keep open the lines of communication necessary to the dominant interests of trade and politics.

Foreign news and the conduct of foreign affairs remained a staple of the London newspaper coverage, receiving what appears at a distance to be an almost excessive amount of attention. However, this material worked at several levels. On one hand it offered the sort of variety and excitement that appealed strongly to newspaper readers across the country. On the other it provided material that related directly to the main themes of political controversy as well as to broad areas of commercial speculation. In combination these interests gave foreign news a peculiar force. The close link between war and sales had been firmly established since the beginning of the century[86] and newspaper proprietors continued to take considerable pains to emphasize their foreign news coverage at times of heightened international tension, even when England herself was not directly involved. At the end of 1733, with the outbreak of war on the Continent, the proprietors of the *General Evening Post* claimed that the enlargement of their paper was to be carried out in response to "several Letters from their Correspondents, desiring by Reason of the present uncertain Situation of Affairs abroad, a fuller and more (particular) Account of Foreign News."[87] Two years later, William Webster felt bound to assure readers of the *Weekly Miscellany* that its literary feature would only be included "as often as Dearth of Foreign News, or the uncertain Posture of Affairs abroad gives us but little Matter of Importance to take Notice of under that Article."[88] The preoccupation with foreign affairs was equally evident in the news sections of the cheap London press. In an issue of his halfpenny *London News* published in July 1724 Parker begged his readers to "excuse the Insertion of Home News before Foreign, for this Time," in the absence of fresh reports,[89] while at the end of the year his protracted serialization of *Arabian Tales* was omitted to allow full coverage of some "surprising News from Thorn which is hardly to be parallel'd."[90] During the 1730s cut-price papers such as the *Penny London Post* followed the complex diplomatic and military maneuvering on the Continent in considerable detail and 1735 handbills for the *Weekly Tatler* assured potential customers that the paper would contain full reports of "the Transactions of both Armies in Italy and on the Rhine, and of the present Breach between Spain and Portugal."[91] After 1739 this general emphasis became even more pronounced and letters containing eye-witness accounts of the major engagements were prominently featured in most papers, the element of patriotic sensationalism providing the cheap press in particular with a major selling point. In 1744 a postscript to the news section of the *Penny London Post*, announcing Admiral Mathews's victory over the French and Spanish fleets at Toulon, described how the English ships "began to cannonade them with such Fury, that in six Hours the Ocean appeared a Sea of Blood, and on the Surface of the Water, nothing but dead Bodies, and Wrecks of the Ships, both Fleets fighting Board and Board. By all we can learn, there has not been for some Centuries past so bloody an Engagement. Letters are expected every hour with the particulars, to which we must refer our Readers."[92]

During the middle years of the eighteenth century the range and depth of the newspaper coverage of foreign affairs was considerably extended. This was partly at least through the intervention of the leading opposition politicians. Walpole's foreign negotiations became a major target for the campaigns in the *Craftsman* during the late 1720s and this momentum, stimulated in the 1730s by the disputes with Spain, was maintained after his resignation as Hanoverian issues became the focus of the opposition campaigns. The provision of news material dealing with foreign affairs could be as potent as any polemical discourse. As the author of the *D'Anverian History* pointed out, "Those who would make any considerable and lasting Impressions on the Minds of the Generality of Mankind, must do it by Relation of Facts." At the same time, the leading papers, benefiting from the injection of bookseller capital, were apparently employing a growing number of overseas correspondents, whose input certainly contributed to an improving foreign news service.

Against this background, sections of the London newspaper press became increasingly involved in providing readers with information features related to the confusing and prolix events that were taking place across the world and that usually cropped up in fragmented and disjointed form in the conventional news paragraphs. Efforts to supply this sort of material were of long standing in the London press. In 1701, a regular program of topical geography was promised in the *New State of Europe,* and eleven years later the author of the *British Mercury* remarked that as *"above a Week may pass without receiving any foreign Mail, it is resolv'd upon such Occasions, to supply that Defect either with Geographical or Historical Accounts of such Places as shall, at that Juncture, be most emminently talk'd of, and which will consequently best answer the Curiosity of the Reader."*[93] However, there does not seem to have been a consistent attempt to give the supplementary content of the London papers a topical ring until the 1730s, when the boom in cut-price publications was accompanied by a marked increase in the volume of serialized material offered to the public. Among the random mixture of literary, historical, and other items, an increasing amount of emphasis was given to extended pieces linked, though not always very closely, with current events abroad. The content of William Rayner's papers clearly reflected this development. In 1737 he announced to readers of his *Morning Advertiser* that, although he had planned to publish a life of Peter the Great, as "the Misunderstanding, which at present between Spain and Portugal has made a great Noise in the World, and may be attended with fatal consequences to the Repose of Europe, we have been desired by many of our Readers to give them some account of the Portuguese. We have accordingly complied with the Request, and shall present them with the History of the Revolutions of Portugal by the famous M. l'Abbe de Vertot."[94] Following the outbreak of war and the highly publicized West Indies campaign, Rayner began to publish the *British Champion; or, Admiral Vernons Weekly Journal*, a 2d. paper that contained a serialized life of the Admiral leading up to an "impartial Relation of his Conduct and Courage in the West Indies, particularly at Porto Bello, Chagre, Carthagena, and other places in America, to revenge our Wrongs, and vindicate the Honour of the British Flag."[95] With the shift in the scene of military activity to the Continent, he introduced in the *Morning Advertiser* a protracted "Description of Flanders, Holland, Germany, Sweden, and Denmark With an Account of what is most Remarkable in those Countries."[96]

During the summer of 1733 the *Daily Journal* offered its readers a mass of extended foreign news features. As well as pieces concerned with the government of the American colonies and the sentence of Cardinal Costia, readers were provided with a protracted and apparently popular account of the involved struggle between the King of France and the Parlement.[97] Descriptions of areas that were currently in the news also appeared occasionally in this active paper. In 1723, for example, an absence of mails prompted the inclusion in the *Daily Journal* of an account of Persia *"by Reason of the Expedition of the Muscovites into these Parts."*[98] Similarly, in 1736 it provided a description of Azoff, recently captured by the Turks, and a footnote on "Badget" following Kouli Khan's coronation.[99] However, it was not until the general increase in page size, which occurred in the mid-1740s, combined with an apparently marked rise in circulation, that this sort of background information became a regular feature of the London press at large. The principal dailies and weeklies, with the exception of the moribund *Gazetteer*, began to include a variety of material of this sort, individual pieces often circulating widely through the different forms of London newspapers. The revolution in Corsica, the shifts in the Continental war, the internal upheavals in Holland, and a number of other variably striking events taking place in 1746 and 1747 were all illustrated by descriptive pieces in the thrice-weekly and daily press.[100]

Whatever the importance of its appeal, coverage of foreign affairs does not in itself seem to have been sufficient to ensure commercial success. In 1729, for example, the proprietors of the derelict *Daily Courant*, which had previously followed a policy of specialization, felt obliged to broaden the news content by the inclusion of domestic reports.[101] This material, which formed a major selling point in several papers and which was focused in the "London" section, was often dominated by items dealing with social topics. Reports on the Royal Family frequently opened the home news and were followed by paragraphs recording the activities of the titled and wealthy as well as of members of the more important professional and commercial groups. This social preoccupation prompted the widespread coverage of sporting events, and during the summer an increasing amount of space was taken up with reports on such matters as horse races and cricket matches.

At the same time, the supply of these items was accompanied, particularly in the cut-price papers, by reports on bizarre events, sexual and romantic happenings, and the miscellaneous circumstances of low life. In their comments on the domestic news service contemporary critics focused their attention on the "London" section. In 1733, Eustace Budgell, introducing his new weekly magazine, the *Bee*, launched a typical attack. He stated that the domestic news published in the London papers was concerned almost entirely with "Robberies, bloody Murders, *Accounts of* Draymen's Carts *that have run over People, with the Adventures of Post-Boys, Tide-Waiters, and Messengers, etc. The Promotions, Deaths and Marriages of the Nobility, Gentry and Clergy, and of the Days when some of the Royal Family go to the* Play House, *or take the* Air. . . ."[102] Budgell was on strong ground in some respects and the "London" news paragraphs in all forms of paper were dominated by exactly these preoccupations. However, equally clearly Budgell, like a number of subsequent historians, was condemning by omission. In fact, as in the case of foreign affairs, the coverage of specific areas of domestic news was improved during the middle decades of the eighteenth century and for much the same reasons. The intervention of the leading opposition politicians, which led to the highlighting of foreign material, also led to an improved supply of information about domestic politics generally and parliamentary activity in particular. The opposition papers continuously emphasized the legitimate constitutional role of public opinion and pressed the people's right to know the details of events both at home and abroad.[103] Consequently, the London press became involved in a protracted attempt to open up the proceedings in Parliament.

During the parliamentary session quite effective control continued to be maintained over the reporting of debates, and during 1728 and 1729 comprehensive action was taken against the printer of the *Gloucester Journal* and the authors of the leading London newsletters for breech of privilege.[104] These steps were accompanied by a firm resolution to act against further violation and consequently the only in-session reports appearing in the London papers consisted of brief opposition news paragraphs. These occasionally contained detailed information and in January 1740, for example, the *London Evening Post*, in announcing the defeat of a Place Bill, supplied the voting figures.[105] More often such items were tantalizingly oblique, as when the *Champion* reported at the beginning of the following session that "Last Night the Disputes of the famous Political Club were carried on with such Eagerness and Obstinacy, that they did not break up till between one and two o'Clock this Morning: On which Occasion it may be decently said, Blessed are they who hunger and thirst for Righteousness sake."[106]

Nonetheless, a clear outline of proceedings could be obtained from the political essay-papers, which often included discussion of measures pending or under consideration in terms exactly parallel to those used in Parliament. Such discussion was rejected on principle in the ministerial papers, although they were inevitably drawn into the same area of debate. As William Arnall remarked, in defending his own reported attendance in the gallery of both houses, "I can truly say, that I never was inclined to fatigue myself with attendances in either House of Parliament, till the *Authors and Patrons of the Craftsman,* by their Misrepresentations of those Proceedings, made it absolutely necessary for me to be present on those Debates, without which I could not possibly have engaged with Writers who allowed themselves such Liberties with the Proceedings of Parliament."[107] Comments of this sort was sometimes supplemented by the publication of speeches from earlier sessions. In 1745, for example, the author of the *Craftsman* stated, "There being a strong Report in Town that a Motion will be soon made in Parliament for repealing the *Septennial Act,* and restoring our ancient Constitution by frequent *new Parliaments,* I cannot entertain my Readers, better, at this Juncture, than by some Extracts from a Speech made in the *House of Commons,* when the Act for *triennial Parliaments* was repeal'd."[108] While the Stage Licensing Bill was pending, *Common Sense* contained an abstract of Lord Chesterfield's famous speech delivered in the House of Lords a few days before,[109] and it seems possible that the substance of recent speeches was quite often incorporated in the leading political essay-papers.

With the Summer adjournment, parliamentary restraint virtually lapsed in spite of the reassertion of privilege in 1738.[110] From 1730 the uninformative *Votes* and the cautious accounts in the *Political State* and the *Historical Register* were supplemented by the growing number of "debates" which formed a popular feature of most new magazines.[111] No attempt was made in any London newspaper to publish postdated reports, perhaps largely because the inclusion of piecemeal accounts would have been both confusing and costly of space. At the same time, individual speeches from the previous session occasionally appeared as propaganda items. During the 1741 recess four issues of *Common Sense* contained Sandys's speech for the removal of Walpole from office on grounds of corruption, the author announcing, "The *LONDON MAGAZINE of* MAY *hath given us a* SPEECH *made upon the Occasion of a certain Motion, which deserves to be read by all the world: We shall therefore give it the Publick, as a full Answer to all that hath been said or can be said by those modest Gentlemen who pretend there was no Proof.*"[112] Such extended accounts were rare although most opposition papers carried occasional short items of the type, usually extracted from the *London Magazine.*[113]

From the late 1720s newspapers on both political sides began to carry end-of-session summaries as part of their propaganda campaigns. The first of the *Craftsman's* reports appeared in June 1727 and consisted of what was later described in the *Free Briton* as "a partial, invidious, malicious Review of the publick Proceedings, intersperced with *Secret History* and *Private Scandal.*"[114] In June 1729 the *Craftsman's* report ended with a double column entry showing on one side the ministry's financial measures and on the other the Acts, Motions, and Resolutions of the opposition, thus "doing Justice to *both Parties,* by ascribing to each the Honour of *those Acts,* which properly belong to them."[115] The *Craftsman's* summaries sometimes appeared in response to ministerial accounts and in 1732 the author expressed ironic surprise that the usual panegyrics on Walpole's parliamentary measures were not forthcoming.[116] However, these reviews remained more characteristic of the leading opposition papers. In May 1740, for example, the *Champion* gave the heads of the dealings of the last Parliament "In which, almost at a single Glance, the material Merit of both Parties, stripp'd of all the Disguises of Flattery on one Hand, or Malignity on the other may be seen and summ'd up by the Light of their own Conduct,"[117] while four years later the *Westminster Journal* supplied a detailed financial balance sheet on the basis of the last Parliament.[118] These summaries seldom contained extended reviews of items of legislation and, although immediately after the recess of 1733 two issues of *Fog's Weekly Journal* contained detailed quotations from the proposed Excise Bill,[119] no comparable items seem to have appeared in the London press during this period.[120]

All forms of London newspaper carried a variety of occasional lists often concerned with civil or military officers, shipping or "horse matches," and occasionally providing a more obvious public service. Following the outbreak of the forty-five, for example, the front page of two issues of the *London Evening Post* carried a list of tradesmen willing to accept bank notes.[121] However, the most extended and important of such items had political overtones and reflected the close links between the London press and all kinds of political activity. Polling lists issued to detect fraudulent voting during parliamentary and local elections in London appeared occasionally during the 1720s and 1730s, the dailies publishing especially extended issues for this purpose.[122] The general elections in particular also prompted the appearance of a good deal of information concerned with M.P.'s generally. The practice of supplying an account of the national results as they came in had been established since the beginning of the century, and most forms of newspaper continued to do so, now and then providing detailed polling figures.[123] Similarly, complete lists of M.P.'s, sometimes provided as soon as all the returns were known, continued to be published as an occasional feature of the leading dailies and thrice-weeklies. In March 1736 a double issue of the *London Daily Post* contained a current list of members "so contriv'd as to hang up in Coffee-houses, and to be seen at one View."[124] The publication of post-election reports was accompanied in the opposition press by an attempt to provide readers with a guide to the political sympathies of individual M.P.'s. The first lists of this type seem to have appeared in the press during the election of 1722, when the *London Journal,* Mist's *Weekly Journal,* and the *Post-Boy* all distinguished the names of the successful Whig and Tory candidates as the returns came in by using differentiated type.[125] The emergence of the Whig opposition during the mid-1720s probably confused the issue sufficiently to deter any London paper from making similar distinctions during the election of 1727. However, in 1734 the *London Evening Post,* which had previously distinguished the politics of the London officials,[126] used the same technique on M.P.'s during the general election. The distinction between members was indicated as the results came in by the established use of italics for ministerial supporters and roman letters for opposition sympathizers, the Excise vote, it was later stated, being "the chief (though not the sole) Guide for the Members rechosen."[127] At the end of June a complete list was published separately, including "several Curious Particulars never before printed in any List of Parliament," which was at once reprinted by public demand and later reissued in the *Post.*[128] During the 1741 election the classification of incoming names in the opposition press prompted a brief parallel attempt in the *Gazetteer,*[129] and subsequently both the *London Evening Post* and the *Craftsman* issued complete distinguishing lists of M.P.'s that also met with an enthusiastic reception.[130]

The range of up-to-date parliamentary information was further extended by the risky and occasional publication of division lists, which usually appeared in the opposition papers as a guide to electors, and were often spiced with information on the places held by M.P.'s. The author of the *Craftsman's* parliamentary summary in 1729 regretted that it was not current practice to provide more of this sort of material, including "a particular List of the Names of all such Members as voted on *either side.*"[131] Although in March 1722 the votes on the Peerage and Septennial Bills were published in a supplement to the *St. James's Journal,*[132] the latter also appearing in two issues of Mist's paper, [133] similar items were avoided in the opposition press for the rest of the decade.[134] It was not until the rundown to the election of 1734 that emphasis again began to be placed on this material in the London newspapers. Following the summer adjournment, the excise vote was immediately advertised as appearing in the *Whitehall Evening Post,*[135] and a few weeks later it was published in two consecutive issues of *Fog's Weekly Journal* under the title of *The List.*[136] The heightened political tension at this point stimulated the publication of an unusual amount of privileged information in *Fog's.* The excise list was followed by an account of the Lords voting "for and against an Enquiry into the Frauds of the South Sea Company," while two weeks later the paper published a letter including the names of the speakers for and against "a standing Army."[137] The following April it was announced that "as the Publick will expect, we shall say something upon Elections, I think we cannot caution them better whom to chuse, than by a List of those who Voted for and against Repealing the Septennial Bill."[138] This sort of material made effective propaganda and was evidently very popular, but it had to be used with caution. A voting list on the highly unpopular Spanish Convention was published in 1739 but failed to appear in any of the London papers,[139] although the printers of both the *Craftsman* and *Common*

Sense advertized it as a separate publication and continued to do so at the
end of the next two sessions. The most striking use of a division list outside
an election context was made in the *Westminster Journal* in February 1743
when, below a garbled account of the December debate on the Hanoverian
troops, the paper published a list of the House of Commons showing how
each member had voted on the issue.[140] This apparently unprecedented
breach of privilege was ignored by the House and, in spite of the ostensible
risks of providing such information, none of the division lists seems to have
provoked a prosecution.

The high level of demand for material concerned with foreign affairs
and domestic politics brought together the interests of politicians and
newspaper proprietors and sharpened the coverage in both areas. However, against this active background the London newspapers continued to
provide more static forms of news and information in which the elements
of controversy and propaganda were replaced by an alternative appeal.
Among a variety of standard themes, coverage of crime stood out as a
recurrent element in the domestic news offered in all forms of London
newspaper. During the 1720s, crime had become a subject of peculiar
emphasis in some papers. John Applebee's *Original Weekly Journal* rapidly
became noted for its regular accounts of criminals,[141] and proceedings of
particular interest were occasionally given front-page treatment in less
committed publications. This appeared most strikingly in the coverage of
Christopher Layer's trial for high treason provided by the officially sponsored *London Journal.* During February 1723 two twelve-page issues and
one eight-page issue of the paper as well as three extended supplements,
two of twelve and one of six pages, were devoted to a verbatim account of
the proceedings.[142] Such comprehensive treatment was extremely unusual
and while a few cases continued to be featured in this section of the
press,[143] coverage was generally limited to conventional news reports.
Nonetheless, even when the amount of space was curtailed in 1725, current
crime evidently remained a necessary ingredient of the news. The author
of the *Weekly Miscellany,* for example, announced in 1733 that "some of the
Papers mention other Robberies, and Commitments thereupon, which we
purposely omit, as thinking them too trifling for our Design; and the full
Account we shall give Monthly of every Sessions at the Old-Baily, will, we
believe, be taking sufficient Notice of such obscure Miscreants, as fall under
the Lash of publick Justice, except in very flagrant Cases."[144]

If the emphasis placed on crime in the full-priced press was sometimes
limited, the subject was consistently treated with morbid enthusiasm in the
cheap London papers. The biographies and dying words of recently executed criminals rapidly became a staple element in their supplementary
content. In the *London Spy Revived,* special pains were taken over these
accounts, which were given consistent prominence on a second sheet,[145]
and the penny thrice-weeklies of the 1740s frequently offered this material
as their leading item. In 1745 the author of the *Penny London Post* an-

nounced that "the Ordinary of Newgate's new Editor of the Dying Speeches being determined to out-do even the Ordinary himself, we have been desired to insert his Account, which we have done accordingly, verbatim, that the Publick may see the Excellence of his Performance."[146] The first pages of three consecutive issues were devoted to these extracts. A good deal more space in the cheap London papers was devoted to individual or, more often, serialized accounts of criminals. Such items were sometimes published as an adjunct to the main serial, itself occasionally composed of a record of earlier notable hearings.[147] In 1738, for example, the *London Farthing Post,* while featuring the popular but obsolete trial of Christopher Layer, also included short accounts and serializations of recent proceedings. Even minor cases seem to have been greatly in demand and were occasionally given precedence over an established serial,[148] while reports of the more sensational proceedings were extended *ad nauseam* in a variety of cut-price papers. During 1744 the notable legitimacy case between James Annesley and the Earl of Anglesey ran for seven months as the lead in the *Penny London Morning Advertiser,*[149] and the following year the apparent popularity of this material encouraged the publication of a related perjury case that filled the front page for a further three months.[150] However, the most newsworthy trials of mid-century, arising out of the collapse of the Jacobite rebellion of 1745, proved rather more difficult to handle. The most consistent attempt to provide a record of the proceedings was made by Alexander McCulloh, printer of the *General London Evening Mercury* and the *Extraordinary Gazetteer,* who announced in the former in May 1746 that "a great many of our Readers being desirous to have the TRYALS at the Old Bailey, etc. continued in the Paper, as usual, we hope it may not be disagreeable to the whole, especially when those of the Rebels come to Hand, in which particular Care will be taken to have them punctually inserted."[151] McCulloh subsequently serialized the trials of the leading Jacobites in both his papers, although by the inclusion of the Lord High Steward's speech in passing sentence, he directly breeched the privilege granted to the printer S. Billingsby by the House of Lords. As a result he was taken into custody by Black Rod and obliged to publish a humble recantation in the press.[152] Conventional crime coverage, interspersed with bizarre cases from earlier periods, remained characteristic of the content of cheap and printer-owned papers, and this material was given a good deal of prominence in their advertisements.[153]

The coverage of crime, which received such a heavy emphasis in sections of the London press, had a general appeal to readers across society, providing an effective mixture of news and information, instruction and entertainment. Within the generalist content of the London newspapers no other news material offered such variety of detail and range of human interest, and the early employment of reporters to cover the assize circuits and the London prisons reflected its importance to the economics of the press.[154] At the same time, the London newspapers offered a range of routine commercial information aimed primarily at the trading community. This material, consisting of a combination of unadorned accounts of the movement of shipping and economic lists, became a particularly pervasive element in the content of the full-priced publications and underlined their dependence on this area of readership.

Ship news had been a feature of the content of the London newspapers since the seventeenth century and paragraphs containing information on arrivals and departures at ports in the British Isles and elsewhere were appearing regularly in all forms by the mid-1720s. Their inclusion in the London weeklies in spite of the inevitable delay in publication reflected a widespread demand for this material. In 1724 James Read's *Weekly Journal* contained a letter from a Limehouse reader who remarked that

> Happening t'other Day into a Coffee-house, I met with a *St. James's Evening Post,* and observ'd that in it you gave an Account of What Ships are Enter'd Inwards, and Cleared Out at the Custom House. Now, you must know, Sir, that I am your constant Customer for *Journals,* but live in a Part of the World where we seldom see your *St. James's Post:* but at the same Time, not only myself, but some of my Neighbours, have some Concern in Shipping so that we should be glad to see an Account of it in your *Journals,* in doing which you'll oblige
> Your constant Readers
> A, B, C, D, E, F, G, etc.[155]

Even after the reduction of 1725, Read's paper carried a regular "Ship News" section below the "London" reports. Similarly, the back page of the *Weekly Register* initially contained a very full table of shipping movements, which it was hoped would "be very acceptable to such as are concerned in Trade, or who have Friends on Voyages."[156] However, this feature was gradually curtailed as the balance of the papers' content shifted and ship news remained primarily a feature of the thrice-weeklies and dailies. In 1728 the *Daily Journal* became the first paper of its type to introduce a separate heading,[157] and the proprietors continued to take special pains to emphasize the quality of their reports. With the *Journal's* collapse in 1737, the feature was transferred, with some formality, to the related *Daily Gazetteer*[158] which, it was subsequently claimed, was of particular value to "the *Mercantile* Part of the World."[159] By the 1740s paragraphs of ship news had become the leading item in both the *London Daily Post* and the *Daily Advertiser,* as well as a separately identified element in most of the thrice-weeklies.[160]

The tabular information that concluded the news sections of the majority of London papers consisted of a variable combination of standard items. The times of high and low water at London Bridge, an abstract of the popular bills of mortality, and the list of bankrupts from the *Gazette* were very widely offered. This section had a predominantly commercial emphasis and a variety of economic information in tabular form was published throughout the press. This almost invariably included a current quotation of stocks[161] and, more erratically, an account of the prices of grain and other commodities, usually as recorded at Bear Key.[162] Publications consisting entirely of commercial lists had appeared in the capital since the previous century[163] and remained in circulation at least into the 1720s.[164] Such papers, often issued as a form of advertisement, probably sold very few copies.[165] However, while conventional news paragraphs and forms of supplementary content were the mainstay of a viable circulation, an element of this tabular material also remained a useful selling point and by the mid-1720s had become an integral part of newspaper content. In several of the new weeklies and thrice-weeklies routine economic material was given special prominence. The *Universal Spectator,* the *Weekly Register,* and the *London Evening Post* all initially contained an unusual range of tabulated material, while during the mid-1740s such enlarged papers as the *Whitehall Evening Post* carried long lists of prices and related items. In the London dailies the emphasis on advertising content often restricted the space available for news reports and kept the tabular content to a minimum. Even so, a serious attempt to revive the old form of specialist register was made in the *Daily Advertiser.* In place of the news the paper initially contained an account of the price of stocks, of the course of the exchange, of bankrupts, of all imports and exports, and also of the unclaimed letters at the Lombard Street Post Office. In spite of this comprehensive coverage, it was soon found desirable to strike a more conventional and popular balance by the inclusion of news reports. This required a corresponding reduction in the number of tables and by 1740 the *Advertiser,* like its immediate rivals, only carried the times of high water and the price of stocks.[166]

The news sections of the London papers, with their stereotyped layout and carefully graded reports, represented only a small part of the coverage available through the press. Every part of a newspaper could contribute to the provision of news and information; and essays, correspondence, features, and editorial comment all combined to produce a reasonably effective, if socially limited, view of the contemporary scene. Even the advertising sections, with their equally ordered and overlapping content, supported the conventional provision. In 1736 a contributor to *Fog's* remarked that he never gave up his paper in the coffee-house until he had "with great Accuracy perused the Advertisements, which take up the latter End of it, for I look upon them as Pieces of *Domestick* Intelligence, much more interesting than those paragraphs which our Daily Historians, generally give us, under the Title of Home News.—"[167] The line dividing material published in the news and advertising section of individual papers was often blurred,[168] and as the semi-ironic essayist suggested, the content of the paid notices and advertisements provided a useful adjunct to coverage in other forms. Considerable pains were taken to check the content of this material. However, the topical appeal of the newspaper advertisements was underlined by the way in which they continued to provoke frequent official and private legal action.[169]

Electioneering during London and national contests was vigorously conducted through paid-for notices published in the press, and these items, containing a variety of political comment, often dominated the leading papers.[170] At the same time, the advertising sections were frequently prefaced by material inserted by government departments, providing information on most aspects of local and national administration. These official notices, usually laid out in italics, were paralleled by items inserted by such economic and social organizations as the City companies and cultural societies announcing meetings, elections, and other business of general concern. Among the most popular advertisements were those concerned with current entertainment. According to the editor of the *London Daily Post, "those Papers which contain the greatest Number of* PLAY BILLS, *and other Accounts of Public Diversions are always most called for,"*[171] and by cornering the market in theatrical advertisements, prominently displayed in the first two columns of page one, the proprietors of this paper offset some of the worst side effects of specialist advertising.[172] The other full-priced papers continued to carry advertisements for horse races, cricket matches, musical events, and other entertainments in London and the provinces, and it was this sort of item that was most frequently inserted among the news reports.

However, the bulk of the information made available through newspaper advertising remained commercial in character. In 1715 the author of the *British Mercury* pointed out that his paper would contain *"a Weekly Account of what Houses, Lands, Goods, and Wares, are to be bought or sold, and what lost or stollen, and of all other Businesses of Moment in way of Traffick,"* stressing that it would help "to advance Trade both in Town and Country." It was on the basis of this sort of advertising program that the notable success of the *Daily Advertiser* was established and the initial appeal for advertisements was made to *"the Person who is desirous to make known his Want, either to Buy or Sell, Let or Hire, or recover any thing lost."*[173] The miscellaneous advertising of goods and services, shading off into such personal items as matrimonial appeals,[174] continued in most full-priced papers and advertisements for auctions and lotteries remained a common commercial denominator between all forms. Although its engagement with the current scene gave newspaper advertising much of its appeal, the financial structure of the press encouraged the dominance of bulk advertising of limited topicality. The frequent preponderance of essentially stereotyped advertisements for books, pamphlets, and related publications and also for quack medicines seems to have had a damaging effect on a number of full-priced papers. The prevalence in the weeklies of such items as "an Infallible Remedy for Broken Winded Horses," "Nelson's True Cure of Fresh Claps," and new editions of *Onania, Or The heinous Sin of Self-Pollution* seems to have caused considerable problems. In 1746 it was found necessary to announce in *Old England* that "in order to make Room for other Advertisements . . . the Medicinal Advertisements shall be, occasionally confined to the last Page."[175] Several of the full-priced dailies under bookseller ownership, which were stuffed with the house advertisements of their proprietors as well as medicinal notices, failed to provide the sort of topical variety that the public demanded. It seems possible that this advertising defect played as great a part in the decay of such papers as the *Daily Journal,* the *Daily Post,* and the *Daily Gazetteer* as any inadequacy in their news coverage.

In spite of the inevitable deficiencies arising from the problem of checking material, the constant threat of prosecution, and the exigencies of popular taste, the London papers provided readers with a reasonable coverage of events at home and abroad. The errors and distortions that inevitably cropped up were far less damaging than the ironic abuse of contemporaries suggested. Later in the century Horace Walpole remarked that the London papers, "though always full of lies, seldom fail to reach the outline at least of incidents,"[176] and this grudging accolade could as easily have been applied during the earlier period. By providing a constant flow of current information, the London papers oiled the wheels of commerce and politics and had become by mid-century a vital adjunct to the conduct of affairs at the middling and upper levels of English society.

Part 2: Instruction and Entertainment

The material deployed through the London newspapers with the intention of providing readers with instruction and entertainment as opposed to news, information, and political comment, covered a broad front. Nonetheless a pattern of output emerges that not only provides an indication of the tastes and interests of proprietors and readers but also offers a commentary on the ebb and flow of all forms of newspaper content. The pressure of competition after 1695, which drew many newspaper proprietors into the potentially difficult area of politics, led others to exploit alternative lines of interest. During Queen Anne's reign a number of papers appeared whose appeal was based on material concerned with the social and cultural preoccupations of the middle and upper ranks of society and in particular with the supposed interests of women. The identification and build-up of a substantial female readership was of considerable importance to all sections of the London press, and material concerned with manners and morals, romance and marriage, and the circumstances of family life became an increasingly important element in newspaper content. The spectacular success of the essay-sheets the *Tatler* and *Spectator,* based at least in part on their appeal to a female audience, remained a dominant commercial model. At the same time, the demand for general information presented in a light and entertaining manner, which reinforced the appeal of the newspaper as an aid to self-help education, stimulated the publication of a lot of highly miscellaneous material. The notion of combining a variety of non-contraversial items with other forms of coverage began to be explored during the early years of the century, although often in a rather uncoordinated way. The character of some of this supplementary content was indicated in 1707 when Charles Povey attempted to diversify the content of his *General Remark on Trade*. He announced that

> for the further Improvement of our Paper to a general Acceptation, there shall be inserted, Instructions for Gentlemen to judge of the most nice and intricate Pieces of Art, as Painting, Jewellery, etc. Likewise curious Discoveries in several Arts and Sciences, Delightful Experiments in the Mechanicks, Observations for Sports-men, etc. All done by the most ingenious Men of the Age. To render it acceptable to the Female Sex also, we shall give them Receipts for Distillery, Sweet-meats, Compositions of curious Dishes according to the Season, all perform'd in the nicest Manner, which a Lady of Quality will oblige us with from her own Collection, with many other Things, New and Entertaining for both Sexes.[1]

However, for the most part, the major newspapers appearing daily or thrice-weekly did not become involved in the wholesale publication of this sort of material and only included letters, poems, and other short fillers as the supply of news fluctuated. The main impetus to the devlopment of supplementary content in news-carrying publications was provided by the emergence of the extended journals and cut-price thrice-weeklies after 1712. The need to fill the mandatory six pages evoked a variable response. On the one hand a section of the London press, particularly the cheap papers, became involved in the publication of a mass of secondhand material in serial form. On the other the new journals began to offer the original material, usually in essay form, which became a characteristic feature of their content.

Serialization, however, was not pioneered in the cut-price papers. Faced with the sudden need to fill four additional pages, the proprietors of the *British Mercury* seem to have been initially nonplussed. After leaving page six of their extended paper blank for several issues, they began to offer as the leading item a rather peculiar, pseudo-oriental piece entitled *A Voyage Into Another World*, which was to be continued "if acceptable."[2] It was in fact carried on until December, when it was succeeded by a similar item, ultimately given the title of *The Ungrateful Spaniard: or, the Adventures of Donna Isabella*.[3] Extended pieces, in which rather indigestible fact was interspersed with more racy material, continued to appear for three years as the lead in the *Mercury*. However, a satisfactory formula does not seem to have been established and the problem of catering to a very wide range of newspaper readers, not yet accustomed to this sort of content, was summed up at a time when the paper was facing greatly extended competition. In a long title notice it was stated that *"there are solid Readers, who read for Information; and there are others more Mercurial, who value not a Book any farther, than for the Diversion and Amusement it affords. The Design of this Paper, is, as far as practicable, to please all Readers; which cannot be hop'd but by a Succession of Variety. The History of the World in it, was acceptable to many, and at last grew tedious to some. It was follow'd by the Rover, an entertaining Piece, not disagreeable to others. Next follow'd Geography, an abridgement, not without its Use, but heavy to such as seek for Entertainment: And the Accounts of Tunis, Tripoly, and Algier, could not but please some. It is intended now to find such Subjects, as may be short and pleasing; so that by constant Change, something may touch every different Genius."*[4] Only two of these short pieces appeared in the *Mercury*,[5] after which no further attempts were made to supplement the news content and a few weeks later the struggle to maintain newspaper publication was abandoned.

The low-key market research undertaken through the *Mercury* suggested the virtues of a flexible approach to supplementary content and probably reinforced the move among the proprietors of other journals toward the inclusion of a mixture of original essays. Nonetheless, as the lower reaches of newspaper publications were developed toward the end of the decade, serialization was established as a crucial form of content. The owners of the cheap, six-page thrice-weeklies, attempting to pare their costs to the bone, needed a large amount of entertaining, low-cost material. The serial represented an effective solution and by 1720 most if not all the cheap newspapers were offering a variety of such items more or less legitimately obtained. In October 1720 the author of the *Penny Weekly Journal*, introducing his paper to the public, remarked that "since Authors have so ingeniously Pleased their Readers, by various Performances taken from the Tryals of State Criminals; Arabian Nights Entertainments; Robinson Crusoe of York, Mariner and others," he would begin to serialize Ned Ward's *Matrimonial Dialogues*, "which indeed Merit the Praise of the Learned, and the Acceptance of every Body, being as Natural and Easy to be understood by the meanest Capacities."[6] The apparent success of this form of content probably prompted its reappearance in the full-priced press, and during the early 1720s James Read introduced a substantial element of serialization into his *Weekly Journal*. As well as a regular feature entitled the *Fairy Tatler*,[7] two full-scale serials were launched: in April 1721 the first of a protracted series of *State Trials*,[8] and in August an equally extended *History of England*. These were ostensibly added in response to a reader's letter urging "that you may constantly employ a Part of your Paper, which you seem to have to spare, to a very good purpose, and I think to a much better than I see in Many of those Weekly Entertainments call'd *Journals*, where Paper and Print is very often little better than thrown away, or made use to an ill purpose."[9] The publication of these serials alongside supplementary essays, letters, and poems on a variety of topics, clearly provided a major part of the appeal of Read's paper although giving rise to some problems in presentation. In 1723 it was announced that "several of our Readers having complain'd that our Account of the Kings of England, and also of the State Trials, have not been so entertaining as we would desire, by Reason of the Shortness of them, and the scantiness of the Paper rendering it impossible to make them longer, while they are both in one, we have resolv'd, for the time to come to insert them seperately, in every other Paper, as that having more Room to be succinct and particular, and also to conclude at the properest Periods, we hope to give at once more Instruction and Satisfaction."[10]

Extended pieces were not adopted by any rival papers and Read himself rapidly wound up his serials in favor of a conventional essay following the reduction of space in 1725.

Read's slightly uneasy flirtation with the serial may have been prompted by his family involvement in the cheap press, where this material continued in extensive use, not least because of its potential appeal to women readers. In April 1724 George Parker published a letter in his paper that embodied the accepted female view of this form of supplementary content. The notional writer, "Philo-Romance," referring to an interruption in the publication of the *Arabian Nights Entertainment,* accused Parker of having,

> very much disoblig'd me and a great many more of the Fair (or at least weaker) Sex, by your indirect Practices of late; in postponing the History of the Royal Lovers, for an Account of the Committments of a Parcel of Goal-Birds to the Marshalsea (as you did the other Day) but which is still worse (when this Morning we were big with Expectation of hearing how *Prince* what d'ye call him recover'd his Talisman, and all things were in a fair Way to be set right again) to fob us off with the Epitaph of an old Man of Fourscore, tho' he had been Lord Mayor, yet had no Lady Mayoress, which shows he had no great Veneration for our Sex; I can assure you, if your learned Readers are not more diverted with it than your unlearned you might 'een have kept it to your self: Pray let us have no more of these irregularities for the future, nor our diverting History interrupted by your Trifles or dismal Ditties.[11]

However disingenuous such an item may be, it suggests the sort of audience Parker had in mind, and in spite of the sharp reduction in space after the tax adjustment of 1725, his paper and the papers of his competitors continued to carry large amounts of fiction and related material in serial form.

In the upper reaches of the London press, particularly in the journals, news was increasingly supplemented by a variety of original items in verse and prose, either supplied by a house writer or sent in by way of the extended circle of correspondents that grew up around such publications. This material, scattered initially through the six folio pages, rapidly became an integral feature of journal content. In 1716 a notice in the first issue of the *Charitable Mercury* promised "to make the Paper acceptable to all sorts of

Readers by inserting as Occasion shall offer, any Essay that shall come to hand, for the Entertainment of the Publick of both Sexes and all Conditions."[12] By 1720 original essays and letters were published as the leading items in all the London weeklies, with political comment providing a major theme in the more popular papers. Political material was never isolated in an individual publication, and a conglomeration of other topics was included to diversify the content. This prolixity was important to papers appearing under individual ownership and was based on the need to establish and maintain a very far-flung readership. Politics emerged by the 1720s as the most effective stimulus to sales, but already essay-sheets devoted to alternative themes, manners and morals, or religion, or the theatre and literature, had all proved commercially viable. Few attempts to combine this sort of specialist essay content with weekly news coverage were made before the end of the 1720s, when the intervention of the booksellers led to the appearance of a sequence of new weekly journals picking up and exploiting each of these nonpolitical themes.

One strand of alternative specialization was drawn directly from the program of social and moral improvement that had underpinned the massive success of the *Tatler* and *Spectator*. Use of the old titles and characters had continued to crop up at different levels of the London press, and the use of the original essay itself owed a great deal to its refinement in these publications. It was in avowed imitation of its illustrious predecessor that the *Universal Spectator* was established in 1728. The paper's leading essay, like those of its short-lived rival, the *What-D'Ye-Call-It*, were generally light in tone and explicitly aimed at a female readership.[13] The material on which this appeal was based was essentially noncontroversial. In its initial advertisement the *Universal Spectator* offered "the Progress of Wit and Humor, Free from Politicks and Raillery, Religious Controversy or Dulness"[14] and, for the most part, the published essays steered clear of contention. In 1728 a set of political verses sent in from Exeter was rejected, though the correspondent was invited to supply alternative material.[15] A few weeks later a notice stated that although several letters had been received "*relating to the Affairs of private Families, it is proper to acquaint our Correspondents that every Thing of that kind is directly contrary to the Design of this Paper, and therefore no Body must take it amiss that they are not inserted. One Gentlemen in particular, who has sent four or five Letters about a certain Lady's Misfortunes must excuse our meddling with Matters of such a Nature.*"[16] The sort of topics that were handled in the paper appeared from the first advertisement to carry a content list. "This Number," it stated, "will contain a lively Description of a Happy Married State: With the Ill-consequences attending Quadrille. Also a Copy of Verses on the death of Lora, a Lady's Parrot."[17] Subsequently, the essays published in the *Universal Spectator* were dominated by material on romantic situations and marital or family problems, and the essays offered in the *What-D'Ye-Call-It* were to be similarly concerned with vice and virtue, love, dress, and gallantry.[18] The emphasis on morality and social improvement took a more serious turn in the leading essays of a number of London weeklies, which adopted a variety of literary devices to attract readers. The author of the *British Journal*, for example, which in 1730 dropped its obsessive political line and appeared under new subtitle of the *Traveller*, announced that his intention was "again to travel thro' various Lands, to research the Annals of past Ages, and to exhibit such examples of Virtue as may incite an Emulation in the living to render Praise to the dead by a strict imitation of them."[19] A similar, rather daunting program appeared two years later in a title notice to the *Universal Spy*, which opened with a pompous statement on party writers, who failed

> *to persuade and lead their fellow Countrymen to a noble Reflection on themselves, the rectification of those Abuses, under which they labour, and the Instilling of manly and virtuous Principles: It is therefore proposed, That a Method entirely Novel, and never yet attempted in the Way of a Journal, shall, under the Title Above, be pursued, (that is) That all the Excellencies and Imperfections of human Life shall be displayed by way of* Simile, Fable, *or* Vision.[20]

Linked with the ostensibly more serious content of this type and still appearing within the *Tatler* and *Spectator* framework were the leading essays that dealt directly with religion, an area of controversy that continued to figure prominently in the upper regions of the press.[21] Religious topics, which had previously characterized a number of London essay-sheets, including the very popular *Independent Whig*[22] and the *Protestant Advocate*, formed the dominant theme of several full-priced journals during the 1730s. The *Weekly Miscellany*, established by the extremist clergyman William Webster, perhaps with some Church of England support, was both the earliest and longest lived of these papers. In spite of the claim implicit in the title and the inclusion of a well-developed literary section, the leading essays were almost exclusively theological. As the putative author, Richard Hooker, remarked severely to a light-hearted correspondent, "The primary End of the *Miscellany* is to guard the Minds of the People against Attempts of Infidels to introduce a universal Irreligion and Immorality; and to defend the Church of *England* against the united Efforts of Infidels and Sectaries to destroy it."[23] The bulk of the paper's essay comment was directed against the Protestant dissenters, although occasional forays were made against other religious groups, particularly Catholics and Methodists, and into the field of profound morality. An entirely contrary set of religious principles formed the basis of the essays published in the *Old Whig*, set up in 1735 by the ex-bookseller and dissenting minister Samuel Chandler as a vehicle for essays on behalf of the dissenting groups. The paper, which ran an extended campaign against the restrictive Acts supported by the *Miscellany*, at once embarked on a protracted wrangle with the rival paper on such matters as subscription and the power of the clergy. A third religious position was taken up in the *London Journal*. After the close of its political crusade in 1738, the essays published in the paper, as well as those appearing in its short-lived rival, were devoted almost entirely to religious topics considered from a distinctly unorthodox point of view.[24] In 1736 a contemporary remarked of the author that some people "think he has too much Religion while a great Party among the Clergy think he has none at all."[25]

The involvement of the book trade in the projection and support of the new range of specialist weeklies was most evident in those journals in which the leading essay was focused on contemporary literature. The link between newspaper content and current publications was long established. Lists and abstracts of new books and pamphlets had appeared separately since the 1690s,[26] and the sort of information that they contained has been incorporated in newspapers at least since the beginning of the century. However, increasingly comprehensive efforts were made to provide readers with full literary coverage. In 1721, for example, it was announced in the *Gentlemen's Journal* that the paper would contain "*an Account of Books, Pamphlets, etc. that are publish'd every Week, whereby those who are Encouragers of Learning, will in a few Minutes, Receive that Information which otherwise they must spend Hours in searching after.*"[27] The following year the introduction to the *St. James's Journal* promised to supply readers with "*Abstracts of the most curious Pieces that are published all over* Europe, *in what language or Faculty soever, especially such as relate to the* Belles Lettres; *and as nothing material contained in them shall be omitted, 'tis to be hoped, as they will require much less Time and Expense, they will not be less useful than the larger volumes.*"[28] All the full-priced forms attempted something of the kind later in the decade and while, for example, the *Daily Courant* contained occasional foreign literary announcements,[29] the thrice-weekly *Evening Journal* offered "the Student, the Merchant, and the Politician" a regular account of the new books published both in England and abroad.[30]

However, literary coverage continued to be focused in the weeklies. This emphasis was most clearly evident in two London journals: the *Weekly Medley,* published in 1729 and subsequently subtitled the *Literary Journal,* and the *Weekly Miscellany,* published in 1732. Both papers contained a variably extended account of books published on the Continent under separate national headings, readers of the *Miscellany* being invited to observe "the Extensiveness of our Correspondence, the Earliness of our Intelligence, and the Usefulness of this Part of our Design."[31] They also both carried a conventional list of new English titles, those advertised in the *Miscellany* itself being distinguished "in such a Manner that they can't escape the Eye of the most superficial Reader." The way in which these conventional forms of content could merge into an overall literary scheme was again clearly indicated in the *Miscellany.* It was stated that "if any Piece greatly *Useful,* or greatly *Censurable,* shall come out, it will be a proper Subject for our Animadversion in the *Letter* or *Essay,* and so become Part of our *principal Design.*" During the late 1720s and early 1730s a series of weeklies under bookseller ownership were published in London, carrying a larger than usual volume of essays on literary subjects. *The Knight Errant,* the *Weekly Medley*, the *Weekly Register* and, most importantly, the *Grub Street Journal* were all papers of this type. The *Grub Street Journal*, for example, although engaged in a long series of miscellaneous controversies,[32] was avowedly published with the aim of exercising a critical censorship over various forms of output.[33] The title of its short-lived successor, the *Literary Courier of Grub Street*, itself indicated the continued emphasis on essays with a literary theme.[34]

The sudden boom in the publication of nonpolitical essay-papers was short lived. From the early 1730s the steady increase in direct competition from the London magazines, and to some extent the provincial newspapers, proved particularly damaging.[35] At the same time, a wider range of nonpolitical material was becoming available through the mushroom growth of cut-price publications.[36] The amorphous weeklies published at this level and standing mid-way between the magazines and the conventional journal combined very variable serialization with a mass of original nonpolitical items aimed at a broadening readership. The variety of this content was suggested in the case of Robert Walker's *Weekly Tatler* which, published in two sheets at 1½d., offered a historical vindication of the Stuarts in serial form with "some entertaining Letters and Tales collected from the *Persian Tales*, *Tales of the Fairies*, etc. with original Poems, Songs, Epigrams, Satyrs, Lampoons, Panegyricks, Amours, Intrigues, etc. And the best and freshest Account of all Authentick Domestick and Foreign News." On the second large sheet he provided "a Collection of the best Comedies, Tragedies and Operas, which have not hitherto been printed at a reasonable Price."[37] The growing demand for all forms of factual information was also catered to in the ambiguous weekly newspapers. The *Weekly Oracle*, appearing in 1734, guaranteed readers that the first sheet would "always contain some Moral or Instructive Essay in Prose or Verse, either Original or extracted from the best Authors,"[38] as well as the news. However, the second sheet was given over to the sort of question-and-answer service that had proved popular at the beginning of the century.[39] According to the introduction, a special panel consisting of a clergyman, doctor, a lawyer, a mathematician "of a truly mechanical Head and Genius," a philosopher, a virtuoso specializing in the study of insects, and a man of fashion had been assembled to deal with readers' questions. These covered a wide and generally educational area and the team were asked to assess the population of London, to state whether glass was poisonous, to give rules for pleasing in conversation, and so on.[40] Even in the farthing dailies the popular serials were frequently accompanied by variations on the nonpolitical content of the full-priced papers. The *London Farthing Post*, for example, regularly included a romantic poem, sometimes serialized through several issues,[41] while *All Alive and Merry* ran a series of mercifully short jokes under the subtitle of the *British Jester*.[42]

The build-up in pressure, which by the end of the 1730s had led to the collapse of a large proportion of nonpolitical weeklies, including such an initially successful venture as the *Grub Street Journal*, stimulated variable modifications in the content of the survivors. Both the main printer-owned weeklies ceased to carry an original essay and turned again toward the serial. The shifts in the character of the leading items carried by *Read's Weekly Journal* and Applebee's *Original Weekly Journal* after 1725 followed a similar pattern, although with slightly different timing. Regular publication of a leading political essay, for and against the administration respectively, was followed by a change of emphasis to light, largely nonpolitical material and finally to the adoption of long-term serialization. Applebee's journal was the first to introduce a substantial element of this sort of extended item, and from the late 1720s the paper's supplementary content was dominated by serializations of foreign fiction, sometimes specially translated for this purpose.[43] In 1732 Read also again began to publish serials in his paper, apparently with some success. The first issue that offered this form of content, containing the opening of Voltaire's *Life of Charles XII*, was said to have been reprinted by public demand,[44] and subsequently the paper, which outlived all its nonpolitical rivals, based its supplementary appeal on extended serialization that was issued from 1733 on a supplementary sheet.[45]

Among the papers that continued to offer original essays within a variable program of instruction and entertainment, the pressure of competition that built up during the 1730s led almost inevitably toward the area of political controversy. In the more serious weeklies attempts were sometimes made to counter commercial pressure by lightening the heavy moral tone. As the author of the *Universal Spectator* remarked, "a poignant Discourse, which is at the same Time light and carries its moral concealed so that few perceive it, sells twice as well as the most elaborate piece of Morality."[46] This commercial diagnosis, which underlay the paper's national success[47] was clearly forced on the proprietors of the religious-essay papers. In the final issue of the *Old Whig* readers were assured that it would reappear in a new guise, "wherein a greater Latitude and Variety of Subjects may arise for the Instruction and Amusement: In which it shall be our Business to lead our Readers not only to true Opinions, but Scenes of Action in publick and private life."[48] On the other hand, Webster's reluctance to publish light essay material in the *Miscellany* kept the paper on the brink of disaster throughout the 1730s. The emergence of Methodism at the end of the decade provided a topical theme for renewed theological invective.[49] However, the inclusion of a slightly higher proportion of genuinely miscellaneous material at this point[50] suggests a belated attempt to boost readership by lightening the tone. Webster's efforts in this direction were extended when his paper was taken over in 1741 and, while the advertisements for the *New Weekly Miscellany* continued to offer essays on religion and morality, "Humours, Fashions etc." were added to the list of topics to be regularly handled.[51] Such efforts seem, at best, to have offered a temporary respite and the *Miscellany* was soon absorbed in the political struggle.

The adoption of a political line could involve a variety of local circumstances, including the ideological commitment of the proprietors. However, the appearance of opposition material in a previously neutral essay paper was almost always linked to declining commercial circumstances and represented, in part at least, an attempt to maintain a position in the crowded market. Between 1737 and 1742 a ¹⁄₁₂ share in the *Universal Spectator* slumped in value from £23 to £2. 2s.[52] and although the character of its essay content remained largely unchanged, vigorously partisan material was injected at this point into its news section. The final collapse of the paper in 1746 underlined the swing in public taste and it was characteristic of the shift in the content of this section of the press that its correspondents were recommended to apply to the predominantly political *Westminster Journal.*[53]

From the late 1730s changes in the character of supplementary content were also evident in other areas of the London press. While the long-term literary and historical serials continued to appear in the cut-price weeklies and also the farthing dailies until their suppression in 1743, this material became less characteristic of the penny thrice-weeklies. In 1742 a serialized life of Cromwell began to appear in *Rayner's London Morning Advertiser*[54] and in 1746 a "Collection of Letters, on various Subjects, to eminent Persons" began a long run in the *Penny London Post.*[55] However, in papers of this type the emphasis shifted increasingly to news and current affairs features interspersed with a variety of individual or short-term items on a wide range of miscellaneous topics. Some of these conformed to the traditional pattern of social and moral improvement. For example, at the end of 1743 consecutive issues of the *Universal London Morning Advertiser* contained essays under the headings "DEPORMITY *not always a Sign of an* Ill Man" and "*of* PATIENCE *and* POWER *over our* Passions,"[56] and such material continued to crop up occasionally in this section of the press usually with a more popular and lighter tone.[57] More frequent were the random items providing factual information on a very wide range of topics. In one week in March 1745 the *Penny London Post* carried an essay on the uses of the microscope, an account of a rattlesnake, and the first of a series of items on hurricanes, earth-quakes, and similar phenomena.[58]

The same sort of combination appeared in the extended and overlapping content of the full-priced thrice-weeklies and dailies. A variable number of non-political items in verse and prose had become a regular part of the content of these papers since the 1720s, the *Daily Journal* in particular becoming associated with this material.[59] In the mid-1740s, with the general increase in page size, a new element of original content in the form of short essay features began to be introduced. An early attempt to provide such material through a daily paper had been made in 1736 and 1737 when Aaron Hill's theatrical essay-sheet, the *Prompter,* had been incorporated in the *Daily Journal.* But is was not until the alarms of the Jacobite rebellion that this sort of original item came into widespread use, appearing under such running titles as the *Briton,* the *Subject,* the *Fool,* and the *Ventilator: Or, Universal News Monger.*[60] Many of the features were shared between publications, the *Fool,* for example, appearing irregularly in the *Gazetteer* in

1746 and reappearing in the thrice-weekly *General London Evening Mercury*. The content was very miscellaneous, ranging across politics and those areas of instruction and entertainment which had become familiar in other sections of the press. The publication of short factual pieces, which paralleled the extended use of news backgrounds, also became characteristic of the principal thrice-weekly and daily papers at the end of this period. During September and October 1747, for example, the flourishing *General Advertiser* provided readers with an account and defense of the Copernican system, followed by short essays headed "*The* PROGRESS *of* PHYSICKS, *or* NATURAL PHILOSOPHY," "*Of the* BAROMETER *and* THERMOMETER," and "*Of the* AIR PUMP."[61] The usual combination of items in this section of the press was reflected in the proprietor's instructions to the printer of the *General Evening Post* to include pieces of Postlethwaite's *Dictionary* as well as material from the racy nonpolitical essay-sheets, the *World* and the *Connoisseur*.[62]

Through the London newspapers of the middle decades of the eighteenth century, contemporaries received a clear but limited view of the world. Whatever the range of the items of news and information, the perspective was invariably that of the dominant elites and in particular of the respectable businessmen who controlled the organization of the press. The emphasis within this area of content was invariably on those materials which facilitated and encouraged the activities of the trading community, whether through coverage of foreign affairs, the provision of commercial information, or the supply of a comprehensive range of advertisements. At the same time, until the early 1740s the supplementary content of the London papers, published in different forms and at different market levels, extended access to areas of the dominant culture, the materials of which formed the proprietors' main stock in trade. Through the press the frontiers of cultural participation were pushed back, although the tone never wavered and, even in the cheap press, the values of the establishment were never challenged. Publication of cut-price newspapers was not ideologically motivated, and the heavy emphasis on areas of conventional literature underlines the sharp distinction between these papers and their radical counterparts produced at the end of the century. As the alternative forms of periodical publication were developed, largely through the exploitation of forms of material originating in the London newspapers themselves, and as the booksellers' control of the press became more effective, so a good deal of the diversity of newspaper content disappeared. Increasingly news and advertising became the main line of provision and it was the dailies and thrice-weeklies, in which this material was focused, that came through the 1740s in the greatest strength. Although the range of supplementary items that they carried was increasing, their content was predominantly routine and businesslike and their success exemplified the process of "commercialization" that was at work within the London press, defining its character and shaping all the forms of material that it carried.

10

The London Press in Mid-Century

By 1750 the London newspapers formed part of a spectrum of periodical output competing for readers within a national market and opening up new social and geographical areas that could offer mutual commercial benefits. The provincial journals, which had begun to appear early in the century, continued their erratic growth, reaching a high point of forty-two separate weeklies in 1746. Often set up by printers whose skills were acquired in the capital and who took the London papers as a model for their own, as well as for the source of much of their material, the local press formed an interlocking network of publications that by mid-century covered a large part of the nation. At the same time, the monthly magazines published in London also grew in number and popularity, offering a low-price compendium of material which, if no longer by 1750 drawn entirely from the newspapers, followed a similar pattern and were directed at an overlapping readership.

Against this background the total circulation of the London newspapers continued to rise, possibly accelerating toward mid-century. Although this process cannot be pinned down in detail, some guidelines for an overall assessment have already been established. On one hand are the comparatively prolix figures for Queen Anne's reign, resurrected from Robert Harley's papers and providing an accurate account of circulation for short periods early in the century.[1] On the other is the nonspecific, but still useful, record of the gross number of newspaper stamps sold annually between 1750 and 1756.[2] Such figures are entirely lacking for the intermediate period, but it is possible on the basis of the few available statistics, as well as of the sort of hypothetical calculations already described, to trace some of the shifts in the circulation levels of different forms and to indicate the way in which the marked growth in readership took place.

During the 1720s and early 1730s, political circumstances led to a dominance of the weekly journals. The *Craftsman's* sale of about 13,000 copies weekly may have represented a ceiling in this area, although earlier claims for both the *London Journal* and *Mist's* suggest even higher figures. How-

ever, this market supremacy was comparatively short-lived, and while by
the late 1730s the *Craftsman* was selling less than 5,000 copies, it seems
unlikely that even the most successful political journals of this and the
subsequent decade were able to stabilize their circulation at a much higher
level. During the late 1730s and early 1740s the most dramatic expansion
apparently took place among the cheap unstamped papers, and the contemporary estimates to a total of 50,000 or 60,000 copies circulated weekly,
although perhaps exaggerated, suggest the impact of the boom in sales at
this level. The almost complete suppression of these illegal publications in
1743 benefited the legitimate papers and during the mid-1740s the area of
greatest sales success shifted to the primarily news-carrying sections of the
London press. In 1746 the circulation of the *London Daily Post* was rapidly
approaching 2,500 copies per day and it seems likely that its very successful
rival, the *Daily Advertiser,* was achieving an even higher figure. By the
mid-1740s the *London Evening Post* was probably selling over 5,000 copies
per issue and, even if the claim in the *Penny London Post* of a circulation of
7,000 copies was more optimistic than accurate, it seems reasonable to
suppose that its level of sales was also over 5,000.

Taking these figures as a rough guide, a tentative estimate can be made of
the annual total sale of the London newspapers in 1746. Allowing the five
dailies an average circulation throughout the year of 1,500 copies per issue,
the six thrice-weeklies an average of 2,500 copies, the five weeklies an
average of 3,000 copies, and the two principal cut-price thrice-weeklies an
average of 3,500 copies, the weekly sale would have amounted to 100,000
and the annual total to over five million copies. This account makes no
allowances for either the *Daily Post* or the *Universal Spectator,* which were
dropped during the year, or for other related forms of publication such as
essay-sheets and the Moribund news letters. The number of newspaper
stamps purchased in 1750 amounted to 7,313,266, of which some two
million were used for provincial papers, and the similarity of the figures,
allowing for the unusual demand of the mid-1740s, seems to suggest that
these speculative and probably conservative estimates have at least some
basis in fact. Consequently it is possible to assert that on Saturdays during
1746 at least 45,000 papers were sold, about twice the number published at
any time during Queen Anne's reign. Allowing for the moderate estimate
of ten readers per paper, this could have meant a *de facto* readership of not
far short of half-a-million. At the same time, although the London newspapers were distributed nationally, the most marked rise in circulation took
place among the daily and cut-price papers, whose sale was focused in the
capital and consequently the main impact of this dramatic growth was
probably felt in London itself. Aspinall refers disparagingly to the
"ridiculously small circulation" of the eighteenth-century newspapers.[3]
However, in basing his view on the sale of the mass-produced juggernauts
of a later period, Aspinall, like many subsequent historians, overlooked the

virtual revolution of the scale of newspaper distribution that had already taken place by 1750.

What did the considerable mid-century totals imply about the character of the readership? Can the high numerical level be taken to indicate a substantial extension in the range of individuals and groups reached by the London papers? These are questions that it is peculiarly difficult to answer, given the patchy and fragmented nature of the evidence. It seems likely that a large proportion of the total circulation increase can be accounted for by a higher level of intake among the middle and upper ranks, who clearly continued to form the backbone of the readership. To some extent this was achieved by an extended provincial sales. The rising number of copies passing through the Post Office suggests a growing demand among country readers who could afford the relatively high cost of the publications produced in London. According to Cranfield, the provincial readership of the papers published in the capital consisted largely of "the local gentry the clergymen and the town magnates,"[4] and the consistent preponderance of readers at this social level and above is also indicated in a few surviving subscription lists. The seventy individuals supplied by Charles Delafaye during Queen Anne's reign included ten members of the peerage, three knights, two bishops and eight other clergymen, three mayors, a judge and an attorney, five government and four military officers, as well as a further eighteen "esquires." The customers supplied with newspapers by Robert Gosling during the 1730s came from similar social backgrounds, and the subscription lists of the *Craftsman* were composed entirely of leading members of both houses of Parliament.

London circulation levels were also rising, largely, it appears, through increased sales within the trading community, whose concerns figured so extensively in the content of the newspapers. Direct evidence of personal interest at the upper levels is hard to come by but can be glimpsed in the dairy of Stephen Monteage, a city merchant active in the South Sea Company from the 1730s to the 1750s.[5] Monteage's outlay on newspapers was small, seldom exceeding £1 a year, presumably because of their general availability through his office and the coffee-house, but at the same time his long-term readership of the *Daily Advertiser* is constantly evident. Until 1740 his diary was regularly prefaced with items of news, recipes, and poems taken from the paper,[6] while individual entries continued to refer to news reports of particular interest, such as deaths and bankruptcies.[7] During 1746 the nonspecific entries in his accounts for newspapers and related items, the *Sessions Papers*, and trials of the rebels, increased and the regular outlay of 6d. a week suggests his personal subscription to the *Daily Advertiser* at this point.[8] Whatever the importance of Monteage's mercantile contemporaries in extending newspaper purchase, the build-up in circulation of the full-priced papers, particularly the dailies, was probably centered on less exalted commercial groups. Here again direct evidence of the

identity of subscribers is lacking and one of the few clues to the composition
of newspaper readership at this level comes from outside the trade through
the activity of the proprietors of the insurance companies earlier in the
century. Between 1705 and 1715 Charles Povey and his successors offered
potential policy holders the incentive of a commercially orientated newspaper at a very reduced rate. In the case of the important *British Mercury,*
which had achieved a total circulation of nearly 4,000 copies by 1715, this
was set by the Sun Insurance Company at 6d. a quarter.[9] It seems likely that
a majority of subscribers took advantage of the special rate and therefore
that the table of about 3,500 policy-holders published in the *Mercury* in
1714 was virtually a subscription list to the paper itself.[10] Although the
composition was very varied, including, for example, several peers and a
large number of "gentlemen," the bulk consisted of booksellers, shoe-
makers, bakers, coal merchants, weavers, and a mass of other self-employed tradesmen, shopkeepers, and craftsmen. A newspaper was clearly
considered an effective draw, and it seems likely that in mid-century a large
proportion of the readers of the full-priced forms were drawn from this
sector.[11] While the rising circulation levels can to some extent be accounted
for by greater penetration of such established groups, it seems clear that
new interests were also involved. The extent to which women readers were
targeted in the content of all forms of London newspapers suggests their
importance in maintaining and increasing sales. It is impossible to quantify
any such development and it is even harder to pin down the process by
which newspaper intake was extended among groups previously excluded
by considerations of cost and problems of literacy. In this area the emergence of the cut-price newspapers of the second decade probably provided
a major stimulus. The main target group of these papers was ostensibly the
lower reaches of the trading community. James Read's *Penny Post* was
subtitled the *Tradesman's Select Pacquet,* William Heathcote's *London Post,* the
Tradesman's Intelligence, and William Rayner's *Oxford Journal,* also the *Tradesman's Intelligence.* However, their readership certainly extended into less
conventional areas. Acording to the author of the *British Mercury,* writing in
1712, "*the meanest of Shopkeepers* and *Handicrafts*" were particularly suscepti-
ble to the newspaper habit,[12] and the purchasers of the cut-price papers
probably came to include a growing number of individuals drawn from the
floating population of servants, street traders, laborers, and comparable
groups, although their involvement remains almost entirely submerged.[13]

In London in particular the range of potential newspaper purchasers
was increasing as developments in the press coincided with those in society
at large. During a period of slowly rising wages, which were at their highest
in the capital and which seldom fell below 10/- a week,[14] regular purchase
of a London paper was within the reach of all but the poorest. Prior to 1725
subscription to an extended "post" or six-page journal could amount to
1½d. or 1d. a week, while the subsequent development of the unstamped
press meant that every copy of a thrice-weekly or daily paper could be

The Politician, by William Hogarth; the original n.d. but after 1735. It shows a London tradesman reading the *Gazetteer.*

obtained for a weekly outlay of as little as 1½d. or 1¼d. Even after the suppression of 1743, a number of legitimately stamped thrice-weekly or weekly papers were still available at the cost of 3d. and 1½d. a week respectively. These very low prices, which were not paralleled anywhere in the provinces and which were combined with a wide accessibility, suggest that the London readership reached a long way down the social scale by the mid-1740s.

An apparent rise in the literacy rate was also increasing the number of potential newspaper readers at this level and, to some extent, the cut-price publications were cashing in on developments in formal education. These were centered in the fashionable and rapidly expanding Charity School movement initiated in London in 1698. Within six years 32 of the parishes of London and Westminster had schools specifically aimed at providing the children of the poor with a rudimentary educational background, including reading skills, and in June 1704, 2,000 selected pupils walked in procession to a service at St. Andrew's Holborn.[15] By 1729 the number of Charity Schools in London and Westminster had risen to 132, taking in 5,225 children, while in the adjacent counties of Middlesex, Surrey, and Kent at least a further 111 schools had been set up by the late 1720s.[16] How far such institutions helped to extend the already massive demand for printed materials that had appeared in the long-term sale of almanacks and chapbooks is not clear.[17] But it seems that the papers themselves provided a stimulus to literacy and were also, in a sense, creating their own readers. As E. A. Wrigley has pointed out, "Life in London probably encouraged a certain educational achievement in a wider spectrum of the population than might be expected," and the cheap press provided an important aid to the process of educational self-help.[18] The element of practical instruction was also identified within the full-priced papers and was most marked in a variety of foreign-language publications. The French edition of the *British Mercury*, for example, was claimed to be "taken in by divers English, for the easier acquiring of the French Tongue,"[19] while in 1729 the *Weekly Medley*, published in a parallel French and English test, was advertised as "very useful for Schools."[20] However, the cut-price papers, with their wide range of supplementary content, had a more direct impact in this area. According to George Parker, petitioning Parliament against the tax of 1725, the halfpenny paper was of particular value "to the poorer sort of People, who are Purchasers of it by Reason of its Cheapness, to divert themselves, and also to allure therewith their Young Children, and entice them to reading."[21] Similar claims continued to be made in the papers themselves and in 1751 the *British Spectator*, a new publication selling at 1d., was described as of value to all readers but *"especially Youth, as it will induce them to read; which they are debarr'd from, (more's the Pity) because their well meaning Parents can't afford to lay out too much Money at once."*[22]

It therefore seems likely that the substantial circulation levels of mid-century were linked to a quite broad-based readership and the London newspapers apparently remained an accepted feature of life among the most obscure social groups. Within the spectrum of clubs formed by the humblest urban workers[23] the newspapers probably continued to supply most of the material "for Discourse and Speculation,"[24] and in 1758 Dr. Johnson claimed that "all foreigners remark, that the knowledge of the common people of England is greater than that of any other vulgar. This superiority we undoubtedly owe to the rivolets of intelligence, which are continually trickling among us, which every one may catch, and of which every one partakes,"[25] While some parallel extension of readership was probably also taking place in the provinces, the conditions did not exist locally for the sort of downward growth that was evident in London, and it is significant that Cranfield, in attempting to illustrate provincial development, was often thrown back on examples that referred specifically to the capital.[26]

The extended readership seems to have survived the suppression of the unstamped newspapers and the subsequent rundown of the legitimate, penny publications, both of which circumstances were symptoms of the capture of the London press by the interests of commerce and politics. By 1750 the implications of the bookseller takeover were clear enough. The injection of capital had had some beneficial effects. In the short term bookseller investment had breathed some life into the essay-carrying papers of the 1720s and 1730s, while in the long term their financing of the dailies and thrice-weeklies underwrote the recruitment of additional personnel and contributed to a general rise in the standard of news coverage. Equally, bookseller management resulted in the emergence of a greater overall stability within the London press, and the mushroom growth of newspapers of the earlier years was replaced by a smaller number of durable publications that provided some continuity of approach. To set against these apparent advantages was the general closing down of access to the press and the gradual squeezing out of competition. To an extent this was carried through by the bookseller proprietors themselves, whose influence over distribution and advertising was crucial in the suppression of rival publications. However, their actions were substantially reinforced by the implicit support of the political establishment. The sequence of parliamentary acts which pushed up prices and destroyed fringe elements of the London press were the product of concerted action from both directions. The Act of 1725, which was directed at the extended journals and cut-price thrice-weeklies standing outside the developing network of bookseller control, brought a large category of successful publications firmly into line and removed much of their commercial advantage. The later Act of 1743 was more directly repressive, blotting out the cheap, unstamped papers that represented an alternative line of competition. In both cases, as in 1712, the politicians, eager to deal with potential vehicles of extremism and sedition, found their interests and those of the booksellers developing in tandem. Uniformity and stability were to the commercial advantage of the well-financed and respectable papers in which bookseller interest was focused, and the legal process, working obliquely across the press, also helped to maintain a mutually desirable state of equilibrium. The threat of private as well as political action encouraged a high level of self-censorship and prevented the use of personal comment and other forms of controversial material as the basis for an alternative appeal.

The gradual tightening of the booksellers' grip on the London press was clearly expressed through the careers of the most active of the independent entrepreneurs of the 1720s and 1730s. After his release from prison William Rayner continued in the newspaper business, concentrating his output in the apparently popular penny thrice-weekly that had appeared under his name. However, by the end of the 1740s both he and his paper disappear from view. This may have been the result of personal circumstances. On the other hand, he can hardly have failed to see the way things were moving in the trade and as a skillful opportunist may simply have transferred into the mainstream of newspaper ownership. The various shares held at his death in 1761 certainly seem to indicate this sort of maneuver. Similarly, Robert Walker, whose personal finances may have been even less stable, moved out of newspapers altogether and by the mid-1740s had adopted a mixed output based on low-key pamphlet material.

Through their control of the London newspapers the booksellers were also able to reconstruct the hierarchy of function that existed elsewhere in the trade. Authors and printers were, if not entirely subordinated, at least slotted into an organization in which their freedom of action was severely restricted. The newspapers were never a central concern of the book-trade shareholders, whose main commercial interests lay in other forms of output. This can, to some extent, explain why the conduct of most papers was left in the hands of the printer and, at the same time, why the publications themselves remained so static in form and layout. Even so, the newspapers came to be of considerable importance to the book trade generally in ways which extended beyond the channel they supplied for advertising and the modest but regular income they produced. The newspaper shareholders seem to have become an important part of the infrastructure of the trade and it is possible to suggest that these groups of like-minded business colleagues superseded the less coherent "congers" that had coordinated the activities of the trade since the seventeenth century. By 1750 the London press was a stable and respectable institution run by clubs of increasingly prosperous booksellers who, in combination, can be seen as the first press establishment. John Nichols, the benevolent and learned proprietor of shares in a variety of London papers toward the end of the century provides an apposite personal contrast with the multifarious projectors of the earlier decades.

This emphasis on stasis cannot conceal the newspaper's continuing importance as an active and reactive medium. All successful London publications stood at the center of circles of correspondents, known and unknown, who continuously deluged the papers with contributions of one sort or another. A proportion of the essay material published in the press was generated in this way and the editorial comments in some papers suggests an almost overwhelming input from readers. In 1727 the author of *Mist's Journal* stated bluntly, "Mr. Mist receives daily a great Number of Packets from his Friends, as well as Strangers, containing Pieces of Poetry, Scandal, Controversy, etc. desiring them to be inserted; whereas the Paper being of a certain Gage, cannot hold the 20th Part of what is sent; nor is it consistent with the Business of this Journal to publish Things that no way concern the Publick; and, 'tis hoped, that no Person hereafter will expect a particular Reason, or private Letters from him to satisfy them why he rejects any such Pieces, or why he judges them unfit for his Paper; A Matter that must take up all his Time."[27] Debate through the press was concerned with a bewildering range of subjects and issues, but the interaction between newspapers and readers was most fully developed in the area of politics. Through the London press, opposition groupings established circuits of political communication, linking all sections of the political community and placing the newspaper itself at the center of the political process.[28] This active role of the press in society made it a potentially unstable instrument in the hands of its commercial and political controllers. Throughout its history the newspaper press has veered between the forces of stability and change. If in the age of Walpole the emphasis was on an increasingly commercial stability, the channel for social and political change remained firmly open.

Notes

Preface

1. E.g., F. Knight Hunt, *The Fourth Estate*, 2 vols. (London, 1850); Alexander Andrews, *The History of British Journalism*, 2 vols. (London, 1859); H. R. Fox Bourne, *English Newspapers*, 2 vols. (London, 1887).

2. Analagous to the use of newspapers in literary research is the quarrying of the London press for material on such specialist topics as music and the theater.; e.g., R. McGuiness, "Newspapers and Musical Life in Eighteenth-Century London," *Journal of Newspaper and Periodical History* 1 (1984): 29–36.

Chapter 1: The Shaping of the London Newspaper

1. For an examination of the circumstances leading to the lapse, see Raymond Astbury, "The Renewal of the Licensing Act in 1693 and its Lapse in 1695," *Library*, 5th ser., 33 (1978): 296–322.

2. *The Printers' Case: Humbly submitted to the Consideration of the Honourable House of Commons* [1712]. *B.M.* 369, Saturday 2 August 1712. See the list of papers appearing in 1709 in J. Nichols, *Biographical and Literary Anecdotes of William Bowyer* (London, 1782), 493.

3. See G. A. Cranfield, *The Development of the Provincial Newspaper 1700–1760* (Oxford: Clarendon Press, 1962), 7–8, 28–29, 48; R. Munter, *The History of the Irish Newspaper 1685–1700* (Cambridge: at the University Press, 1967), 17.

4. A number of petitions to Parliament urging some form of compulsory registrations appear in Lincolns Inn Library, M.P. 102.

5. F. S. Siebert, *Freedom of the Press in England, 1476–1776* (Urbana: University of Illinois Press, 1952), 306–8.

6. It has been suggested that the Act was introduced mainly as a revenue-raising device. Alan Downie, "The Growth of Government Tolerance of the Press to 1790," in *Development of the English Book Trade, 1700–1899*, ed. Robin Myers and Michael Harris (Oxford: at the Polytechnic Press, 1981). However, this does not seem an adequate explanation, given the long-term maneuvering of the political and commercial interest groups. For a full account of the Act of 1712, its application, and the variable forms of evasion, see D. F. Foxon, "The Stamp Act of 1712," Sanders Lectures 1978, unrevised text.

7. E.g., *A Proposal for Restraining the Great Licentiousness of the Press Throughout Great Britain and for Redressing the many Abuses and Mischiefs thereof* [1710]. This contained suggestions for suppressing newspapers by depriving them of their advertising revenue.

8. *B.M.* 369, Saturday 2 August 1712. See also *The Spectator*, ed. D. F. Bond, 5 vols. (Oxford: Clarendon Press, 1965), 4, 62–65.

9. See J. M. Price, "A Note on the Circulation of the London Pres, 1704–1714," *Bulletin of the Institute of Historical Research* 31 (1957): 215–24. Also H. L. Snyder, "The Circulation of Newspapers in the Reign of Queen Anne," *Library*, 5th ser., 23 (1968): 206–35. Snyder provides a fuller analysis and his account is preferred in subsequent notes. See also H. L. Snyder, "A Further Note on the Circulation of Newspapers in the Reign of Queen Anne," *Library*, 5th ser, 31 (1978): 387–89.

10. The advertisement duty was not payable by newspapers registered as pamphlets.

11. *Pax* 2808, Saturday 9 May 1713; *F.P.* 3375, Saturday 16 May 1713.

12. John Toland, *Proposal for Regulating the News-papers* (1717). Printed in L. Hanson, *Government and the Press 1695–1763* (Oxford: Clarendon Press, reissue, 1967), 135–38.

13. *D.P.* 214, Wednesday 8 June 1720–218, Monday 13 June 1720.

14. Broadsheets 232 (6), London University Goldsmiths Library.

15. *B.M.* 369, Saturday 2 August 1712. The last page was initially left blank. See below, chap. 9.

16. *B.M.* 528, Saturday 13 August 1715.

17. *B.M.* 566, Wednesday 2 May 1716, final issue prior to the publication of the *Historical Register*.

18. *N.L.* 1, Saturday 7 January 1716.

19. The papers produced by Robert Mawson and Nathaniel Mist. Developments in other sections of the press seem to have put an end to this practice.

20. Notice in *L.J.* 123, Saturday 2 December 1721.

21. See comment in *W.J. or S.P.* Saturday 16 December 1721.

22. First issue in the Burney collection 103, Monday 25 November 1717. Heathcote had already produced the *Weekly Remarks*, first published at the end of 1715 and suppressed.

23. For a rambling account of the timing of the publication of both papers, see *P.L.N.* 1,003, Wednesday 21 April 1725. According to Parker, Heathcote's paper was suppressed by the authorities following his failure to pay the advertising duty, but was subsequently resurrected.

24. Printed for the author by E. Midwinter.

25. List in J. Nichols, *Literary Anecdotes of the Eighteenth Century,* 8 vols. (London, 1812–15), 1: 288–312. Those mentioned are "Heathcot's, Baldwin's-gardens, Parkers, Salisbury-court, Reads, White Fryers, Fleet-street."

26. *P.L.N.* 1,000, Wednesday 14 April 1725. *P.L.N.* 992, Friday 26 March 1725, contains a vigorous attack on an unidentified "Tonsor" of Salisbury Court for his part in the campaign.

27. *M.W.J.* 1, Saturday 1 May 1725. Page one reprinted in S. Morison, *The English Newspaper* (Cambridge: at the University Press, 1932), 102.

28. Cranfield, *Provincial Newspaper,* 20.

29. *Reasons humbly offer'd to the Parliament in behalf of several Persons concern'd in Paper making, Printing and Publishing the Half-penny News-Papers. . . .* (London; n.d.). Printed in *P.L.N.* 988, Wednesday 17 March 1725, and cited below as *Reasons.*

30. *W.J. or B.G.* 5, Saturday 29 May 1725.

31. *P.L.N.* 1,000, Wednesday 14 April 1725; 1,001, Friday 16 April 1725.

32. *P.L.N.* 1,005, Saturday Evening, 24 April 1725.

33. A reprint of the titles of the *Weekly Journal, or Saturday Post* and the *London Journal* appears in Morison, *English Newspaper,* 96.

34. *Gaylard's Journal,* produced by the same printer.

35. *West. J.* 20, Saturday 28 November 1741.

36. Notice in *L.E.P.* 141, Saturday 2 November 1728.

37. *M.W.J.* 3, Saturday 17 May 1725; 306, Saturday 5 June 1725; *W.J. or B.G.* 7, Saturday 12 June 1725; *B.J.* 224, Saturday 7 January 1727.

38. *D.J.* 1,838, Monday 5 December 1726; *D.P.* 22,152, Monday 12 December 1726. *The Daily Post Boy* was appearing in the same form by the early 1730s.

39. *D.J.* 2,190, Friday 19 January 1728.

40. There was also some difficulty in obtaining stamped paper of the necessary size. *D.J.* 2,192, Tuesday 23 January 1728.

41. Title notices in *D.J.* 2,201, Thursday 1 February 1728; 2,219, Thursday 22 February 1728; 2,220, Friday 23 February 1728.

42. Advertisement for *L.E.P.* in *U.S.* 268, Saturday 24 November 1733 and for *G.E.P.* in *C.* 386, Saturday 1 December 1733.

43. *D.C.* ca. Friday 2 January 1730. A number of issues are missing from the Burney collection at this point.

44. *T.B.P.* 1731–34, 65. He also suggested a restriction on the number of lines in each advertisement.

45. The type area of the *Craftsman* was enlarged from ca. 10″ × 8″ in 1727 to ca. 13¼″ × 9″ in 1732. No further increase took place and all the journals of this period remained within these measurements.

46. The type area of the *London Evening Post* was enlarged most strikingly; from ca. 10½″ × 7″ in 1728 to ca. 16¼″ × 9½″ in 1744.

47. The type area of the *London Daily Post* and *General Advertiser* was enlarged to ca. 13¾″ × 9½″ by the early 1740s. The area in the four-page issues was slightly smaller.

48. See advertisement in *U.S.* 256, Saturday 7 September 1733.

49. *C.* 2, Friday 9 December 1726. In the mid-1750s six-page essay-papers, such as the *Monitor*, were registered as pamphlets, and official acceptance of this evasion perhaps reflected a change in the political atmosphere.

50. *L.M.* 2 (1733): 261–63. See R. M. Wiles, *Serial Publicaton in England before 1750* (Cambridge: at the University Press, 1957), 55–56.

51. Wiles, *Serial Publication,* 58–60.

52. Advertisement for the *Penny London Post* in U.S. 256, Saturday 7 September 1733 and for *Heathcote's Intelligence* in *D.A.* 816, Thursday 13 September 1735. *Read's Weekly Journal* was published with a second sheet from 447, Saturday 13 October 1733.

53. Advertisement in *L.D.P.* 351, Wednesday 17 December 1735.

54. *D.G.* 1,204, Tuesday 1 May 1739.

55. The evidence for this is oblique but while the *O.L.P.* was printed by Bridget Buckeridge, the A.O. returns 1735–1741 show her regularly paying advertisement duty for a halfpenny paper. The only surviving run for this period is an irregular series in the Guildhall Library from Monday 24 July 1738 to 38 Wednesday 11 October 1738.

56. According to the author of the *Daily Gazetteer,* some newspaper proprietors were claiming exemption from the tax on the grounds that they were printing on less than a half-sheet, a marginal defense that may sometimes have been used in this section of the press, *D.G.* 1,204, Tuesday 1 May 1739.

57. Thursday 14 December 1738–Monday 2 April 1739, Guildhall Library.

58. *C.* 647, Saturday 2 December 1738.

59. *L.E.P.* 1,724, Saturday 2 December 1738.

60. *D.P.* 6,001, Monday 4 December 1738. The author of the *Daily Gazetteer* assessed the total number of unstamped papers distributed weekly at 60,000, *D.G.* 1,204, Tuesday 1 May 1739.

61. "The humble Petition of Daniel Pratt, Printer and Stationer over against Northumberland house in the Strand," 2 May 1743, B.L. Add. MSS. 33,054, ff. 189–90. Application for post of overseer of the press.

62. *Royal Oak Journal, All Alive and Merry: or, the London Daily Post, London Evening Post,* and *Robin Crusoe's Journal.* It seems likely that the *Champion: or, London Evening Advertiser* was also a farthing paper, although the *London Morning Advertiser* and the *Universal Weekly Journal,* also listed by Pratt, were not.

63. *C.* 559, Saturday 31 December 1737; 751, Saturday 22 November 1740; *L.E.P.* 1,991, Saturday 16 August 1740.

64. *C.* 647, Saturday 2 December 1738.

65. Printed and sold by J. Harwood in Goulding Lane, near Playhouse Yard. Printed for T. Mouleson, in Turnmill Street.

66. An uncatalogued item at the British Library dated Friday 17 June 1737.

67. *D.G.* 1,204, Tuesday 1 May 1739. See also 1,202, Saturday 28 April 1739.

68. Wiles, *Serial Publication,* 51.

69. B.L. Add. MSS. 33,054 ff. 189–90. Cf. comparable developments in the early nineteenth century described in Patricia Hollis, *The Pauper Press* (London: Oxford University Press, 1970), 194–202.

70. *D.G.* 515, Wednesday 16 February 1737 contained an enthusiastic report of £10 fines imposed by the Lord Mayor and Aldermen.

71. *L.E.P.* 1,970, Saturday 28 June 1740. See also *C.* 751, Saturday 22 November 1740.

72. A denial of reports of his prosecution for unstamped papers appeared in *L. and C.J.* 114, Tuesday 3 March 1741. Cf. recurrent Stamp Office action against the provincial printer Edward Farley between 1736 and 1742, P.R.O.: T.1, 54, 3 December 1741–29 March 1748, 59–60.

73. 15 December 1740, C.U.L.: C.(H.) MSS. 75, 28/1.

74. *T.B.P.* 1742–45, 242, 24 February 1742.

75. *L.E.P.* 2,540, Saturday 18 February 1744. Cf. arrests in Bristol, Cranfield, *Provincial Newspaper,* 197.

76. *T.B.P.* 1742–45, 291, 29 June 1743; 318, 28 September 1743.

77. See *L.E.P.* 2,645, Saturday 20 October 1744; *P.L.M.A.* 203, Wednesday 15 August 1744.

78. *T.B.P.* 1742–45, 492, 28 June 1744.

79. *The Case Between the Proprietors of News-Papers and the Subscribing Coffee-Men. Fairly Stated* (London, 1729), 13.

80. See below, chap. 3.

81. Advertisements in *D.P.* 421, Saturday 4 February 1721. *Pasquin* 28, Monday 22 April 1723 contained ironic remarks on a coffee-house project to suppress "the Redundance of Public Papers," as did Read's *Weekly Journal,* Saturday 11 February 1721.

82. The three pamphlets concerned contain a good deal of useful material on the trade of both groups and are entitled:

(1) *The Case of the Coffee-Men of London and Westminster* (London, n.d.).

(2) *The Case Between the Proprietors of News-Papers, And the Subscribing Coffee-Men. Fairly Stated* (London, 1729).

(3) *The Case Between the Proprietors of News-Papers and the Coffee-Men of London and Westminster, fairly Stated* (London, n.d.).

83. *the Case of the Coffee-Men,* 15.

84. Ibid., 13.

85. Ibid., 19–25.

86. *The Case Between the Proprietors of Newspapers and the Subscribing Coffee-Men,* 17–19.

87. *Observations on the First Six of the Morning and Evening Papers, Published by the Subscribing Coffee-Men of London and Westminster* (London, n.d.).

88. A.O.3, 1730. *Grub Street Journal* 8, Thursday 26 February 1730.

89. Advertisement for the *Champion* explaining its change of publication time in *Ch.* 64, Thursday 10 April 1740.

Chapter 2: The Distribution of the London Newspapers

1. *Penny Post* 1, Tuesday 19 July 1715.

2. Cranfield, *Provincial Newspaper,* 31.

3. *G.S.J.* 417, Thursday 22 December 1737.

4. *D.G.* 2,039, Wednesday 30 December 1741.

5. Toland in Hanson, *Government,* 137.

6. N.d., C.U.L.: C. (H.) MSS. 75, 16/3

7. *The Case between the Proprietors of News Papers and the Coffee-Men of London and Westminster,* 6.

8. Reference to new proprietors in *L.E.P.* 160, Saturday 14 December 1728. The paper seems to have ceased publication early in 1736.

9. See the G.P.O. notices published in the press during 1741. Also Howard Robinson, *The British Post Office* (Princeton: Princeton University Press, 1948), 103.

10. Advertisement in *O.E.* 179, Saturday 4 October 1746.

11. G. A. Cranfield, "The London Evening Post, 1727–1744," *Historical Journal* 8 (1965): 16–30.

12. *B.M.* 502, Saturday 12 February 1715.

13. Cranfield, *Provincial Newspaper,* 123.

14. Realey, "The *London Journal* and its Authors, 1720–1723," *Bulletin of the University of Kansas* 5 (1935): 10–11.

15. In *Pasquin* 42, Friday 14 June 1723 it was announced that publication during the parliamentary recess would be weekly instead of twice-weekly while the final issue of the *Senator* 32, Tuesday 28 May 1728, coincided with the end of the session. See also comment in the advertisement for the *Auditor* in *D.J.* 4048, Monday 7 January 1734 and the statement in the *Weekly Oracle* that *"As the Encouragement given to this Paper has been chiefly among Persons in polite Life; and as the Season of the Year is now come on, which usually calls such to more agreeable Scenes than the Town can afford, we think it proper to suspend for a Time, the Progress of our Work, and shut up the Mouth of our Oracle, who has been always unwilling to answer the Impertinences of the Vulgar: but we promise our Readers that we will be ready to attend them again in the Winter Season."* Bound, undated copies of the supplement in the Burney collection.

16. *C.* 45, Saturday 13 May 1727.

17. *W.M.* 312, Saturday 16 December 1738.

18. *C.* 600, Saturday 7 January 1737; 820, Saturday 20 March 1742.

19. *West. J.* 246, Saturday 16 August 1746.

20. Until all surviving issues are available for comparison it will not be possible to establish accurately whether separate editions were produced and to discover whether major content variations took place. For some oblique comment on possible changes in the leading essay, see *West. J.* 220, Saturday 15 February 1746. It is also uncertain whether the full-priced Thursday journals were distributed to the provinces on Tuesday, as in the case of Robert Walker's cheap *London and Country Journal.*

21. No news-carrying weekly seems to have appeared on a Tuesday, although Walker's cut-price *Weekly Tatler* appeared on Monday. Rev. D. Lysons, "Collectanea," 2, f. 48, B.L. department of printed books.

22. Ibid., f. 21.

23. K. G. Burton, "The Early Newspaper Press in Berkshire 1723–1855," M.A. thesis, University of Reading (1954), 70.

24. R. M. Wiles, *Freshest Advices* (Columbus: Ohio State University Press, 1965), 170. For the extensive sale of the *Newcastle Journal* and *Derby Mercury* in London during the Jacobite crisis, see Cranfield, *Provincial Newspaper*, 200.

25.

York Courant	Ward and Chandler	*C.* 653, Saturday 13 January 1739
Salisbury Journal	T. Astley	*G.A.* 1,314, Monday 23 July 1739
Leeds Mercury	J. Clarke	*G.A.* 1,683, Monday 17 March 1740
Reading Mercury	J. Kemp and J. Winder	*L.E.P.* 2,402, Saturday 2 April 1743
Norwich Mercury	M. Cooper	*G.A.* 2,712, Friday 1 July 1743
York Courant	W. Bickerton	*G.A.* 3,031, Wednesday 1 August 1744
Birmingham Gazette	Baldwin and Jefferies	*G.A.* 3,581, Friday 18 April 1746.

26. *D.J.* 2,201, Thursday 1 February 1728.

27. Parallel runs are preserved in the British Library and the Bodleian Library.

28. For some account of these papers, see Cranfield, *Provincial Newspaper*, 54–55, and Wiles, *Freshest Advices*, 7–8.

29. E.g., *The Compleat Historian: or, the Oxford Penny Post; The Country Tatler: or, the Daily Pacquet.*

30. Not all those included on the imprints of the full-priced papers necessarily handled these orders, and a clear distinction was sometimes made between those taking in advertisements and others, perhaps as proprietors, willing to accept orders. E.g., the *London Daily Post* in 1734.

31. *D.A.* 1, Wednesday 3 February 1731.

32. *D.A.* 22, Saturday 27 February 1731.

33. William F. Belcher, "The Sale and Distribution of the British Apollo," in *Studies in the English Periodical*, ed. Richmond P. Bond (Chapel Hill: University of North Carolina Press, 1957), 78, 84, 93–95. *Diverting P.* 27, Saturday 28 April 1705.

34. *W.M.* 263, Friday 6 January 1738; *L.D.P.* 3,535, Monday 24 February 1746.

35. Examination of Catherine Brett, 19 September 1728, P.R.O.: S.P. 36, 8/153; examination of Edward Pickard, 23 October 1739, S.P. 36, 50/19.

36. For a valuable analysis of the development of trade publishing, see Michael Treadwell, "London Trade Publishers, 1675–1750," *Library*, 6th ser., 4 (1982): 99–134.

37. N.d. (ca. 1734), C.U.L.: C.(H.) MSS. 75, 15.

38. Ibid.

39. The publishers apparently handled a very large proportion of each edition of their papers and it seems possible that they sometimes organized delivery to individual subscribers. However, there is no clear evidence of any such direct contact.

40. The mercuries themselves organized the collection of copies. A number of small-scale businesses described specifically as "news-shops" were apparently scattered through the London area. See advertisements in *E.P.* 386, Thursday 31 January 1712, *D.J.* 905, Monday 16 December 1723.

41. The proprietors of these shops were among the first to take delayed advantage of the 1764 extension of the right to send newspapers through the post free of charge. Their continued importance as distributors was also reflected in the concern of the proprietors of the *General Evening Post* with their prompt supply, Daniel Stow to Mr. Freeling, 4 June 1811, G.P.O. Ref. 1/18A. See also W. S. Lewis MSS., 9 February 1780.

42. Books printed here during the late 1720s and the 1730s usually appeared with the joint names of E. and R. Nutt on the imprint, although by 1728 Mrs. Nutt was nearly 70 years old. Petition of Elizabeth Nutt, n.d., P.R.O.: S.P. 36, 9/249.

43. Edward Deacon, *The Family of Deacon and Meres* (Bridgeport, Conn., 1891), 13.

44. Information of Robert Amey, 5 April 1740, P.R.O.: S.P. 36, 50/266. Examination of Robert Amey, 28 June 1737, B.L. Add. MSS. 32, 690, f. 329.

45. Examination of William Hewitt, 12 August 1721, P.R.O.: S.P. 35, 28/9(1).

46. Papers seized 31 January 1727, C.U.L.: C.(H.) MSS. 74, 28. The account shows that she received 400 copies of the first pamphlet collection but does not itemize any newspaper intake.

47. *A Complete Collection of State Trials*, ed. T. B. Howell, 34 vols. (London, 1816–26), 17, col. 644.

48. *C.* 746, Saturday 18 October 1740 contained an account showing £40 paid by Mrs. Dodd for July 1738.

49. P.R.O.: S.P. 36, 50.19.

50. Examination of Mary Dowe, 2 July 1739, P.R.O.: S.P. 36, 48/32.

51. Accounts of the *Alchymist,* 12 February 1737–14 May 1737, B.L. Add. MSS. 32,690, f. 318. Mrs. Nutt took in about 150, returning over half, while Mrs. Charlton received about 190 copies and returned over three quarters.

52. C.U.L.: C.(H.) MSS. 74, 28. *C.* 746, Saturday 18 December 1740.

53. Information of George Chordsey, 8 April 1740, P.R.O.: S.P. 36, 50/282.

54. Howell, *State Trials,* 17, cols. 645–46.

55. Examination of John Brett, 2 July 1739, P.R.O.: S.P. 36, 48/39.

56. *C.S.* 111, Saturday 17 March 1739.

57. *C.J. or O.C.* 714, Saturday 13 October 1739.

58. The mercuries' discount was perhaps too high to allow the distribution of the cheapest London papers through their shops.

59. *Reasons.*

60. Ibid. A number of these "miserable Creatures" cropped up in the reports of arrests in 1743 including Frances Karver, alias Blind Fanny, *L.E.P.* 2,487, Thursday 18 October 1743. For an account of a number of London hawkers at the beginning of the century see *The Mercury Hawkers in Mourning* (London, 1706), Society of Antiquaries, London.

61. *C.* 893, Saturday 6 August 1743.

62. *L.E.P* 2,487, Tuesday 18 October 1743.

63. Cranfield, *Provincial Newspaper,* 198–99. Wiles, *Freshest Advices,* 117, 126–27.

64. 1740, C.U.L.: C.(H.) MSS. 75, 28/1.

65. *P.L.P.* 312, Monday 29 April 1745.

66. *P.L.P.* 405, Monday 2 December 1745, *passim.*

67. Cranfield, *Provincial Newspaper,* 193.

68. *C.* 886, Saturday 18 June 1743.

69. E.g., *W.O.* 51, Saturday 22 November 1735.

70. *W.M.* 111, Saturday 25 January 1735. Richard Clements and Mr. Thirlborne, booksellers in Oxford and Cambridge, handled the collected essays published in 1736, conceivably implying a link with the *Miscellany* itself, *W.M.* 190, Saturday 5 August 1736.

71. P.R.O.: S.P. 35, 28/15, quoted in Realey, *"London Journal,"* 46.

72. *W. Spy* 3, Saturday 8 April 1732.

73. E.g., *L. and C.J.* 79, Tuesday 1 July 1740. Advertisement for Daffy's Elixir, distributed by Walker and sold by dealers in Warwick, Birmingham, Nottingham, Leicester, Northampton, Ipswich, Bury, Stow, Devizes, Cirencester, Bristol, Bath, Colchester, Chelmsford, Salisbury, Chippenham, "and by the several Persons who serves Books and News-papers, printed in London by R. Walker."

74. Wiles, *Freshest Advices,* 127–28.

75. P.R.O.: C. 108/19; Gentleman's Ledger B., 1730–40 Bodleian Library MSS. Eng. Misc. c.296.

76. *C.* 123, Saturday 2 November 1728.

77. C.U.L.: C.(H.) MSS. 74, 72. *The Craftsman* is not specified, and the lists may have referred to the collections of essays from the Journal republished in pamphlet form.

78. Clerk's Memorial, 20 December 1791, G.P.O. Ref. 1/18A.

79. For the scale of charges, see Robinson, *British Post Office,* 96–97. Various attempts were made by the proprietors of publications appearing twice weekly or more often to reduce postage costs by publishing a combined issue once a week, e.g., *N.S.E.* 1, Friday 23 May 1708.

80. *C.* 126, Saturday 30 November 1728.

81. In 1761 the imprint of the *St. James's Chronicle* included the clerks among those taking in provincial orders

82. 30 June 1788 House of Commons *Report of the Commissioners,* 7 (1806), 10th Report, 888. Jamineau claimed to have "formerly been Consul at Naples twenty-five years."

83. Jamineau was also responsible for the insertion of Post Office notices in the press. He received a fee of 1/-for each one published.

84. Cranfield, *Provincial Newspaper,* 200–201. *Wiles Freshest Advices,* 117–18.

85. By the end of the century such competition had become a feature of the struggle between the clerks and the commercial dealers, Stow to Freeling, G.P.O. Ref. 1/18A.

86. 24 April 1755, 29 May 1756, W. S. Lewis MSS.

87. Advertisement in *F.W.J.* 152, Saturday 2 October 1731.

88. *G.S.J.* 168, Thursday 15 March 1732.

89. Advertisements in *G.S.J.* 125, Thursday 25 May 1732 and *W.R.* 113, Saturday 10 June 1732.

90. See below, chap. 8.

91. H. M. C. Egmont, *Diary,* 1, 434, 16 November 1733.

92. *H. of C.J.* 29, 998.

93. I have published a full analysis of this material in "Newspaper Distribution during Queen Anne's Reign," in *Studies in the Book Trade* (Oxford: Oxford Bibliographical Society, 1975), 139–51.

94. On the Huguenot connections see G. C. Gibbs, "Some Intellectual and Political Influences of the Huguenot Emigrés in the United Provinces, ca. 1680–1730," *Bijdragen en mededelingen betreffende de geschiedenis der Nederlanden,* 90 (1975): 2:255–87.

95. C.U.L.: C.(H.) MSS. 75.20 n.d. John Chricheley supplied the office until 1732.

96. Capt. James Maule to Payzant, 26 January 1728, P.R.O.: S.P. 36, 5/65.

97. Mr. Byde to Payzant, 25 November 1729, P.R.O.: S.P. 36, 16/27.

98. J. Collier to Newcastle, 28 March 1730, B.L. Add. MSS. 32691, f. 97.

99. The extensive trade in counterfeit franks, uncovered by the Select Committee of 1764, may have been linked directly with newspaper distribution, although this is not stated, *H. of C.J.,* 29, 997.

100. Following the suppression of his post the clerks' charges were apparently halved. Clerks' Memorial, G.P.O. Ref. 1/18a.

101. 5% by the early nineteenth century, Stow to Freeling, ibid.

102. Edmund Barres to Mr. Woodcock (June) 1779, Postal History Society Records.

103. Clerk's Memorial, G.P.O. Ref. 1/18A.

104. *H. of C.J.* 29:998.

105. In 1791 the cost of delivery was assessed at between ½d and 2d, Clerks' Memorial, G.P.O. Ref. 1/18A.

106. P.R.O.: S.P. 35,49/38, 62/23; S.P. 36,6/220, 11/236. 18/62. These were addressed to a number of his political supporters in Sussex.

107. L. Payzant to J. Payzant, 23 March 1725, P.R.O.: S.P. 35, 55/86.

108. See below, chap. 7.

109. Some figures showing the level of Post Office distribution in 1704 are discussed in J. R. Sutherland, "Circulation of Newspapers and Literary Periodicals in the Eighteenth Century," *Library,* 4th ser., 15 (1935): 111.

110. *H. of C.J.* 26: 462–65. See comment in *L.E.P.* Saturday 22 February 1735; Thursday 27 February 1725.

111. *H. of C.J.* 29: 997–1000.

112. Clerk's Memorial, G.P.O. Ref. 1/18A.

113. *W.J. or S.P.* 234, Saturday 20 April 1723.

114. *W.J. or S.P.* 279, Saturday 29 February 1724.

115. *P.* 116, Friday 13 March 1724.

116. William Maitland, *The History and Survey of London,* 2 vols. (London, 1756), 2: 735.

117. *The Case of the Coffee-Men,* 15.

118. *The Case Between the Proprietors of the News Papers And the Subscribing Coffee-Men,* 9. See also the advertisement for a new coffee-house taking in all the papers in *L.D.P.* 2916, Tuesday 20 March 1741.

119. *A Trip Through London: Containing Observations on Men and Things,* 3d ed. (London, 1728), 6–7.

120. *The Case Between the Proprietors of the News Papers And the Subscribing Coffee-Men,* 16; *The Case of the Coffee-Men,* 17.

121. For some ironic comment on distribution to such houses see *W.J. or B.G.* Saturday 11 February 1721; *G.S.J.* 148, Monday 30 October 1732.

122. Advertisement in *L.S.R.* 127, Monday 16 May 1737 and *Catalogue of Prints and Drawings in the British Museum,* Division 1, Personal and Political Satires, 2, 1689–1733 (London, 1873), 604.

123. *W.H.* 48, Saturday 6 March 1742.

124. *Spectator* 10, Monday 12 March 1711.

125. *The D'Anverian History of the Affairs of Europe, For the memorable year 1731,* 2d ed. (London, 1732), 81. Cited below as *D'Anverian History.*

Chapter 3: The Finances of the London Press

1. See below, chap. 4.

2. R. L. Haig, *Gazetteer* (Carbondale: Southern Illinois University Press, 1960), 272.

3. *The Political Journal of George Bubb Doddington,* ed. J. Carswell and L. A. Dralle (Oxford: Clarendon Press, 1965), 111.

4. All the material in the *Grub Street Journal* proprietors' ledger is printed in *Publishing History* 4 (1978): 95–112. References here and throughout will be made to the Queens College manuscript itself, in this case 26 August 1730, *passim,* Q.C. MSS. 450. The original agreement is missing from the ledger.

5. Another letter, B.L. Add. MSS. 32690, ff. 323, 324. Neither item is dated but they were seized with other material on 17 June 1737.

6. 6 January 1770, 8 January 1770, B.L. Add. MSS. 38729, ff. 165/166. The entry for 12 January 1770, B.L. Add. MSS. 38728, f. 130, indicates agreement on a call of 10 guineas each. In 1761 a payment of £7. 17s. 6d. made by Thomas Lowndes to Henry Baldwin was described as "his Subscription towards the Support of the *St. James Chronicle* and the *London Spy and Reads Weekly Journal* at the Rate of Five Guineas for one 20th Share," Bodleian Library MSS Eng. Misc. C., 297.

7. The survival of a bill for one of Robert Walker's cheap two-sheet weeklies indicates both their general use and the form that they took. It gives a rundown of the contents of the *Weekly Tatler, and English Theatre* to be published on Monday 12 May 1735, ending with a money-back offer to unsatisfied readers. Lysons, "Collectanea," 2, f. 48.

8. 28 August 1730, 7 May 1731, *Q.C.* MSS. 450. B.L. Add. MSS. 32690 f. 318. Similar charges were made by the printer Charles Ackers, *A Ledger of Charles Ackers,* ed. D. F. McKenzie and J. C. Ross, (Oxford: Oxford Bibliographical Society, 1968), 48, 126.

9. Ibid., 169, 175.

10. B.L. Add. MSS. 32,690, f. 318.

11. For an indication of the impact of handbill advertising, see *W.O.* 1, Saturday 7 December 1734. They were very extensively used for political purposes and during the Westminster election of 1748, 227,500 handbills and other ephemeral items were produced in the Bedford interest by six London printers, including Richard Francklin, N. Rogers, "Aristocratic Clientage, Trade and Independency in Popular Politics in Pre-Radical Westminster," *Past and Present* 61 (1973): 70–106.

12. 28 August 1730, Q.C. MSS. 450.

13. Ibid. Cf. the continuous use of newspaper advertising on behalf of the *Hyp Doctor* and the *Weekly Miscellany.*

14. 28 August 1730, Q.C. MSS. 450.

15. Advertised in *L.D.P.* 1575, Monday 12 November 1739.

16. *D.A.* 1, Wednesday 3 February 1731.

17. *D.A.* 22, Saturday 27 February 1731. See *D.P.* 7, Saturday 10 October 1719. The first six issues of this paper were given away.

18. *D.A.* 1, Wednesday 3 February 1731. See also Friday 26 November 1731.

19. *D.A.* 22, Saturday 27 February 1731, *passim.*

20. *L.C.* 467, Saturday 27 December 1746, *passim.*

21. See below, chap. 4.

22. *E.E.P.* 32, Thursday 13 March 1740.

23. See the account of the prosecution of *Mist's Journal* that appeared in *U.S.* 21, Saturday 1 March 1729 and P.R.O.: S.P. 36, 44/87 and 91.

24. The statement by Samuel Neville in 1728, that he was employed in setting the advertisements for the *Daily Post* seems to imply a second compositor, but there is some ambiguity, P.R.O.: S.P. 36, 5/95.

25. In 1721 an extended edition of the *London Journal* was worked off by a journeyman, an apprentice, and two pressmen, P.R.O.: S.P. 35, 28/9.

26. For some variation in the allotment of work by the printer of the *Craftsman,* see the examination of Henry Stapleton, 13 December 1737, P.R.O.: S.P. 36, 44/91.

27. I have printed the various accounts of the *Craftsman* that survive among the Cholmondeley (Houghton) MSS. in "Figures Relating to the Printing and Distribution of the Craftsman 1726–1730," *Bulletin of the Institute of Historical Research* 43 (1970): 233–42. Similar charges for the printing of Steele's *Englishman* appear in George Aitken, *Life of Sir Richard Steele,* 2 vols. (London, 1889), 2: 70–71 and in C. Blagden, "Henry Rhodes and the Monthly Mercury," *Book Collector* 5 (1956): 343–53.

28. 28 August 1730, Q.C. MSS. 450.

29. 21 September 1733, ibid.

30. B.L. Add. MSS. 32,690 f. 318.

31. Subsequent printing costs for a basic unit of 1,000 copies:
St. James's Chronicle (1761), £3. 7s. R. and M. Bond, "Minute Books," 25.
Public Advertiser (1765), £3.13s. 6d. B.L. Add. MSS. 38,169.
London Packet (1773), £3. 3s B.L. Add. MSS. 38,728.
Gazetteer (1783), £3.19s. 6d. Haig, *Gazetteer,* 209
Gazetteer (1793), £ 4. 6s. 6d. Ibid.
The rate of increase per token was 3/6 for the *Public Advertiser* and 3/9 for the *Gazetteer.*

32. 8 September 1779, W. S. Lewis, MSS.

33. 15 September 1779, ibid.

34. An amusing description of the return of various London papers to the Lincoln's Inn office appears in the *G.S.J.* 147, Thursday 26 October 1732 and 148, Monday 30 October 1732.

35. Harris, "Figures," 238. During Queen Anne's reign a similar proportion of issues of the *London Gazette* remained unsold, Snyder, "The Circulation of Newspapers," 226–29.

36. 2 May 1743, B.L., Add. MSS. 33, 054 ff. 189–90.

37. Comment on other difficulties arising out of the need for country printers to deal, regardless of distance, with the Lincoln's Inn office appears in Cranfield, *Provincial Newspaper,* 238–39.

38. W. S. Lewis MSS. A table of discounts on penny stamps prefaces the *General Evening Post* ledger.

39. Morison, *English Newspaper,* 104.

40. *L.J.* 431, Saturday 4 November 1727. The identity of the mill referred to is not clear. It seems possible, though only as speculation, that the Mr. Johannet who supplied the printers of the *Grub Street Journal* also supplied the printers of other London newspapers, 5 January 1733, *passim,* Q.C. MSS. 450.

41. *O.E.* 189, Saturday 13 December 1746. Cf. the later efforts of the *General Evening Post* proprietors to keep up the quality of paper.

42. Harris, "Figures," 238.

43. 28 August 1730, *passim,* Q.C. MSS. 450. For a full account of the composition of reams and quires, see W. Sale, *Samuel Richardson, Master Printer* (Ithaca: Cornell University Press, 1950), 24–25. Subsequent paper costs per ream: *General Evening Post* (1757), 16/-, W. S. Lewis MSS. *Public Advertiser* (1765–71), 25/-, B.L. Add. MSS. 38. 169. *Gazetteer* (1784), 30/-, Haig, *Gazetteer,* 150.

44. Slightly later estimates of provincial printers cited by Cranfield put the cost of paper for a four-page publication at about ¼d, Cranfield, *Provincial Newspaper,* 238.

45. *The Printers Case: Humbly submitted to the Consideration of the Honourable the House of Commons* (London, n.d.).

46. Accounts 1765–71, B.L. Add. MSS. 38,169.

47. 3/6d per ream in 1774 and 4/- per ream in 1783, Haig, *Gazetteer,* 150.

48. *Reasons.*

49. *Ibid.* The paper's quality and size made it, according to Parker, unfit for any other use, *P.L.N.* 989, Friday 19 March 1725.

50. For some discussion of the employment of editorial personnel, see chaps. 6 and 9.

51. See below, chap. 4.

52. B.L. Add. MSS. 38, 169. This paper was first published as the *London Daily Post and General Advertiser* in 1735.

53. *L.D.P.* 1, 4 November 1734, *passim*. In 1726 the proprietors of the *Daily Journal* apparently established a similar though more limited advertising concession with the Lincolns Inn and Haymarket Theatres, *D.J.* 1834, Wednesday 30 November 1726.

54. December 1766, B.L. Add. MSS, 38,169.

55. Cf. Later *Gazetteer* payments in Haig, *Gazetteer*, 222–23.

56. Wiles, *Freshest Advices*, 163. Burton, "The Early Newspaper Press in Berkshire," 55.

57. *The Case of the Coffee-Men*, 23.

58. Haig, *Gazetteer*, 31.

59. ¼d. was apparently the amount received by the hawkers of the penny newspapers of Queens Anne's reign, P. G. M. Dickson, *Sun Insurance Office* (London: Oxford University Press, 1960), 25. The arrangements made by the proprietors of the unstamped papers remain obscure.

60. *C.A.*, 3,535, Monday 24 February–3,540, Saturday 1 March 1746.

61. N.d., C.U.L.: C.(H). MSS. 75.15.

62. Harris, "Figures," 238. This was also the rate paid during the 1760s for publication of the *Public Advertiser*.

63. 28 August 1730, 7 May 1731, Q.C. MSS. 450.

64. The charge of 3d for the weekly *True Patriot* in 1745 was justified at length by Henry Fielding in his introduction and was probably a major cause of the paper's collapse early the following year. *The True Patriot*, ed. M. Locke (London: Macdonald, 1965), 35–36.

65. Harris, "Figures," 238.

66. This makes no allowance for editorial expenses.

67. Nichols, *Literary Anecdotes*, 5, 169.

68. 28 August 1730, Q.C. MSS. 450. This again makes no allowance for editorial expenses.

69. *Treachery, Baseness and Cruelty Display'd to the Full: In the Hardships and Sufferings of Mr. Henry Haines, Late Printer of the Country Journal, Or, Craftsman* (London, 1740), 27. Cited below as *Treachery, Baseness*.

70. See below, chap. 7.

71. *D'Anverian history*, p. 80 includes a reference to the income from the *Craftsman* when selling 10,000 copies.

72. Harris, "Figures," 240.

73. H.M.C. Portland MSS., 8, 187–88.

74. The only indication of the level of sale of an old-style thrice-weekly appeared in John Peele's publication estimates of 1734 in C.U.L.: C.(H.) MSS. 75,1 5. No fee is stipulated but if this can be assumed to have been, as in the case of a single-leaf *Craftsman*, about 2/- per thousand, the average circulation of the *Whitehall Evening Post* at this time would have been about 1,200 copies per issue.

75. *D.J.* 4,205, Wednesday 10 July–4,214, Saturday 20 July 1734.

76. Haig, *Gazetteer*, 124–25.

77. 8 September 1779, *passim.*, W. S. Lewis MSS.

78. *P.L.P.* 321, Monday 29 April 1745.

79. On the basis of Peele's estimates the *Daily Post* and the *Daily Post Boy* would each have had an average circulation of about 1,200 copies a day, C.U.L.: (H). MSS. 75, 15.

80. For comment on the methods used when demand exceeded the capacity of the press, see William B. Todd. "The Printing of Eighteenth Century Periodicals With Notes on the *Examiner* and the *World*," *Library*, 5th ser., 10 (1955): 49–54.

81. *G.A.* 3,535, Monday 24 February 1746. Usual publication time was 6:00 A.M.

82. For a general view of the main elements of advertising content, see R. B. Walker, "Advertising in London Newspapers, 1650–1750," *Business History* 15 (1973): 112–30.

83. W.J. 4, Saturday 22 May and 5 Saturday 29 May 1725.

84. 17 March 1726, C.U.L.: C.(H). MSS. 75, 1a/1, 1a/2.

85. Audit Office accounts reprinted by A. Aspinall in "Statistical Accounts of the London Newspapers during the Eighteenth Century," *English Historical Review* 63 (1948): 208. The first year after the 1725 Act for which records survive is 1729. The figures quoted are for sums "Paid at the Head Office" and therefore, presumably, largely made up of payment for London papers.

86. *C.* 45, Saturday 12 May 1727.

87. *C.* 200, Saturday 2 May 1730.

88. Cf. Cranfield, *Provincial Newspaper*, 236.

89. *D'Anverian History*, 31.

90. Parker's *Reasons* suggests an average of three advertisements per issue in the ½d. papers and there are no signs of an increase.

91. The only attempts to evade the advertising duty seem to have taken place among the cheap unstamped papers, *P.L.N.* 1,003, Wednesday 21 April 1725. B.L. Add. MSS. 33054, ff. 189–90.

92. The *British Mercury* was apparently unique in carrying charges set by the number of letters used, 1/- for 200, 1/3 for 250, 1/6 for 300, *B.M.* 87, Friday 13 October 1710. For internal and unpublished variations in the rate charged by the proprietors of the *Grub Street Journal*, see 1 March 1733, Q.C. MSS 450.

93. Guildhall Library.

94. A letter published in the *Daily Advertiser* in full, probably by mistake, ends "You'll oblige me if you can let me know the lowest Price of a good Puff," *D.A.* 4117, Wednesday 28 March 1744.

95. *U.S.* 20, Saturday 22 February 1729.

96. 28 August 1730, 7 January 1731, Q.C. MSS. 450.

97. 29 April 1731, 1 November 1733, ibid.

98. 21 April 1735, ibid.

99. 12 November 1736, ibid.

100. 1/- advertisements were entered by J. Shuckburgh, T. Woodward, Edward Cave, E. Symon, J. & J. Pemberton, J. Roberts, S. Harding, H. Williamson, T. Osborne, T. Cooper.

101. See a letter in *G.S.J.* 410, Thursday 3 November 1737.

102. These remain largely the same and in 1746 were A. Millar, E. Withers, R. Dodsley, T. Astley, C. Hitch, T. Wotton, J. Hodge, J. Davidson, G. Woodfall, M. Cooper.

103. *The Case of the Coffee-Men*, 16.

104. *The Case Between the Proprietors of News-Papers And the Subscribing Coffee-Men*, 16.

105. *G.E.P.* 398, Saturday 17 April 1736.

106. The largest number of advertisements contained in a single-leaf issue was 36, yielding £2.13.6d. after tax, *L.D.P.* 2,599, Friday 18 February 1743. The largest number in a double issue was 58, yielding £3.10s. *L.D.P.* 2,896, Saturday 25 February 1744.

107. *Report of the Commissioners* 7 (1806): 888.

108. 30 May 1785, 29 August 1755, 27 February 1756, 29 May 1756, W. S. Lewis MSS. The proprietors of the *St. James's Chronicle* also had considerable difficulty in this area and in 1771 were owed over £200 for advertisements, Richmond P. Bond and Majorie N. Bond, "The Minute Book of the St. James's Chronicle," *Studies in Bibliography* 28 (1975): 31–32.

109. Gentlemen's Ledger B., f. 14, Bodleian Library MSS.

110. 11 March 1731, Q.C. MSS. 450.

111. 2 June 1734, ibid. Some provincial advertisers continued to pay their newspaper bills in kind, Cranfield, *Provincial Newspaper*, 233–34.

Chapter 4: The Booksellers and Group Ownership

1. For subsequent remarks on the London book trade I have relied largely on Terry Balanger's very useful Ph.D. diss. "Booksellers' Sales of Copyright: Aspects of the London Book Trade, 1718–1768," Columbia University, 1970. Belanger has printed some of this material in "Booksellers' Trade Sales, 1718–1768," *Library*, 5th ser., 30 (1975). References here and throughout are to his dissertation.

2. The real profits in the trade came from ownership of copyright rather than from retail sale. Belanger, "Booksellers' Sales," 18–19.

3. For a detailed study of this group known as the "Wholesaling Conger," see Norma Hodgson and Cyprian Blagden, *The Notebook of Thomas Bennet and Henry Clements* (Oxford: Oxford Bibliographical Society, 1956).

4. For details of the "Printing" and "Castle" congers, see Belanger, "Booksellers' Sales," 13–15.

5. The Wholesaling Conger dealt in books rather than copyrights, an old fashioned approach that probably led to its collapse, Belanger, "Booksellers' Sales," 13.

6. Such complex forms of ownership were virtually unknown outside London. Munter, *Irish Newspaper*, 36.

7. The offer to Defoe of a share in *Dormers News-Letter* made in 1716 may indicate an established practice. Cf. similar vestigial combinations in Dublin in the 1730s, Munter, *Irish Newspaper*, 36.

8. John Heptinstall a "Citizen and Stationer of London," James Brooke a stationer on London Bridge, John Woodward a bookbinder, Thomas Norris a bookseller at the "Looking Glass" on London Bridge. Dickson, *Sun Insurance Office*, 268–69.

9. Printed trade sale catalogues began to be issued regularly from about 1718 while the "Castle" conger had been set up the previous year following the success of the "Printing" group, Belanger, "Booksellers' Sales," 14–15, 32.

10. In 1718 a ¹⁄₂₀ share in the *Daily Courant* was purchased at the booksellers' trade sales. This appears in the earliest of a long series of annotated catalogues kept by the firms of Longman and Ward. In referring to items entered in these catalogues I shall use the system of consecutive numbering adopted by Belanger, in this case sale 2, lot 38. For the *Whitehall Evening Post*, see W. Lee, *Defoe: His Life and Recently Discovered Writings, 1716–1729*, 3 vols. (London, 1869), 1: 285, and for the other papers P.R.O.: S.P.35.18/113, 117. It seems possible that the ten booksellers and one printer listed in a special edition of the *Daily Journal* advertising a new publication were the paper's proprietors in the mid-1720s, *D.J.* 1,692, Friday 17 June 1726.

11. See above, chap. 3.

12. L/W. Sale 57, lot 57.

13. B.L. Add. MSS. 38,729 f. 255.

14. L/W. Sale 44 MSS. entry p. 4.

15. L/W. Sale 97, lot 25. The reason for this slump is obscure.

16. R. and M. Bond, "Minute Books," 30.

17. 7 March 1734, 4 April 1834, 3 October 1734 *passim*, Q.C. MSS. 450.

18. 17 October 1766, 23 December 1777, W. S. Lewis MSS. R. and M. Bond, "Minute Books," 28–29.

19. *H.D.* 59, Tuesday 25 January 1732.

20. Wiles, *Serial Publication*, 115–16.

21. *G.M.*, 9 (1739): 111–12; advertisements by Cave in *G.S.J.* 167, Thursday 8 March 1733; 169, Thursday 22 March 1733, *passim*.

22. *R.L.M.A.* 1223, Wednesday 15 December 1742.

23. *The Bee*, 1(1733): 28.

24. *Ch.* 64, Thursday 10 April 1740: *E.E.P.* 32, Thursday 13 March 1740.

25. *N.J.* 4, Saturday 29 March 1746.

26. *T.P.* 17, Tuesday 25 February 1746. The decision by *G.E.P.* partners to stop the progress of the *London Chronicle* indicated the formal character of such action, 13 May 1757, W. S. Lewis MSS.

27. *H.D.* 59, Tuesday 25 January 1732.

28. 4 March 1736, B.L. Add. MSS. 27,784.

29. A written deputation prior to sale was insisted on by the proprietors of the *Grub Street Journal*, 27 January 1732, Q.C. MSS. 450.

30. Multiple share holdings, as in the *Grub Street Journal*, can upset this very generalized picture.

31. 7 January 1731, Q.C. MSS. 450.

32. For the *General Evening Post* see October 1766, *passim*, W. S. Lewis MSS.

33. Ninety-eight sales took place between 1718 and 1742, and the existing catalogues, covering most of this run, show only twenty-one newspaper share transactions.

34. 3 August 1732, Q.C. MSS. 450.

35. Haig, *Gazetteer*, 96 shows the same restriction to have formed part of the agreement of the *G.E.P.*

36. *D.J.* 2288, Monday 13 May 1728: *H.D.* 59, Tuesday 25 January 1732.

37. *L.E.P.* 67, Saturday 11 May 1728.

38. This may also apply to the third paper printed by Nutt, the *Universal Spectator*.

39. Charles Ackers was printer of all three, and the imprints and advertising of the two newspapers suggest that the same booksellers had an interest in both. For further comment on the ownership of the *Weekly Register* and the *London Magazine*, see *A Ledger of Charles Ackers*, 4–11. Also comment in *G.S.J.* 168, Thursday 15 March 1732 and *W.R.* 113, Saturday 10 June 1732.

40. P.R.O.: T.I, 255/88. *D.J.* Monday 8 October 1733.

41. Nichols, *Literary Anecodtes*, 1: 300.

42. See below, chap. 5.

43. Sale, *Samuel Richardson*, 53.

44. E.g., *L.D.P.* 503, Friday 11 June 1736; 1018, Thursday 2 February 1738.

45. Sale, *Samuel Richardson*, 62. He does not identify the second paper.

46. P.R.O.: T.I. 255/88. C.U.L.: C.(H.) MSS. 75, 15. The prominent publisher Thomas Cooper appeared on the imprint of the *Daily Courant* and the *Daily Gazetteer*, which may imply some share in these papers.

47. Woodward's interest in the *Free Briton* is implied from C.U.L.: C.(H.) MSS. 75, 15 and from the fact that only his advertisements appeared in the paper together with Peele's.

48. Wether this was John Walthoe Sr. or Jr. remains obscure.

49. Tovey is not identified in Plomer's *Dictionary of Booksellers and Printers* or in any more recent list of booksellers.

50. *L.E.P.* 1,243, Thursday 6 November 1735. Similar attacks appeared in 1,244, Saturday 8 November and subsequent issues.

51. Nichols, *Literary Anecdotes*, 5: 168. *W.M.* 444, Saturday 27 June 1741.

52. His circular letter to the Bishops was published in *W.E.P.* 3,330 Saturday 24 June 1738.

53. *G.A.* 740, Tuesday 21 October 1746.

54. Examination of Charles Bennet, 28 June 1737, B.L. Add. MSS. 32,690, ff. 335–36.

55. P.R.O.: S.P. 35, 18/117.

56. B.L. Add. MSS. 27,784, f. 27.

57. On the original imprint, notice was given that the paper could be ordered through a variety of booksellers and printers, of whom the first was T. Wood, who had an office at the Covent Garden Theatre.

58. R. and M. Bond, "Minute Books," 22.

59. P.R.O.: C. 104, cited in Haig, *Gazetteer*, 276–77.

60. This is difficult to pin down but the *ad hoc* rulings in the ledger on such matters as share dealing and the election of the treasurer settled in the *Gazetteer* agreements seem to support the view.

61. R. and M. Bond, "Minute Books," 22. The *Grub Street Journal* ledger does contain the financial statements presented at the first two general meetings. 28 August 1730, 7 May 1731, Q.C. MSS. 450.

62. December 1766 is complete in the ledger and although it is possible that the pages have been extracted more recently, this sort of casual approach to accounting seems to fit mid-eighteenth-century practice.

63. 6 June 1734, Q.C. MSS. 450. The first general meeting was at the Angel Tavern, Temple Bar; there is no record of the location of the second.

64. 13 December 1754, W. S. Lewis MSS. The expenses of the *Gazetteer's* Treasurer during the 1770s and 1780s are indicated in Haig, *Gazetteer*, 150.

65. 7 January 1731, Q.C. MSS. 450.

66. 23 December 1778, W. S. Lewis MSS. Also 14 April 1778, *passim*.

67. Cf. similar *Gazetteer* practice, Haig, *Gazetteer*, 150.

68. Angel Tavern, Temple Bar; John's Coffee-house, Sheer Lane; Rainbow Coffee-house, Cornhill; St. Paul's Coffee-house, St. Paul's Churchyard; Half-Moon Tavern, Aldersgate Street; Devil Tavern and Mitre Tavern, Fleet Street; Peele's Coffeehouse, Fleet Street; Sunderland's Coffee-house, Warwick Lane; Goldsmith's Arms, Carey Lane; Castle Tavern, Paternoster row; Oxford Arms, Ludgate Street.

69. There were some variations and as well as those listed above the Golden Lion, North Street, the London Punch House, and, in 1739, the Southampton Coffee-house, Chancery Lane, were also included.

70. 1 November 1753, Q.C. MSS. 450.

71. Nichols, *Literary Anecdotes*, 9: 665.

72. 1 November 1733, Q.C. MSS. 450. The only negative vote recorded in the ledger was made by Richard Russel on this occasion. In the event, Huggonson held office for a double term of six months.

73. 2 May 1734, ibid. Brotherton's refusal of office was recorded in the entry for 12 October 1735 and further attempts to tighten up the system were made at a general meeting held on 13 May 1736.

74. Pressure was placed on the printer to send in the advertisement accounts promptly, 11 March 1731, ibid.

75. Ibid. A block of eight of these accounts presented 12 August 1731 and 4 May 1732 appears at the end of the ledger showing the shareholding of each partner.

76. 23 October 1730; 7 May 1731, ibid.

77. This was obliquely indicated in 1718 by Thomas Warner's payment of the writers contributing to Nathaniel Mist's journal, P.R.O.: S.P. 35, 13/28, 31, 32, 33.

78. The earliest known is still the agreement between Mary Say and the proprietors of the *Gazetteer* printed in Haig, *The Gazetteer*, 276–80.

79. 1 June 1732, Q.C. MSS. 450.

80. 6 July 1732, ibid.

81. 3 August 1732, ibid.

82. 6 September 1733, ibid.

83. 21 September 1733, ibid.

84. 11 September 1766, W. S. Lewis MSS.

85. 20 December 1770, 22 February 1771, 10 April 1782, ibid.

86. 27 January 1732, 5 August 1736, Q.C. MSS. 450.

87. 5 January 1733, ibid. For an account of the Johannet family, see A. R. Shorter, *Paper Making in the British Isles* (Newton Abbot: David and Charles, 1971).

88. 29 July 1779, 12 July 1780, 12 February 1785, *passim*, W. S. Lewis MSS.

89. 7 September 1732, Q.C. MSS. 450. It appeared on *G.S.J.* 150, Thursday 9 November 1732.

90. 5 September 1734, ibid.

91. 6 February 1735, ibid.

92. 3 July 1735, ibid.

93. 12 January 1780, W. S. Lewis MSS. The entry for 9 February 1780 contained a report stating that the present circulation level was usual.

94. 17 January 1781, ibid. Their main publication problem was getting the paper to the Post Office on time, although this was the responsibility of the printer.

95. Some account of this division appears in J. T. Hillhouse, *The Grub Street Journal* (New York: Benjamin Blom, reissue, 1967), 12–13.

96. See below, chap. 6.

97. 15 August 1737, Q.C. MSS. 450.

98. 30 August 1754, W. S. Lewis MSS.

99. 17 September 1754, ibid.

100. E.g., 2 October 1766, 17 October 1766 on the inclusion of a list of fairs and a literary review, ibid.

101. E.g., 23 December 1778, 13 September 1780, ibid.

102. 8 May 1782, ibid.

103. C.U.L.: C. (H.) MSS. 75, 15.

104. 21 March 1785, W. S. Lewis MSS.

105. *An Historical View of The Principles, Characters, Persons, etc. Of The Political Writers to Great Britain* (London, 1740), 28. Cited below as *An Historical View.*

106. *W.J.* 94, Saturday 25 February 1727.

107. *Treachery, Baseness,* 9.

108. *O.E.* 2, Saturday 12 February 1743.

109. *C.* 746, Saturday 18 October 1740.

110. *A Short State of the Case. . . .* (London, 1754), 2. Also *C.* 751, Saturday 22 November 1740. See also the claim in *F.B.* 293, Thursday 19 June 1735 that similar financial backing was provided for the *London Evening Post.*

111. 21 April 1735, Q.C. MSS. 450.

112. 4 August 1737, ibid. Cf. agreement at the same meeting to launch a prosecution against Mr. Staples for the pamphlet *Grub-Street Versus Bowman.*

113. Helen Sand Hughes, *The Gentle Hertford, Her Life and Letters* (New York: Macmillan Co., 1940), 203–5.

114. For an account of the series of political and private law suits facing the proprietors of the *St. James's Chronicle,* see R. and M. Bond, "Minute Books," 32–36.

115. *W.M.* 444, Saturday 27 June 1741. R. and M. Bond, "Minute Books," 38.

116. 25 November 1731, Q.C. MSS. 450. There seems to be no mention in the minutes of the pamphlet collection described in Hillhouse, *Grub Street Journal,* 22.

117. 2 March 1732, ibid. See advertisement in *C.S.J.* 115, Thursday 16 March 1732 asking for correctiions and stating that the volume was in the press. No indication of the reasons for

the delay appears in the minutes.

118. 5 September 1734, ibid.

119. 3 July 1735, ibid.

120. 9 December 1736, ibid.

121. 4 April 1737, ibid.

122. Wilford had been declared bankrupt in 1735, and the assignment of his share may have resulted from this. The share continued to be held in common by the partners. 15 August 1737, ibid.

123. Meetings recorded on 2 May 1737, 5 May 1737, 6 May 1737, 4 August 1737.

124. 12 November 1736, Q.C. MSS. 450.

125. 10 December 1737, ibid.

126. 28 February 1739, 9 March 1739, ibid.

127. Arrangements for the accommodation of shareholders in the *Daily Gazetteer* transferring to the new *London Gazetteer* appeared in the agreement of 1753.

Chapter 5: The Newspaper Printers

1. For comment on the key role of the printer in the development of the provincial newspaper, see Cranfield, *Provincial Newspaper*, 48.

2. *The Case of the Free Workmen-Printers, Relating to the Bill For Preventing the Licentiousness of the Press* [1704]. Cf. *Reasons humbly offer'd to the Consideration of the Honourable House of Commons* [1712]. This petitioner estimated that while in 1676 there were thirty printing houses, the number had since doubled. Also the comprehensive list of printers supplied to Robert Harley in 1705. H. L. Snyder, "The Reports of a Press Spy for Robert Harley," *Library*, 5th ser., 22 (1967): 336. Also Michael Trendwell, "London Printers and Printing Houses in 1705," *Publishing History* 7 (1980): 5–44.

3. Nichols, *Literary Anecdotes*, 1: 288–321. For further information based on this list see Ellic Howe, *The London Compositor 1785–1900* (London: Bibliographical Society, 1947), 36–39, and for comment on its shortcomings, T. Gent, *The Life of Mr. Thomas Gent, Printer of York* (London, 1832), 141–42. Evidence for redating in K. I. D. Maslen, "Samuel Negus, His List and 'His Case,'" *Library*, 6th ser., 4 (1982): 317–20.

4. *Letters of David Hume to William Strahan*, ed. G. B. Hill (Oxford, 1888), 47.

5. Howe, *The London Compositor*, 36.

6. Haig, *Gazetteer*, 276–80.

7. T. C. Duncan Eaves and B. D. Kimpel, *Samuel Richardson* (Oxford: Clarendon Press, 1971), 42.

8. Deacon, *The Families of Deacon and Meres*, 12.

9. These included a variety of monthly and other occasional publications.

10. MSS. pamphlet, n.d., C.U.L.: C.(H.) MSS. 73.44/3.

11. Examination of R. Walker 31 December 1729, B.L. Add. MSS. 36,138, ff. 171–75. A confession to the ruse appears in f. 179.

12. Bodleian Library MSS. Eng. Misc. C., 141.

13. In 1759 the printer William Faden received a fourteen-year royal license to print the daily *Publick Ledger* and subsequently agreed to farm the paper for three years, paying the partners £360 p.a. which amounted to £15 on each share, Plomer, *Dictionary*, and Charles Welsh, *A Bookseller of the Last Century* (London, 1885), 43–44. See also Henry Baldwin's initiative in establishing the *St. James's Chronicle*, R. and M. Bond, "Minute Books," 17.

14. 26 June 1731, 15 August 1737, Q.C. MSS. 450. See below, chap. 6.

15. Haig, *Gazetteer*, 93–100. Minutes in the 1780s complaining of the quality of the printing, W. S. Lewis MSS.

16. See below, chap. 7.

17. *I.L.J.* 1, Saturday 19 July 1735, "Printed by T. Pape, at W. Wilkins in Lombard-street."

18. *D.J.* 4,329, Monday 21 July 1735.

19. For some rather confused speculation on their background, see T. C. Duncan Eaves and Ben D. Kimpel in "Two Notes on Samuel Richardson," *Library* 5th ser., 23 (1969): 243–47.

20. The initial bifurcation apparently occurred on Saturday 5 November 1737. Both appeared with the same title until Saturday 26 November. The publication of *Old Common Sense* was attributed in one account to an unidentified "Bookseller, at Temple Bar," P.R.O.: S.P. 9,35/32–35.

21. Letter in *C.* 593, Saturday 19 November 1737.
22. *C.S.* 42, Saturday 19 November 1737. *O.C.S.* 43, Saturday 26 November 1737.
23. Letter in *C.* 595, Saturday 3 December 1737.
24. *L.E.P.* 1598, Saturday 11 February 1738.
25. This is obliquely suggested by an Audit Office entry of 1739, which debits his business associate John Standen with *Common Sense.* In the last issue readers were recommended to change to Rayner's *Original Craftsman.*
26. *D.G.* 1,646, Saturday 27 September 1740: 1,652, Saturday 4 October 1740.
27. *C.* 746, Saturday 18 October 1740.
28. Her name appeared on the imprint from *C.* 617, Saturday 6 May 1738.
29. The first paper printed by Thomas Hinton under this agreement was *C.* 646, Saturday 25 November 1738.
30. The first paper printed by Goreham in the Burney Collection is *C.* 653, Saturday 13 January 1739.
31. Haines was apparently released at the end of his two year sentence, perhaps on the strength of his account of the shortcomings of the *Craftsman's* proprietors, *D.G.* 1711, Friday 12 December 1740.
32. As business manager of a paper under a limited form of ownership, the publisher also occasionally took this sort of unilateral action. In 1728, for example, Thomas Warner refused to give up the *Flying Post* to its sole proprietor and continued to produce a parallel paper, *D.J.* 2,174, Monday 1 January 1728.
33. For a split in the *Monitor* in 1762, see R. R. Rea, *The English Political Press in Politics 1760–1774* (Lincoln: University of Nebraska Press, 1963), 33–34. Also in the *General Evening Post* in 1770, Haig, *Gazetteer*, 93–100.
34. Haig, *Gazetteer*, 279.
35. Ibid.
36. Poll Book of the City election of 1727. Advertisement in *D.P.* 5,152, Thursday 18 March 1736, with thanks the following day.
37. *D.P.* 6,609, Wednesday 12 November 1749.
38. *D.J.* 3,831, Friday 13 April 1733.
39. *D.J.* 3,986, Monday 8 October 1733.
40. *A.O.W.J.* Saturday 16 July 1720.
41. *M.W.J.* 1, Saturday 1 May 1725.
42. *R.W.J.* 282, Saturday 15 August 1730. Copies appeared under both titles on this date.
43. *Baldwin's London Journal* and the *Craftsman or Grays inn Journal,* R. and M. Bond, "Minute Books," 38.
44. To Lord Townshend, n.d., P.R.O.: S.P. 35, 34, 78 (b).
45. Gent, *Life*, 111.
46. Howe, *London Compositor*, 35–36.
47. Gent, *Life*, 140, 142. He worked for Henry Woodfall, among others.
48. Cf. a similar informality in the provinces, Cranfield, *Provincial Newspaper*, 50.
49. Gent does not identify the paper but it seems likely that the reference is to the *Oxford Post*, which first appeared in December 1717 and which was "Printed for and by Francis Clifton in Little Wild Street."
50. Gent, *Life*, 85–86. For comment on extensive activity in this area during the early 1720s, see P.R.O.: S.P. 35, 24/97 and 25/94.
51. Gent, *Life*, 86–87.
52. *C.* 751, Saturday 22 November 1740.
53. *P.L.N.* 988, Wednesday 17 March 1725.
54. Wiles, *Serial Publication*, 63.
55. Stationers' Company Records, "Apprentices Register," 1710–46.
56. Advertisement in *L.J.* 372, Saturday 10 September 1726, *passim.*
57. For some analysis of Walker's career see Wiles, *Serial Publication*, 68–73 and Cranfield, *Provincial Newspaper*, 51–56.
58. Will proved 16 November 1761, P.R.O.
59. *The Dunghill and the Oak* (London, 1728), was "Printed for R. Walker and W.R." and subsequently their names were linked on the imprints of several pamphlets.
60. *D.J.* 3,147, Friday 5 February 1731; John Pullen was a second witness.
61. This location appears in P.R.O.: S.P. 36, 39/76, which is misplaced in the records and belongs to 1729, not 1736 as cited by Plomer.

62. *D.J.* 3564, Friday 19 February 1731. Advertisement for *Iago Display'd.*

63. *D.A.* Friday 21 September 1733.

64. For a short list of Rayner's publications, see the *Inquisitor* (London, 1731). At the same time, a number of publications with romantic themes appeared with E. Rayner on the imprint, suggesting another area of specialization; see *Memoirs of Love and Gallantry* (London, 1732), and *D.J.* 3,513, Saturday 8 April 1732.

65. *D.C.* 8271, Tuesday 27 July 1731.

66. P.R.O.: S.P. 36, 15/100, 16/38, *passim.*

67. General warrant, 5 July 1731, P.R.O.: S.P. 44, 82.

68. A very fully account appeared in *L.E.P.*774, Thursday 16 November 1732.

69. For further reference to the circumstances leading up to his sentence, see *The Friendly Writer, and Register of Truth* (London, 1732), 11–12.*L.E.P.* 780, Thursday 30 November 1732. *C.* 346, Saturday 17 February 1733.

70. I am grateful to Alan Sterenberg at the British Library for providing me with a print-out of Rayner imprints through the *Eighteenth-Century Short Title Catalogue.* For a view of the research implications of this project see M. Crump and M. Harris, eds., *Searching the Eighteenth Century* (London: British Library, 1984). The imprint of *The Opera of Operas* (London, n.d. but ca. 1733), states "printed for William Rayner prisoner in the King's-Bench, and to be sold at the Theatre, and likewise at the Printing-Office in Marigold Court."

71. For an account of the rules see Edward Walford, *Old and New London,* 6 vols. (London, 6 1876), 6: 65.

72. J. Lyons to Sir R. Walpole, 15 October 1734, C.U.L.: C.(H.) Corres. 2,356. Similar activity was evident within the rules of the Fleet prison.

73. Examinations of Doctor Gaylard, P.R.O.: T.S. 11/1027/4315.

74. Ibid. and *H. of C.J.,* 23: 713.

75. P.R.O.: S.P. 36. 50/29., examination of B. N. Defoe.

76. *G.L.M.A.* 983, Friday 1 January 1742.

77. *T.B.P.* 1739–41, 29 January 1741, 519.

78. Unless there were two William Rayners involved, which seems unlikely.

79. Advertisement in *U.S.* 256, Saturday 1 September 1733.

80. *D.A.* Thursday 13 September 1733. On the 21st he announced publication of a new series of State Trials.

81. The first issue of the *Royal Oak Journal* was advertised in *D.P.* 5,311, Friday 30 January 1736.

82. The first known issue is number 57, dated Monday 3 May 1736.

83. Advertisement for the sixth issue in *C.* 647, Saturday 2 December 1738.

84. *R.M.A.* 183, Monday 21 February 1737.

85. *R.M.A.* 184, Wednesday 23 February 1737.

86. P.R.O.: S.P. 36,15,100.

87. See the advertisements in *L.D.P.* Wednesday 4 February 1736: *D.J.* Tuesday 2 March 1737 *passim.*

88. Wiles, *Serial Publication,* 44–45.

89. Wiles, *Freshest Advices,* 55. The *Maidstone Journal.*

90. Cranfield, *Provincial Newspaper,* 54.

91. *D.P.* 3674, Tuesday 29 June 1731.

92. 29 August 1734, B.L. Add. MSS. 28,275, f. 319. A full account of Walker's part in this episode appears in Wiles, *Serial Publication,* pp. 19–21. For a reference to Rayner's piratical *Gentleman's Magazine,* see *G.M.* 5 (1735): iv.

93. Gaylard had worked for Mist and was the printer of at least one overtly Jacobite newspaper while a warrant was issued against Ilive and one of the Applebees, among others, for publishing the Pretender's declaration, 8 December 1745, P.R.O.: S.P. 44. 83.

94. *H. of C.J.,* 22, 713.

95. Gaylard also claimed that soon after joining Rayner in 1734 he had produced some Jacobite material for Nixon, T.S. 11,1027 and 4315.

96. Examination of Charles Bennet, 28 June 1737, B.L. Add. MSS. 32,690, f. 335.

97. Examination of John Standen, 23 October 1739. P.R.O.: S.P. 36.50/21.

98. Examination of B. N. Defoe, 19 November 1739. P.R.O.: S.P. 36.50/29.

99. P.R.O.: S.P. 36.50/16 and 19.

100. This seems to be implied in C.U.L.: C.(H.) MSS. 73, 44/3

101. Imprint of *The Sixteenth Epode of Horace Imitated* (London, 1739). Also comment in *C.* 746, Saturday 18 October 1740.

102. P.R.O.: S.P. 36,50/29.

103. Evidence of Rayner's connection with the evening paper appears in P.R.O.: S.P. 36, 50/282.

104. Examination of de Coetlogan, 17 January 1740, P.R.O.: S.P. 36, 50/33.

105. Wiles, *Serial Publication*, 68–69. Rayner, like Walker, was also active in the publication of trials and criminal biographies, which were a staple of the lower levels of the trade. See Michael Harris, "Trials and Criminal Biographies," in *Sale and Distribution of Books from 1700*, ed. R. Myers and M. Harris (Oxford: at the Polytechnic Press, 1982).

106. *O.C.* 647, Saturday 2 December 1738, *passim.*

107. Advertisement in *L.M.A.* 949, Monday 12 October 1741. The printer Henry Goreham seems to have been associated with Rayner.

108. The paper's adoption of the title of a successful rival in 1744 was characteristic of his approach, *P.L.M.A.* 203, Monday 13 August 1744.

109. Nichols, *Literary Anecdotes*, 6:447–48.

110. *L.M.A.* 1235, Friday 14 January 1743. In May 1744 Rayner received a license to print, publish, and sell William Friend's *Family Bible, Or, the Old and New Testament Explained by Way of Question and Answer*, B.L. Add. MSS. 33,054, ff. 215–18.

111. L.M., 30 (1761): 561, William Rayner, late of White Friars, printer. His will was signed on 16 November and his executor was the apothecary George West.

112. 13 May 1761, B.L. Add. MSS. 38,730,f. 11. R. and M. Bond, "Minute Books," 17.

113. The Walker imprints in the British Library fall from a peak of 71 items in the 1730s to 20 items in the 1740s.

Chapter 6: The Journalists

1. For some account of these authors, see "A Secret History of the Weekly Writers," in *The Life and Errors of John Dunton*, ed. J. Nichols, 2 vols. (London, 1818), 2: 423–39.

2. C.U.L.: C. (H) MSS. 75, 16/1–4.

3. J. R. Sutherland, *Defoe*, 2d ed. (London: Methuen, 1950), 215, 225, 226.

4. *W.J. or S.P.* 65, Saturday 8 March 1718 *passim.* W. Lee, *Defoe*, 1: xii.

5. 17 January 1740, P.R.O.: S.P. 36,50/33.

6. The essay-sheet, with lower production costs and profit threshold, apparently re mained viable as an individual enterprise.

7. Wilbur Cross, *The History of Henry Fielding*, 3 vols. (New Haven: Yale University Press, 1918), 1: 250.

8. Examination of John Purser, 25 July 1737, P.R.O.: S.P. 36, 41, 240.

9. *W.M.* 444, Saturday 27 June 1741.

10. To George Ducket, Sunday 6 April 1718, B.L. Add. MSS. 36,722, ff. 183–84.

11. For authorship attributions of the *Universal Spectator*, see the marked copies kept by the editor Henry Baker and now held by the Bodleian Library.

12. *D'Anverian History*, 81.

13. Attempts to isolate elements in the authorship of the *Craftsman* through an analysis of the initial letters printed below each essay in the collection of 1757 have not thrown much light on this problme. E.g., G. Barber, B. Litt. thesis "A Bibliography of Henry Saint John Viscount Bolingbroke," Oxford, 1967. See also Simon Varey, ed., *Lord Bolingbroke's Contributions to the Craftsman* (Oxford: Clarendon Press, 1982).

14. *The Political Journal of George Bubb Doddington*, 218. To David Mallet, 30 December 1753, B.L. Add. MSS. 32,733 f. 614.

15. 21 November 1733, H. M. C. Egmont, *Diary*, 1: 444.

16. Arnall to Sir R. Walpole, 10 August 1734, C.U.L.: C.(H.) Corres., 2,306.

17. *L.E.P.* 1,333 Thursday 3 June 1736.

18. Alexander Pope, *The Dunciad*, ed. James Sutherland, 3d ed. (London: Methuen, 1963), 134.

19. H. M. C. Egmont, *Diary*, 3 : 323–24.

20. 12 April 1733, C.U.L.: C.(H.) Corres. 1965.

21. 10 October 1734, ibid., 2486.

22. 11 October 1735, ibid., 2487.

23. 23 October 1735, ibid., 2493.

24. 2 November 1735, ibid., 2504.

25. A few notes from Courteville, who seems previously to have contributed to both the *Daily Courant* and the *London Journal*, appear in the Walpole correspondence, but they are scattered and do not imply much personal contact. There is nothing either to or from Pitt.

26. *An Historical View*, 15–18; J. Ralph, *A Critical History of the Administration of Sir Robert Walpole* (London, 1743), 505.

27. *Universal Spy; or, the Royal Oak Journal Reviv'd*, 2 Saturday 6 May 1732.

28. *Bob Lynn against Frank Lynn* (London, 1732), 16.

29. See below, chap. 8.

30. [James Miller] *An Epistle for Dick Poney, Esq.* (London, 1742), 9–10. Cf. *Correspondence of Alexander Pope*, ed. George Sherburn, 5 vols. (Oxford: Clarendon Press, 1956), 4: 179, n. 1. A. Pope to J. Swift, 17 May 1739.

31. *Verres and His Scribblers: A Satire in Three Cantos* (London, 1732).

32. *C.* 474, Saturday 2 August 1735.

33. James Watson to Charles Delafaye, 11 March 1728, P.R.O.: S.P. 36. 5/184.

34. *D'Anverian History*, 31.

35. *True Patriot*, 23–25.

36. Seized by the messengers 28 June 1739, P.R.O.: S.P. 9, 35.

37. P.R.O.: S.P. 9, 35/21, 37, 77, 137, *passim.*

38. 6 April 1732, Q.C. MSS. 450.

39. 2 January 1736, ibid.

40. *W.J. or S.P.* 272, Saturday 11 January 1724.

41. Haig, *Gazetteer*, 86–89, 92–93, 162–63.

42. Examination of John Purser, 25 July 1737, P.R.O.: S.P. 36, 41/240; S.P.36, 50/29. Cf. the £1 a week paid to Alexander Justice, author of the *British Mercury* from October 1710 to December 1711, Dickson, *Sun Insurance Office*, p. 37.

43. Examination of T. Warner, 1 November 1718, P.R.O.: S.P. 35, 13/33.

44. 17 January 1740, P.R.O.: S.P. 36, 50/33. Cf. the offer of half a guinea to readers for any full-page contribution published in *N.W.M.* 1, Saturday 18 July 1741.

45. C.U.L.: C.(H.) MSS. 73, 44/3..

46. *Treachery and Baseness*, 28. *C.* 746, Saturday 18 October 1740.

47. *Treachery, Baseness*, pp. 19–20. According to Thomas Davies, the most Amhurst ever received from Pulteney was "a hogshead of claret," T. Davies, *The Characters of George the First, Queen Caroline, Sir Robert Walpole, Mr. Pulteney, Lord Hardwicke, Mr. Fox and Mr. Pitt reviewed* (London, 1777), 43.

48. O.E. 2, Saturday 12 February 1743.

49. J. Ralph, *The Case of Authors by Profession and Trade, Stated* (London, 1758), 32. T. Davies, *The Characters*, 42–44.

50. 4 May 1743, London Unviersity, Stuart Papers (Microfilm), vol. 249/113.

51. Ralph, *Case of Authors*, 32.

52. 26 March 1730, C.U.L.: C.(H.) Corres. 1703.

53. See [Paul Chamberlen], *A Letter to Richard Arnald, alias Francis Walsingham, Esq.* (London, 1731), 12.

54. A claim in the *Craftsman* in August 1730 that Arnall had been seen flaunting a Treasury bill for £312.18s.6d. in the Exeter Exchange Coffee House, although vigorously denied in the *Free Briton* as a put-up job to discredit him with Walpole, may suggest the timing of his new prosperity, *F.B.* 39, Thursday 27 August 1730, 40, Thursday 3 September 1730, *passim.*

55. *T.B.P.* 1735–38, 170.

56. *L.E.P.* 1333, Thursday 3 June 1736.

57. *Ch.* 145, Thursday 16 October 1740.

58. *A Plain Narrative of Facts*, 6.

59. To the King, n.d., C.U.L.: C.(H.) MSS. 75, 16/4. Other requests to Walpole 16/1, 16/2, 16/3.

60. *T.B.P.* 1729–30, 13, 6 February 1729.

61. The nature of the payments made to John Henley remains obscure. See a report of his £100 p.a. pension in *C.S.* 4 March 1738. Also J. Nichols, *History of Leicestershire*, 4 vols. (London, 1795–1811), 2: 261.

62. S.P. 36.11/89. *L.E.P.* 221, Thursday 8 May 1729.
63. *C.* 273, Saturday 25 September 1731.
64. *L.E.P.* 552, Saturday 12 June 1731.
65. 6 December 1732, C.U.L.: C.(H.), Corres. 1931.
66. Ralph, *The Case of Authors*, 38.
67. N.d., C.U.L.: C.(H.), Corres. 3,041.
68. *C.* 659, Saturday 24 February 1739; included in a news item announcing a place given to Richard Morley, a supposed author of the *Gazetteer.*
69. 28 July 1744, C.U.L.: C.(H.) Corres. 3181a. Hardwicke's refusal, dated 4 August, is printed in William Coxe, *Memoirs of the Life and Administration of Sir Robert Walpole Earl of Oxford*, 3 vols. (London, 1798), 3: 601.
70. *G.S.J.* 140, Thursday 7 September 1732.
71. N.d., C.U.L.: C.(H.), Corres. 1507.
72. 12 September 1734, C.U.L.: C.(H.), MSS. 73. 29/1.
73. N.d., ibid., 73, 73.
74. *C.S.* 169, Saturday 26 April 1740. B.L. Add. MSS. 32,687 f. 524, contains a reference to an author of the *Daily Courant*, who probably wrote for the *Craftsman.* See also C.U.L.: C.(H.) Corres. 2388, n.d.
75. *An Historical View*, 27–29. *F.B.* 38, Thursday 20 August 1730; 39, Thursday 27 August 1730, *passim.* See also an equivocal letter from Francklin to Wilkins apparently implying his authorship of essays in the *London Journal*, 6 November [?], C.U.L.: C.(H.) 74, 45.
76. Realey, "London Journal," 17.
77. 25 March 1730, C.U.L.: C.(H.) Corres. 2712.
78. 11 October 1737, C.U.L.: C.(H.) Corres. 2712. Cf. his undated petition for Royal Bounty, C.(H.) 81, 181/1 and 2.
79. 19 October 1739, P.R.O.: S.P. 36, 48/173b.
80. W. Arnall to Sir R. Walpole, 10 August 1734, C.U.L.: C.(H.) Corres. 2,306.
81. 2575, 5 June 1736, C.U.L.: (C.(H.) Corres, 2575. For a comparable career structure, see Graham C. Gibbs, "Abel Boyer Gallo-Anglus Glossographus et Historicus 1667–1729; from tutor to author, 1689–1699," *Proceedings of the Huguenot Society of London* 24 (1983): 46–59.
82. C. 832, Saturday 12 June 1742.
83. Lord Orford to Lord Chancellor, 28 July 1744, C.U.L.: C.(H.) Corres. 3181a.
84. N.d. B.L. Add. MSS. 32733, f. 616.

Chapter 7: The Press and Politics

1. Alan Downie, *Robert Harley and the Press* (Cambridge: at the University Press, 1979).
2. Linda Colley, *In Defence of Oligarchy* (Cambridge: at the University Press, 1982).
3. For some analysis of the content of Mist's paper as well as information about Mist himself, see Paul Chapman, "Jacobite Political Argument in England, 1714–1766," Ph.D. diss., Cambridge University, 1984.
4. Hanson, *Government*, 66.
5. *C.G.* 36, Friday 15 July 1726, reprinted in 42, Monday 1 August 1726. The essay was used in the preface to the collected edition of the *Crafsman* in 1731. The author of *An Historical View* stated that the *Country Gentleman* was sunk into the *Craftsman* but the nature of any relationship remains obscure. The first number of the *Craftsman* appeared on Monday 5 December 1726 and the last of the *Country Gentleman* on Monday 26 December 1726.
6. C.U.L.: C.(H.) MSS. 74, 72.
7. *C.* 45, Saturday 13 May 1727.
8. *D.G.* 1800, Friday 31 July 1741.
9. *S.* 8, Tuesday 5 March 1728.
10. *W.J.* 224, Saturday 6 September 1729.
11. *Liberty and the Craftsman* (London, 1730), 3.
12. *D'Anverian History,* 79.
13. Harris, "Figures," 233–42.
14. *C.* 9, Monday 2 January 1727. Publication announced in *C.* 14, Monday 16 January 1727.
15. There is slight doubt about the nature of the sums appearing against each grouping of four issues, but it seems likely that they represented the overall profit.

16. *Treachery and Baseness,* 20.

17. The popularity of the *Craftsman* was also reflected in notices in the paper claiming that exorbitant prices were being charged on the false ground of scarcity and that allied pamphlet material was being pirated or faked, *C.* 66, Saturday 7 October 1727; 82, Saturday 27 January 1728; 137, Saturday 15 February 1729; 177, Saturday 22 November 1729.

18. *D'Anverian history,* 80–81.

19. Realey, "London Journal," 23–26.

20. See below, chap. 8.

21. These papers were listed among defeated opponents in the *C.* 494, Saturday 20 December 1735. I have not found any other reference to the *Plain Man.*

22. *B.J.* 1, Saturday 20 January 1728.

23. See above, chap. 6.

24. The *British Journal* appeared without the subtitle from 100, Saturday 29 November 1729. It finally ceased publication sometime in 1731 after continuing to carry occasional essays in support of the ministry.

25. The paper had contained a number of political essays in the late 1720s and the radical changes in format had apparently been prompted by an attempt to fit such material into the paper as a regular feature, *D.J.* 2,189, Thursday 18 January 1728.

26. J. C. Sainty, *Officials of the Secretaries of State 1660–1782* (London: University of London, Athlone Press, 1973).

27. 13 December 1728, P.R.O.: S.P. 36, 9/110. Gray's request for the position. His appointment was reported in *L.E.P.* Saturday 14 December 1728.

28. Nichols, *Literary Anecdotes,* 8, 294.

29. L/W sale 22, MSS. entry, 3. See comment on the *Daily Courant's* decline in *W.J. or S.P.* 237, Saturday 11 May 1723.

30. Nichols, *Literary Anecdotes,* 8, 294.

31. See *C.S.* 57, Saturday 4 March 1738.

32. *C.* 381, Saturday 20 October 1735.

33. *Liberty and the Craftsman,* 4.

34. *H.D.* 1, Tuesday 15 December 1730.

35. C.U.L.: C.(H.) MSS. 74, 72. See above chap. 2.

36. For the account of the original arrangements, see P.R.O.; T.1, 255. Cal.88 n.d.

37. T.B.P. 1729–30, 170.

38. See William Arnall's account reprinted in Hanson, *Government,* frontispiece.

39. First recorded payment, *T.B.P.* 1731–34, 210.

40. *T.B.P.* 1731–34, 538.

41. Account for the *Free Briton* June 1733–June 34, C.U.L.: C.(H.) 75,7/1.

42. *T.B.P.* 1731–34, 530.

43. Account for the *Free Briton* July–September 1734, C.U.L.: C.(H.) MSS 75,8/1. Account for the *London Journal* March 1734–February 35, C.(H.) MSS. 75, 9. *T.B.P.* 1731–34, 539, 564 *passim.*

44. None of the pamphlets referred to below, for which accounts exist among the Walpole papers, appear among other similar items in the Treasury records.

45. See the account published in *C.* 265, Saturday 31 July 1731.

46. William Webster, *A Plain Narrative of Facts* (London, 1758), 6.

47. See the vigorous but highly inconclusive denial of any financial link in *R.W.J.* 333, Saturday 7 August 1731.

48. Eustace Budgell, *A Letter to the Craftsman* (London, 1730), 26–27.

49. R. Courteville to Walpole 4 October [?], C.U.L.: C.(H.) Corres. 3,231.

50. For an analysis of this material see Michael Harris, "Print and Politics in the Age of Walpole," in *Britain in the Age of Walpole,* ed. Jeremy Black, (London: Macmillan, 1984), 199–200.

51. *Craftsman,* 14 vols. (London, 1731 and 1737), 11: 224. The pamphlet quoted was *A Review of the Excise-Scheme,* which was included as an appendix to this volume.

52. See below, chap. 8.

53. *G.E.P.* 1, Tuesday 2 October 1733. *L.E.P.* 919, Thursday 11 October 1733.

54. Sale, *Samuel Richardson,* 54–58.

55. C.U.L.: C.(H.) MSS. 75, 15.

56. *R.M.A.* 100, Wednesday 11 August 1736. A copy is preserved among the State papers, P.R.O.: S.P. 36, 39/74. There are no clear indications of any action against the paper.

57. See handbills for the first issue Monday 12 May 1735. Lyson's "Collectanea," 2, f. 48.

58. Harris, "Print and Politics."

59. *F.B.* 99, Thursday 21 October 1731.

60. John Smith to the Duke of Newcastle, September 1732, B.L. Add. MSS. 32, 687, ff. 518–21.

61. *D.G.* 360, Saturday 21 August 1736; 413, Friday 22 October 1736; 416, Tuesday 26 October 1736.

62. *Treachery and Baseness*, 20.

63. *L.E.P.* 1,284, Tuesday 10 February 1736.

64. Mist to Mr. Cameron of Locheal, 11 July 1736, P.R.O.: S.P. 36, 39/21. The letter, probably stopped at the Post Office, describes Mist's visit to a Jacobite club and contains complaints of "a little Business, few Friends and much Idleness."

65. This condition is referred to in *An Historical View*, 19–20.

66. *C.S.* 1, Saturday 5 February 1737. Abandonment of politics announced in *F.* 401, Saturday 10 July 1736.

67. C.U.L.: C.(H.) MSS. 75, 15.

68. P.R.O.: T.I. 303 Cal. 88. My dating seems to be confirmed by a reference to the official circulation of the papers standing at 2,200 copies.

69. W. Arnall to Sir R. Walpole, 10 August 1734, C.U.L.: C.(H.) Corres. 2,306.

70. The *London Journal* seems to have been dropped before the end of 1738, while the *Corn Cutters' Journal* was apparently abandoned in 1741.

71. See allocation of days for their respective essays; *D.G.* 1, Monday 30 June 1735.

72. Payments made to John Peele for unspecified services that continued until 1738 may conceivably have been connected with the *London Journal, T.B.P.* 1735–38, 352.

73. The volume of the *Gazetteer* for 1741 in the Burney Collection is in this four-page form, with the second title replaced by an abstract design.

74. *T.B.P.* 1735–38, 55. This calculation assumes that no writing fee was included and that each paper cost the ministry 2d.

75. Although the *Gazetteer* is not named for 1738, the payments to John Walthoe probably refer to the paper.

76. *L.E.P.* 1,190, Saturday 5 July 1735.

77. *Memoirs of the Times In A Letter to a Friend in the Country* (London, 1737), 34.

78. *L.E.P.* 1,444, Thursday 17 February 1737.

79. G. H. James, "The Jacobite Charles Molloy and *Common Sense*," *Review of English Studies*, new ser., 4 (1950).

80. Ibid., 144.

81. Advertisement in *L.E.P.* 1,490, Thursday 2 June 1737. P.R.O.: S.P. 36, 41/240.

82. Ibid., 145.

83. The evidence connecting Chesterfield and Lyttleton to all the papers is clear enough and is referred to in the *D.N.B.*, Fielding's position is more ambiguous. His connection with *Common Sense* can be directly established by the presence among Molloy's papers of an essay in his handwriting. For the argument linking him with the *Craftsman*, see Martin C. Battestin, "Four New Fielding Attributions: His Earliest Satires of Walpole," *Studies in Bibliography* 36 (1983).

84. *C.S.* 108, Saturday 24 February 1739. See also advertisement for vol. 2 of the collected edition of the essays in *C.S.* 110, Saturday 10 March 1739.

85. See below, chap. 8. The heterogeneous nature of the paper's political associations may have contributed to the management problems.

86. *O.C.S.* 86, Saturday 30 September 1738.

87. *D.C.*, 1,590, Thursday 24 July 1740.

88. The original publisher, Thomas Cooper, was well known for handling pro-ministerial or neutral papers, while Fielding's political position at this time is highly ambiguous, and the tenor of the early essays does not suggest a primarily political approach.

89. Comment on its poor financial state in *Ch.* 9, Tuesday 4 December 1739; 14, Saturday 15 December 1739; 25, Thursday 10 january 1740; 88, Thursday 12 June 1740.

90. An announcement of the change in policy appeared in *U.S.* 703, Saturday 27 March 1742. Between 1737 and 1742 a ¹/₁₂ share in the paper had slumped in value from £23 to £2.2s., L/W. 56, lot 57; 97, lot 24.

91. *W.M.* 444, Saturday 27 June 1741.

92. The *New Weekly Miscellany* was said to be written by a nephew of Richard Hooker, the pseudonym used by Webster.

93. *West, J.* 1, Saturday 28 November 1741. The stimulus of the election is stated to have

been the cause of this change in an advertisement for a collection of essays in *West. J.* 294, Saturday 18 July 1747.

94. *H. of C.J.*, 24: 180–81, 230.

95. *L.M.*, 12 (1742): 621. *T.B.P.* 1742–45, 102–3, 233, 341.

96. 29 March 1744, B.L. Add. MSS. 32,702, ff. 268–69.

97. *L.E.P.* 2,228, Saturday 20 February 1742.

98. *D.G.* 2,085, Monday 22 February 1742.

99. *C.* 817, Saturday 27 February 1742.

100. *C.* 819, Saturday 13 March 1742.

101. *Ch.* 362, Saturday 6 March 1742.

102. *D.G.* 2,085, Monday 22 February 1742.

103. Haig, *Gazetteer*, 19.

104. *Ch.* 422, Saturday 31 July 1742.

105. *W.J.* 54, Saturday 3 December 1742.

106. *C.* 854, Saturday 6 November 1742.

107. *W.J.* 54, Saturday 3 December 1742.

108. R. Courteville to J. West 5 March 1747, B. L. Lansdowne MSS. 841 ff. 151–52.

109. Horsley contributed the short essays appearing under the general title of *The Fool*.

110. *D.P.* 7,535, Friday 28 October 1743, *passim*.

111. A.O. 3, 1746–47. The end of variations in advertisement duty payments, which often mark the end of publication.

112. The timing of Amhurst's retirement is not clear and he may have been replaced by Thomas Cooke before 1742. It was claimed that he died of a fever on 27 April of that year, T. Cibber, *The Lives of the Poets of Great Britain and Ireland*, 5 vols. (London, 1753), 5:337.

113. Francklin apparently remained proprietor and his advertisements continued to be carried prominently into the mid-1740s.

114. *O.E.* 1, Saturday 5 February 1743.

115. *C.S.* 314, Saturday 19 February 1743.

116. 17 March 1743, P.R.O.: S.P. 44, 83.

117. A reference to Purser appears in the third number in a collected edition, and his dual responsibility appears 15 March 1743, in P.R.O.: S.P. 44, 83.

118. B. Cowse, Jane Morgan, and H. Morgan, whose names replaced Purser's on the imprint, were all linked with his office.

119. The last copy in the Burney Collection is *C.S.* 351, Saturday 5 November 1743.

120. *O.E.* 101, Saturday 12 January 1745.

121. *W.J.* 165, Saturday 25 January 1745.

122. *O.E.* 103, Saturday 26 January–108, Saturday 2 March 1745.

123. *O.E.* 109, Saturday 9 March 1745.

124. 4 May 1743, London University, Stuart Papers (Microfilm) vol. 249/113.

125. Carte to the Pretender's secretary, suggesting the application of about £2,000 a year for "a well write paper, and seasonable pamphlets, and to support them in case of prosecutions," ibid., Box 1/299 n.d. (ca. 1749).

126. To Lord Holland, 8 November 1743. B.L. Add. MSS. 51,390.

127. *Catalogue of Prints and Drawings in the British Museum*, Div. 1, 2: 463. *O.E.* 20, Saturday 18 June 1743.

128. The number of reprints from each paper is difficult to establish. *West.J.* 65, Saturday 19 February 1743 contains an advertisement for three publications containing eight essays from the paper, while at least sixteen issues of *Old England* were reprinted before the end of 1743: 1–9, 10, 33, 34, 36, 38, 39, 40.

129. See below, chap. 8.

130. *O.E.* 101, Saturday 12 January 1745; cf. an ironic comment in Saturday 23 June 1744, in which the author claimed to be at the head of "three hundred and fifty or four hundred Persons (including Devils and all) who get their Bread by this Paper." This might include all those involved in an extensive distribution network.

131. *N. and Q.*, 198 (1953): 441.

132. *G.M.* 12 (1746): 431.

133. A run of the *Craftsman* from 7 October 1749 to 30 December 1752 originally held by the Parochial Library of St. Leonards Shoreditch was discovered in the mid-1970s, T. Brown, *Library*, 5th ser., 29 (1974): 460.

134. Lord Harrington to the Attorney General, 9 September 1746, P.R.O.: S.P. 44, 83. S.P. 36, 107/26, 33, 35, *passim*.

135. *West. J.* 222, Saturday 1 March 1746.
136. *O.E.* 189, Saturday 13 December 1746.
137. Cibber, *Lives of the Poets,* 5: 13–14.
138. B. L. Landsdowne MSS. 841, ff. 151–52.

Chapter 8: Political Control of the Press

1. See also chap. 1.
2. *D.G.* 774, Tuesday 27 December 1737 *passim.* Comment in *C.S.* 49, Saturday 14 January 1738.
3. *Ch.* 362, Saturday 6 March 1742.
4. *Reasons humbly offer'd to the Consideration of the Honourable House of Commons* [1712].
5. *The Printers' Case.*
6. C.U.L.: C.(H.) MSS. 75, 1a/1 and 21 n.d. Cf. earlier variations on the same theme in *A Proposal for Restraining the Great Licentiousness of the Press* [1710].
7. C.U.L.: C.(H.) MSS. 75.21. Cf. similar plan put forward by an anonymous correspondent 9 March 1722, P.R.O.: S.P. 35. 30/52.
8. The approach is similar to that adopted by the coffee-men in their struggle against the general increase in newspapers in the late 1720s; see chap. 1.
9. Snyder, "Reports of a Press Spy," 326–45. Also Michael Treadwell, "A Further Report from Harley's Press Spy," *Library,* 6th ser., 2 (1980): 216–18.
10. *H. of C.J.,* 20: 143. Cf. reference to money spent by the Messenger of the Press on its behalf in S.P. 44,81, 2 July 1722, 76. A variety of plans for establishing an official oversight of new publications are preserved in the State Papers, including one submitted on behalf of the printer Francis Clifton, P.R.O.: S.P. 35,24/75, 27/22.
11. Anthony Cracherode to Lord Townshend, 7 April 1722, P.R.O.: S.P. 35.31/17.
12. *T.B.P.* 1720–28, 391.
13. Hanson, *Government,* 39.
14. P.R.O.: S.P. 36,8/218, 13/115, 29/13.
15. 29 November 1733, B.L. Add. MSS. 32,689, ff. 58–59.
16. N.d., C.U.L.: C.(H.) Corres. 3,178. Cf. earlier delays in payment in P.R.O.: S.P. 36.16/29.
17. A. Pope, *Epilogue to the Satires* (London, 1738), line 1; P. Whitehead *Manners* (London, 1739), 13; *A Dialogue Which Lately Pass'd Between The Knight and His Man John* (London, n.d.), lines 6–10.
18. To Newcastle, 29 March 1744. B.L. Add. MSS. 32,702, ff. 268–69.
19. A number of reports submitted by semi-literate informers during the early 1720s are preserved among the State Papers, the letters of Richard Shaw cropping up most regularly, P.R.O.: S.P.35,51/34,35. At the same time, both Edmund Curll and John Henley were also active in this dubious area; *G.M.* 68, pt. 1 (1798): 190–92.
20. There are no clues to the identity of Smith, conceivably his real name, although in one letter he gives a forwarding address as "Mr.Howson's a Stationer over against Exeter Exchange in the Strand."
21. September 1732, B.L. Add. MSS. 32,687, f. 514.
22. N.d., f. 527, ibid.
23. 17 October 1732, ff. 528–29, ibid.
24. 17 April 1733, P.R.O.: S.P. 36,29/156.
25. Edmund Curll claimed in 1722 that the publisher of the *Freeholders Journal* regularly supplied him with prepublication copies for scrutiny, P.R.O.: S.P. 35, 31/39.
26. Some incomplete remarks on his career in A. S. Limouze "Dr. Gaylards Loyal Observator Reviv'd," *Modern Philology* 48 (1950): 97–103. See also 25 May 1722, T.I. 239/64; 25 June 1723, P.R.O.: S.P. 44, 81.
27. *T.B.P.* 1735–38, 18 May 1738. P.R.O.: T.S. 11,1027, 4315. See above, chap. 5.
28. Manuscript pamphlet, n.d., 19, P.R.O.: S.P. 36,46/284.
29. P.R.O.: S. P. 36,78/62, 84/138, 164, 166, 90/185. Cf. Hanson, *Government,* 39, for comment on the payment of wives earlier in the century.
30. Cf. the brief career of James Watson as a ministerial informer following his arrest in 1728; P.R.O. S.P. 36, 5/187 *passim.*
31. E.g., *Bob Lynn Against Franck-Lynn,* 18.
32. *C.* 820, Saturday 20 March 1742.

33. B.L. Add. MSS. 36, 139, ff. 148–49. P.R.O.: S.P. 36, 28/219, 46/11. The presentments appeared in the political press as propaganda items, *F.W.J.* 226, Saturday 24 May 1728; *D.C.* 9,256, Thursday 8 July 1731; *L.E.P.* 1,125, Tuesday 4 February 1735 (a presentment of 1723); *D.G.* 630, Thursday 30 June 1737.

34. *C.* 321, Saturday 26 August 1732, 582, Saturday 3 September 1737: *C.S.* 39 Saturday 29 October 1737, *O.E.* 102, Saturday 19 January 1745.

35. Hanson, *Government*, 31.

36. Guildhall Library MSS. 214/4. One of the unlisted warrants appears in P.R.O.: S.P. 44, 82, directed against the personnel of the *Original Craftsman* in 1739.

37. Charles Delafaye to [Townshend] 29 March 1722, enclosing two warrants, one asked for, the other sent on the undersecretary's initiative, P.R.O.: S.P. 35, 30/67.

38. Paxton's report to Newcastle on the arrest of Kelly as author of *Fog's* 20 July 1737, P.R.O.: S.P. 36, 41/206. See also reference to Paxton's efforts in this area in S.P. 36, 46/284.

39. For their joint reputation in the lower levels of the newspaper world during the late 1720s, see reference to murder threats by "Mistes Men" in an informer's letters to Delafaye. P.R.O.: S.P. 36, 15/70, 148, 16/28.

40. Buckley's successor, the under secretary Edward Weston, though not so active in this area, was subsequently concerned in many newspaper prosecutions.

41. Cf. Paxton's successful prosecution of William Rayner in 1733.

42. P.R.O.: T. 54, 1741–48, 19. Those prosecutions listed by Paxton were against Marshall, Prine, Ebsall, Bowen, Cotton, Gaylard, Philips Sr. and Jr., Sarah Philips, Redmain, Cotton, Earbery, Curll, Woolston, Murray, Meighan, Kerr, Perry, Francklyn, and Mist under an escape warrant.

43. See P.R.O.: T.S. 11, 5, 338/1, 076, 3, 422/944, 178.

44. Hanson, *Government*, appendixes 2 and 4, 139, 146.

45. See comment in *C.* 582, Saturday 3 September 1737.

46. Hanson, *Government*, 51–52. Cf. the directive to avoid the prosecution of authors in 1723, ibid., 66.

47. P.R.O.: S.P. 36, 41/240, 48/1.

48. Realey, "London Journal," 19. Advertisement in *D.J.* 3,147, Friday 5 February 1731. Delafaye to the Attorney General, 15 September 1729, B.L. Add. MSS. 36, 137, ff. 265–66.

49. Committal order 29 June 1737, P.R.O.: S.P. 44, 82. See also S.P. 36, 46/284.

50. P.R.O.: S.P. 36, 50/33; 15 April 1740, S.P. 44,82.

51. Committal order to Newgate and bail, 21 March 1743, P.R.O.: S.P. 36, 60/109. Guthrie did not have to find this amount since the question of the legality of giving sureties for good behaviour, raised by Francklin in 1731 and again by Amhurst in 1737, had not been settled and provided a technical loophole, Sir. D. Ryder to Lord Cartaret, 22 March 1743, S.P. 44, 83.

52. N. Paxton to [Delafaye], 20 June 1738, P.R.O.: S.P. 36, 45/326.

53. *L.E.P.* 772, Saturday 11 November 1732. 13 February 1737. King's Bench Affidavits Hilary 11 GII., *C.S.* 55, Saturday 18 February 1738. *C.S.* 70, Saturday 3 June 1738.

54. 17 April 1727, p. 480; P.R.O.: S.P. 44, 81.

55. 22 July 1737; B.L. Add. MSS. 32, 690.

56. *Treachery and Baseness*, 11.

57. *C.* 605, Saturday 11 February 1738. B.L. Add MSS 33, 052, f. 150.

58. P.R.O.: S.P. 9, 35.

59. A system of registration was regularly canvassed at the beginning of the century and Walpole may have contemplated some further action in this direction, C.U.L.: C.(H.) 73, 48, n.d.

60. 28 June 1737, B.L. Add. MSS. 32, 690, f. 335.

61. *Oxford Post* 9, Tuesday 6 January 1718.

62. 15 July 1729, P.R.O.: S.P. 36, 13/86. Cf. a notice in *C.* 137, Saturday 15 February 1729, warning against piracy.

63. P.R.O.: S.P. 36, 13/86, 15/82. C.U.L.: C.(H.) MSS. 74, 79. S.P. 36, 50/264.

64. Hanson, *Government*, 55.

65. *W.J.* 5, Saturday 29 May 1725.

66. *C.* 586, Saturday 10 October 1737. Cf. the arrest of Gent in Hanson, *Government*, 48.

67. *L.E.P.* 1,508, Saturday 16 July 1737. The *Craftsman* of this date did not appear; see notice in *L.E.P.* 1,510, Thursday 21 July 1737, promising continued publication.

68. *C.* 582, Saturday 3 September 1737.

69. *C.* 597, Saturday 17 December 1737. *L.E.P.* Saturday 10 December 1737. *Treachery, Baseness*, 13–14.

70. *Treachery, Baseness,* 16–17.

71. P.R.O.: S.P. 35, 29/31.

72. 3 August 1738, P.R.O.: S.P. 44, 83.

73. 24 April 1732, P.R.O.: S.P. 44, 82. No printer was asked to find such substantial bail as was imposed in the early 1720s; Hanson, *Government,* 54.

74. The problem of establishing a case without the assistance of official witnesses to publication appeared in the failure to pin a charge on Edward Farley for reprinting the notorious essay from Mist's paper in the *Exeter Journal,* Cranfield, *Provincial Newspaper,* 144–45.

75. *C.* 73, Saturday 25 November 1727, *passim.* Hanson, *Government,* 23, 67.

76. *C.* 582, Saturday 3 September 1737.

77. See the account of the trial of Mist's workmen in *U.S.* 21, Saturday 1 March 1729.

78. List of prisoners in custody, P.R.O.: S.P. 36, 8/67.

79. List of prisoners in custody of the Messengers, 10 December 1737, P.R.O.: S.P. 36, 44/79. Warrant against named personnel, 10 December 1737, S.P.44, 82.

80. P.R.O.: S.P. 36, 8/254.

81. *C.* 578, Saturday 6 August 1737.

82. *C.* 586, Saturday 1 October 1737.

83. 6 February 1738, P.R.O.: S.P. 36, 45/97.

84. 18 March 1738, B.L. Add. MSS. 33, 052, f. 151.

85. 17 April 1738, 31 May 1738, P.R.O.: S.P. 44, 82.

86. James Ford to Newscastle, 30 May 1740, B.L. Add. MSS. 32, 693, ff. 300–301. Also P.R.O.: S.P. 36, 8/67.

87. *T.B.P.* 1739–41, 7.

88. Hanson, *Government,* 52.

89. *O.W.J.* Saturday 26 April 1718 contains a notice inserted by Phillip James *"Bookseller, and late Barber"* who had been accused of acting as an informer for 10/- a week *"by which Report my Business is prejudiced, my Family damag'd and my Life threatened."*

90. *L.E.P.* 226 Tuesday 20 May 1729.

91. See above, chap. 3.

92. E.g., the *Hyp Doctor.*

93. To Newcastle, 26 May 1731, P.R.O.: S.P. 36 23/134. Cf. Mrs. Nutt's undated petition S.P. 36, 9/249.

94. Petition to Newcastle, 17 October 1728, P.R.O.: S.P. 36, 8/238.

95. 24 April 1732, P.R.O.: S.P.: S.P. 44, 82.

96. In an advertisement in *D.J.* 3, 165, Friday 26 February 1731, "Mrs." Rayner reported the seizure of her entire stock of *Iago display'd,* offering the author's name but also suggesting that if the action had been taken without authority she would initiate legal proceedings herself.

97. Lord Harrington to Attorney General, 12 January 1731, P.R.O.: S.P. 44, 83.

98. Report of her acquittal in *L.E.P.* Saturday 1 March 1729.

99. P.R.O.: S.P. 36 and S.P. 44 *passim. C.* 16, 31, 36, 140, 158, 160, 215, 217, 235, 236.

100. 17 April 1727, p. 480, P.R.O.: S.P. 44, 61. *C.* 32, 34, 36.

101. P.R.O.: S.P. 36 and 44 *passim. M.* 170, 171, 175, 177/8.

102. P.R.O.: S.P. 36 and 44 *passim. F.W.J.* 83, 95, 100, 198.

103. Cranfield, *Provincial Newspaper,* 143.

104. 27 July 1729, P.R.O.: S.P. 44, 82. S.P. 36, 13/101. 115, *passim.* 22 July 1729, S.P. 43, 79.

105. P.R.O.: S.P. 44, 82, 83 *passim. C.* nos. 440, 442, 443.

106. *D.G.* 630, Saturday 30 June 1737.

107. P.R.O.: S.P. 36 and 44, *passim.* The numbers of the papers under attack were *A.* 21, *C.* 574, *F.W.J.* 7, *C.* 596. *O.C.S.* 44.

108. William Coxe, *Memoirs of the Administration of the Right Honourable Henry Pelham. . . .* 2 vols. (London, 1829), 1: 203.

109. P.R.O.: S.P. 36 and 44, *passim. O.E.* 6 and 7, *C.S.* 317.

110. Ibid. *O.E.* 52, 110.

111. P.R.O.: S.P. 36, 5/187, 191; 6/232. His presence in France is noted in *H.W.J.* 171, Saturday 27 July 1728.

112. *C.* 3, Monday 12 December 1726.

113. *C.* 6, Friday 23 December 1726.

114. *C.* 16, Monday 23 January 1727.

115. *C.* 304, Saturday 29 April 1732.

116. See above, chap. 5.

117. William Kittoe to Mr. Farley, 9 September 1728. P.R.O.: S.P. 36, 8/115.

118. *The Bee* 1 (1733): 9–10.

119. B.L. Add. MSS. 32,687, f. 526, n.d.

120. Monday 29 March 1744, B.L. Add. MSS. 32, 702, f. 268.

121. *O.E.* 179, Saturday 4 October 1746. Cf. similar comments in *O.E.* 181, Saturday 29 November 1746; *O.E.* 188, Saturday 6 December 1746.

122. *Liberty and the Craftsman*, 4. Cf. comment in *The Town Spy* (Gloucester, 1725), 22; *O.E.* 126, Saturday 6 July 1745.

123. *D'Anverian History*, 80. The same author also claimed that "the taking them up by the Messengers, and binding them over for three Terms," cost the printers, at most, four guineas, ibid., 79.

124. One of the usual replies was to cite Bolingbroke's record of prosecution during Queen Anne's reign. See the full accounts in *F.B.* 110, Thursday 5 January 1732; 112, Thursday 12 January 1732; 291, Thursday 5 June 1735. See also notice on continued publication of *Mist's* in *D.J.* 2,394, Tuesday 10 September 1728.

125. Sir John Willes to [Newcastle], 23 December 1734, P.R.O.: S.P. 36, 33/147.

126. 25 October 1718, P.R.O.: S.P. 35, 18/31. Repeated in S.P. 35, 39/67.

127. *F.B.* 213, Thursday 29 November 1733. Probably a reference to the rejection of the *Daily Courant* for its pro-excise comment.

128. *C.* 37, Monday 10 April 1737.

129. *C.* 19, Friday 10 February 1727.

130. Warrant v. James, 3 July 1735, P.R.O.: S.P. 44, 82.

131. 4 July 1735, P.R.O.: S.P. 44, 82.

132. 9 July 1735, P.R.O.: S.P. 36, 35/117.

133. *A Letter to a Member of Parliament in the North* (London, 1729), pp. 17–18. Copy in B.L. Add. MSS. 36, 138 and P.R.O.: S.P. 36, 16/38.

134. *C.S.* 117, Saturday 28 April 1739. Letter from an M.P. and petition to the Post-Master General, P.R.O.: S.P. 9, 35/165.

135. *Ch.* 151, Thursday 30 October 1740.

136. *T.B.P.* 1721–28, p. 68.

137. *C.* 82, Saturday 27 June 1728. See also *C.* 122, Saturday 2 November 1728.

138. *Gloucester Journal* 10 September 1728, in Cranfield, *Provincial Newspaper*, 146.

139. N.d., C.U.L.:C.(H.) MSS. 75, 19.

140. This ran for over a month. *L.E.P.* 919, Thursday 11 October–935 Saturday 17 November 1733. The word *forc'd* was changed to *Impos'd* in 921.

141. *L.E.P.* Saturday 27 October 1733.

142. The first of a series of advertisements appeared at the end of the parliamentary session, informing readers that the printer would supply them with the paper at the increased price of 2d. plus postage, *L.E.P.* Saturday 13 April 1734.

143. *L.E.P.* 935, Saturday 17 November 1733. Similar notices in the *Universal Spectator* make no mention of the political issue, *U.S.* 268, Saturday 24 November 1733.

144. *L.E.P.* 998, Saturday 13 April 1734.

145. Edward Carteret to Newcastle, sending William Wye's newsletter discovered by Bell among the clerk's papers, 10 January 1733, P.R.O.: S.P. 36, 29/9.

146. *Ch.* 88, Thursday 5 June 1740.

147. For some views of this process at work within English society at large during the eighteenth century, see N. Mckendrick, J. Brewer, and J. H. Plumb, *The Birth of a Consumer Society: The Commercialisation of Eighteenth-Century England* (London: Europa, 1982).

Chapter 9: The Content of the London Newspapers

PART 1: NEWS AND INFORMATION

1. Haig has some interesting but rather disconnected comments in his study of the *Gazetteer*, while Wiles, in his book *Freshest Advices*, does little to add to Cranfield's findings, although providing more extensive quotation.

2. *B.L.* 369, Saturday 2 August 1712.

3. For a brief account of these sources see K. Ellis, *The Post Office in the Eighteenth Century* (Oxford, 1958), 61.

4. Memorandum n.d., C.U.L.: C.(H.) 75, 19.

5. *D'Anverian History,* 5.

6. 4 May 1743, London University, Stuart MSS (microfilm), vol, 249/113.

7. 30 December 1753, B.L. Add. MSS. 32, 733, f. 614.

8. *G.A.* 3,511, Monday 27 January 1746. Similar comment appeared in the paper itself, *The True Patriot,* ed. Locke, 25.

9. See John Dunton's account of De Fonvive's foreign correspondents, who were said to be supplying the *Post Man* during Queen Anne's reign. *Life and Errors of John Dunton,* ed. J. B. Nichols, 2 vols. (London: 1818), 2: 428.

10. *W.J. or S.P.* 34, Saturday 3 August 1717.

11. It seems likely that Mist's Jacobite connections contributed to the supply of material from abroad.

12. *D.J.* 4,040, Friday 28 December 1733, and a series of issues of the *L.D.P.* during 1735. The claims in the *Post-Boy* for an exclusive Hague correspondent were apparently supported in 1735 by the Post Office check of material sent to the proprietors from Holland, Newcastle to the Postmaster General, 9 July 1735, P.R.O.: S.P. 36, 35/117.

13. *D.J.,* 5,386, Thursday 12 July 1735; cf. 5,387, Friday 13 July 1733. According to an ironic comment in the *Daily Post,* the printer sometimes put an old news item in inverted commas "to intimate to our Proprietors, that extraordinary postage must be allowed for it . . . ," *D.P.* 888, Friday 3 August 1722.

14. *D.J.* 2,414, Thursday 3 October 1728.

15. *L.E.P.* 141, Saturday 2 November 1728.

16. *B.J.* 156, Saturday 11 September 1725.

17. For some comment on the employment of London and local correspondents by a printer of local papers, see Wiles, *Freshest Advices,* 204–6; Cranfield, *Provincial Newspaper,* 262.

18. 27 February 1756, W. S. Lewis, MSS.

19. 13 September 1780, 11 October 1780, 14 August 1781, ibid.

20. *Some Memoirs of the Life of Abel, Toby's Uncle* (London, 1726), 42.

21. See John Dunton's ambiguous description of the employment of news gatherers on the *Post Man* earlier in the century, *Life and Errors of John Dunton,* 2: 428–29.

22. *Case of the Coffee-Men,* 5. See also a description of one of the reporters, "the Fellow with the Black Wig," 8.

23. *W.M.* 268, Friday 10 February 1738.

24. For the later development of the system see 10 February 1779, W. S. Lewis MSS., and Haig, *Gazetteer,* 178–79.

25. *F.P. or W.M.* 12, Saturday 21 December 1728.

26. *W.J. or B.G.* Saturday 12 September 1724. For an earlier ironic account of Mist's news sources, see the news-bill in *W.J. or B.G.* Saturday 28 December 1717.

27. *Case of the Coffee-Men,* 5–12.

28. *The Town Spy, Or A View of London and Westminster,* 22.

29. P.R.O.: S.P. 35, 34, 78 (b) 2.

30. E.g., *C.* 290, Saturday 23 January 1732. Paragraph rejected in spite of an enclosed half guinea. See also the marriage notice apparently sent in to Molloy P.R.O.: S.P. 9, 35/82.

31. *B.M.* 369, Saturday 2 August 1712.

32. See above, chap. 2.

33. Occasional criticism of the quality of these papers appeared in the press and elsewhere, e.g., *E.P.* 3, Friday 27 January 1727, also P.R.O.: S.P. 47, 79.

34. John Oldmixon *The History of England* (London, 1735), 491. He also refers to invented news "printed in the Article from the *Hague.*"

35. *D'Anverian History,* 61.

36. A precisely similar process was described in the *Daily Journal* in an attack on the *Post Boy's* news content, *D.J.* 2, 753, Monday 3 November 1729.

37. *L.E.P.* 1,466, Saturday 9 April 1737. Cf. the original scheme by the Pretender to establish a paper in Antwerp; James, "Charles Molloy," 144.

38. Stephen Whatley, in a petition probably dating from the late 1720s, claimed that the low ebb of the *Flying Post* had forced him "to the Drudgery of Translating for two or three other Publick Papers as well as his own." C.U.L.: C.(H.) MSS. 75, 16/2 n.d. In 1768 Charlotte Foreman, in a series of letters to John Wilkes, claimed to be translating for the *London Evening Post* at 9/- a week as well as for the *Gazetteer,* B.L. Add. MSS. 30, 270, ff., 52, 117.

39. For example the *St. J.E.P.; G.E.P.; W.E.P.* See also the *P.L.P.*

40. J. Nichols, *The Rise and Progress of the Gentleman's Magazine* (London, 1821), 5.

41. Cranfield, *Provincial Newspaper*, 82.

42. *L.E.P.*, 1,931, Saturday 29 March 1740; *D.P.* 6,414, Saturday 29 March 1740. *L.E.P.* 2,116, Thursday 4 June 1741; *G.E.P.* 1,049, Saturday 13 June 1741; 1,054, Thursday 26 June 1741.

43. Cranfield, *Provincial Newspaper*, 83.

44. E.g., *L.E.P.* 1,733, Saturday 23 December 1738; 2,022, Tuesday 28 October 1740; *D.P.* 6,394, Thursday 6 March 1740.

45. Dr. Gaylard on the news content of *Mist's*, P.R.O.: S.P. 35, 34/78(b)(2). Many of the pre-1725 journals aimed at a comprehensive provision of material and were intended to be bound up at the end of the year. This was emphasized by the use in some of the older weeklies, including those owned by Mist and Read, of consecutive page numbering running into thousands, rather than separately pageing each issue.

46. Cf. the similar content of the publication attacking the coffee-house newspapers that appeared from 1728.

47. E.g., *D.J.* 3,068, Thursday 5 November 1730. Cf. similar ironic treatment of published news in the *Alchymist* in 1737 and the *True Patriot* in 1745.

48. *W.H.* 10, Friday 19 June 1730.

49. In 1740 an advertisement for the *Champion* claimed that ten of its news paragraphs had appeared verbatim in the previous *Craftsman*, *Ch.* Thursday 10 April 1740.

50. E.g. Advertisement in *D.P.* 2,869, Saturday 30 November 1728.

51. R. and M. Bond, "Minute Books," 38.

52. 5 April 1740, P.R.O.: S.P. 36, 50/264.

53. *L.E.P.* 132, Thursday 10 October 1728.

54. *L.E.P.* 2,845, Thursday 30 January 1746. See also *D.P.* 8,239, Monday 27 January 1746.

55. *O.E.* 179, Saturday 4 October 1746.

56. *C.* Foreman to John Wilkes, 2 March 1769, B.L. Add. MSS. 30, 870, f. 117.

57. P.R.O.: S.P. 9, 35/208.

58. E.g., *P.L.N.* 975, Monday 15 February 1725.

59. *F.B.* 198, Thursday 6 September 1733.

60. *D.C.* 8,807, Monday 12 May 1729.

61. *P.L.N.* 964, Wednesday 20 January 1725.

62. *P.L.N.* 977, Friday 19 February 1725.

63. *W.M.* 1, Saturday 16 December 1732.

64. *N.J.* 1, Saturday 22 March 1746.

65. For some hostile comment on this practice and other criticisms of news layout, see *G.S.J.* 184, Thursday 5 July 1733; 190, Thursday 16 August 1734; 194, Thursday 13 September 1734.

66. See George Gordon's instructions to the printer of the *National Journal* in 1746 on "how to place or Range the Articles of News," quoted in full in Hanson, *Government*, 146.

67. The extent of the costs was indicated on the accounts of the *Grub Street Journal*, which offered a number of full-page illustrations during the early 1730s. The first of these was a print of the arms of the city companies, and the entry on the ledger for "graving the Plate, cutting the Arms," and for "Rolling-Press Work" showed an outlay of £8.13s, 7 May 1731, Q.C. MSS. 450.

68. E.g., *W.J.* or *S.P.* Saturday 17 August 1717, full page-1 map of part of Turkey; *W.J.* or *B.G.* Saturday 17 August 1717 smaller version of the same. *W.J.* or *B.G.* Saturday 13 May 1721, political cartoon on the South Sea Company, reprinted Saturday 20 May 1721. *W.J.* or *B.G.* Saturday 9 May 1724, diagrams of the lunar eclipse.

69. Advertisement in *D.P.* Saturday 11 February 1727.

70. Q.C. MSS. 450, 7 May 1731. *G.S.J.* Thursday 3 December 1730. *The Grub Street Journal* initially contained an unusual amount of illustrated material. Cf. the publication of a series of obscure cuts in the *Hyp Doctor* in 1731.

71. *Ch.* 86, Saturday 31 May 1740; 87, Tuesday 3 June 1740.

72. *L.E.P.* 2,116, Thursday 4 June 1741; *G.A.* 3,070, Saturday 15 September 1744; *W.J.* 232, Saturday 10 May 1746; 258, Saturday 8 November 1746.

73. *West. J.* 207, Saturday 16 November 1745, "The Pope's Scourge" published separately in a sheet of writing paper at 3d.

74. The use in the *Champion's* news section of such ironic classifications as "Rumours,"

"Ministerial Puffs," and "Prophecies" was merely an extension of the usual approach.

75. E.g., The *Observator*, and the *Medley*.

76. C. 113, Saturday 31 August 1728. Cf. the occasional "headlining" of specially interest-ing items in such advertisements as that for the *London Evening Post* in *D.P.* 2,726, Monday 17 June 1728.

77. Cf. the use of the *Craftsman's* initial letter as a constant reminder of the main areas of dispute in foreign affairs, *C.* 89, Saturday 16 March 1728–146, Saturday 19 April 1729.

78. *D.A.* 4,427, Monday 25 March 1745–4,432, Saturday 30 March 1745.

79. *G.A.* 3,397, Saturday 28 September 1745–3,498, Saturday 11 January 1746.

80. *P.L.P.* 378, Monday 30 September 1745–425, Friday 17 January 1746. Cranfield, *Provincial Newspaper*, p. 78.

81. E.g., *W.J.* 26, Saturday 29 November 1746.

82. E.g., notices in the *Flying Post or Post Master* 1,005, Thursday 16 October 1701 and the *New State of Europe* 22, Saturday 8 November 1701. See also Morison, *English Newspaper*, 61–68, 75, 76.

83. *The Whitehall Evening Post* and the *General Evening Post* were among the first to appear in this form.

84. 4 April 1778, 23 December 1778, 8 May 1782, W. S. Lewis MSS.

85. Reflected in the use of this classification in their subtitles.

86. See the remarks in the *Hawkers New-Year's Gift*.

87. Advertisement in *C.* 386, Saturday 1 December 1733.

88. *W.M.* 112, Saturday 1 February 1735. Cf. offer of regular index of foreign affairs in *W.M.* 1, Saturday 16 December 1732.

89. *P.L.N.* 890, Friday 31 July 1724.

90. *P.L.N.* 952, Wednesday 23 December 1724. Cf. the similar interest in the *Daily Journal*, *D.J.* 1,216, Saturday 12 December 1724.

91. Lyson, "Collectanea," 2: 48.

92. *P.L.P.* 135, Monday 5 March 1744.

93. *B.M.* 369, Saturday 2 August 1712. See also *Ch.M.* 1, Saturday 7 April 1716 and the similar combination of news and "Remarks" in a number of newly established journals of this date, including the *Weekly Remarks* and *Robins Last Shift*.

94. *R.M.A.* 166, Wednesday 11 January 1737.

95. Advertisement in *R.M.A.* 949, Monday 12 October 1741.

96. Concluded in *R.M.A.* 1,213, Monday 22 November 1742.

97. *D.J.* 3,889, Wednesday 13 June 1733; 3,914, Wednesday 11 July 1733. Reprinted in short form in the *Weekly Miscellany* and if, as seems likely, Cranfield has the date wrong, also in the *Derby Mercury*, Cranfield, *Provincial Newspaper*, 69. It was followed by a similar account of ecclesiastical struggles in France, *D.J.* 3,987, Thursday 4 October 1733.

98. *D.J.* 891, Friday 29 November 1723, continued erratically to 902, Thursday 12 De-cember 1723; 903, Friday 13 December 1723, contained a related piece.

99. *D.J.* 5,747, Monday 26 July 1726; 5,802, Tuesday 28 September 1736.

100. *G.A.* 3,715, Wednesday 24 September 1746; 3,888, Tuesday 14 April 1747; 3,891, Friday 17 April 1747. *St.J.E.P.* 5,817, Saturday 2 May 1747; 5,853, Saturday 25 July 1747.

101. *D.C.* 8,606, Monday 12 May 1729.

102. The *Bee*, 1 (1733): 242.

103. Harris, "Print and Politics," 205.

104. *H of C.J.*, 21: 85, 104, 106, 117, 119, 227, 238.

105. *L.E.P.* 1,906, Thursday 31 January 1740.

106. *Ch.* 326, Saturday 12 December 1741.

107. *F.B.* 137, Thursday 13 July 1732. Comment on Amall's attendance in *C.* 300, Saturday 1 April 1732; 362, Saturday 9 June 1733.

108. *C.* 400, Saturday 2 March 1734.

109. *C.S.* 18, Saturday 4 June 1737.

110. *H. of C.J.*, 23, 148.

111. Comment on the popularity of debates appeared in the *Bee* 2 (1734): 117.

112. *C.S.* 228, Saturday 20 June 1741·231, Saturday 11 July 1741.

113. *W.M.* 289, Friday 7 July 1738; *Ch.* 104, Saturday 12 July 1740; *D.P.* 7, 258, Thursday 9 December 1742; 7,457, Friday 29 July 1743. On the party links of the *Gentleman's* and *London Magazines*, see E. Cave to Sir R. Walpole, 12 January 1741, C.U.L.: C.(H.) Corres. 3,116.

114. *F.B.* 137, Thursday 13 July 1732. *C.* 49, Saturday 10 June 1727.

115. *C.* 156, Saturday 28 June 1729.

116. *C.* 313, Saturday 1 July 1732. Ministerial reviews appeared in *R.W.J.* 115, Saturday 22 July 1727; *B.J.* 75, Saturday 7 June 1729; *L.J.* 774, Saturday 27 April 1734.

117. *Ch.* 85, Thursday 29 May 1740; cf. *Ch.* 430, Thursday 19 August 1742 and *R.L.M.A.* 1,166, Thursday 19 August 1742.

118. *W.J.* 132, Saturday 2 June 1744; cf. 182, Saturday 25 May 1745.

119. *F.W.J.* 241, Saturday 16 June 1733: 242, Saturday 23 June 1733.

120. In-session action by Parliament was taken against William Rayner in 1736 for publishing the Gin Act.

121. *L.E.P.* 2,792, Saturday 28 September 1745–2,793, Monday 1 October 1745.

122. Polling lists appeared in a supplement to the *St. James's Journal* 17, Wednesday 25 April 1722; *D.P.* 1,622, Monday 7 December 1724; *D.J.* 1,211, Monday 7 December 1724; *D.J.* 2,120, Tuesday 31 October 1727 (two eight-page papers); *D.P.* Extraordinary 4,545, Tuesday 9 April 1734; *D.J.* Extraordinary, Tuesday 9 April 1734; *L.D.P.* 480, Saturday 15 May 1736; 481, Monday, 17 May 1736.

123. The reports in the *Daily Journal* in 1734 were unusually comprehensive in this respect.

124. Advertisement in *L.E.P* 1,300, Thursday 18 March 1736. The list appeared in *L.D.P.* 431, Friday 19 March 1736.Cf. similar items in *L.D.P.* 62, Tuesday 14 January 1735; *G.E.P.* 338, Saturday 29 November 1735.

125. *L.J.* 139, Saturday 24 March 1722–144, Saturday 28 April 1722. *W.J. or S.P.* 175, Saturday 31 March 1822–179, Saturday 28 April 1722. *Post Boy* 5,096, Thursday 22 March–5,110, Tuesday 24 April 1722.

126. *L.E.P.* 186, Saturday 15 February 1729; 513, Saturday 13 March 1731.

127. *L.E.P.* 1,022, Saturday 8, June 1734. The method was initially followed in the *Craftsman*, *C.* 409, Saturday 4 May.

128. *L.E.P.* 1,031, Saturday 29 June 1734. Advertisements in Tuesday 2 July, Thursday 11 July. Modified lists appeared as propaganda items in *L.E.P.* 1,019, Saturday 1 June; 1,022, Saturday 8 June. Reissue of complete list in *L.E.P.* 1,331, Saturday 29 May 1736. For criticism of the method, see *F.B.* 244, Thursday 4 July 1734.

129. Distinctions continued to *D.G.* 1,851, Saturday 23 May 1741.

130. *L.E.P.* 2,128, Thursday 2 July 1741. *C.* 786, Saturday 25 July 1741. Advertisement for reissue as a separate publication: *C.* 804, Saturday 28 November 1741. Criticism in *D.G.* 1,907, Wednesday 29 July 1741 *passim.* Cf. Subsequent long lists of those meeting in the country interest, e.g., *L.E.P.* 2,225, Saturday 13 February 1742; 2,228, Saturday 20 February 1742.

131. *C.* 156, Saturday 28 June 1729.

132. *St.J.J.* Supplement 8, Friday 16 March 1722.

133. *W.J. or S.P.* Saturday 17 March 1722; Saturday 24 March 1722.

134. Votes on the civil list and the Hessian troops were among other lists appearing as separate publications.

135. Advertisement in *D.J.* 3,888, Thursday 14 June 1733.

136. *F.W.J.* 244, Saturday 7 July 1733; 245, Saturday 14 July 1733. Cf. the advertisement for a separate list in black and red in *C.* 408, Saturday 27 April 1734.

137. *F.W.J.* 247, Saturday 28 July 1735.

138. *F.W.J.* 286, Saturday 27 April 1734; 287, Saturday 4 August 1734.

139. For its partial publication in the provinces, Cranfield, *Provincial Newspaper,* 162.

140. *West J.* 64, Saturday 12 February 1743.

141. M. Shugrue, "Applebee's Original Weekly Journal: An Index to Eighteenth Century Taste," *Newberry Library Bulletin* 6 (1964): 111–14. *W.J. or S.P.* 237, Saturday 1 May 1723. Applebee also produced the *Ordinary of Newgate's Account* containing the biographies and last dying words of executed criminals.

142. *L.J.* 185, Saturday 9 February 1723; 186, Saturday 16 February 1723; 187, Saturday 23 February 1723. One of the supplements is dated Saturday 2 February 1723; the other two carry no date.

143. E.g., *L.E.P.* 92, Tuesday 9 July 1728; *U.S.* 188, Saturday 8 April 1731.

144. *W.M.* 5, Saturday 13 January 1733.

145. See comment in *L.S.R.* 195, Friday 3 October 1737.

146. *P.L.P.* 346, Wednesday 17 July 1745–348 Monday 22 July 1745.

147. Cf. the widespread use of the collections of State Trials during the 1720s and 1730s, as in the *P.L.P.*, which incorporated some of the main crimes in its title area; *P.L.P.* 89, Wednesday 4 March 1734.

148. E.g., *P.L.P.* 279, Friday 8 February 1745.

149. *P.L.M.A.* 109, Monday 9 January 1744–183, Friday 29 June 1744. The case was also serialized in *L.C. and C.J.* from 46, Saturday 17 March 1744.

150. *U.L.M.A.* 301, Friday 5 April 1745–343, Wednesday 10 July 1745.

151. *G.L.E.M.* 482, Tuesday 27 May 1746.

152. *G.A.* 3,684, Saturday 16 August 1746. For provincial ramifications of similar action, see Cranfield, *Provincial Newspaper*, 163–65. McCulloh also published biographies of the leading rebels with some success; *G.L.E.M.* 518, Thursday 21 August 1746.

153. See the notice advertising the next issue of the *British Spy* in *P.L.P.* 329, Friday 7 June 1745.

154. For some account of this activity, see Harris, "Trials and Criminal Biographies."

155. *W.J. or B.G.* Saturday 8 August 1724.

156. *W.R.* 10, Friday 19 June 1730.

157. *D.J.* 2,311, Saturday 8 June 1728.

158. Title notice in *D.G.* 541, Monday 11 April 1737–567, Monday 18 April 1737.

159. *D.G.* 2,085, Monday 22 February 1742.

160. Cf. the development of *Lloyds List,* appearing twice-weekly from 1740.

161. A specific exclusion of this item was announced in the *Evening Entertainment* in 1727.

162. Prices at provincial markets were occasionally included, while the *Daily Journal* obtained the exclusive right to publish the Assize of Bread for the City, *D.J.* 2,037, Tuesday 25 July 1727.

163. See John J. McCusker, "The Business Press in England before 1775," *Library,* 6th ser., 8(1986): 205–31.

164. E.g., *Proctor's Price Courant, Robinson's Price Courant, Price of Stocks.*

165. Snyder, "Circulation of Newspapers," 213–14.

166. See the later and unsuccessful attempts to compile a commercial register for inclusion in the *Daily Gazetteer,* described in Haig, *Gazetteer,* 49–50.

167. *F.W.T.* 380, Saturday 14 February 1736.

168. Deliberately in the inclusion of paid items among the news paragraphs.

169. Kings Bench records reveal a constant stream of private actions, often on account of advertisements.

170. Linked with these items were the mock advertisements containing satirical comment on personalities and events, which cropped up erratically in the political papers and occasionally elsewhere. See the warning of the nonacceptance of such items in *B.M.* 505, Saturday 5 March 1715.

171. *L.D.P.* 1, Monday 4 November 1734.

172. During the 1720s and early 1730s the *Daily Post* and the *Daily Journal* had been the main vehicles for these notices, and subsequently the *Daily Post* and the *Daily Advertiser* continued to provide short notices of the day's theatrical performances as a service to readers.

173. *D.A.* 1, Wednesday 3 February 1731.

174. For comment on the inclusion of such items see *C.S.* 324, Saturday 30 April 1743.

175. *O.E.* 189, Saturday 13 December 1746.

176. To Sir Horace Mann, 21 December 1773, *Horace Walpole's Correspondence,* ed. W. S. Lewis, 48 vols. (New Haven: Yale University Press; London and Oxford: Oxford University Press, 1937–83), 23: 236.

PART 2: INSTRUCTION AND ENTERTAINMENT

1. *G.R.T.* 240, Monday 8 September 1707.

2. *B.M.* 381, Wednesday 22 October 1712.

3. For the notice of republication, see *B.M.* 395, Wednesday 28 January 1713 and for the separate republication of other items, *B.M.* 424, Wednesday 19 August *passim.*

4. *B.M.* 519, Saturday 11 June 1715. Cf. comments on the problem of variable taste in *B.M.* 471, Wednesday 14 July 1714; 484, Wednesday 13 October 1714, 500, Saturday 21 January 1715.

5. In the same issue *The Definition of Justice According to an Arabian Poet* and in the following, *Antiquity of Drinking Healths, and other Customs relating to Drinking.*

6. *P.W.J.* 1, Saturday 29 October 1720. Comment on the popularity of the series appeared in the first issue in amended form, *London Mercury* 16, Saturday 11 February 1721. At

least one attempt was made to produce a single-leaf publication containing only a serial; see *The Narrative* 1, Thursday 12 November 1719.

7. From Saturday 9 December 1721.

8. *W.J.* or *B.G.* Saturday 15 April 1721.

9. Ibid., Saturday 5 August 1721.

10. Ibid., Saturday 20 July 1723.

11. *P.L.N.* 842, Friday 10 April 1724.

12. *Ch.M.* 1, Saturday 7 April 1716.

13. E.g., *U.S.* 703, Saturday 27 March 1742. Also advertisement in *L.J.* 752, Saturday 24 November 1733.

14. E.g., *D.J.* 2,416, Saturday 5 October 1728.

15. *U.S.* 4, Saturday 2 November 1728.

16. *U.S.* 15, Saturday 18 January 1729.

17. Advertisement for no. 3 in *D.J.* 2,433, Friday 25 October 1728.

18. Advertisement in *L.J.* 752, Saturday 24 November 1733.

19. *B.J.* 152, Saturday 28 November 1730.

20. *The Universal Spy: or Aesop the Fabulist* 1, Saturday 25 March 1732. A further alternative to the variable combination of instruction and entertainment in the full-priced weeklies was provided by the occasional foreign-language papers, sometimes in parallel texts, as in the *Flying Post: or the Weekly Medley* 1, Saturday 5 October 1728.

21. The subject had marked political overtones, and the Protestant dissenters became the focus of a good deal of propaganda in the sponsored papers, particularly during the rundown to the 1734 election.

22. Essays from this paper passed through seven editions between 1721 and 1743.

23. *W.M.* 27, Saturday 16 July 1733.

24. During the paper's political period a series of essays on religious topics were contributed by its principal author, the free-thinker James Pitt, and the ministry was caused some embarrassment in 1729 when one of these items, appearing under the pseudonym of "Socrates," was presented for blasphemy by the Middlesex Grand Jury, *L.J.* 508, Saturday 26 April 1729; the presentment was published in *F.W.J.* 35, Saturday 24 May 1729.

25. *Memoirs of the Times*, 34.

26. See D. Foxon, "Monthly Catalogues of Books Published," *Library*, 5th ser., 18 (1963): 223–28.

27. *G.J.* 3, Saturday 15 April 1721.

28. *St. J.J.* 1, Thursday 3 May 1722.

29. *D.C.* 8,476, Monday 9 December 1728; 8,480, Friday 13 December; 8,495, Tuesday 31 December, *passim.*

30. *E.J.* 7, Friday 8 December 1727.

31. *W.M.* 1, Saturday 16 December 1732. See also comment in 55, Saturday 29 December 1733 and 272, Friday 7 March 1738.

32. J. T. Hillhouse, *Grub Street Journal.*

33. *G.S.J.* 1, Thursday 8 January 1730. *Memoirs of the Society of Grub Street*, 1: iv.

34. January to July 1738.

35. In 1737 the collapse of the *Grub Street Journal* and the decline of all similar publications was attributed directly to the rise of the magazines; *Memoirs of the Society of Grub Street*, 1, 12.

36. The best account of this output appears in Wiles, *Serial Publication*, 15–74.

37. Lysons, "*Collectanea*," 2, 48. It seems possible that Walker added the news sheet to his collection of plays to offset the serious competition they faced as conventional part publications. See Wiles, *Serial Publication*, 19–20.

38. *W.O.* 1, Saturday 7 December 1734.

39. *Studies in the English Periodical*, 40.

40. Cf. *The Country Oracle: and General Review*, advertised as printed for T. Cooper in *L.D.P.* 2,036, Friday 17 April 1741.

41. E.g., *L.F.P.* Wednesday 21 February 1739–Tuesday 6 March 1739.

42. These were occasionally the vehicle for political comment; e.g., *A.A.M.* Tuesday 21 October 1740.

43. Wiles, *Serial Publication*, 40.

44. *R.W.J.* 372, Saturday 6 May 1732.

45. Advertisement in *St.J.E.P.* 2,854, Thursday 20 September 1733. See ironic comment in the *Bee* 1 (1733): 29.

46. *U.S.* 67, Saturday 17 June 1730.

47. For comment on the reprinting of the paper's essays in the provincial press, see Cranfield, *Provincial Newspaper*, 103, 105, 187.

48. *O.W.* 160, Thursday 20 March 1738.

49. Methodism also stimulated the publication of the propagandist *Christians Amusement*, which in 1741 became the *Weekly History*. It was characteristic of developments in the press as well as of the movement itself that these were ld. essay publications. Neither carried a conventional news section and among the London newspapers only the *Daily Advertiser* gave the Methodists consistent support. See comment in the advertisement for the *Weekly Miscellany* in *G.A.* Saturday 15 September 1739, and also *Ch.* 103, Thursday 10 July 1740; *L.E.P.* 2,511, Tuesday 13 December 1743.

50. E.g., *W.M.* 304, Saturday 21 October 1738; 353, Saturday 29 September 1739; 365, Saturday 22 December 1739.

51. *L.D.P.* Friday 10 July 1741.

52. L./W. 57, lot 57; 63, lot 55; 88, lot 39; 89, lot 54; 97, lot 24.

53. *West.J.* 222, Saturday 1 March 1746.

54. *R.L.M.A.* 1,216, Monday 29 November 1742, *passim*.

55. The first issue in the Burney Collection containing this serial is *P.L.P.* 441, Wednesday 26 February 1746.

56. *U.L.M.A.* 105, Friday 20 December 1743; 106, Monday 2 January 1744.

57. E.g., *L.M.A.* 103, Monday 26 December 1743; *P.L.P.* 301, Wednesday 3 April 1745; *G.L.E.M.* 490, Tuesday 17 June 1746.

58. *P.L.P.* 297, Monday 25 March 1745–299, Friday 29 March 1745.

59. See the editorial comment in *D.J.* 2,263, Saturday 13 April 1728. Also *A Collection of Recipes and Letters lately inserted in the Daily Journal* (London, 1730).

60. The *Briton* in the *Daily Gazetteer* from Thursday 5 September 1745 republished in the *General Evening Post* from Thursday 19 September 1745. The *Subject* in the *General Advertiser* from Saturday 18 October 1745.

61. *G.A.* 4,018, Thursday 10 September 1747; 4,024, Thursday 17 September 1747; 4,059, Thursday 29 October 1747; 4,060, Friday 30 October 1747.

62. 27 September 1754, W. S. Lewis MSS.

Chapter 10: The London Press in Mid-Century

1. Snyder, "Circulation of Newspapers."

2. Cranfield, *Provincial Newspaper*, 175–76.

3. A. Aspinall, *Politics and the Press 1780–1850* (London: Home and Van Thal, 1949), 7.

4. Cranfield, *Provincial Newspaper*, 181–82.

5. The Diary of Stephen Monteage, 8 vols., 1733 to 1760, Guildhall Library MSS. 205.

6. The volume for 1738, for example, opened with several cures and poems taken from the *Daily Advertiser* and also an epitaph from the *London Journal*.

7. Ibid., 25 June 1733, 1, p. 155; 10 October 1733, 253; 15 December 1746, 7, 334.

8. It seems possible that over the years Monteage himself contributed to the paper, although the only reference to any literary output occurred in April 1739, when he recorded the publication of a romantic poem in the *Lady's Magazine*, 28 April 1739, 3, 82.

9. Notice at the head of each issue. See the earlier terms in *B.M.* 125, Wednesday 10 January 1711.

10. *B.M.* 451, Wednesday 24 February 1714–456, Wednesday 31 March 1714. Names, occupations, and policies only.

11. In Hogarth's *Beer Street* the two prosperous butchers have a copy of the *Daily Advertiser* on the table beside them.

12. *B.M.* 369, Saturday 2 August 1712.

13. For comment on such devices as group purchase and hire of copies, which extended access at the lowest levels, see chap. 2.

14. Dorothy George, *London Life in the Eighteenth Century* (London: Kegan Paul & Co., 1925), 166.

15. H. G. Jones, *The Charity School Movement* (Cambridge: at the University Press, 1938), 57, 59.

16. Ibid., Appendix 1, 57. List of Charity Schools in England as returned in the Account

of Charity Schools for 1724, 364–71. See the report of 5,300 Charity School children in procession in *L.E.P.* 1,478, Saturday 7 May 1737.

17. Margaret Spufford, *Small Books and Pleasant Histories; Popular Fiction and its Readership in Seventeenth Century England* (Cambridge: at the University Press, 1982).

18. E. A. Wrigley, "A Simple Model of London's Importance in Changing English Society and Economy, 1650–1750," *Past and Present* 37 (1967): 51. Cf. the large number of primers and reading aids advertised in the newspapers, almanacks, and elsewhere during this period.

19. *B.M.* 125, Wednesday 13 January 1711.

20. Advertisement in *C.* 129, Saturday 10 January 1729. Cf. *La Steffata Italiana: or, the Italian Post,* 1729, and *Mercurius Latinus,* 1746.

21. Reasons, misleadingly cited and badly misdated in Cranfield, *Provincial Newspaper,* 89.

22. Advertisement in *L.M.P.P.* Wednesday 2 October 1751.

23. For comment on such clubs see *W.J. or S.P.* 234, Saturday 20 April 1723; M. Crosley, A Tour to London, 2 vols. (London, 1772), 1: 150; Madame Fiquet du Bocage, *Letters Concerning England, Holland and Italy,* 2 vols. (London, 1770), 1: 37.

24. See Dr. Johnson's introduction in *G.M.,* 10 (1740).

25. *Idler* 7, Saturday 23 May 1758.

26. Cranfield, *Provincial Newspaper,* 185–89.

27. *M.W.J.* 126, Saturday 16 September 1727.

28. Harris, "Print and Politics."

Bibliography

Sources

I. MANUSCRIPT MATERIAL

Public Record Office

State Papers Domestic   Miscellaneous.   S.P.9. 35, 217.
                         George I   S.P.35. 1–76
                         George II   S.P. 36. 1–107
                         Regencies   S.P.43. 71–83
                         Entry Books, Criminal   S.P. 44. 81–83.
Treasury Papers   TI. 255
Treasury Miscellaneous   T.54. 34
Treasury Solicitors' Papers   T.S. 11, 944, 1001, 424, 157, 1027, 124, 125
Seditious Cases, Miscellaneous Papers   T.S. 24. 4
Audit Office, Stamp Duties General Account   A.O.3. 950–53
Post Office Comptrollers Accounts   A.O.3. 796
Kings Bench Papers   Affidavits   K.B.1. 3–8
                      Indictments   London and
                           Middlesex.   K.B.10. 19–27
                      Crown Rolls   K.B.28. 92–174
                      Precedents   K.B. 33. 6–10
Chancery, Masters Exhibits   C. 103, 108, 110, 114
Prerogative Court of Canterbury, List of Inventories   Prob. 3

British Library

Miscellaneous Letters   Lansdowne MSS. 841
Bagford Collection   Harleian MSS. 5,935, 5,940, 5,942, 5,954, 5,958
T. Burnet Correspondence   Add. MSS. 36,772
Hardwick Papers   Add. MSS. 36,137, 36,138, 36,139
Junius Papers   Add. MSS. 27,784
Liverpool Papers   Add. MSS. 38,334
Newcastle Papers   Add. MSS. 33,054, 32,687, 32,689, 32,690,

32,691, 32,692, 32,693, 32,694, 32,695, 32,701, 32,702, 32,816, 32,922, 32,925, 33,052, 33,054
Original Assignments   Add. MSS. 38,728, 38,729, 38,730
William Strahan Papers   Add. MSS. 4,800
Jacob Tonson Correspondence   Add. MSS. 28,275
Sir Charles Hanbury Williams Correspondence   Add. MSS. 51,390
John Wilkes Papers   Add. MSS. 30,870
Henry Woodfall Accounts   Add. MSS. 38,169

General Post Office Record Office

Newspaper Privilege of the Clerks of the Roads   G.P.O. Ref. 1. 18A
Treasury Letter Books, 1742–60   Post 1/8

Stationers Hall

Apprentices Index, 1640–1748
Apprentices Register Book, 1666–1727
Apprentices Register Book, 1728–62
Entries of Copies, 1710–46

Guildhall Library

Stephen Monteage Diaries   MSS. 205
John Wilkes Papers   MSS. 214

London University Library

Stuart Papers (Microfilm Holdings)   Vol. 142/141
                                    Vol. 249/113
                                    Box 1/299

Bodleian Library, Oxford

Gentleman's Ledger B   MSS. Eng. Misc. C. 296

Queens College Library, Oxford

Grub Street Journal, Proprietors' Ledger   MSS. 450

Cambridge University Library

Walpole Papers   Cholmondeley (Houghton) MSS. 73, 74, 75, 81
Walpole Correspondence   Cholmondeley (Houghton) Corres.

W. S. Lewis Collection, Yale

General Evening Post, Proprietors' Ledger   [No reference]

II. Printed Material

London Newspapers

The following alphabetical list is not intended to be comprehensive and includes only those papers seen during the course of this study. The bulk are preserved in the Burney Collection in the British Library or in the Nichols and Hope Collections in the Bodleian Library, although a few are scattered through other London repositories. Each paper is listed under its original title with subsequent variations given in brackets and with the abbreviations used in the footnotes in front of each name. Papers not mentioned in any other published list are marked thus [*] and are followed by their year of publication and location.

A.	*The Alchymist; or, Weekly Laboratory** 1737, Public Record Office
A.A.M.	*All Alive and Merry; or, the London Daily Post*
	The Auditor
	The British Apollo
B.J.	*The British Journal*
B.M.	*The British Mercury* (*The British Weekly Mercury*)
	The British Spectator and London Penny Tatler
	The Censor; or, Muster-Master-General of all the news-papers printed in Great Britain and Ireland
Ch.	*The Champion; or, British Mercury* (*The Champion; or, Evening Advertiser*)
	The Charitable Mercury and Female Intelligence; Being a Weekly Collection of all the Material News Foreign and Domestick
	*The Christian Priest** 1720, Burney Collection
	The Christian's Amusement; Containing Letters Concerning the Progress of the Gospel both at Home and Abroad. (The Weekly History; or an Account of the most Remarkable Particulars Relating to the Progress of the Gospel)
C.S./O.C.S.	*Common Sense; or, the Englishman's Journal* (*Old Common Sense*)
C.C.J.	*The Corn Cutters Journal*
C.G.	*The Country Gentleman*
	*The Country Tatler; or, The Daily Pacquet** 1739 Bodleian Library
	The Covent Garden Journal
C.	*The Craftsman* (*The Country Journal; or, the Craftsman*)
D.A.	*The Daily Advertiser*
D.C.	*The Daily Courant*
D.C.	*The Daily Gazetteer*
D.J.	*The Daily Journal*
D.P.	*The Daily Post*
	The Diverting Post
	*The English and French News Journal** 1723, Burney Collection

	The Englishman
E.E.P.	*The Englishman's Evening Post and Universal Advertiser*
	The Evening Entertainment
E.P.	*The Evening Post (B. Berington's Evening Post. The Old Evening Post)*
	*The Evening Post** 1740, Burney Collection [a farthing paper]
F.P.	*The Flying-Post (The Flying Post; or, Weekly Medley)*
F.P. or P.A.	*The Flying-Post; or, the Post-Master*
F.B.	*The Free Briton*
F.J.	*The Freeholders Journal*
G.E.P.	*The General Evening Post*
	The General London Evening Mercury
G.R.T.	*The General Remark on Trade*
G.J.	*The Gentleman's Journal*
G.S.J.	*The Grub Street Journal*
	The Humours of the Age; or, Dean Swift's New Evening Post
H.D.	*The Hyp Doctor* [This paper underwent multiple subtitle changes not listed here]
I.L.J.	*The Independent London Journalist (The Independent London Journal)*
	The Independent Whig
	The Jacobites Journal
	Jones Evening News Letter
	The Knight Errant
L.C.G.S.	*The Literary Courier of Grub Street*
L. and C.J.	*The London and Country Journal*
L.C.	*The London Courant; or, New Advertiser*
L.D.P. and G.A. G.A.	*The London Daily Post and General Advertiser (The General Advertiser)*
L.E.P.	*The London Evening Post*
L.F.P.	*The London Farthing Post*
	The London Gazette
P.L.N./P.P.P.	*The London News; or, the Impartial Intelligencer (Parker's London News. Parker's Penny Post)*
O.L.P.	*The London Post; or, Tradesman's Intelligence (The Original London Post; or, Heathcotes Intelligence)*
L.S.R.	*The London Spy Revived*
L.T.	*The London Tatler*
	The Loyal Observator Revived; or, Gaylard's Journal (The Loyal Observator; or, Collins Weekly Journal)
	The Merchants Remembrancer (Whistons Weekly Remembrancer)
W.M. N.W.M. West J.	*The Miscellany; Giving an Account of the Religion, Morality and Learning of the Present Time (The Weekly Miscellany. The New Weekly Miscellany. The Westminster Journal; or, the New Weekly Miscellany)*

	The Narrative; or the delightful and melancholy history of Leucippe.* 1719, Burney Collection
N.J.	*The National Journal; or, the Country Gazette*
N.L.	*The News Letter*
N.S.E.	*The New State of Europe*
	The Nonsense of Common Sense
	The Observator
	The Occasional Writer
O.E.	*Old England; or, the Constitutional Journal*
O.W.	*The Old Whig*
O.W.J.	*The Original Weekly Journal (Applebees Original Weekly*
A.O.W.J.	*Journal)*
O.P.	*The Oxford Post; or, Ladies New Tatler*
P.	*Pasquin*
P.L.P.	*The Penny London Post*
	The Penny Post
	The Penny Post; or, Tradesman's Select Pacquet
	The Penny Weekly Journal; or, Saturday Entertainment (The London Mercury; or, Great Britain's Weekly Journal)
P.B./D.P.B.	*The Post-Boy (Pax, Pax, Pax; or, a Pacifick Post-Boy. The Daily Post Boy)*
P.M.	*The Post-Man. (Oedipus; or, the Post-Man Remounted)*
	The Prompter
R.M.A.	*Rayner's Morning Advertiser (London Morning*
L.M.A.	*Advertiser. Generous London Morning*
G.L.M.A.	*Advertiser. Rayner's London Morning Advertiser.)*
R.L.M.A.	
St.J.E.P.	*St. James's Evening Post*
	St. James's Post
	The St. James's Journal
S.	*The Senator*
	The Spectator
	The Tatler
	Terrae Filius
L.J.	*The Thursday's Journal (The London Journal)*
	The True Briton
	The Universal Journal
U.L.M.A.	*The Universal London Morning Advertiser (Penny London*
P.L.M.A.	*Morning Advertiser. Penny London Post; or, the Morning*
P.L.P.	*Advertiser)*
or M.A.	
U.S.	*The Universal Spectator and Weekly Journal*
	The Universal Spy; or, Aesop the Fabulist
	The Universal Spy; or, the Royal Oak Journal Reviv'd
W.J. or B.G.	*The Weekly Journal; or, British Gazetteer (Read's Weekly Journal; or, British Gazetteer)*
W.J.	*The Weekly Journal; or, Saturday's Post (Mist's Weekly*
or S.P./M.W.J.	*Journal. Fog's Weekly Journal)*

F.W.J.	
W.O.	*The Weekly Oracle; or, Universal Library*
W.R.	*The Weekly News and Daily Register (The Weekly News and Register. The Weekly Register)*
	Weekly Remarks, and Political Reflections Upon the Most Material News Foreign and Domestick
	The What-D'Ye-Call-It
W.E.P.	*The Whitehall Evening Post*
W.E.P. or L.I.	*The Whitehall Evening Post; or, London Intelligencer*

Magazines

	The Bee; or, Universal Weekly Pamphlet
	The Friendly Writer and Register of Truth
G.M.	*The Gentleman's Magazine; or, Monthly Intelligencer*
L.M.	*The London Magazine; or, Gentleman's Monthly Intelligencer*
	The Political State of Great Britain

Contemporary Works, Correspondence, Private and Official Papers

A Ledger of Charles Ackers. Edited by D. F. McKenzie and J. C. Ross. Oxford Bibliographical Society, 1968.

The Notebook of Thomas Bennet and Henry Clements. Edited by N. Hodgson and C. Blagden. Oxford Bibliographical Society, 1956.

Bob-Lynn Against Franck . . . Lynn: Or, a full History of the Controversies and Dissensions in the Family of the Lynns. London, 1732.

Lord Bolingbroke's Contributions to the Craftsman. Edited by S. Varey. Oxford: Clarendon Press, 1982.

Boswell, James. *The Life of Samuel Johnson, L1.D.* Edited by G. B. Hill. 6 vols. Oxford: Clarendon Press, 1964.

Budgell, Eustace. *A Letter to the Craftsman from Eustace Budgell Esq.* 2d ed. London, 1730.

Calendar of Treasury Papers, 1720–28. Edited by J. Redington. London: H.M.S.O., 1889.

Calendar of Treasury Books and Papers, 1729–1745. Edited by J. Redington and W. Shaw. 5 vols. London: H.M.S.O., 1897–1903.

The Case Between the Proprietors of News-Papers, and the Coffee-Men of London and Westminster fairly Stated. London, n.d.

The Case Between the Projectors of News-Papers, and the Subscribing Coffee-Men fairly Stated. London, 1729.

The Case of the Coffee-Men of London and Westminster. . . . London, n.d.

The Case of the Free Workmen-Printers: Relating to the Bill for Preventing the Licentiousness of the Press. [1712].

The Case of the Members of the Sun-Fire-Office, London relating to the Duties on News-Papers. London, 1712.

Chamberlayne, John, *Magnae Britanniae notitia; or, The present state of Great Britain.* London, editions 1726–46.

[Chamberlen Paul.] *A Full Answer to That Scandalous Libel, The Free Briton of July 1 That was pretended to be written by one Francis Walsingham Esq; alias Ar = n = ld, Clerk.* London, 1731.

A Letter to Richard Arnald, alias Francis Walsingham, Esq: In Answer to his unparalled'd Scurrility and Falsehood In The Free Briton of Sept. 30, 1731. London, 1731.

Cibber, Theophilus. *The Lives of the Poets of Great Britain and Ireland.* 5 vols. London, 1753.

An Apology for the Life of Mr T—— C—— Comedian. London, 1740.

The Tryal of Colley Cibber Comedian, etc. . . . For Writing a Book intitled An Apology for his Life. London, 1740.

A Collection of Recipes and Letters lately inserted in the Daily Journal. London, 1730.

A Complete Collection of State Trials. Edited by T.B. Howell. 34 vols. London, 1816–26.

The D'Anverian History of the Affairs of Europe, for the memorable Year, 1731. London, 1732.

Davies, Thomas. *The Characters of George the First, Queen Caroline, Sir Robert Walpole, Mr. Pulteney, Lord Hardwick, Mr. Fox and Mr. Pitt reviewed.* London, 1777.

De Saussure, César. *A Foreign View of England in the Reigns of George I and George II.* translated and edited by Madame Van Muyden. London: John Murray, 1902.

A Dialogue White lately pass'd between The Knight and His Man John. London, n.d.

Discontent or An Essay on Faction, a Satire. London, n.d.

Doddington, George Bubb. *The Political Journal.* Edited by John Carswell and L. A. Dralle. Oxford: Clarendon Press, 1965.

Dunton, John. *The Life and Errors of John Dunton.* Edited by J. Nichols. 2 vols. London, 1818.

Manuscripts of the Earl of Egmont, Diary of Viscount Percival, afterwards First Earl of Egmont. 3 vols. London: H.M.S.O., Historical Manuscript Commission, 1920–23.

Fielding, Henry. *The True Patriot.* edited by M. Locke. London: Macdonald, 1965.

——. *The Jacobite's Journal and Related Writings.* Edited by W. B. Coley. Oxford: Clarendon Press, 1974.

Gent, Thomas. *The Life of Mr. Thomas Gent, Printer, of York.* London, 1832.

Haines, Henry. *Treachery, Baseness and Cruelty Display'd to the Full in the Hardships and Sufferings of Mr. Henry Haines, late Printer of the Country Journal or Craftsman.* London, 1740.

The Hawkers New Year's Gift: To all their Worthy Masters and Mistresses. London, 1727.

Hervey, John, Lord, *Memoirs of the Reign of George the Second.* Edited by R. Sedgwick. 3 vols. London: private publication, 1931.

House of Commons Journals. vols. 20–25, 1722–50.

House of Commons Reports of Commissioners. vol. 7. 1806.

Letters of David Hume to William Strahan. Edited by G. B. Hill. Oxford, 1888.

Liberty and the Craftsman: A Project for Improving the Country Journal. London, 1730.

Lysons, Rev. D. "Collectanea." 2 vols., a collection of newspaper cuttings and other ephemeral items. N.d. British Library.

[Marforio]. *An Historical View of the Principles, Characters, Persons etc. of the Political Writers in Great Britain.* London, 1740.

Memoirs of the Society of Grub Street. 2 vols. London, 1737.

Memoirs of the Times in a Letter to a Friend in the Country. London, 1737.

The Mercury Hawkers in Mourning. London, 1706.

[Miller, J.] *An Epistle from Dick Poney, Esq; Grand-Master of the Right Black-Guard Society of Scald-Miserable-Masons from his House in Dirty Lane, Westminster, to Nick P———n, Esq. . . .* London, 1742.

"The Minute Books of the Partners in the *Grub Street Journal.*" *Publishing History* 4 (1978).

Montague, Lady Mary Wortley. *The Nonsense of Common Sense.* Edited by R. Halsband. Evanston: Northwestern University, Studies in the Humanities 17, 1947.

The National Journal or Country Gazette. A collection of political and humorous letters, poems and articles of news, publish'd in . . . the *National Journal.* London, 1748.

Observations on the First Six of the Morning and Evening Papers. Publish'd by the Subscribing Coffee-Men of London and Westminster. London, 1729 (first of an occasional publication).

Observations on the Writers of the Craftsman. London, 1730.

Pope, Alexander. *The Dunciad.* Edited by J. Sutherland. 3d ed. London: Twickenham ed. Methuen, 1963.

———. *Imitations of Horace.* Edited by J. Butt. 3d ed. London: Twickenham ed., Methuen, 1963.

———. *The Correspondence.* Edited by G. Sherburn. Oxford: Clarendon Press, 1956.

Manuscripts of the Duke of Portland. 9 vols. London: H.M.S.O., Historical Manuscripts Commission, 1891–1923.

The Printers' Case: Humbly submitted to the Consideration of the Honourable House of Commons. [1712].

The Printers' Proposals for a Regulation of the Press, A Proposal for Restraining the Great Licentiousness of the Press, Throughout Great-Britain and for Redressing the many Abuses and Mischiefs thereof. [1710].

Purefoy Letters, 1735–1753. Edited by G. Eland. 2 vols. London: Sidgwick and Jackson, 1931.

Ralph, James. *The Case of Authors by Profession or Trade, Stated, With Regard to Booksellers, the Stage, and the Publick.* London, 1758.

———. *A Critical History of the Administration of Sir Robert Walpole, Now Earl of Orford.* London, 1743.

Reasons humbly offer'd to the Consideration of the Honourable House of Commons. [1712].

Reasons humbly offer'd to the Parliament, in behalf of several Persons concern'd in Paper making, Printing and Publishing the Half penny News Papers, against the Bill now depending, for laying a Penny Stamp upon every half Sheet of all News-Papers. London, 1725.

The Remonstrance, Containing some Account of the Lives and Characters of our Present Political Writers. London, 1735.

A Short State of the Case, with Relation to a Claim made by Richard Francklin, Bookseller, on David Mallet, Esq. London, 1754.

The Town Spy: Or, a View of London and Westminster Written by a Foreigner. Gloucester, 1725.

A Trip through London: Containing Observations on Men and Things. 3d ed. London, 1728.

Tripe, Dr. Andrew. *Some Memoirs of the Life of Abel, Toby's Uncle.* London, 1726.

Verres and his Scribblers, a Satire in Three Cantos. London, 1732.

Walpole, Horace. *The Correspondence.* Edited by W. S. Lewis et al. 48 vols. New Haven: Yale University Press; London and Oxford: Oxford University Press, 1937–83.

Webster, William. *A Plain Narrative of Facts, or, the Author's Case fairly and candidly stated, by Way of Appeal to the Publick.* London, 1758.

Later Works

I. BOOKS AND ESSAYS

Aspinall, A. *Politics and the Press, 1780–1850.* London: Home and Van Thal, 1949.

Aitken, G. *Life of Sir Richard Steele.* 2 vols. London, 1889.

Blagden, C. *The Stationers Company.* London: George Allen and Unwin, 1960.

Bond, R. P. *The Tatler, the Making of a Literary Journal.* Cambridge, Mass: Harvard University Press; London: Oxford University Press, 1971.

Brewer, J. *Party Ideology and Popular Politics at the Accession of George III.* Cambridge: at the University Press, 1976.

[Burn J. H.]. *Catalogue of a Collection of Early Newspapers and Essayists, formed* by the late John Hope Esq, and presented to the Bodleian Library by the late Frederick William Hope. Oxford, 1865.

The New Cambridge Bibliography of English Literature. Edited by G. Watson. Cambridge: at the University Press, 1971–77. Esp. vol. 2, 1660–1800, "Periodical publications."

Catalogue of Prints and Drawings in the British Museum. Division 1, Personal and Political Satires. Edited by F. G. Stephens. 4 vols. 1870–83. Esp. vol. 2, 1689–1733, and vol. 3, pt. 1, 1734–50.

Christie, I. R. "British Newspapers in the Later Georgian Age." In *Myth and Reality in Late Eighteenth-Century British Politics and Other Papers.* London: Macmillan, 1970.

Cochrane, J. A. *Dr. Johnson's Printer.* London: Routledge and Kegan Paul, 1964.

Colley, L. *In Defense of Oligarchy.* Cambridge: at the University Press, 1982.

Collins, A. S. *Authorship in the Age of Johnson.* London: R. Holden and Co., 1927.

Coxe, W. *Memoirs of the Life and Administration of Sir Robert Walpole, Earl of Oxford.* 3 vols. London, 1798.

———. *Memoirs of the Administration of the Right Honourable Henry Pelham.* 2 vols. London, 1829.

Crane R. S., and F. B. Kaye. *A Census of British Newspapers and Periodicals, 1620–1800.* 2d ed. Chapel Hill: University of North Carolina Press, 1966.

Cranfield, G. A. *The Development of the Provincial Newspaper, 1700–1760.* Oxford: Clarendon Press, 1962.

Cross, W. *The History of Henry Fielding.* 3 vols. New Haven: Yale University Press, 1918.

Davis, R. M. *The Good Lord Lyttelton.* Bethlehem Pa.: Times Publishing Co., 1939.

Dickinson, H. T. *Bolingbroke.* London: Constable, 1970.

Dickson, P. G. M. *The Sun Insurance Office.* London: Oxford University Press, 1960.

Downie, A. "The Growth of Government Tolerance of the Press to 1790." In *Development of the English Book Trade, 1700–1899,* edited by R. Myers and M. Harris. Oxford: at the Polytechnic Press, 1981.

———. *Robert Harley and the Press.* Cambridge: at the University Press, 1979.

Eaves, T. C. D., and B. D. Kimpel. *Samuel Richardson, a Biography.* Oxford: Clarendon Press, 1971.

Ellis, K. *The Post Office in the Eighteenth Century, a Study in Administrative History.* London: Oxford University Press, 1958.

Ewald, W. B. *The Newsmen of Queen Anne.* Oxford: Basil Blackwell, 1956.

George, M. D. *English Political Caricature to 1792.* 2 vols. Oxford: Clarendon Press, 1959.

Goldgar, B. H. *Walpole and the Wits.* Lincoln: University of Nebraska Press, 1976.

Graham, W. *English Literary Periodicals.* reprint ed. London: Frank Cass, 1966.

Greenwood, J. *Newspapers and the Post Office.* London: Postal History Society, Special Series Publication 26, 1971.

Haig, R. L. *The Gazetteer: 1735–1797.* Carbondale: Southern Illinois University Press, 1960.

Handover, P. M. *A History of the London Gazette.* London: H.M.S.O., 1965.

Hanson, L. *Government and the Press, 1695–1763.* Oxford: Clarendon Press, reissue 1967.

———. *Contemporary Printed Sources for British and Irish Economic History, 1701–1750.* (Cambridge: at the University Press, 1963).

Harris, M. "Journalism as a Profession or Trade in the Eighteenth Century." In *Author-Publisher Relations During the Eighteenth and Nineteenth Centuries,* edited by R. Myers and M. Harris. Oxford: at the Polytechnic Press, 1983.

———. "The Management of the London Newspaper Press During the Eighteenth Century," *Publishing History* 4 (1978): 95–112.

———. "Newspaper Distribution during Queen Anne's Reign." In *Studies in the Book Trade.* Oxford: Oxford Bibliographical Society, 1975.

———. "Print and Politics in the Age of Walpole." In *Britain in the Age of Walpole,* edited by J. Black. London: Macmillan, 1984.

———. "Trials and Criminal Biographies; a Case Study in Distribution." In *Sale and Distribution of Books from 1700,* edited by R. Myers and M. Harris. Oxford: at the Polytechnic Press, 1982.

Henderson, A. J. *London and the National Government, 1721–1742.* Durham, N.C.: Duke University Publications, 1945.

Hillhouse, J. T. *The Grub Street Journal.* New York: Benjamin Blom, reissue 1967.

History of Parliament, *The House of Commons 1715–1754.* Edited by R. Sedgwick. 2 vols. London: H.M.S.O., 1970.

Hollis, P. *The Pauper Press, a Study in Working-Class Radicalism of the 1830's.* London: Oxford University Press, 1970.

Howe, E. *The London Compositor.* London: Bibliographical Society, 1947.

———. *The London Society of Compositors.* London: Cassell and Co., 1948.

Hughes, H. S. *The Gentle Hertford, Her Life and Letters.* New York: Macmillan Co., 1940.

Jones, M. G. *The Charity School Movement.* reprint ed. Cambridge: at the University Press, 1964.

Kramnik, I. *Bolingbroke and his Circle.* Cambridge, Mass: Harvard University Press, 1968.

Laprade, W. T. *Public Opinion and Politics in Eighteenth-Century England.* New York: Macmillan Co., 1936.

Lee, W. *Defoe: His Life and Recently Discovered Writings, 1716–1729.* 3 vols. London, 1869.

Lillywhite, B. *London Coffee Houses.* London: George Allen and Unwin, 1963.

Loftis, J. *The Politics of Drama in Augustan England.* Oxford: Clarendon Press, 1963.

Mckendrick, N., J. Brewer, and J. H. Plumb. *The Birth of a Consumer Society: the Commercialisation of Eighteenth-Century England.* London: Europa, 1982.

McLeod, W. R. and V. B. *A Graphical Directory of English Newspapers and Periodicals, 1702–1714.* Charlottesville: West Virginia, 1982.

Milford, R. T., and D. M. Sutherland. *A Catalogue of English Newspapers and Periodicals, 1622–1800.* Oxford: Oxford Bibliographical Society, 1936. [An interleaved copy with extensive manuscript additions is available at the Bodleian Library]

Morison, S. *The English Newspaper.* Cambridge: at the University Press, 1932.

Munter, R. *The History of the Irish Newspaper.* Cambridge: at the University Press, 1967.

Newsletters to Newspapers: Eighteenth-Century Journalism. Edited by D. H. Bond and W. R. McLeod. Morgantown, W. Va.: School of Journalism, West Virginia University, 1977.

Nichols, J. *An Account of the Rise and Progress of the Gentleman's Magazine.* London, 1821.

———. *Biographical and Literary Anecdotes of W. Bowyer.* London, 1782.

———. *History and Antiquities of Leicestershire.* 4 vols. London, 1795–1811.

———. *Literary Anecdotes of the Eighteenth Century.* 9 vols. London, 1812–1815.

Nichol Smith, D. "The Newspaper." In *Johnson's England,* edited by A. S. Turbeville. 2 vols. Oxford: Clarendon Press, reprinted 1952.

Pargallis S., and D. J. Medley. *Bibliography of British History: The Eighteenth Century, 1714–1789.* Oxford: Clarendon Press, 1936.

Perceval, M. *Political Ballads Illustrating the Administration of Sir Robert Walpole.* Oxford: Clarendon Press; Oxford Historical and Literary Studies 8, 1916.

Perry, T. W. *Public Opinion, Propaganda, and Politics in Eighteenth-Century England.* Cambridge Mass.: Harvard University Press, 1962.

Pinkus, P. *Grub St. stripp'd bare.* London: Constable and Co., 1968.

Plomer, H. R. *A Dictionary of the Printers and Booksellers Who Were at Work in England, Scotland and Ireland from 1668 to 1725.* London: reprinted by the Bibliographical Society, 1968.

Plomer, H. R., G. H. Bushell, and E. R. McC. Dix. *A Dictionary of the Printers and Booksellers who were at Work in England, Scotland and Ireland from 1726 to 1775.* London: reprinted by the Bibliographical Society, 1968.

Plumb, J. H. *Sir Robert Walpole the Making of a Statesman.* London: Cresset Press, 1956.

Plumb, J. H. *Sir Robert Walpole the King's Minister.* London: Cresset Press, 1960.

The Press in English Society from the Seventeenth to the Nineteenth Centuries. Edited by M. Harris and A. J. Lee. Rutherford, N.J.: Fairleigh Dickinson University Press, 1986.

Rea, R. R. *The English Press in Politics, 1760–1774.* Lincoln: University of Nebraska Press, 1963.

Realey, L. C. *The Early Opposition to Sir Robert Walpole, 1720–1727.* Lawrence: University of Kansas Humanistic Studies 4, nos. 2, 3, 1931.

Robinson, H. *The British Post Office, a History.* Princeton: Princeton University Press, 1948.

Rogers, P. *Grub Street.* London: Methuen, 1972.

Sale, Jr., W. *Samuel Richardson Master Printer.* Ithaca: Cornell University Press, 1950.

Shorter, A. R. *Paper Making in the British Isles, An Historical and Geographical Study.* Newton Abbot: David and Charles, 1971.

Siebert, F. *Freedom of the Press in England 1476–1776.* Urbana: University of Illinois Press, 1952.

Spufford, M. *Small Books and Pleasant Histories.* Cambridge: at the University Press, 1982.

Straus, R. *Robert Dodsley—Poet, Publisher, and Playwright.* London: John Lane; New York: John Lane Co., 1910.

Studies in the English Periodical. Edited by R. P. Bond. Chapel Hill: University of North Carolina Press, 1957.

Sutherland, J. R. *Defoe.* 2d ed. London: Methuen, 1950.

Timperley, C. H. *A Dictionary of Printers.* London, 1839.

Watt, I. P. *The Rise of the English Novel.* London: Chatto and Windus, 1957.

Wood, K. K., and H. P. Bond. *Studies of British Newspapers and Periodicals from their Beginning to 1800.* Chapel Hill: University of North Carolina, Studies in Philology extra series, no. 2, 1946.

Welsh, C. *A Bookseller of the Last Century.* London, 1885.

Wiles, R. M. *Serial Publication in England before 1750.* Cambridge: at the University Press, 1957.

Wiles, R. M. *Freshest Advices: Early Provincial Newspapers in England.* Columbus: Ohio State University Press, 1965.

II. ARTICLES AND NOTES

Aspinall, A. "Statistical Accounts of the London Newspapers in the Eighteenth Century." *English Historical Review* 63 (1948).

Astbury, R. "The Renewal of the Licensing Act in 1693 and its Lapse in 1695." *Library,* 5th ser., 33 (1978).

Battestin, M. C. "Four New Fielding Attributions: His Earliest Satires of Walpole." *Studies in Bibliography* 36 (1983).

Belanger, T. "Booksellers Trade Sales, 1718–1768." *Library*, 5th ser., 30 (1975).

Blagden, C. "Henry Rhodes and the Monthly Mercury." *Book Collector* 5 (1956).

Bond, R. P., and M. N. Bond. "The Minute Books of the St. James's Chronicle." *Studies in Bibliography* 28 (1975).

G. A. Cranfield. "The London Evening Post, 1727–1744: a Study in the Development of the Political Press." *Historical Journal* 6 (1963).

———. "The London Evening Post and the Jew Bill of 1753." *Historical Journal* 8 (1966).

Downie, A. "An Unknown Defoe Broadsheet on the Regulation of the Press?" *Library*, 5th ser., 33 (1978).

Gibbs, G. C. "Some Intellectual and Political Influences of the Huguenot Emigrés in the United Provinces, c. 1680–1730." *Bijdragen en mededelingen betreffende de geschiedenis der Nederlanden* 90 (1975), vol. 2.

Harris, M. "Figures Relating to the Printing and Distribution of the Craftsman, 1726–1730." *Bulletin of the Institute of Historical Research* 43 (1970).

———. "The Management of the London Newspaper Press during the Eighteenth Century." *Publishing History* 4 (1978).

James, G. H. "The Jacobite, Charles Molloy, and Common Sense." *Review of English Studies*, n.s. 4 (1953).

Joshi, K. L. "The London Journal 1719–1738." *Bombay University Journal* 9 (1940).

Kenny, R. W. "James Ralph: an Eighteenth Century Philadelphian in Grub Street." *Pennsylvania Magazine of History and Biography* 64 (1940).

Limouze, A. S. "Dr. Gaylard's Loyal Observator Reviv'd." *Modern Philology* 48 (1950).

McCusker, J. J. "The Business Press in England before 1775." *Library*, 6th ser., 8(1986).

Periodical Post-Boy. Edited by J. R. Sutherland. 1 (1948).

J. M. Price, "A Note on the Circulation of the London Press, 1704–1714." *Bulletin of the Institute of Historical Research* 31 (1958).

Realey, C. B. "The London Journal and its Authors, 1720–1723." *Bulletin of the University of Kansas* 5 (1935).

Rogers, N. "Aristocratic Clientage, Trade and Independency: Popular Politics in Pre-Radical Westminster." *Past and Present* 61 (1973).

Shipley, J. B. "On the Date of the Champion." *Notes and Queries* 198 (1953).

Shugrue, M. "Applebees Original Weekly Journal: an Index to Eighteenth-Century Taste." *Newberry Library Bulletin* 6 (1964).

Snyder, H. L. "The Reports of a Press Spy for Robert Harley: New Bibliographical Data for the Reign of Queen Anne." *Library*, 5th ser., 22 (1967).

————. "The Circulation of Newspapers in the Reign of Queen Anne." *Library*, 5th ser., 23 (1968).

————. "A Further Note on the Circulation of Newspapers in the Reign of Queen Anne." *Library*, 5th ser., 31 (1976).

Sutherland, J. R. "The Circulation of Newspapers and Literary Periodicals, 1700–1730." *Library*, 4th ser., 15 (1934).

Todd, W. B. "The Printing of Eighteenth Century Periodicals; with Notes on the Examiner and the World." *Library*, 5th ser., 10 (1955).

Treadwell, M. "A Further Report from Harley's Press Spy." *Library*, 6th ser., 2 (1980).

————. "London Trade Publishers 1675–1750." *Library*, 6th ser., 4 (1982).

Walker, R. B. "Advertising in the London Newspapers, 1650–1750." *Business History* 15 (1973).

Wrigley, E. A. "A Simple Model of London's Importance in Changing English Society and Economy, 1650–1750." *Past and Present* 37 (1967).

III. Theses and Dissertations

Barber, A. D. "Edward Cave, Samuel Johnson and the Gentleman's Magazine." Ph.D. diss., Oxford University, 1982.

Barber, G. "A Bibliography of Henry Saint John Viscount Bolingbroke." B.Litt. thesis, Oxford University, 1963.

Belanger, T. "Booksellers' Sales of Copyright; Aspects of the London Book Trade, 1718–1768." Ph.D. diss., Columbia University, 1970.

Burton, K. G. "The Early Newspaper Press in Berkshire." M.A. thesis, Reading University, 1954.

Chapman, P. "Jacobite Political Argument in England, 1714–66." Ph.D. diss., Cambridge University, 1984.

Limouze, A. S. "A Study of Nathaniel Mist's Weekly Journal." Ph.D. diss., Duke University, 1947.

Peacock, H. A. "The Techniques of Political Controversy in the Early Eighteenth Century Periodicals, with Particular Reference to the Craftsman." M.A. thesis, London University, 1951.

Index

Acts: copyright (1710), 65; Gin (1737), 96; Habeas Corpus (1679), repeals of, 149, 150; hawkers and pedlars (1698), 29; Licensing, lapse of (1695), 19, 65, 155; Stage Licensing (1737), 134, 147; Stamp (1712), 19–21, 23, 52, 135, 195; Stamp (1725), 22, 23, 25–27, 52, 53, 195; Stamp (1743), 195; Stamp (1757), 52; triennial Parliaments (1694), repeal of, 170; Vagrancy (1743), 30

Alchymist, The; or, Weekly Laboratory, 39, 49, 50, 52, 71, 85, 96, 97, 100, 125, 140, 147, 148

All Alive and Merry, 95, 185

Amhurst, Nicholas, 70, 79, 87, 102, 105, 107, 110, 123, 130, 140, 141

Anglesey, Richard, 6th Earl of, 174

Annesley, James, 174

Applebee, Edward, 95

Applebee, Elizabeth, 98

Applebee, George, 98

Applebee, John, 20, 90

Applebee family, 90

Applebees Original Weekly Journal. See *Original Weekly Journal, The*

Aris, Samuel (printer), 76, 148

Arnall, William, 102, 103, 108, 109, 111, 117, 122, 124, 125, 170

Aspinall, Arthur *(Politics and the Press),* 7, 190

Attorney General, 151

Audit Office, 27, 94, 95, 97, 98

Baker, Walter, 49, 50, 52, 85, 96, 142

Baldwin, Henry (printer), 89, 98, 161

Banks, John, 132

Bavius, Mr., 106

Bayle, Mr., 89

Bayle's *Dictionary,* 67

B. Berrington's Evening Post. See *Evening Post, The*

Bee, The, 27, 169

Bell, Joseph, 120, 127, 151, 153

Bennet, Charles, 96, 97, 142

Bernard, Mr., 105

Berridge, Virginia, 8

Bew, John, 77

Billingsby, S. (printer), 174

Bingley, Mr., 105, 148

Birmingham, Warws, 41

Birt, Samuel, 68

Blackheath, Kent, 73

Bolingbroke, Henry St. John, Viscount, 19, 102, 114, 118, 122, 136; and *Hague Letter,* 147

Bond, Marjorie, 73

Bond, Richmond, 73

Boston Gazette, The, 159

Bowyer (printer), 76, 85

Brett, John, 38, 39

Briscoe (printer), 21

Bristol, Glos, 41

British Champion, The; Or, Admiral Vernon's Weekly Journal, 98, 168

British Intelligencer, The, Or Universal Advertiser, 30, 98

British Journal, The, 103, 117, 120, 157, 183

British Library, 98

British Mercury, The (The British Weekly Mercury), 20, 21, 35, 66, 155, 158–59, 167, 177, 179–80, 192, 194

British Mercury, The; or Weekly Pacquet, 94

British Observator, The, 27

British Oracle, The, 71

British Spectator, The, 194

Broadbottom, Jeffrey, 130–32

Brotherton, Mr., 75, 76

Buckley, Samuel, 117, 139, 156

Budgell, Eustace, 27, 120, 169
Burnet, Gilbert (bishop of Salisbury),
(*Travels*), 106
Burnet, Thomas, 101
Burridge, Richard, 99
Burton, William, 144

Caledonian Mercury, The, 160
Cambridge, 41; Theater coffee-house
in, 41
Cambridge University "News Carriers,"
42
Carte, Thomas, 108, 131, 156
Carter, Joseph, 145
Carteret, Edward, 152
Carteret, John, Lord, 131, 132
Cato's Letters, 114
Cave, Edward, 43, 67, 159
*Champion, The; or, British Mercury (The
Champion; or, Evening Advertiser),* 23,
34, 50, 68, 100, 101, 105, 109, 126,
127, 129, 132, 134, 152, 153, 164,
169, 171
Champion, The; or, Evening Advertiser. See
Champion, The; or, British Mercury
Chandler, Samuel (bookseller), 183
Charitable Mercury, The, 181
Charlton, Worcs, 91
Chesterfield, Philip, 4th Earl of, 125,
170
Cibber, Theophilus, 68, 72
Citizen, The, 116
Clarke, Mr., 75
Clarke, John, 145
Clay, John, of Northampton, 41
Clifton, Francis, 90, 142, 143
Commons, House of, 96, 173
*Common Sense; or, the Englishman's Jour-
nal (Old Common Sense),* 39, 86, 87,
106, 123, 125, 130, 140, 141, 147–49,
152, 153, 162, 170, 173
*Compleat Historian, The; or the Oxford
Penny Post,* 94
Concanen, Matthew, 110
Connoisseur, The, 78, 188
Cooper, Thomas, 38
Corn Cutters Journal, The, 71, 110, 117,
119, 124, 126
Country Gentleman, The, 114
Country Journal, The, 35
Courteville (Courtevil), Ralph, 103,
109–11, 129, 133
Cowell, Mr., 142
Cracherode, Anthony, 137

Craftsman, The, 26, 28, 35, 36, 39–41, 43,
48, 51–55, 58, 68, 70, 78, 84, 85, 87,
90, 91, 96, 97, 102, 104, 107, 109–11,
114–17, 122, 123–25, 129, 130, 132,
135, 137, 139, 141–44, 146–52, 156,
159, 161, 167, 170–72, 189–91
Cranfield, G. A., 8, 155, 195
Curll, Edmund, 25
Curran, James, 8

Daily Advertiser, The, 26, 31, 37, 50, 51,
57, 58, 72, 79, 120, 126, 129, 165,
175–77, 190, 191
Daily Courant, The, 22, 34, 36, 56, 66, 67,
70, 71, 88, 89, 92, 104, 117, 119, 124,
156, 162, 163, 168, 184
Daily Gazetteer, The, 8, 27, 29, 36, 45, 53,
54, 56, 69–72, 74, 76, 80, 81, 84–89,
103, 104, 106, 107, 109, 115, 123–25,
127, 129, 133, 134, 153, 161, 162,
168, 172, 175, 178, 193
Daily Journal, The, 22, 23, 25, 26, 31, 36,
56, 60, 66, 67, 70, 84, 89, 91, 117,
121, 156, 168, 175, 178, 187
Daily Post, The, 22, 23, 25, 28, 34, 38–40,
66–69, 72, 78, 84, 85, 88, 117, 121,
133, 147, 152, 160, 161, 178, 190
Daily Post Boy, The, 54, 59, 67, 71, 84,
121, 147, 152
D'Anverian History, 58, 116, 167
Dartford, 41
Davidson, Joseph, 68
de Coetlogan, Dennis, 49, 71, 97, 100,
107, 125, 138, 140, 141
Defoe, Daniel, 99, 107
Defoe, Norton, 97, 107, 110, 140, 141
de Fonvive, 56
Delafaye, Charles, 44, 45, 63, 139, 159,
191
Deptford, 41
Derby Mercury, The, 160
Dodd, Mrs. Anne, 38, 39, 146
Doddington, Bubb, 49, 110
Dormer's News Letter, 99
Dublin, 45

Earbery, Matthias, 104, 141
Egmont, John, 1st Earl of, 103
Emmonson (printer), 85
Englishman, The, 36
*Englishman's Evening Post and Universal
Advertiser, The,* 34, 126
Evans, Mr., 109
Evening Journal, The, 184

Evening Post, The (B. Berrington's Evening Post, The Old Evening Post), 45, 147
Examiner, The, 33
Excise Office, 51
Exeter, 182
Extraordinary Gazette, The, 161
Extraordinary Gazetteer, The, 34

Fancourt, Mr., 67
Fielding, Henry, 8, 100, 101, 105, 125; *Welch Opera*, 96
Fleetwood, Henry, 42, 114
Flying Post, The, 33, 34, 109, 120
Flying Post, The; or, the Post Master, 20
Fog's Weekly Journal. See *Weekly Journal, The; or, Saturday's Post*
Ford, James, 145
Foreman, Charlotte, 161
Francklin (Francklyn), Richard (bookseller), 42, 70, 78, 79, 85, 87, 114, 122, 140–43, 146–50
Fraser, James, 30
Frederick, Prince of Wales, 125
Free Briton, The, 38, 71, 103, 116, 117, 119, 123, 124, 151, 162, 170
Freeport, Sir Charles, 110
Freethinker, The, 101

Gardner, Mr. (printer), 96
Gavin, Anthony, 110
Gaylord, Dr. (printer), 89, 92, 96, 97, 138, 158; wife of, 138
General Advertiser, The. See *London Daily Post and General Advertiser, The*
General Evening Post, The, 25, 34, 42, 43, 52, 56, 59–63, 66, 67, 73–78, 84, 85, 121, 157, 160, 165, 166, 188
General London Evening Mercury, The, 188
General Remark on Trade, The, 179
Generous London Morning Advertiser, The. See *Rayner's Morning Advertiser*
Gent, Thomas, 90
Gentleman's Journal, The, 27
Gentleman's Magazine, The; or, Monthly Intelligencer, 43, 67, 132
George II (king of England), 109, 147
Gilliver, Lawton, 75, 76, 79
Gloucester Journal, The, 160, 169
Goldgar, Bertrand, 8
Gordon, Thomas, 104, 111, 131, 156
Goreham, Henry (printer), 87
Gosling, Robert, 42, 63, 68, 191

Gosport, 157
Gover, Mr., 76
Grange, James Erskine, *styled* Lord, 125
Gray, Samuel (printer), 117
Greenwich, 41; Harding's coffee-house in, 41
Griffin, Benjamin, 72
Griffin, Samuel, 145
Griffiths, Ralph, 75
Grub Street Journal, The, 34, 43, 49–53, 55, 60, 63, 66–69, 73–77, 79–81, 83, 85, 100, 101, 106, 121, 160, 164, 185
Guthrie, William, 102, 126, 130–32, 141

Haig, R. L., 8, 72, 109, 129
Haines, Henry (printer), 55, 78, 79, 87, 88, 97, 107, 116, 141–45, 149
Haines, Margaret (sister of Henry), 87
Hampstead, 73
Hampton Court, 141
Hanbury Williams, Sir Charles, 131
Hanson, Laurence, 7, 108, 136, 137, 139; *Government and the Press, 1695–1763*, 136
Harding, Samuel, 79
Hardwicke, Philip Yorke, Lord (lord chancellor), 141, 147
Harington, William, Lord, 110
Harley, Robert, 113, 136
Heathcote, William, 21
Henley, John, called "orator," 67, 68, 110, 117, 119, 137, 150
Hertford, Algernon Seymour, *styled* Earl of, 79
Hertford, Frances Seymour, *styled* Countess of, 79
Hill, Aaron, 71
Hinde Cotton, Sir John, 114
Hinton, T. (printer), 41
Hinton, W. (printer), 41
Historical Register, The, 85, 170
Historical View, An, 78, 104
Hogarth, William, 193
Horsley, William, 129
Huggonson, John (printer), 52, 75–77, 85, 106
Hyp Doctor, The, 67, 110, 119, 120, 126

Ilive, Abraham, 92, 95, 96
Ilive, Jacob, 95
Independent London Journalist, The, 86
Independent Whig, The, 183
Ipswich, Suff, 41

James, George (printer), 71, 152
Jamineau, Isaac, 43, 45, 54, 63
J.C., 79
Jekyll, Sir Joseph, 114
Jenour, Matthew (printer), 66
Johnson, Samuel, 195

Kelly, John, 99, 107, 125, 140
Kings Bench Halfpenny Post, The, 95
Knell, Robert, 145
Knight Errant, The, 66, 70, 184

Lady's Curiosity, The; Or Weekly Apollo, 94
Layer, Christopher, 173, 174
Lee, Alan, 8
Lewis, John (printer), 47
Lewisham, 41
Lintot, Bernard, 68, 117
List, The, 172
Literary Courier of Grub Street, The, 81, 185
Littleton, Mr., 110
London: Albermarle Street, Ballard's Coffee-house, 148; Aldersgate, 95; Bank of England, 51; Bartholomew Close, 86; Bear Key, 176; Bedford Coffeehouse, 75; Billingsgate, Gun Tavern, 73; Bow Street, 142, 143; Bridge, 175; Bridges Street, Cocoa Tree Chocolate house, 148; Chancery Lane, 40, 88, 97; Charing Cross, 38, 145; Charity Schools, 194; City of, Common Council of, 89, 108; Clerkenwell (Clarkenwell) Bridewell, 30; Covent Garden, 149; Covent Garden theater, 54; Customs House, 51; Devereux Court, 91; Drury Lane theater, 54; Falcon Court, 92; Falcon Tavern, 106; Fleet prison, 90; Fleet Street, 75; George Tavern, 91; Globe Tavern, 75; Goodman's Fields theater, 54; Hart Street, 87; Haymarket theatre, 54; Horn Tavern, 75; India House, 51; King's Bench, 141; King's Bench prison, 87, 91, 92, 97, 148, 150; Lincoln's Inn, 30; Lombard Street, 89; Lombard Street post office, 176; Ludgate Street, Oxford Arms, 75; Newgate prison, 100, 140, 141, 143, 144, 146; Newgate Street, Salutation Tavern, 75; Old Bailey (Baily), 38, 40, 84, 97, 173, 174; Paternoster Row, 148; Royal Exchange, 38, 51, 145, 151; Royal Society House, 67; St. Andrew by the Wardrobe parish, 158; St. Andrews Holborn parish, 91; St. Anne's Blackfriars parish, 158; St. Paul's, 75; the Savoy, 38; Shakespeare Tavern, 75; South Sea House, 51; Strand, Marigold Court, 91, 92; Temple Bar, 38, 39, 75, 76, 145; White Friars, 86; Wine Office Court, 97–98
London and Country Journal, The, 37, 41
London Courant, The; or, New Advertiser, 23, 51, 158
London Cryer, The, 68
London Daily Post and General Advertiser, The (The London Post Boy and General Advertiser. The General Advertiser), 26, 54, 57–61, 72, 95, 171, 175, 176, 188, 190
London Evening Advertiser, The, 29
London Evening Post, The, 23, 25, 28–29, 34, 35, 38–40, 56, 67, 70, 71, 84, 88, 109, 121, 123, 124, 126, 127, 133, 142, 145, 147, 152, 153, 157, 159–62, 169, 171, 172, 176, 190
London Farthing Post, The, 28, 174, 185
London Gazette, The, 20, 33, 44, 63, 117, 159, 175
London Gazetteer, The, 49
London Journal, The, 21, 22, 35, 38, 39, 41, 45, 46, 52, 55, 58, 70, 71, 84, 86, 88, 89, 103, 104, 108, 109, 110, 114, 116, 117, 119, 120, 123, 124, 157, 161, 173, 183, 189
London Magazine, The, 44, 70, 170
London Mercury, The; or, Great Britain's Weekly Journal. See *Penny Weekly Journal, The; or, Saturday's Entertainment*
London Morning Advertiser, The. See *Rayner's Morning Advertiser*
London News, The; or, the Impartial Intelligencer (Parker's London News. Paker's Penny Post), 21, 23, 24, 163, 166
London Packet, The, 50
London Post, The; or Tradesman's Intelligence (The Original London Post; or, Heathcotes Intelligence), 21, 23, 27, 28, 33, 192
London Spy Revived, The, 173
London Tatler, The, 94
Lords, House of, 174
Lyons, John, 92
Lyttelton, George, 125

McCulloch, Alexander (printer), 174
Madden, Rev. Samuel, 110
Mahoney, Ann, 30, 40
Maidstone newspaper, 95
Mallet, David, 102, 108, 111, 132, 156
Manufacturer, The, 99
Martyn, John, 100
Maryland Gazette, The, 159
Mathews, Edward (admiral), 166
Mawson, Robert, 20, 21
Meere, Hugh (printer), 38, 66, 72
Memoirs of the Society of Grub Street, 80
Mercurius Latinus, 158
Meres, John (printer), 35, 88, 142, 143, 161
Midwinter, E. (printer), 21
Millar, A., 68
Mills, John, 72
Mist, Nathaniel (printer), 89, 105, 114, 115, 123, 125, 142, 148, 156, 197
Mist's Weekly Journal. See *Weekly Journal, The; or, Saturday's Post*
Molloy, Charles, 86, 102, 105, 108, 125, 130, 140, 141
Monday's Daily Journal, 163
Monteage, Stephen, 191
Monthly Oracle, The; or Gentlemans Magazine, 95
Moore, "Puff," 41
Morison, Stanley, 7
Morning Advertiser, The, 94, 95, 122, 167
Morpeth, Henry Howard, *styled* Lord, 114
Motte, Benjamin, 42
Munter, Robert, 8

National Journal, The; or, the Country Gazette, 68, 131, 148, 163
Negus, Samuel, 22, 84, 88
Neville, Samuel (printer), 153
Newcastle, Thomas, Duke of, 28, 45, 46, 127, 137, 138, 141, 146, 147, 149, 151, 152
Newcastle Journal, The, 160
News Letter, The, 21
New State of Europe, The, 167
New Weekly Miscellany, The (The Westminster Journal, Or, The New Weekly Miscellany), 126, 186
Nichols, John, 70, 75, 98, 159, 196
Nicholson, John (printer), 30
Nixon, Robert, 96, 138
Nutt, Elizabeth (widow of John), 38, 39
Nutt, John (printer), 38

Nutt, Richard (printer), 38, 70, 84, 85, 88, 141, 146; father-in-law of, 84, 88

Observator, The, 82
Oedipus; or the Post Man Remounted. See *Post Man, The*
Old Common Sense, 130. See also *Common Sense; or, the Englishman's Journal*
Old England; or, the Constitutional Journal, 36, 52, 108, 130–2, 137, 141, 147, 150, 151, 178
Old Evening Post, The. See *Evening Post, The*
Oldmixon, John, *159*
Old Whig, The, 121, 183, 186
Onslow, Arthur, 114
Original Craftsman, The, 38, 39, 97, 107
Original London Post, The; or, Heathcotes Intelligence. See *The London Post, The; or, Tradesman's Intelligence*
Original Weekly Journal, The (Applebees Original Weekly Journal), 20, 35, 66, 89, 164, 173, 186
Owen, Edward (printer), 117
The Oxford Journal, The; or, the Tradesman's Intelligence, 192
Oxford Post, The, 90, 142

Palmer, Samuel, 76
Paris-à-la-Main, 44
Parker, George, 21–23, 40, 53, 91, 95, 163, 166, 181, 194
Parker's London News. See *London News, The; or, the Impartial Intelligencer*
Parker's Penny Post. See *London News, The; or, the Impartial Intelligencer*
Parliament, House(s) of, 170
Pasham, of Northampton (bookseller), 41
Pasquin, 47, 116
Pax, Pax, Pax; or a Pacifick Post Boy. See *Post Boy, The*
Paxton, Nicholas, 103, 104, 127, 128, 136, 137–40, 149
Payne, Thomas (printer), 142
Payzant, James, 45
Peele, John, 38, 55, 71, 78, 86, 108, 116, 122–24, 140
Penny, Robert, 27
Penny London Morning Advertiser, The, 30, 174
Penny London Post, The, 26, 40, 57, 94, 165, 166, 173, 187, 190

Penny Post, The; or, Tradesman's Select Pacquet, 21, 42, 90, 192
Penny Weekly Journal, The; or, Saturday's Entertainment (The London Mercury; or, Great Britain's Weekly Journal), 21, 180
Perry (printer's workman), 141, 144
Philipps, Erasmus, 114
Phillips, Ambrose, 101
Pickard, Edward, 38, 97
Pierce, Mrs., 39
Pitt (Pitts), James, 99, 102, 103, 108, 109, 111, 125
Plain Man, The, 116
Political State of Great Britain, The, 54, 170
Pope, Alexander, 125
Portsmouth, 157
Post Boy, The (Pax, Pax, Pax; or, a Pacifick Post Boy), 20, 33, 34, 71, 159, 164, 171
Postlethwayte, Mr.: *Dictionary of Trade and Commerce,* 77–78, 188
Post Man, The (Oedipus; or the Post Man Remounted), 33, 34, 56
Post Master, The, 33, 56
Postmaster General, 43
Post Office, 33, 36, 42–46, 48, 54, 63, 117, 119, 120, 123, 125, 127, 139, 151–53, 191; clerks of the road, 43–46, 63, 152
Pratt, Daniel (printer), 28, 29, 52
Prompter, The, 187
Protestant Advocate, The, 183
Public Advertiser, The, 53, 54, 73
Publishing History, 73
Pulteney, William, 79, 102, 108, 114
Purser, James, 86, 87
Purser, John, 86, 87, 100, 140, 141, 143

Ralph, James, 100, 102, 104, 105, 108, 132
Randal, Thomas, 145
Ratley, Mr., 75
Rayner (Rainer), E., 92
Rayner, W. (surgeon), 91
Rayner, William, 87, 88, 90–98, 100, 107, 130, 138, 167, 168, 196
Rayner's Halfpenny Post, 94
Rayner's Morning Advertiser (The London Morning Advertiser. The Generous London Morning Advertiser), 26, 58, 67, 98, 187
Rayner's Penny Post, 94
Read, James (printer), 21, 22, 27, 52, 58, 90, 142, 164, 180, 181, 186

Read, Thomas (son of James), 90, 94
Reading Mercury, The, 36
Read's Weekly Journal; or, British Gazetteer. See *Weekly Journal, The; or, British Gazetteer*
Reynall, Richard, 63
Richardson, Samuel (printer), 70, 71, 84, 86, 133
Robe, Thomas, 58, 135
Roberts, James, 38, 55, 77
Robinson, Charles, 145
Rock, Dr., 150
Rogers, Pat, 8
Roper, Abel, 65
Royal Oak Journal, The; Or, Rayners General Magazine, 94
Rushout, Sir John, 114
Russel (Russell), Richard, 75–77, 80, 100, 106
Ryder, Sir Dudley (attorney-general), 29, 40, 147

St. James's Chronicle, 66, 67, 72–74, 89, 98, 161
St. James's Evening Post, 20, 45, 46, 63, 66, 90, 98, 120, 147, 159, 161, 175
St. James's Journal, 135, 172, 184
St. James's Post, 33, 66, 175
St. James's Weekly Pacquet, 94
Sandys, Samuel, 114, 170
Say, Charles (printer), 89, 161
Say, Mary, 84, 88
Say family, 85
Secretary of State, office of, 41, 44, 46, 117, 120, 137–40, 145, 152, 156
Senator, The, 115, 116
Sessions Papers, The, 191
Shakespeare, William: *The Merry Wives of Windsor,* 96
Sharpe, John, 137
Siebert, Frederick: *Freedom of the Press in England, 1476–1776,* 136
Smith, Jeremy More, 79
Smith, John, 137, 138
South Sea Company, 172
Southwark, Surr, 92, 94, 95, 97
Spectator, The, 33, 48, 126, 178, 182, 183
Spens (printer), 85
Stamp Office, 52, 64, 95; commissioners of, 26–30
Standen, John (printer), 40, 97, 111
Stanley, Sir Edward, 42
Stapleton, Henry, 145
Strahan, William, 84

Stuart, James, the Pretender, 108, 125, 131
Sun Insurance Company, 192
Sun Insurance Office, 66

Tatler, The, 33, 178, 182, 183
Thompson, Roger, 107
Toland, John, 21, 34
Tonson, Jacob, 96
Touchit, Thomas, 126
Tovey, Mr., 71
Townshend, Charles, Viscount, 105, 136
Traile, John, of Worcestershire, 63
Treasury, the, 94, 104, 108, 109, 119, 120, 123, 127, 136, 140; lords of, 152; secretary of, 123; solictor of, 28, 137, 140
True Briton, The, 114, 116, 142
True Patriot, The, 105, 156

United Provinces: British minister to, 159
Universal London Morning Advertiser, The, 187
Universal Spectator and Weekly Journal, The, 34, 38, 63, 66, 85, 88, 101, 126, 132, 161, 176, 182, 186, 187, 190
Universal Spy, The, 23, 41, 104, 141, 148, 183
Universal Weekly Journal, The, 94
Utrecht Gazette, The, 159

Vander Esch, Henry, 72, 79, 120
Venn, Richard, 102
Vernon, Edward (admiral), 168
Vertot, abbé de, 168
Voltaire, François Marie Arouet de: Life of Charles XII, 186
Votes, The, 63, 170

Walker, Amy, 145
Walker, Robert (printer), 29, 37, 41, 85, 91, 92, 94–98, 140, 142, 196
Walpole, Horatio, 44, 178
Walpole, Sir Robert, 9, 38, 92, 102–4, 108–11, 113, 114, 116–18, 127, 130, 136, 159, 164, 167, 171
Walsingham, Francis, 104, 109, 124
Walthoe, John, 71
Ward, Ned: Matrimonial Dialogues, 180
Warner, Thomas (printer), 38, 148
Watson, Mr., 76

Webster, William, 55, 71, 100, 109, 126, 166, 186
Weekly History, The, 47
Weekly Journal, The, 20, 21
Weekly Journal, The; or, British Gazetteer (Read's Weekly Journal; or, British Gazetteer), 22, 27, 35, 89, 115, 116, 120, 146, 147, 158, 175, 180, 186
Weekly Journal, The; or, Saturday's Post (Mist's Weekly Journal. Fog's Weekly Journal), 21, 23, 35, 38, 47, 51, 55, 58, 66, 78, 86, 89, 98, 99–100, 106, 107, 114, 115, 123, 125, 138, 140, 144, 149, 152, 158, 164, 171, 172, 189, 197
Weekly London Journal, The, 45
Weekly Medley, The, 184, 185, 194
Weekly Miscellany, The, 35, 36, 41, 42, 55, 71, 84, 100, 109, 121, 126, 157, 163, 166, 173, 183, 184, 186
Weekly News and Daily Register, The (The Weekly News and Register. The Weekly Register), 36, 70, 120, 121, 160, 175, 176, 185
Weekly News and Register, The. See Weekly News and Daily Register, The
Weekly Oracle, The; or, Universal Library, 27, 41, 185
Weekly Pacquet, The, 20
Weekly Register, The. See Weekly News and Daily Register, The
Weekly Tatler, The, 122, 166, 185
West, James, 129
Western Flying Post, The, 36
Westminster: Charity Schools, 194; Westminster Hall, 51
Westminster Journal, The, 23, 126, 129, 131, 132, 171, 173, 187. See also New Weekly Miscellany
Weymouth, 157
Wharton, Philip, Duke of, 146
What-D' Ye-Call-It, The, 36, 182
Whatley, Stephen, 34, 99, 107, 109, 120
Whitehall Evening Post, The, 23, 43, 45, 54, 56, 63, 66, 67, 99, 122, 172, 176
Wight, Isle of, 157
Wilcox, Susannah, 40
Wilde, Mr., 75
Wiles, R. M., 8, 27, 91, 94, 95
Wilford, John (stationer), 75, 77, 80, 152
Wilkins, William (printer), 70, 84, 86, 89, 99, 108, 116, 123, 124
Wilson, Robert, 145
Wine Office, 104

Wolfe, John (printer), 148, 149
Woodfall, Henry (printer), 53, 57, 73
Woodward, Thomas (bookseller), 68, 71, 152
World, The, 78, 188

Wrigley, E. A., 194
Wyndham, Sir William, 42, 114

Young, Dr., 110
Young, Sir William, 110